the worm, the germ, and the thorn

J.S. Macaulay

Isabel Henderson, photographed at the old ruined church of Abercromby, Balcaskie House, Fife – one of the sites visited on a Pictish Arts Society field-trip, 26 May 1996

the worm the germ and the thorn

Edited by David Henry

Pictish
and related studies
presented to
Isabel Henderson

The Pinkfoot Press

Balgavies, Angus

1997

First published in Scotland in 1997 by

The Pinkfoot Press

Balgavies, Forfar, Angus DD8 2TH

ISBN 1 874012 16 4 pbk

ISBN 1 874012 17 2 hbk

Supported by

The Pictish Arts Society

27 George Square, Edinburgh EH8 9LD

Front Cover *Incorporating a detail from a cross-slab from Woodrae, Aberlemno, Angus, of a serpent-tailed monstrous beast devouring a human (after Allen and Anderson 1903, III, fig 258c, p 245)*

Typeset and designed at The Pinkfoot Press

Printed by Burns Harris and Findlay Ltd, Dundee

This volume
is respectfully dedicated to

Isabel B. Henderson

MA (Abdn) BA PhD (Cantab) FSA FSA Scot

to mark her retirement from teaching
and to acknowledge her outstanding contribution
to Pictish studies

Presented on the occasion of
The St Andrews Sarcophagus Conference
held in
The Royal Museum of Scotland
Edinburgh
27 September 1997

Contents

Acknowledgements

The publishers would like to thank the Pictish Arts Society for its timely support which allowed this volume to stay on course for publication. We are especially grateful to Mrs Marjorie O. Anderson and to Sheriff Stuart O. Kermack for their generosity, without which this volume could not have gone to press. We would also like to thank those contributors who patiently endured a long interval between submission of their papers and eventual publication. The editor apologises for this unexpected hiatus, only too aware that originally their contributions were required in rude haste. Several contributors have given practical help and advice, namely: Barbara Crawford, Tom E. Gray, John Higgitt, Elisabeth Okasha, Edwina Proudfoot, Anna Ritchie, and Ross Trench-Jellicoe; but Carola Hicks deserves a special mention and thanks for her extra work in compiling the Bibliography of Isabel Henderson. We are also grateful to George Henderson for his help and silence, and lastly to Isabel Henderson herself, for her support of The Pinkfoot Press and for providing the opportunity for this written celebration.

Illustrations

We gratefully acknowledge permission to reproduce the following photographs and illustrations:

Frontispiece – Ross Trench-Jellicoe
Sally M. Foster: **1** – Batsford and Historic Scotland
Edwina Proudfoot: **1**, **6**, **9a**, **9b**, **10a**, **10b**, **11**, **12**, **13**, **14**, **15**, **16**, **17** – Tom E. Gray; **3**, **4**, **5**, **8** – Trustees of the National Museums of Scotland; **18a**, **18b**, **18c**, **18d** – Tom E. Gray and Perth Museums and Art Galleries
J.N. Graham Ritchie: **1**, **2**, **3** – The Royal Commission on the Ancient and Historical Monuments of Scotland
Ian G. Scott: **1** – The Royal Commission on the Ancient and Historical Monuments of Scotland
Niall M. Robertson: **3**, **4**, **5a**, **5b**, **7**, **8a**, **8b**, **9**, **10**, **13**, **14**, **15**, **16** – Tom E. Gray
Jane Hawkes: **3**, **3a**, **4**, **4a** – Tom E. Gray and Cultural Services, Angus Council
Douglas Mac Lean: **1a**, **1b**, **2**, **3**, **4a** , **4b**, **4c**, **4d**, **5** – The Royal Commission on the Ancient and Historical Monuments of Scotland

Unacknowledged illustrations are the property of contributors or The Pinkfoot Press. Illustrations are not to scale except where indicated in the caption.

Contributors

Dr J.R.F. Burt
  5 Veere Park, Culross, Fife KY12 8NE

Dr Barbara E. Crawford
  Dept of Mediaeval History, University of St Andrews, St Andrews, Fife KY16 9AL

Dr Katherine Forsyth
  Dept of History, University College London, Gower Street, London WC1E 6BT

Dr Sally M. Foster
  Historic Scotland, Longmore House, Salisbury Place, Edinburgh EH9 1SH

Tom E. Gray
  5 Clerwood Park, Edinburgh EH12 8PW

Dr Jane Hawkes
  Dept of Fine Art, University College Cork, Ireland

David Henry
  The Pinkfoot Press, Balgavies, Angus DD8 2TH

Dr Carola Hicks
  Newnham College, Cambridge CB3 9DF

John Higgitt
  Dept of Fine Art, University of Edinburgh, 19 George Square, Edinburgh EH8 9LD

Stuart McHardy
  Scottish Language Resource Centre, A.K. Bell Library, Perth PH2 8EP

Dr Douglas Mac Lean
  1108 Highland Avenue, Northfield, MN 55057, United States of America

Professor Emeritus W.F.H. Nicolaisen
  Dept of English, University of Aberdeen, King's College, Aberdeen AB9 2BU

Professor Elisabeth Okasha
  Dept of English, University College Cork, Ireland

Edwina Proudfoot
  St Andrews Heritage Services, Westgate, Wardlaw Gardens, St Andrews, Fife KY16 9DW

Dr Ian Ralston
  Centre for Field Archaeology, University of Edinburgh, Old High School, 15 Infirmary Street, Edinburgh EH1 1LT

Dr Anna Ritchie
  50 Spylaw Road, Edinburgh EH10 5BL

Dr J.N. Graham Ritchie
  Royal Commission on the Ancient and Historical Monuments of Scotland, John Sinclair House, 16 Bernard Terrace, Edinburgh EH8 9NX

Niall M. Robertson
  22 Letham Road, Perth PH1 2AP

Ian G. Scott
  3 Saxe-Coburg Street, Edinburgh EH3 5BN

Dr Ross Trench-Jellicoe
  101 Sibsey Street, Lancaster LA1 5DQ

Introduction

This collection of studies was originally intended to mark the retirement from teaching of Isabel Henderson, after a distinguished career as lecturer and tutor at Newnham College, Cambridge. However, that event occurred two years ago and, as publication of this volume has been unavoidably delayed, it seems more appropriate to offer it now in recognition of Dr Henderson's outstanding contribution to Pictish studies.

By happy coincidence, the late arrival of this volume also allows us to celebrate the thirtieth anniversary of the publication of Isabel's influential classic text *The Picts,* which appeared in 1967, twelve years after the publication of the ground-breaking collection of studies *The Problem of the Picts,* edited by Dr Frederick Wainwright. It was these two books that laid the foundation for modern Pictish studies and, such is their enduring influence, they remain the standard by which publications on the subject are judged.

While paying tribute to those works here, comparison between this volume and either of them should be avoided. This is really a different kettle of fish monsters, being more an opened can of worms (and germs and thorns* perhaps). There was no grand plan behind it and no claims are made for it as a comprehensive synthesis of modern trends in Pictish studies; as a *Festschrift,* it should be viewed as a miscellany taking a form dictated by the current preoccupations and interests of the individual contributors.

Nevertheless, the main areas of study are represented in this collection and, despite an unashamed bias towards sculpture (surely to be expected on this occasion), a certain cohesion is apparent. Each paper presents something new, which should provide stimulus for further study, but which perhaps also indicates that there is still much to be achieved. Pictish studies have come a long way since Wainwright (*et al*) and Henderson started shaping modern attitudes. Today, interdisciplinary study is becoming the norm, not the novelty it was in the 50s, and now the importance of comparative studies is recognised. We have not neglected related studies here, but to have attempted more would have required at least another volume.

Inevitably there are absences from the list of contributors – some due to editorial oversight, not to deliberate exclusion; some due to the other commitments of potential contributors, never to an unwillingness to participate.

One of the most significant boosts to the recent advancement of Pictish studies was the creation of the Pictish Arts Society in 1988. Most of the contributors are members, and it is a measure of the Society's regard for Isabel Henderson that it has contributed to this volume by supporting its production.

Since retiring, Isabel has been even busier than before and we look forward eagerly to sharing more of her characteristically inspired writings on the Picts and their art. All of the contributors owe much to Isabel's scholarship and no matter how each of them primarily regards her – as scholar, teacher, colleague or friend – they are united in writing in her honour with great respect and deep affection. I join them in wishing her a long, happy and fruitful retirement.

August 1997

David Henry
The Pinkfoot Press

---

* The source of the title can be found within the book itself. It is from an imaginative self-description of the Picts, and one we would not readily subscribe to, but, judging from the sculpture, its language seems to echo some of the evident concerns of the period under examination here.

Are the Dark Ages Still Dark?

Barbara E. Crawford

Having adopted the term 'Dark Age' for the title of two Conference publications I am following the path trod by many other editors in using it as a term of convenience for books which span several centuries of the early medieval era and which include contributions concerning different disciplines (1994; 1996). The most impactfull of such publications was that entitled simply *The Dark Ages*, (ed David Talbot-Rice 1965). The editor of this sumptuous volume also contributed a chapter on 'The Myth of the Dark Ages' in which he admits that both text and illustrations belie the connotation of darkness. As the book includes such literate and civilised societies as the Carolingian and the Byzantine, the title does indeed seem something of a misnomer.

The continued use of the term by researchers in many different branches of early medieval studies testifies to its convenience: Dark-Age numismatics (Grierson 1979), Dark-Age sculpture (Close-Brooks and Stevenson 1982), Dark-Age economics (Hodges 1982), Pictish studies in Dark-Age Northern Britain (Friell and Watson eds 1984), place-names and settlement patterns in Dark-Age Scotland (Whittington 1974–75), Dark-Age naval power (Haywood 1991), and Dark-Age biographies (Williams, Smyth and Kirkby, 1991).

In general the term has been much used by presenters of television programmes. Michael Wood went 'In Search of the Dark Ages' in 1980. *The Making of Britain* series presented in 1984, was also called *The Dark Ages* and both these were limited to the peoples and cultures of the British Isles in the early medieval period using the term in its more usual context. Later in the 1980s Frank Delaney went a very long 'Walk in the Dark Ages', from the rocky outpost of Skellig Michael through Britain and Europe to Istanbul. Lloyd and Jennifer Laing reject the validity of the

term in relation to Celtic Britain and Ireland by adding the subtitle 'The Myth of the Dark Ages' to their book although saying that 'there is some justification in speaking of the 'Dark Ages' in the former province of Britannia, since it is an ill-documented period following a well-documented one' (1990, 13). The term is meaningless for those areas which were untouched by Roman control where 'documentation had never existed' (ibid, 13–14). They do use it frequently thereafter, however, particularly in relation to art, and also referring to 'Dark Age Celts' (p.15). This contradiction between intent and usage raises the issue of whether it **is** reprehensible for academic authors to continue to use the term 'Dark Age' or whether its usefulness outweighs the disrepute in which the term is now held in some (mostly archaeological) quarters. Should its usefulness as a term which evokes the barbarian centuries of the newly-Christian era be limited to TV series and publications with a popular appeal? Or can its use be justified with reference to academic publications and historians' terminology?

In opening up this issue I will be referring to an article in *Antiquity* written nearly 50 years ago by F.T. Wainwright in which he discusses 'problems and policies' in relation to the Dark Ages (1949) which Isabel Henderson first brought to my notice. It therefore seemed appropriate to contribute some thoughts on the question of this term in relation to the study of early medieval society north of the Border to a volume marking her retiral. So many of Wainwright's points about the need for inter-disciplinary understanding in this period of history have been exemplified in Isabel's own work. Wainwright's use of the term is central to his theme, which he made particularly his own: the need for co-ordination of history, archaeology and place-names in an age when there is very little history, and the historian looks to other disciplines for evidence to help fill out our sparse understanding of the period after the withdrawal of the Roman armies from Britain. In popular publications the term is extended to the whole of the pre-Norman Conquest period, even though the literate culture which grew up in Anglo-Saxon England after the Conversion to Christianity provides, if not a wealth, then a sufficiency of documentary evidence for the historian to use, and renders the concept of a 'dark age' difficult to hold.

Wainwright's Dark Ages were dark primarily from the point of view of the historians' need of a historical synthesis based on disciplines in which they had no expertise. Wainwright himself of course was one of the very few of his generation who **did** attempt to conduct his researches into the early medieval period of the British Isles in a truly inter-disciplinary way. In the *Antiquity* article he is urging his academic reader to see the need for co-operative research and for understanding fellow researchers' problems with their material. He also argued a case for the establishment of a Dark-Age research institute manned by experts in the different disciplines who could co-ordinate their work and 'secure planned and permanent co-operation' rather than 'casual mutual assistance'.

There would seem no doubt that that need is still with us 50 years on and that Wainwright's call for more co-ordination was quite prophetic. Should we continue to use the term 'Dark Age' when referring to the period of early history when such co-ordination is a *sine qua non*? Can we (in particular) use it with regard to Scotland?

It is in respect of the British Isles that the term appears to have originated in the Enlightenment attitudes of the seventeenth century. References to the 'intellectual darkness' of the age after the Roman imperial administration collapsed and barbarian hordes swept into the province of Britannia and created a new order start to appear (*OED*). It is not often used by Continental historians however (and it is interesting to note that M. Daniel-Rops's *L'Eglise des Temps Barbares*, was translated into English as *The Church in the Dark Ages* (1959)). Of course the darkness of Merovingian France or Visigothic Spain is merely opaque considering the survival of historical works and the evident continuity of Latin as a written language. As far as Britain is concerned however, the break between the culture of the classical world and the society of

Germanic settlers is deep and wide, despite several recent attempts to bridge that gap with continuity and survival themes. In any case the intellectual darkness has not been lifted, despite the valiant efforts of the Cambridge school of Celticists.

This is a darkness created by our ignorance, not by barbarism (Smith 1984, 2). As historians, art historians, archaeologists we do not condemn these societies as barbarous any longer. A more general anthropological awareness helps us to compare them with other societies at a similar state of development: there are many lessons to be learned from comparison with tribal societies.

Increased archaeological knowledge makes us vastly better informed about the way of life and living standards than ever before – in many respects much the same as earlier or later periods of prehistory. The sculptural evidence from Anglo-Saxon, Scottish and Pictish societies provides a wealth of material for studying the religious imagery, the intellectual contacts and the craftsmen's skill in these societies; evidence which Isabel's lectures and publications have illuminated far beyond any previous understanding of these art-forms. The techniques and artistry of the metalworkers of all these 'Dark-Age' societies surpasses most things that have been created in any other era of prehistory in these islands. We should certainly be very wary of denigrating the achievements of the period by using the term 'Dark Age' pejoratively.

For historians however these centuries remain exceedingly dark, due to the lack of illumination cast by historical sources. Wainwright could boldly say in 1949 'there are political, social, economic, artistic, literary and linguistic problems which archaeology alone can never solve' (1949, 76) and to him these gaps in our evidence were a peculiarly Dark-Age problem. Today's archaeologists could – and do – argue that the advances made in discovery and excavation from this same period render the term 'Dark Age' inadequate: that it is no darker than any other prehistoric period and that the historical sources which do exist are only a hindrance to our understanding of the material source evidence. They would probably suggest that we could live without the political, social, economic, artistic, literary or linguistic problems! The trouble is, we have sufficient evidence for all of these facets to give **some** material for a historical synthesis. We also have contemporary societies in Europe which are more fully literate, and from which written sources have survived to a much greater degree. This evidence can be used for comparative purposes, whether it is to understand the position of kings or the role of the early monastic orders. Here we have a methodological clash of attitudes between the practitioners of the different disciplines and their priorities, and they may be irreconcilable.

Turning to Scotland we have to ask if the validity of the term 'Dark-Age' to describe those centuries of the post-Roman era is indeed questionable – as the Laings would argue for Celtic Britain as a whole. Certainly the impact of the Roman world on tribal society was less important than in southern Britain. The British and Pictish peoples maintained their traditional way of life probably little influenced by the period of Roman military conquest. Archaeologists could well argue that the withdrawal of the Roman armies makes little difference to the source material and the introduction of a value-laden term like 'Dark Age' is irrelevant to their methodology – and positively unhelpful.

The archaeologist who has made most contribution to this period has used historical evidence as the basis of his research method. Leslie Alcock (who prefers this to be known as the Early Historic period) has pursued a planned programme of excavation in Scotland tied to those fortified sites which appear in the documentary record and which are therefore known to have been important power centres in a period when very little else is known – historically speaking. By being resolutely inter-disciplinary in combining historical information and research excavation he is exemplifying Wainwright's criterion of the need for co-ordination admirably. Why should Wainwright's terminology not also be used for such co-ordinating activity north of the Border? I am sure that Wainwright himself would not have made any distinction between the different parts of the British Isles in the application of the term. He was briefly lecturer in Dark-Age History in the University of St. Andrews.

There are other respects in which one could argue that this period of north British proto-history is permissibly 'Dark Age'. It is marked by significant tribal invasion, from south east, west and later on, from the north. The mix of ethnic groupings which resulted, and the process in which

these groups fought and settled is according to the pattern of southern Britain and Germanic Europe. The minimal amount of written evidence leads the historian to use other sources, and attempt the inter-disciplinary mode. We know that the Picts were as literate as their Irish cousins (perhaps second cousins!) but their written sources have not survived to anything like the same degree, for some not entirely understood reason (Hughes 1980). We know, in fact, that there is the **potential** for historical synthesis, and the archaeologist has to be prepared for the spindle-whorl with an ogham inscription, and the art-historian has to be prepared for the eroded letters of a memorial on a broken cross-slab found in a churchyard excavation. Finally, the ethos of the age is as heroic and 'barbaric' as other early medieval societies. These factors surely justify the use of the term 'Dark-Age Scotland' although it is noticeable that Scottish historians do not appear to have used it. The cultural use of 'Celtic' has sufficed. (Nor have I yet used it directly, only putting Scotland into the context of 'Dark-Age Britain' and 'Dark-Age Europe'.)

To quote Wainwright once more; 'the full picture of the past will always elude the single-minded approach of the single-minded specialist' (1949, 73). It is because of this very fact, and the necessity of our having to practise our trade alongside our colleagues in the same chronological time zone that justifies the use of the term 'Dark-Age' with respect to the history of Scotland (or what became Scotland) in the centuries after the withdrawal of the Roman armies up to the time when documentary sources become sufficiently available (and that end-date can certainly be argued over!). If it is agreed that it does have any validity then it is a validity relevant to the study of the surviving source material. This is where the peculiarly Dark Age problem lies. And if the use of this term can help to avoid failure of communication, the misunderstanding of other priorities, the inability to present one's subject in an intelligible way or produce a readable synthesis, then it may serve a useful purpose. These are not problems peculiar to the Dark Ages, but they are distinctively relevant to a period where practitioners of many disciplines collide in the same chronological time-frame. The single-minded specialist may not think he works in a Dark-Age environment, but he surely appreciates his inadequacies when faced with the need to utilise the ancillary disciplines to his own, and he should acknowledge that the full picture of the past will only be created by co-ordination – and some sort of synthesis (as urgent today as when Wainwright raised it in 1949) with the other single-minded specialists.

The last word will not be given to Wainwright but to a contemporary archaeologist of the Dark-Age period who, although uneasy with such an epithet (– as with others, such as 'sub-Roman' which have negative implications), nonetheless admits that it 'is still, alas, an evocative and useful term' (Rahtz 1991, 5). All terminology has its defects; of the alternatives for our period such as 'early Christian' or 'early historic', they may serve to exemplify only one aspect of the period. 'Middle Age' itself is a ridiculous concept, and by calling the latter part of the Dark Ages 'The Viking Age' one is mis-using another loaded term! 'Dark Age' should I suggest be allowed to play a useful role in calling to mind the methodological problems inherent in any discussion of the early centuries of our era. It is hoped that Isabel will long continue to practise her skills in combining her knowledge of historical and art-historical sources for the illumination of those of us who try to understand the society and culture of 'Dark-Age Scotland'!

References

CLOSE-BROOKS, J and STEVENSON, RBK 1982 *Dark Age sculpture: a selection from the collections of the National Museum of Antiquities of Scotland.* Edinburgh.

CRAWFORD, BE
– (ed) 1994 *Scotland in Dark Age Europe.* St Andrews.
– (ed) 1996 *Scotland in Dark Age Britain.* St Andrews.

DANIEL-ROPS, M 1959 *The Church in the Dark Ages* (trans of *L'Eglise des Temps Barbares*).

DELANEY, F 1988 *A Walk in the Dark Ages.* London.

FRIELL, JGP and WATSON, WG (eds) 1984 *Pictish studies: settlement, burial and art in Dark Age Northern Britain.* Oxford.

GRIERSON, P 1979 *Dark Age numismatics: selected studies.* London.

HAYWOOD, J 1991 *Dark Age Naval Power.* London.

HODGES, R 1982 *Dark age economics: the origins of towns and trade: A.D. 600–1000.* London.

HUGHES, K 1980 Where are the writings of Early Scotland? In Dumville, D (ed) *Celtic Britain in the Early Middle Ages. Studies in Celtic History*, II, 1–21. Woodbridge.

LAING, L and LAING, J 1990 *Celtic Britain and Ireland, A.D. 200–800. The Myth of the Dark Ages.* Dublin.

RAHTZ, P 1991 Pagan and Christian by the Severn Sea. In Abrams, L and Carley, J (eds) *The Archaeology and History of Glastonbury Abbey*, 3–38. Woodbridge.

SMITH, LM (ed) 1984 *The Making of Britain.* London.

TALBOT-RICE, D (ed) 1965 *The Dark Ages.* London.

WAINWRIGHT, FT 1949 Problems and policies. *Antiquity*, 23, 73–82.

WHITTINGTON, G 1974 Placenames and the settlement pattern of dark-age Scotland. *Proc Soc Antiq Scot*, 106 (1974-75), 99–110.

WILLIAMS, A, SMYTH, A and KIRKBY, DP 1991 *A Biographical Dictionary of Dark Age Britain. England, Scotland and Wales c.500–c.1050.* London.

The Picts: Quite the Darkest of the Peoples of Dark Age Britain?

Sally M. Foster

Isabel Henderson published *The Picts* in 1967 as part of Thames and Hudson's 'Ancient Peoples and Places' series. It was the first popular yet authoritative overview of this Early Historic people. This article briefly reviews the notable contribution Henderson's book made to Pictish studies, highlights some of the many discoveries, developments and changes in perspective which have taken place since, and concludes with thoughts on how Pictish studies might proceed in the future.

The Picts

People have been interested in the history of the Picts since at least the sixteenth century. Yet it is only in the last 40 years that Early Historic studies in Scotland have fully come into their own, with leaps in our knowledge through excavation, field survey, historical, place-name and art-historical research, enhanced by interpretative analyses of this evidence from a variety of differing perspectives. A major landmark was the Dundee conference in 1952 which culminated in the first comprehensive survey of Pictish archaeology, *The Problem of the Picts* (Wainwright 1955). But its contributors could not 'point to a single fortress or to a single dwelling or burial and say with certainty that it was Pictish. The problem lies in the recognition or identification of material as Pictish' (Wainwright 1955, 29–30).

The situation was not much better 15 years later, and the dilemma was perpetuated in *The Picts*: historical and art-historical themes inevitably predominate. Henderson begins (Chapter I) with a discussion about what is meant by the term Picts and the evidence (from Roman and later sources) for the political groupings of Pictland. The contribution of archaeology to recognising the ancestors of the Picts is noted, although few settlements could yet be attributed to the Picts. The history of the Picts (Chapter II) was presented as a series of snapshots, essentially the story of the substantial individuals to whom the meagre documentary sources tantalisingly refer. Chapter III explores pagan beliefs and the evidence for Christianity, while Chapter IV discusses how the 'Irish in Dalriada' came to take over Pictland and what happened to the Picts thereafter. The final chapter concentrates on aspects of Pictish art, 'the only substantial native relic'. The overall tone is upbeat; the Picts are a 'sensitive, aware, intelligent society', full partners in the development of Hiberno-Saxon art.

The Picts drew together current knowledge and made it easily accessible to a wide readership for the first time. Fifteen years after it first appeared, it still provided me, as a student of medieval archaeology, with a vital introduction to the topic. But the subject has now developed, much of the book is inevitably superseded (not least by Henderson's own subsequent research) and a spate of contrasting overviews have recently been published (eg Ritchie 1989; Laing and Laing 1993; Sutherland 1994; Foster 1996).

Pictish studies 1967–1995

The same range of sources exists as in 1967 but new, direct evidence about the Picts, intellectual developments in Early Historic studies and the various component disciplines as a whole, and technological advances, have propelled Pictish studies forward. In so far as number of publications can be used as a crude guide to activity and interest, on the basis of works cited in the 'Pictish Bibliography' (Burt 1995), about 450 relevant publications have been produced since 1967 to the present day, steadily increasing by the decade, whereas only about 300 were published at a broadly constant rate over the previous 120 years. This profound increase, it is suggested, can be attributed to a number of factors: a rise in Scottish political and cultural consciousness, manifested by, amongst other things, an introspective interest in the nation's early history (as witnessed latterly by the foundation of the *Pictish Arts Society*); an increasing academic interest in the Picts (and their neighbours), championed by several prolific, largely university-based proponents (Leslie and Elizabeth Alcock, Lloyd Laing, Chris Morris, Anna Ritchie, Alan Small, Charles Thomas, the late Robert Stevenson and of course Isabel Henderson); and the significant rise in funds for rescue archaeology in the 1970s. But it has to be acknowledged that, despite the soaring number of books and papers written on the subject, the number of landmark publications has been disappointingly few. Aside from the texts singled out for special attention below, these include a useful (although now out-dated) Historical Atlas (McNeill and Nicholson 1975); Charles Thomas's magisterial surveys of early Christian archaeology (1971; 1981); and five sets of conference proceedings which presented some interesting ideas and new material, as well as syntheses and collations of various categories of data (Friell and Watson 1984; Small 1987; Driscoll and Nieke 1988; Armit 1990; Crawford 1994). Regardless, in the light of prevalent ideas (see below), it is possible to attempt to understand how society developed, however transient the evidence for this may eventually prove to be. But this is not the place for a survey of what we (think we) now know or can suggest (see *Picts, Gaels and Scots* – Foster 1996 – for my own attempt to do this), but **why** we know (or do not know) some of the things we do; this is an essential first step to considering how, realistically, our knowledge of the Picts might be progressed in the future.

Study of all the peoples of northern Britain has steadily progressed and our appreciation of the Picts has to be situated within this developing framework for the Early Historic period as a whole. Myths and legends which have clouded modern perceptions of the Picts have been reassessed and current learned opinion largely favours the view that they were 'a typical northwest European barbarian society with wide connections and parallels' (Alcock 1987, 90); at least they were accepted by their neighbours on this basis.

Documentary references to the Early Historic period are few and it is exceedingly unlikely that new (re)discoveries will ever be made (but see Dumville 1976), despite the increasing acceptance that, like their neighbours, the Picts were a literate society. But in the absence of new sources, documentary historians have continued to rework the primary sources (many of which have become available as modern, competent translations, eg Bannerman 1974; Latham 1990; Anderson 1991; although Anderson 1908 and 1922 remain standard references to many of the early sources) producing new historical syntheses and other papers which provide a sound foundation for future enquiry (eg Anderson 1980; Lynch 1992; Smyth 1984). Several trends can be highlighted: the recognition that documents tell as much about the time they were written as the time they purport to describe, hence their reinterpretation with this in mind; the increasing use of later sources to draw inferences about earlier society or to recognise the earlier origins of practices which are only later described; and the use of external sources (particularly from Ireland and Wales) as the basis for interesting yet informed speculation about the nature of Pictish society. For example, work on early forms of administration has led to the recognition of early territories (thanages or shires) and their constituent parts, many of which appear to have a Pictish origin, pre-dating the earliest records for them (Barrow 1973; Driscoll 1991; Grant 1993).

Historians have also reconsidered the nature and identity of the peoples of early Scotland, an issue acutely related to current political concerns about the status and identity of the modern Scottish nation. The Picts are recognised as a geographically extended and diverse peoples, although we still do not know the name(s) they might have used for themselves or their land(s) ('Pictland'), if indeed they recognised such concepts. However, we are now fully confident that the Picts were simply the descendants of the Iron Age tribes of Scotland; it is also no longer fashionable to associate changes in Iron Age architecture with the arrival of new peoples (cf Henderson 1967, 20–4), for example. Although only first documented in AD 297, in historical terms 'Pictish' might be applied to the period from AD 79, if not earlier, when the Romans advanced beyond the Forth-Clyde isthmus into 'Scotland'. However, in practical terms the Picts still only become recognisable as archaeological and historical entities from the sixth century. The period they lived through tends now to be referred to by archaeologists as the Early Historic period in recognition of the availability for the first time of local (in the sense of non-Classical) documentary sources (Alcock 1981, 150), or early Medieval period/Late Iron Age. The Dál Riata (Gaels living in Argyll, Henderson's 'Irish in Dalriada') gradually amalgamated with/took over the Picts (there is no consensus about the precise process), but it is only from *c*900 that they would have recognised themselves as 'Scots' living in Alba; 900 is therefore seen as the more important date than 842/3. The considerable achievements of the Picts are recognised as having laid the foundations for the 'birth' of this new nation. Rather than being a 'lost people', it is argued that aspects of Pictish society continued, including the kingship (Broun 1994a; 1994b).

The ill-founded notion that the Picts, unlike their neighbours, spoke a non-Indo-European language is a present-day myth firmly dispelled by modern research (Forsyth 1995), although yet to fully permeate popular consciousness. Early Historic inscriptions are both the only contemporary written native records and the only documentary source which continues to increase in number, as new examples are either found (such as the ogham-inscribed spindle whorl from excavations at Buckquoy: Ritchie 1977) or recognised on the face of familiar monuments (such as the Dupplin cross: Forsyth in Alcock and Alcock 1992). The inscriptions, both individually and corporately, have also been the subject of modern, authoritative, art-historical, epigraphic and linguistic study which enhances their interpretation and significance through drawing on wider research in these fields, as well as being able to situate the Scottish examples within a broader geographical framework (Higgitt 1982, for example). Katherine Forsyth (1995; 1996) has shown that more of the ogham texts are comprehensible than previously thought and these often contain recognisable Celtic personal names. Some are in P- and some in Q-Celtic, reflecting the increasing gaelicization of Scotland. This is important because the decline of the Pictish language is traditionally attributed to the political events of the ninth century, but this process perhaps began centuries earlier.

The argument for matrilineal succession among the Picts is often justified by the reputed pre-Celtic nature of Pictish society as testified from the language. However, whilst this argument no longer holds, there are alternative strands to the case for this, and learned opinion remains split (see Smyth 1984, 57–75; Sellar 1985; Anderson 1987).

Turning to the archaeological evidence, figure **1** summarises the distribution of recent work and discoveries in Early Historic Scotland. Perhaps some of the greatest advances in Pictish studies since 1967 have come from archaeology, particularly the discovery of sites and associated landscapes through aerial photography. However, a constant problem remains the identification of material as being Pictish. Even when sites have been excavated, they are often poor in artefactual material and there is the additional problem of identifying the material culture as Pictish as opposed to, say, Dál Riata (cf the problems at Dundurn: Alcock, Alcock and Driscoll 1989). Not only is Pictland such a large 'entity' that there is no reason to expect uniformity across it, but a large element of the Pictish cultural repertoire seems to be shared with its neighbours. The material evidence (both structural and artefactual) is also difficult to date in its own right. Material evidence is therefore usually identified as Pictish by virtue of its date and geographical location, a logic with obvious dangers. With the exception of the so-called Pictish symbols, there is little which appears to be exclusive to Pictland and these designs, with their restricted chronological and geographical distribution, are obviously not the sole indicator of whether an area was Pictish or not.

Absolute dating techniques, scarcely applicable when Henderson was writing, are now commonly used. But radiocarbon dating and the less commonly applied thermoluminescence dating, often with brackets of up to several hundred years, do not tend to provide the tightly defined chronologies which are required to synchronise the archaeological evidence with the emergent Early Historic political scene. However, a calendrically-dated dendrochronology covering 7000 years has been constructed using Irish oak, and this has been used to date two Early Historic chronologies in southern Scotland (unpublished work by Anne Crone and Coralie Mills). The existence of these will facilitate the construction and dating of new Scottish material in the future, assuming suitable timbers are recovered.

1 *Distribution of recent work and discoveries in Early Historic Scotland. The timber buildings and most of the souterrains and square barrows are known only from aerial photographs*

Legend:

- souterrain area
- square barrow/cairn area
- □ timber building
- ● significant excavations since 1967
- ○ unenclosed settlement
- + enclosed settlement
- ▲ ecclesiastical site
- burial

50   0   50 kilometres

Courtesy of Batsford and Historic Scotland

Given the problems of absolute dating in the Early Historic period, its use is still usually regarded as secondary in importance to relative dating methods, which are dependent on the (rare) presence of high status items. Few can yet be independently dated from the fourth to seventh centuries. Until very recently, there was little scientific work on identifying and dating more mundane objects such as locally made pottery, but now although distinctive, localised products, have been identified in the northern Hebrides (Lane 1990) and Orkney (MacSween 1990), these do little to resolve the problems of dating sites.

In the first instance, sites are needed to (attempt to) date, but Early Historic sites are notoriously difficult to recognise and virtually impossible to confirm as belonging to this period without excavation (see also above). Modern scientific prospecting techniques can do little to help here. Field walking, a technique which has led to the discovery of many Anglo-Saxon sites in England, is almost guaranteed to be useless in Scotland given the general lack of durable, diagnostic Pictish or other Early Historic material, specifically pottery or coins. Programmes of aerial photographic survey – virtually unknown in Early Historic studies in Scotland prior to 1967 – by the Royal Commission on the Ancient and Historical Monuments of Scotland and individuals – have contributed by far the largest number of potentially relevant 'dots' to the National Monuments Record for Scotland. Rectangular timber buildings and most identified souterrrains and square barrows are known only from aerial photographs (Maxwell 1987) (**1**). The problem is that these sites remain just that – dots about which we know frustratingly little other than that some may relate to Pictish settlement or they may, in fact, be earlier: neither excavated nor analysed in a meaningful fashion (with some notable exceptions: see below). But each new discovery contributes valuably to our expanding database, even if this form of evidence must inevitably remain proscribed by the range of factors (soil-type, climate, land-use, etc.) which will only ever dispose limited parts of Scotland to cropmark production.

Square barrows have been the subject of limited investigation (see Ashmore 1980; Close-Brooks 1984, for example) and appear to belong to the first millennium AD, as could many of the less diagnostic round barrows often found in their vicinity. Upstanding examples are

still, occasionally, being recognised for the first time. Souterrains have a very dense distribution, particularly in Fife, Perthshire, Angus and Kincardineshire, and it is now recognised (again largely from cropmark evidence, but confirmed in some instances by excavation) that these underground storage chambers did not exist in isolation, but were connected to above-ground timber round-houses and other structures (eg Watkins 1980a; 1980b). However, although some of the associated settlement may be late, most are pre-/early Pictish in date, and are best seen as providing the context for Pictish settlement and the development of the early state in the rich, agricultural heartland of southern Pictland. The recognition of souterrains in agricultural land to the north, eg Aberdeenshire, remains rare. Some of the rectangular timber buildings ('halls') are highly likely to be Early Historic in date, but one of the few to be excavated (Fairweather and Ralston 1993) has been demonstrated to belong to the Neolithic period.

In general, since 1967, significant excavation of monuments/landscapes with evidence for Early Historic activity (of any form) has been exceedingly limited. Excavations have usually been very limited in size and geographically restricted. Several purely research-driven programmes of investigation have targeted some of the few known or likely Pictish sites (see below), but most discoveries have been accidental: sites excavated or fortuitously encountered during the course of salvage work in advance of coastal erosion, quarrying, forestry, changes in agricultural land-use or development. It is largely through serendipity, in the light of the opportunities thrown up by rescue archaeology, that we now know more about Pictish fortresses, dwellings and burial than in 1967.

There has scarcely been any work on known ecclesiastical or ritual sites. Place-name studies have been instrumental in identifying the extent of the early church and the likely site of king Nechtán's first Roman-style church has been pinned down to the vicinity of Restenneth, Angus (Barrow 1983). At the time of writing, Professor Martin Carver of York University has finished his first year of fieldwork at Portmahomack, Tarbat, Ross and Cromarty. This was targeted for investigation because a cropmark enclosure may define the site of a Pictish monastery, indicated by the presence of a large assemblage of Pictish carvings including an inscription (Higgitt 1982), although this remains to be confirmed. Exciting new sculptures continue to be discovered (see DES 1994, 82, for cross-slab discovered whilst ploughing near Wester Denoon, Angus, depicting a woman with penannular brooch, for example), and their find spots are sometimes investigated (eg Shepherd and Shepherd 1978), but little is found. Investigations have also taken place around known stones in advance of their removal to secure locations or in advance of protective coverings being placed over them, but only at Sueno's Stone (McCullagh 1995) has significant or meaningful evidence been encountered. Only the roughly pecked and atypical Class I symbol stone from Pool (Hunter 1990) has come, unexpectedly, from an archaeologically dated context.

Long-cist burials continue to be discovered, largely through aerial photography in southern Scotland, but in the absence of burial goods they are difficult to ascribe to particular cultural traditions. However, most excavation has been of settlements. A wide range of unenclosed settlement types has been found (Ritchie 1977; Hunter 1986; Foster 1989; Harding and Armit 1990; Hunter 1990; Driscoll 1991; Ballin Smith 1994; Lowe forthcoming; Rideout 1995; Crawford nd). In the light of these discoveries, re-analysis of artefactual material from earlier excavations and accounts of excavations where material is now lost, has met with limited success in recognising the presence, if not precise nature, of a more widespread Early Historic presence (Foster 1990). Pictish unenclosed settlement does still survive, but remains are often slight and/or overlie more substantial prehistoric remains, and hence they were often missed in the past. Our knowledge of the contemporary landscape between settlements remains negligible, although the few Pictish and other place-names contribute both to the appearance (Fraser 1987) and organisation (Barrow 1973) of the landscape. Palaeo-environmental work is gradually beginning to flesh our evidence for the Pictish economy. Unfortunately, samples to date have often been small and geographically restricted. Far more work is urgently needed here.

The picture is slightly different for enclosed settlement, which has the virtue of often remaining visible, if not easily dated. A successful campaign of trial trenching by Leslie and Elizabeth Alcock from 1974 to 1985 (Alcock and Alcock 1987; 1990; 1992; Alcock, Alcock and Driscoll 1989) has confirmed the identity of some of the high status enclosed settlements whose dates and locations could be inferred from the documentary sources, and other power centres have been partially excavated (eg Ralston 1987), but excavation has largely been restricted to minor trenching of the fortifications rather than the interiors. Work on high status artefactual material, such as Ewan Campbell's (1996) work on imported pottery, has greatly enhanced our understanding of the role which such power centres played in the production and distribution of prestige goods.

Aside from the discovery of new sites, archaeological studies of the Picts have also been characterised, in small but influential measure, by new approaches to the material: the adoption of a multi-disciplinary approach to landscape analysis; and the application of more theoretical approaches to the material evidence. Inevitably this has introduced a new vocabulary and concepts, paralleling archaeological approaches elsewhere. In many instances the emphasis has been on understanding relationships of power, the workings of society and state formation, particularly through an understanding of the strategies used to create, extend and maintain power. The work of Stephen Driscoll (1987) immediately springs to mind. In a study of the Early Historic landscape of Strathearn, he examined the social and political organisation of the early medieval kingdom of Fortriu which eventually became the centre of the medieval kingdom of the Scots. In this he used 'historical evidence bearing on social organisation in early medieval Britain and Ireland in conjunction with archaeological evidence for economic activity to produce a generalised model of early medieval society suitable for Pictland'. This multi-disciplinary approach included attempting to identify which components of the archaeological record, including cropmark sites, could be Pictish, but conclusions were obviously only provisional, in the absence of excavation. Later, in a published paper (Driscoll 1991), he developed this approach, examining the context of centres of royal authority, religious authority and the structure of settlement and the pattern of land use. Margaret Nieke's work on literacy and power (1988) and penannular brooches (1993) similarly reflects the 'Glasgow School', influenced by the teachings of both Professor Leslie Alcock and John Barrett.

In the field of art history, research has been prolific (not least by Henderson herself) leading to an understanding of the development of Insular art and its implications for society as a whole. Very importantly, there have been shifts in art-historical analysis: it now places more emphasis on establishing the context and function of both ornament and subject matter rather than being solely interested in style and the availability of models (although this is important in order to appreciate the external contacts and intellectual horizons of the Picts); major works of art are looked at in conjunction with contemporary religious texts; and the works of art are considered 'as an artefact rather than just a bearer of art' (Henderson 1995). Such shifts in approach have been slow to permeate Pictish studies, but George Henderson's *From Durrow to Kells* (1987) is an excellent example of this. In this vein, interesting and challenging approaches have also come from scholars influenced by anthropology (Jackson 1984 – but see review in Driscoll 1986; and Driscoll 1988a; 1988b; Samson 1992).

There was a brave attempt to attribute the Book of Kells to a scriptorium in eastern Pictland (Brown 1972), but Iona is now the scholars' favourite choice. Published exhibition catalogues and equally lavish conference proceedings present a wealth of descriptive material in an accessible form (Spearman and Higgitt 1993; Youngs 1989). There have not been further spectacular finds in the league of the St Ninian's Isle Treasure, discovered in 1958, but old material has been reworked, and patient analysis of metal-working debris excavated from high status sites such as Dunadd (Campbell and Lane 1993) has important implications for our ideas about how Insular art developed, and the manner in which Celtic and Anglo-Saxon styles amalgamated. However, the primary published source (and classification scheme, albeit with additions) for Pictish sculpture remains Allen and Anderson, published in 1903, although the RCAHMS (1994) has produced a useful hand-list of stones bearing Pictish symbols. Experts remain in disagreement about the date and provenance of many works of art, and the date and function of Pictish symbols remains unresolved, although the subject of much healthy debate.

The future

Put at its simplest, the questions we want and need to ask about the Picts are much the same as for any society, past or present: what happened where, when, why and how? Gaps prevail virtually everywhere in our basic knowledge and we must accept that many questions are unanswerable. Yet the Picts remain 'far from being a worked out seam' (*pace* Henderson 1967, 13): the challenge is to find a sustainable means of mining into this, without destroying the scarce resource itself. There is plenty of extant material for lucrative reworking, but fresh supplies of material are essential. Archaeology clearly provides the best prospect for increasing knowledge in this field.

To do so we need to identify the major research issues which can propel forward the study of the Picts. Being realistic, most new discoveries will continue to arise in the light of reactive work, primarily rescue archaeology – indeed we should welcome the fresh insight and unexpected perspectives these throw up – but we need to be able to make the most of such opportunities. A framework of research issues would not only direct such work, but provide a basis against which results could be assessed. This same framework could also be used to structure proactive work.

GUARD (1994) have suggested a framework for medieval or later rural settlement in Scotland. Research can, in theory, take place at many levels: national – the analysis of particular themes or categories of site over the whole nation; landscape – the analysis of a block of landscape; and local – the examination of a single site or building. A range of principles for research are identified, accompanied by national and regional research themes; this structure, and even some of the identified principles and research themes, are equally applicable to Pictish and other studies. The suggestions made below are my first thoughts on this: a basis on which to develop strategies for my personal research; offered here as the stalking horse for future debate.

Principles for research

1 Long-term strategies are needed which include an integrated range of projects.

2 Whatever the scale of an individual research project, it should be possible to see where this fits into the global picture. This calls for co-ordination and direction.

3 All rescue-derived projects should embrace relevant research issues, as the opportunity arises. Excavation

strategies should recognise that fragile evidence for Early Historic activity may lie just below, if not within, the topsoil.

4   The identification of key issues can only ever relate to our current understanding of Early Historic political circumstances and the range of increasingly sophisticated questions which arise from this. However, it is essential to set up models which can be challenged, leading to a constant refinement and redefinition of the key issues as the subject develops.

5   The most valuable approach will be landscape-based, considering all aspects of the multi-period cultural landscape.

6   This calls for an integrated, inter-disciplinary approach. Of necessity, teamwork must include experts in all periods, because it is neither possible nor ideal, in the first instance, to focus in on chronologically specific components of the cultural landscape.

7   It is essential that any work on the Picts is situated both within the context of the Early Historic peoples of the British Isles and Europe as a whole. The Picts cannot be studied in isolation.

National themes for research

At this stage in our knowledge, it is scarcely possible to identify anything other than national themes for research, since each usually has general application to the various regions of Pictland (however these might be defined) as well as beyond. In many instances, the historical framework, or our perception of it, is also not detailed enough to be able to identify more regionally specific themes. The suggestions below are therefore very general and by no means definitive; nor is it suggested by their inclusion that the necessary evidence potentially exists to answer them: there is inevitably a disparity between the range of academic issues we might wish to respond to and the ability of archaeology (or other available sources) to fully furnish appropriate evidence for these. Few of these themes should or could be considered in isolation and their grouping, is of necessity, only arbitrary.

1 — The structure and workings of society

1.1   The principles of social authority (including kingship) and how certain individuals acquired authority over others.

1.2   The principles of social organisation (including the role of women and children) and its effect on the structure and nature of settlement.

1.3   The origin, definition, extent, physical manifestation and effectiveness of territories, administrative units and other formal land divisions, including recognition of their constituent parts.

1.4   The relative roles of military, political, ideological and economic power in the development of society, and its trajectory towards state formation.

2 — The nature and organisation of settlement

2.1   Chronological sequence for the range of secular monuments which survive from the Pictish period throughout Scotland.

2.2   The impact of prehistoric landuse and monuments on later activities.

2.3   The evolution, nature, development and decline of hilltop power centres and their influence on the structure and organisation of society.

2.4   The evolution, nature and development of non-enclosed power centres and their relationship to enclosed power centres.

2.5   The relationship between Pictish power centres and early urban centres.

2.6   The evolution, nature and development of non-elite settlements.

2.7   The nature and organisation of the landscape, and how natural resources (plant, animal and mineral) were exploited, including transhumance and the use of marginal land.

2.8   Environmental factors and their impact on the economy and settlement forms.

3 — Religious beliefs and associated practices

3.1   Chronological sequence for the range of ecclesiastical monuments which survive from the Pictish period throughout Scotland.

3.2   The nature of pagan belief and associated practice.

3.3   The introduction of Christianity (how, where and when), the structure of the early church and the physical manifestations of its presence.

3.4   The physical manifestations and social consequences of any differences in the various stages of Roman and Columban practice and presence.

3.5   The evolution of burial practice and the impact of Christianity on this.

3.6   The nature of the inter-relationship between the church, secular authorities and the majority of the (rural) population.

3.7   Place-name evidence as a guide to the location, nature and development of the early church, including the presence or absence of the early Columban church.

3.8   The prevalence of literacy and its role in society.

3.9 The contribution of the Picts to Insular art and connection with the art of its neighbours, including elucidation of the date and origin of the Pictish symbols.

3.10 The development of sculpture, including technology and patronage, and its role in society; to extend to a radical re-evaluation of classification schemes.

4 — The nature and effect of external influence or intrusive presence

4.1 The impact of the short-lived Roman presence(s) and withdrawal on later Iron Age and early Pictish society and comparison with impact on different parts of the British Isles.

4.2 The impact of Christianity (in its different forms) on society.

4.3 The language spoken by the Picts and the date and process by which Gaelic successfully infiltrated and permeated all levels of society.

4.4 The cultural awareness and external contacts of the Picts, and the awareness of other peoples of the Picts.

4.5 The nature and impact of Anglian invasion, political and cultural influences on Pictish society, particularly its art.

4.6 The nature and impact of the Viking raiding, invasion and settlement on Pictish society.

4.7 The process by which the Gaels took over Pictland and the impact of this on both society and material culture, especially in light of the suggested dismissal of the 842 cultural landmark.

5 — Trade and economy

5.1 The nature and organisation of specialised craft activities, their technology, source of resources, patronage and circulation.

5.2 The nature and organisation of domestic craft activities, including their technology, source of resources and circulation.

5.3 The role of power centres (and subsequently urban centres) in local and long distance trade, and the nature of this trade.

5.4 Maritime links, communication and transport, and the extent to which the Picts were a sea-based nation.

5.5 The nature and development of North Sea trade and links with the empires of the continental mainland.

Regional themes for research

Stronger regional studies are needed. Most of the above could be applicable at this level, but some are obviously of greater relevance than others. This is not the appropriate place, nor should a sole person be responsible for developing this (or indeed the above!), but several obvious examples can be floated. For example, the presence or absence of the early Columban church in northern Pictland, or the nature of the Roman mission to Pictland (and its impact in southern Pictland, around the Moray Firth and in Orkney) are obvious examples of how national themes could be tailored to the regional level.

Taking this forward

There is no point, in this context, in becoming bogged down in the issue of money: the same problems (i.e. structure of archaeology, lack of funds and suitably qualified personnel with the time and flexibility to undertake the work) beset any type of archaeological endeavour; nor is the absence of funds any excuse for not considering what the best practice might actually be.

In the first instance, there is much work to be done in setting our house in order and fully exploiting the full range of evidence currently available to us. Jack Burt's 'Pictish Bibliography' is an essential adjunct to this. The National Monuments Record for Scotland contains a vast array of information which is of direct relevance to the Picts. There are some practical problems in extracting this: the office-hours of the Record itself effectively prohibit access to all but the (?Edinburgh-based) retired, student or professional researcher, and there are difficulties with interrogating the Record (the staff are enormously helpful and the technology exists, but success is contingent on how sites have been classified over the years, and this is not yet fully standardised). Non-invasive landscape studies of the type undertaken by Driscoll in Strathearn could be extended to many parts of Scotland, particularly where the RCAHMS has recently undertaken detailed ground and/or aerial recording. These could then be complemented by archaeological fieldwork. University students could play an important role in such work. Cropmarks, in particular, are a sorely under-utilised resource. There is a desperate need for imaginative and sustained analyses of the 'dots' in the Record, and for intelligent and challenging 'syntheses' of the material. An improved, standardised recording of the Early Historic sculpture of Scotland as a whole, made more easily accessible, would provide research opportunities for many, enabling this subject to progress by, amongst other things 'further close and comparative study of the physical evidence present in the monuments themselves and in their decoration and imagery' (Henderson 1995). It is to the subject's detriment that the standard reference, however excellent, was published in 1903. Mercifully, it is at least available in modern reprint.

In terms of project types, two main priorities spring to mind: the investigation of functional site types and activities about which we know virtually nothing, such as burial practice, where these have already been identified; and attention to select landscapes. In selecting landscapes for research, attention should be focused on areas which radiate from known power centres, both secular and ecclesiastical, in an attempt to understand the relationship between the majority of the population, potentates and clerics through time. Comparative, geographically diverse landscapes should be selected which are likely to have been the subject of contrasting political developments and cultural stimuli. One aspect of any project should be the development of predictive models for where sealed landscapes and sites may lie preserved. The emphasis should then be on the investigation of sites which have the potential for the recovery of detailed information, particularly waterlogged sites which have the capacity to preserve organic remains: we need to have information about structures, furnishings, environmental data and an accurate/refined dating sequence. Such information will also become a useful tool for preservation and management strategies.

Conclusions

We are still asking – and will probably continue to ask – many of the same questions about the Picts which Henderson posed in 1967. However, as I hope I have demonstrated, Pictish studies need not become introspective nor moribund. Archaeology, in particular, is filling in the gaps; alternative perspectives and fresh ideas are taking the subject slowly forward, but there is an urgent need for intensive research and new fieldwork in many areas.

It is not true any longer to state, as Henderson did in 1967, that the Picts are 'quite the darkest of the peoples of Dark Age Britain'. This is a cap which, despite the best endeavours of Alan MacQuarrie (1993; see also Ritchie 1994), I would pass to the Britons of Strathclyde.

Documentary historians should now stop referring to the Dark Ages in recognition of, and respect for, the vital contribution which other disciplines have – and have the potential – to shed light on the History of the Picts.

Acknowledgements

I am very grateful to Professor Leslie Alcock, Dr David Breeze, Professor Martin Carver, Dr Lesley Macinnes and Rod McCullagh for their comments on an earlier draft of this paper. All inadequacies and remaining errors are the sole responsibility of the author.

Figure **1**, distribution of recent work and discoveries in Early Historic Scotland (Foster 1996), reproduced by kind permission of Batsford and Historic Scotland.

References

ALCOCK, L
– 1981 Early historic fortifications in Scotland. In Guilbert, G (ed) *Hillfort Studies: essays for A.H.A. Hogg*, 150–80. Leicester.

– 1987 Pictish studies: present and future. In Small (ed) 1987, 80–92.

ALCOCK, L and ALCOCK, E A
– 1987 Reconnaissance excavations on Early Historic fortifications and other royal sites in Scotland, 1974–1984: 2, Excavations at Dunollie Castle, Oban, Argyll, 1978. *Proc Soc Antiq Scot,* 117 (1987), 119–47.

– 1990 Reconnaissance excavations on Early Historic fortifications and other royal sites in Scotland, 1974–1984: 4, Excavations at Alt Clut, Clyde Rock, Strathclyde, 1974–75. *Proc Soc Antiq Scot*, 120 (1990), 95–149.

– 1992 Reconnaissance excavations on Early Historic fortifications and other royal sites in Scotland, 1974–85; 5: A, Excavations and other fieldwork at Forteviot, Perthshire, 1981; B, Excavations at Urquhart Castle, Inverness-shire, 1983; C, Excavations at Dunnottar, Kincardineshire, 1984. *Proc Soc Antiq Scot*, 122 (1992), 215–87.

ALCOCK, L, ALCOCK, EA and DRISCOLL, ST 1989 Reconnaissance excavations on Early Historic fortifications and other royal sites in Scotland, 1974–84: 3, Excavations at Dundurn, Strathearn, Perthshire, 1976–77. *Proc Soc Antiq Scot*, 119 (1989), 189–226.

ALLEN, J R and ANDERSON, J 1903 *The Early Christian Monuments of Scotland,* 3 parts. Edinburgh (repr with an Introduction by Isabel Henderson, 2 vols, Balgavies, Angus, 1993).

ANDERSON, A O
– 1908 *Scottish Annals from English Chronicles AD 500– 1286*. London.

– 1922 *Early Sources of Scottish History*. London.

ANDERSON, M O
– 1980 *Kings and Kingship in Early Scotland*. Edinburgh.

– 1987 Picts – the name and people. In Small (ed) 1987, 7–14.

– (ed) 1991 *Adomnan's Life of Columba*. Oxford.

ARMIT, I (ed) 1990 *Beyond the Brochs*. Edinburgh.

ASHMORE, P J 1980 Low cairns, long cists and symbol stones. *Proc Soc Antiq Scot*, 110 (1978-80), 346–55.

BALLIN SMITH, B 1994 *Howe. Four millennia of Orkney prehistory*. Edinburgh.

BANNERMAN, J 1974 *Studies in the History of Dal Riada*. Edinburgh.

BARROW, W S
– 1973 *The Kingdom of the Scots*. London.

– 1983 The childhood of Christianity: a note on some place-name evidence. *Scottish Studies*, 27 (1983), 1–15.

BROUN, D
– 1994a The origin of Scottish identity. In Bjørn, C, Grant, A and Stringer, K J (eds) *Nations, Nationalism and Patriotism in the European Past*, 35–55. Copenhagen.

– 1994b Defining Scotland and the Scots before the Wars of Independence (unpublished paper presented to 'Nationalism and Identity: the search for Scotland' conference, St Andrews).

BROWN, T J 1972 Northumbria and the Book of Kells. *Anglo-Saxon England*, 1 (1972), 219–46.

BURT, J R F 1995 A Pictish Bibliography. In Nicoll, E H (ed) 1995, 33–184

CAMPBELL, E 1996 The archaeological evidence for contacts: imports, trade and economy in Celtic Britain AD 400–800. In Dark, K R (ed) *External Contacts and the Economy of Late Roman and Post-Roman Britain AD 400–800*, 83–96. Woodbridge.

CAMPBELL, E and LANE, A 1993 Celtic and Germanic interaction in Dalriada: the 7th-century metalworking site at Dunadd. In Spearman and Higgitt (eds) 1993, 52–63.

CLOSE-BROOKS, J 1984 Pictish and other burials. In Friell and Watson (eds) 1984, 87–114.

CRAWFORD, I nd *The West Highlands and Islands. A view of 50 centuries*. Cambridge.

CRAWFORD, B (ed) 1994 *Scotland in Dark Age Europe*. St Andrews.

DES = *Discovery and Excavation in Scotland*

DRISCOLL, S T
– 1986 Symbol stones and Pictish ethnography, review of *Symbol Stones of Scotland*. *Scot Archaeol Rev*, 4:1, 59–64.

– 1987 *The Early Historical Landscape of Strathearn: the archaeology of a Pictish kingdom*. (Unpublished PhD thesis, University of Glasgow.)

– 1988a Power and authority in Early Historic Scotland: Pictish stones and other document. In Gledhill *et al* (eds) 1988, 215–36.

– 1988b The relationship between history and archaeology: artefacts, documents and power. In Driscoll and Nieke (eds) 1988, 162–87.

– 1991 The archaeology of state formation in Scotland. In Hanson, W S and Slater, E A (eds) *Scottish Archaeology: new perceptions*, 81–111. Aberdeen.

DRISCOLL, S T and NIEKE, M R (eds) 1988 *Power and Politics in Early Medieval Britain and Ireland*. Edinburgh.

DUMVILLE, D 1976 A note on the Picts in Orkney. *Scot Gaelic Stud*, 12:2 (1976), 266.

FAIRWEATHER, A D and RALSTON, I B M 1993 The Neolithic timber hall at Balbridie, Grampian Region, Scotland: the building, the date, the plant macrofossils. *Antiquity*, 67 (1993), 313–23.

FORSYTH, K
– 1995 Language in Pictland, spoken and written. In Nicoll, E H (ed) 1995, 7–10.

– 1996 *The Ogham Inscriptions of Scotland*. (PhD thesis, University of Harvard)

FOSTER, S M
– 1989 Transformations in social space: Iron Age Orkney and Caithness. *Scot Archaeol Rev*, 6 (1989), 34–55.

– 1990 Pins, combs and the chronology of later Atlantic Iron Age settlement. In Armit (ed) 1990, 143–74.

– 1996 *Picts, Gaels and Scots: Early Historic Scotland*. London.

FRASER, I A 1987 Pictish place-names – some toponymic evidence. In Small, A (ed) 1987, 68–72.

FRIELL, J G P and WATSON, W G (eds) 1984 *Pictish Studies: settlement, burial and art in Dark Age northern Britain*. Oxford.

GLEDHILL, J, BENDER, B and LARSEN, M (eds) 1988 *State and Society: the emergence and development of social hierarchy and political centralisation*. London

GRANT, A 1993 Thanes and thanages from the eleventh to fourteenth centuries. In Grant and Stringer (eds) 1993, 39–81.

GRANT, A and STRINGER, K J (eds) 1993 *Medieval Scotland. Crown, Lordship and Community.* Edinburgh.

GUARD 1994 Medieval or later Rural Settlement (MOLRS) Study: recommendations towards a policy statement. (Unpublished report prepared for Historic Scotland.)

HARDING, D W and ARMIT, I 1990 Survey and excavation in West Lewis. In Armit (ed) 1990, 71–107.

HENDERSON, G 1987 *From Durrow to Kells. The Insular Gospel books 650–800.* London.

HENDERSON, I
– 1967 *The Picts.* London.
– 1995 Pictish art and its place within the history of Insular art. In Nicoll (ed) 1995, 14–19.

HIGGITT, J 1982 The Pictish Latin inscription at Tarbat in Ross-shire. *Proc Soc Antiq Scot,* 112 (1982), 300–21.

HUNTER, J R
– 1986 *Rescue Excavations in the Brough of Birsay 1974–82.* Edinburgh.
– 1990 *Pool, Sanday: a case study for the late Iron Age and Viking Periods.* In Armit (ed) 1990, 175–93.

JACKSON, A 1984 *The Symbol Stones of Scotland.* Kirkwall.

LAING, L R and LAING, J 1993 *The Picts and the Scots.* Stroud.

LANE, A 1990 Hebridean pottery: problems of definition, chronology, presence and absence. In Armit (ed) 1990, 108–30.

LATHAM, R E (ed) 1990 *Bede: Ecclesiastical History of the English People.* Harmondsworth.

LYNCH, M 1992 *Scotland: A New History.* London.

LOWE, C forthcoming Coastal erosion and the archaeological assessment of an eroding shoreline at St. Boniface's church, Papa Westray, Orkney.

MACQUARRIE, A 1993 The kings of Strathclyde, *c*400–1018. In Grant and Stringer (eds) 1993, 1–19.

MACSWEEN, A 1990 The Neolithic and Late Iron Age Pottery from Pool. Sanday, Orkney. (Unpublished PhD thesis, University of Bradford)

MAXWELL, G 1987 Settlement in southern Pictland: a new overview. In Small (ed) 1987, 31–44.

MCCULLAGH, R 1995 Excavations at Sueno's Stone, Forres, Moray, 1990-1991. *Proc Soc Antiq Scot,* 125 (1995), 697–718

MCNEILL, P and NICHOLSON, R 1975 *An Historical Atlas of Scotland c400–c1600.* St Andrews.

NICOLL, E H (ed) 1995 *A Pictish Panorama: the Story of the Picts and a Pictish Bibliography.* Balgavies, Angus.

NIEKE, M R
– 1988 Literacy and power: the introduction and use of writing in Early Historic Scotland. In Gledhill *et al* (eds) 1986, 237–52.
– 1993 Penannular and related brooches: secular ornament or symbol in action. In Spearman and Higgitt (eds) 1993, 128–34.

RALSTON, I B M 1987 Portknockie: promontory forts and Pictish settlement in the North-east. In Small (ed) 1987, 15–26.

RIDEOUT, J 1995 Carn Dubh, Moulin, Perthshire: survey and excavation of an archaeological landscape 1987-90. *Proc Soc Antiq Scot,* 125 (1995), 139–95

RITCHIE, A
– 1977 Excavation of Pictish and Viking-age farmsteads at Buckquoy, Orkney. *Proc Soc Antiq Scot,* 108 (1976-77), 174–227.
– 1989 *Picts.* Edinburgh.
– (ed) 1994 *Govan and its Early Medieval Sculpture.* Stroud.

RCAHMS 1994 Royal Commission on the Ancient and Historical Monuments of Scotland. *Pictish Symbol Stones: A handlist 1994.* Edinburgh.

SAMSON, R 1992 The reinterpretation of the Pictish symbols. *J Brit Archaeol Assoc,* 145 (1992), 29–65.

SELLAR, W D H 1985 Warlords, Holymen and Matrilineal Succession. *Innes Review,* 36, 29–43.

SHEPHERD, I A G and SHEPHERD, A N 1978 An incised Pictish figure and a new symbol stone from Barflat, Rhynie, Gordon District. *Proc Soc Antiq Scot,* 109 (1977-78), 211–22.

SMALL, A (ed) 1987 *The Picts: a new look at old problems.* Dundee.

SMYTH, A 1984 *Warlords and Holymen: Scotland AD 800–1000.* London.

SPEARMAN, R M and HIGGITT, J (eds) 1993 *The Age of Migrating Ideas, Early Medieval Art in Northern Britain and Ireland* (Proceedings of the Second International Conference on Insular Art, Edinburgh, 1991). Edinburgh/Stroud.

SUTHERLAND, E 1994 *In Search of the Picts.* London.

THOMAS, A C
– 1971 *The Early Christian Archaeology of North Britain.* Oxford.
– 1981 *Christianity in Roman Britain to AD 500.* London.

WAINWRIGHT, F T (ed) 1955 *The Problem of the Picts.* Edinburgh (new edn Perth, 1980).

WATKINS, T

— 1980a Excavation of a settlement and souterrain at Newmill, near Bankfoot, Perthshire. *Proc Soc Antiq Scot*, 110 (1978-80), 165–208.

— 1980b Excavation of an Iron Age open settlement at Dalladies, Kincardineshire. *Proc Soc Antiq Scot*, 110 (1978–80), 122–64.

YOUNGS, S (ed) 1989 *'The Work of Angels': masterpieces of Celtic metalwork, 6th–9th centuries AD*. London.

Postscript

Since this paper was completed, in June 1995, the *Atlas of Scottish History* has been updated and reprinted (McNeill and MacQueen 1996) and several other important publications have appeared (such as Crawford 1996). Of particular note is the contribution and increasing profile of place-name studies (see, for example, Taylor 1996). Martin Carver's work at Portmahomack has emerged into a major Heritage Lottery funded enterprise (University of York 1995); archaeological discoveries include the recovery of a range of early medieval sculpture of outstanding craftsmanship, augmenting the existing assemblage and reinforcing the importance of the Pictish establishment there.

Postscript references

CRAWFORD, B E (ed) 1996 *Scotland in Dark Age Britain*. St Andrews.

MCNEILL, P G B and MACQUEEN, H L 1996 *Atlas of Scottish History to 1707*. Edinburgh.

TAYLOR, S 1996 Place-names and the early church in eastern Scotland. In Crawford (ed) 1996, 93–110.

UNIVERSITY OF YORK 1995 *Tarbat Discovery Programme Bulletin No. 1 1995*. University of York, Tarbat Historical Trust, Highland Council.

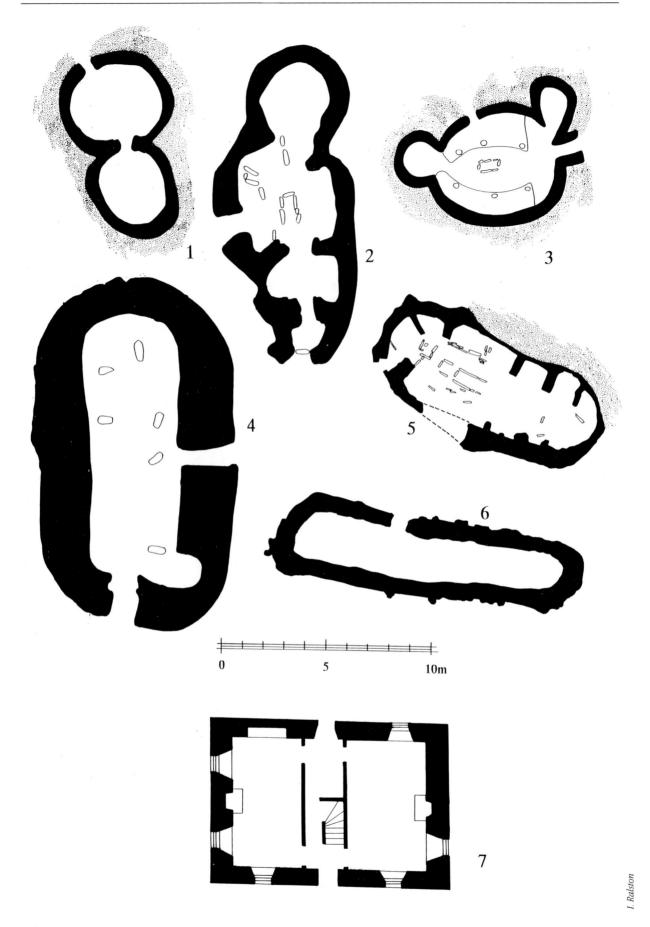

1 *Some typical and atypical Pictish buildings:* **1** *Carlungie, Angus* **2** *Buckquoy, Orkney* **3** *Coileagan an Udail (Udal), North Uist* **4** *Wag of Forse, Caithness* **5** *Howe, Orkney* **6** *Pitcarmick, Perthshire (after Alcock, 1984, Ballin Smith, 1994, and Stevenson, 1991)* *with* **7** *Old Gruline House, Mull ground floor plan (after RCAHMS 1980) of late eighteenth century house as a scalar comparison*

Pictish homes

Ian Ralston

'As the Picts were apparently a heterogeneous people, we should not expect to find a cultural uniformity among them ...' (Wainwright 1955, 87)

Introduction

The late Frederick Wainwright's review of Pictish houses and Richard Feachem's study of fortified settlements (both 1955) form the baseline for all subsequent archaeological approaches to the secular domestic architecture of northern Scotland in the second half of the first millennium AD. Although pervaded with that pessimism which, retrospectively, seems to have been such a characteristic of post-Second-World-War considerations of the archaeological (as opposed to the art historical) aspects of Pictish culture, Wainwright's study in particular perceptively looked forward. He listed some of the several possible categories of settlement units then recognised in the landscapes of Scotland north of the Forth-Clyde isthmus that might in due course be attributable to the Picts.

After the passage of some four decades, the amount and range of evidence available have increased rapidly, indeed almost exponentially, in so doing bolstering Wainwright's salient comments on the likely variability in the settlement record of this period. A major contribution has been provided by the results of aerial survey, mostly undertaken or sponsored by RCAHMS, more particularly of the cropmarked lowlands within the zone. This source of new data continues to offer a counterpoint to the recently-accumulated excavation evidence, for which much of the information on houses has been generated in the North and West, and more particularly from the Orkney Islands. In this essay, submitted with great pleasure in acknowledgement of Dr Henderson's major contribution to other dimensions of Pictish studies, it is on this aspect –

variability in the settlement record – that I should like primarily to focus. This account does not attempt more than a preliminary view on the range of building forms represented in the archaeological record, nor on how they may be interpreted.

Some factors influencing variability in architectural forms

Resources and environment

In itself, the degree of variation manifest in the secular domestic architecture of the first millennium across the great stretch of land between Flanders Moss and Muckle Flugga need occasion no particular surprise. It is, of course, partially conditioned by the availability of building materials, and by environmental factors such as rainfall and wind regimes. Papers in a recent volume summarise our present knowledge of the potential influence of such factors (Edwards and Ralston 1997).

The area encompassed in this account is topographically varied. Some of the most fertile lowlands of Scotland, such as those of the Laigh of Moray and north-east Fife (where, even allowing for millennia of human impact on the vegetation cover, hardwoods for building would still have been obtainable) are included. Much more rugged terrain, the latter characterised in all likelihood by limited supplies of building timber (and that often softwood) in some localities and less tractable stone (such as gneiss) for construction in others is also widely represented.

Even allowing for driftwood, timber for constructional purposes may have been of very restricted availability on some of the off-shore islands. The complex geology and topography of Scotland means that there is no simple south-to-north or similar trend in the qualities of the materials available. For the North, for example, the finely-bedded sandstones, so readily splittable into serviceable flags, of the Caithness plateau and the Orkneys provide an excellent resource for dry-stone building. This had, of course, been appreciated since Neolithic times, as remains visible in the outstanding architectural achievements of some chambered cairns. At Midhowe on Rousay, the wave-cut rock platform, from which slabs would have been prised for both the magnificent stalled cairn and, millennia later, the broch and its surrounding complex constructed just above the shore, illustrates this excellently. The impact of varying lithic resources extended well beyond building; its contribution to the artistic qualities of Pictish sculpture has been the subject of comment (Henderson 1958, 1972; Gordon 1956).

This variability in building styles is also familiar to students of more recent vernacular architecture. Robert Naismith's *Buildings of the Scottish Countryside* (1985), for example, includes a map (Map IV, p.156), which endeavours to present graphically the principal character zones represented in vernacular buildings of pre-Recent times within the country. Overall, some twelve such character sets are identified within Scotland: more than half of these are included within the area that might formerly have been labelled Pictland. The picture is further complicated by the recognition of a second tier of minor variations within these character zones, so that transferring this pattern back in time might well be construed to support the proposition that considerable differences in building types might equally characterise the first millennium AD.

Social, symbolic and other factors

Such variation, however, goes beyond that which might simply be accounted for in terms of the relative accessibility of different resources and the presence of environments of lesser or greater hostility. For more recent times, it would be usual to include consideration of economic, cultural, social and other pertinent factors in the search for explanations for the types of architecture encountered. Buildings are of course far more than simple providers of shelter: encoded in their forms, internal arrangements and decoration (or its absence) are intimations of other cultural and social factors at work. They are thus also signs and symbols (Oliver 1975); and it would be reasonable to

assume that such considerations were also encoded in the architecture of Pictland, even if it difficult for us now to grasp them.

Perspectives of this kind underpin the developing field of the social archaeology of houses (Samson 1990). Whilst, for example, it has long been a truism of later prehistoric studies that there is a marked contrast between British architectural forms, in which round-houses predominate in some areas well into the first millennium AD, and continental types, where rectilinear forms are mainly represented (Harding 1973; Villes 1983; Audouze and Büchsenschütz, 1992), the possible social ramifications of this contrast have not until recently been much explored. Indeed, Classical witness, in particular Strabo's testimony (*Geography,* 4, IV, 3) as to the existence of round-houses in Gaul has continued to obscure the issue. This case is of relevance to the present discussion, if only tangentially, as it proffers an indication of the significance of the external appearance of buildings to foreign observers. Strabo was perhaps simply contrasting the sharp rectilinearity of Mediterranean ashlar structures, seen under bright sunlight, with the altogether doucer outlines of wooden buildings standing under clouded skies further North. Circular forms remain remarkable for their rarity in temperate continental Europe (cf Harding 1974, 48), although – as in the Seine valley – examples are certainly present.

An important perspective on buildings is thus that of the outsider. It is not, however, the only one. Other studies of British Iron Age architecture have in recent years drawn attention to, for example: the perception and signification of house interiors (Barrett 1981); the variable monument-ality of buildings perceived from the exterior, contrasted with how imposing or otherwise they might appear to their inhabitants and their guests (Armit 1990); pathways through domestic complexes and their potential socio-political ramifications, as suggested by access analysis (Foster 1989); and the possible cosmological referents of buildings and their orientations (Parker Pearson 1996; Fitzpatrick 1994; Hill 1995, fig 7a). These contributions illustrate something of the wide range of approaches now being brought to bear by archaeologists, conscious of theoretical stances developed in adjacent disciplines, to the consideration of domestic architecture. Such structures had for long been considered by archaeologists primarily in terms of either seemingly straightforward cultural attributions, or with regard to the technologies vested, and different architectural solutions adopted (Musson 1970), in their construction. Some of the ideas contained in this literature may pertinently be applied to what we know of Pictish domestic architecture: '... given the artefact', as Brunskill expressed it (1982, 18), 'one may, in theory at least, deduce the circumstances in which it was created'.

Another perspective on first millennium AD domestic buildings may be offered by comparisons with sources other than archaeological ones, as has been considered for Irish material (Murray 1979). For a variety of reasons there rehearsed, the correlations between historical document-ation and the evidence recovered by excavation are less than absolute, although some documented features are recognised in archaeological plans of buildings. Such material is however of additional interest in a number of ways: in illustrating (albeit in an assuredly idealised way) the link between social position and architectural forms; and in providing impressions of internal furnishings and decoration and other features – perhaps most notably windows – unlikely to be recovered in many excavation circumstances.

Domestic buildings in Pictland
Variations in plan
Much of the recent commentary on later prehistoric houses has so far been focused on such dualisms as round *versus* rectangular, the monumental against the less imposing, and essentially concentric subdivisions of internal space contrasted with arrangements marked by a prominent central space with attached subsidiary cells. It will be argued below that the architectures of Pictland as presently known provide indications of almost all these threads (**1**). Juxtaposing the results of more recent excavations and surveys with what was already appreciable by Wainwright, it is clear that the domestic buildings of first millennium Pictland demonstrate the co-existence of round, multi-cellular and rectilinear traditions of construction. Thus if buildings are indeed to be seen as signs and symbols, such diversity implies that the messages the buildings conveyed to their inhabitants and their neighbours may equally have been very divergent. Pictland is by no means unique in its

approximately synchronous use of round and rectangular forms, although these may occur in different proportions in different areas. In Ireland, for example, a rectilinear house is abutted against a round *clochan* or beehive-hut with corbelled roof within the ring-fort at Leacanabuile, Co Cork (Edwards 1990, 25 and fig 9d), but Lynn indicates the limitations of the evidence for the strict contemporaneity of the two forms (1978, 31 with table 1). The evidence from Ireland rehearsed by Lynn (1978) and Edwards (1990, 26) points to the increasing adoption of rectilinear forms there from about the eighth century AD, an important change for which the influence of church forms, seemingly there always rectilinear, has been proposed (Lynn 1978). Whilst not excluding other potential sources of external influence, Lynn also pertinently notes that the adoption of different constructional techniques for church architecture may have spilled over into the domestic sphere (1978, 37).

The clustered and the isolated
Further, the characteristics of grouping amongst Pictish structures, as illustrated by more extensive excavation work, again suggest considerable variety in degrees of clustering, as has already been noted by Ritchie (1977). This is best exemplified by the relationships between Pictish structures set within or around complex Atlantic round-houses or brochs, and those in other settings. In the first cases, tight clusters are often apparent, whether within the former broch, as in Professor Harding's excavations at Dun Bharabhat, Lewis, or in partially contiguous arrangements in its immediate vicinity, as at the Howe, on the mainland of Orkney (Ballin Smith 1994). Northern sites lacking evidence for pre-existing structures in the complex Atlantic round-house tradition can display even more complexity: Hunter has recently described the new structures of the second Pictish phase at Pool (Sanday, Orkney) as being 'of a variety of shapes and sizes, all essentially cellular, and all connected by a labyrinth of conjoining passages and openings' (1997, 14). Such patterning offers an immediate contrast with other sites, where the gaps between individual structures are greater. The spacing of structures obtaining in Professor Hunter's excavations on the Brough of Birsay (Hunter 1986) or in the Scotto-Pictish phase mapped by Crawford at the Udal, North Uist, where the 'ventral' buildings were also located some way from the

wheel-house of the previous settlement horizon provide examples.

It has, however, to be acknowledged that repeated use and sequential modifications to buildings at some of these sites may in fact reveal successive phases of decline, or of expansion, rather than the co-existence of numerous serviceable buildings. The evidence for the apparent decline of both Howe and Pool from around the middle of the first millennium is rehearsed by Shepherd (1994, 276–7) and Hunter (1997). Moreover, as Alcock (1984, 17) has already noted, not all secondary occupations associated with earlier major dry-stone buildings in the North and West exhibit such radical changes in their character and layout: the secondary insertion of radial piers within the Broch of Burrian, Orkney, for example, may imply the re-establishment of a community no larger than its Iron Age predecessor on the site.

Behind such differences in the spacing amongst domestic units must lie distinctions in the way human groups organised their daily rounds. Such apparent variation in social patterns at the community scale may be of importance in the further development of wider considerations. For example, the centralising tendencies and emerging political complexity argued to be witnessed by other strands of evidence from first millennium northern Scotland (summarised by Foster 1996), not least from the sculpture itself, may find echoes in such arrangements. It may not be insignificant that another largely new suite of sites – the square barrows and cairns – equally proffer contrasts among sites clustered to varying degrees. At Garbeg, Inverness-shire (Stevenson 1984: Wedderburn and Grime 1984) and some of the Lunan Valley, Angus, examples, such as the cropmark evidence from Invergighty Cottage, the burials are tightly clustered. In others, the graves and their covering mounds seem to be more dispersed. Instances of the latter arrangement are furnished by Greig's important work at Lundin Links, Fife (Close-Brooks 1984, fig 5.11) and by the distribution of square barrows – again known solely from aerial photographs – within the croplands at Pitairlie, Moray District (Shepherd 1993; Shepherd and Grieg 1996, no 46). It may not be entirely idle, in making this connection between houses of the living and the repositories of the dead, to point out that the axial arrangement of conjoined

cairns visible at Lundin Links, has already been noted by Alcock in relation to the arrangement of the houses of the Far North. For cemeteries, too, the accruing evidence essentially post-dates Wainwright's 1955 study, where the eye cast over graves was almost as forlorn as that focused on houses.

Some characteristics of buildings in 'peripheral' Pictland

In terms of Pictish buildings themselves, the principal headway that has been made in recent years has been in 'peripheral' Pictland. A major fillip was furnished by Ritchie's excavations at, and prompt publication of, Buckquoy on Orkney (1977). Since that time, nearly every northern site tackled has served to extend the range of building types marked by the presence of at least dry-stone footings, and continues so to do, as at Traigh Bostadh, Lewis (DES 1996, 113–14 and fig 36). Hunter's excavations at Pool on Sanday, Orkney, provide some of the clearest instances of structural variety, as well as indications of the change to rectilinear forms for domestic buildings – there are early instances also of a byre and courtyard – during his Pictish-Norse interface period (Hunter 1990; Hunter et al, 1993).

All examples of buildings excavated since the 1970s in 'peripheral Pictland' seem to be from unfortified sites, or sites which, if once defensible (as with the more elaborate of the Atlantic complex round-houses), no longer were substantially so during these centuries. At Gurness, on mainland Orkney, for example, the 'Shamrock' building lies outwith the area isolated by the ditches which surround the broch and its adjacent structures. To some extent, the tidal approach to, and cliff outline of much of, the Brough of Birsay on Orkney, make this site an exception to the general lack of concern for defence apparent at may of these locations.

The architecture identified on these northern sites offers an impressive array of forms and groundplans: from informal structures through conjoined circles and multicellular forms, axially arranged on occasion (Alcock 1984, 18), to much more rectilinear outlines, these latter occurring amongst the peripheral buildings at Howe and, as already remarked, at Pool (Sanday). All groundplans are far from reflecting readily-comprehensible layouts, however; Hunter (1997, 8) notes 'the combination of asymmetry, irregularity and disorder' evidenced in some phases at some of these sites. There is also considerable variation in the sizes of buildings that are represented. Those at Udal enclosed areas of the order of 20m² (Alcock 1984, 18), not dissimilar to the floor area of the house of an eighth century freeman of the lowest grade in Ireland, as reconstituted from literary testimony by Murray (1979). Others (eg **1**) are much more substantial.

It is usually considered (eg Ritchie 1995) that the dry-stone footings – in which double-faced walling can often co-exist with elements revetted into midden or pre-existing structures – that constitute the bulk of the surviving evidence would have been complemented externally by divots of turf. The result would have been to produce well-insulated walls, which it is proposed were surmounted by either turf-covered roofs supported on timber frames, as were the Norse structures which sometimes succeeded them (Crawford 1987, 141). More especially in the case of their circular components, roofing may have consisted of stone corbelling. The evidence for repeated rebuilding on some sites, sometimes re-using extent walling, and sometimes based on previously-collapsed stonework, suggests that structural instability was a not-unfamiliar problem. As Foster (1992, 227 and fig 42) has noted, buildings of subrectangular form on the Northern mainland, as at the Wag of Forse, Caithness, may also date to this period.

Many of these houses combine horizontal stonework with upright slabs lining their walls and sometimes forming internal subdivisions. Unlike Norse houses, for which Crawford (1987) has recently suggested that wood was much more substantially employed than has usually been surmised, there does not seem to be a case for arguing for much greater use of wood within most of the northern Pictish period buildings than has standardly been posited. More substantial use of timber should perhaps not be ruled out, however; in this regard, whilst attention has been drawn to the excellent building stone of the Caithness plateau, Zeune (1992, 119) remarks that the hall constructed for Alexander III's visit to Caithness in 1263 was of timber.

The Pictish 'heartlands'

Timber architecture and nails in forts and elsewhere

Timber architectures have generally been less well served by recent excavation programmes, although even in their case there are numerous intimations of additional types, for some of which more secure evidence can be anticipated: timber halls, considered further below, are a case in point. In the meantime, as an indication of the carpentry and other skills potentially represented in domestic Pictish timber buildings, fortifications still provide much of the strongest evidence, and offer a complement to other structural detail recovered in excavations furth of Pictland.

This set of evidence is interesting in a number of ways. First, the use of iron spikes to hold together the internal timber framework within the defences at Burghead, Moray (Edwards and Ralston 1978, with earlier references), and, on the south-western margin of Pictland, at Dundurn (Alcock *et al* 1989) surely represents – as it does in the *murus gallicus* tradition (Ralston 1995) of late Iron Age continental Europe – conspicuous consumption of these items, and thus an intimation of the possible importance of iron production. Whilst the use of iron nails, sometimes of relatively standardised lengths (Vaginay and Guichard 1988, 150–1), becomes a recurrent feature of house architecture in the nearer continent from about the second century BC, or even a little earlier, there are relatively few signs of this development even a millennium later in northern Scotland. Evidence is not, however, entirely absent. Howe on Orkney, for example, offers indications of both greater use of nails, more particularly during Phase 7 of that site's sequence, and some regularity in their lengths (Ballin Smith 1994, 217–8, 226), and nails were also recovered in quantity within one of the principal buildings of the Pictish-Norse interface period at Pool, Sanday (Hunter *et al* 1993, 279). It is of course possible that this seeming tardiness in the use of nails in buildings may have as much to do with iron's reduced survival possibilities in many Scottish soil conditions, as with its real level of use.

Carpentry

As regards woodwork itself, the carbonised timbers within the rampart framework at the Green Castle, Portknockie, Moray, display evidence for both half-check and mortise joints (Ralston 1987, figs 4-5). There are parallels for complex jointing within fortifications far to the south at South Cadbury (Alcock 1982). These British sites share with examples to the East on the continent the renewed, indeed more elaborate, construction of Holz-Erde-Mauer-style fortifications, as previously found in later prehistory, and which culminate there in defences of around 1,000 AD at Behren-Lübchin in the former East Germany (Schuldt 1989) and Naszacowice (Poland) (Poleski 1992, Abb 17). It is a reasonable assumption that such sophistication in woodworking may also have been employed in some Pictish domestic architecture, the more so given the quality of timberwork, displayed in the mortised palisades that are a late feature the first millennium crannog at Buiston, Ayrshire (Crone 1991; 1993), as well as that known for example from wetland contexts, notably through the work of the Archaeological Wetland Unit in Ireland (Edwards 1990). Similarly, the Irish literary records (Murray 1979) and the remarkable-preserved seventh century structures at Deer Park Farms, Glenarm, Co Antrim, provide additional evidence for the sophisticated use of woods and wattling.

Earthfast timbers, post-pads and sleeper beams

Lastly, it may also be remarked that there are some indications of a further major development in timber architecture at this time. Throughout Scottish later prehistory, the construction of timber buildings seems to have remained substantially dependant on earthfast timbers, set in postholes, even if, once built, the buildings were quite capable of continuing to stand without reliance on this feature, as Reynolds (1994, 13) has been able to demonstrate at the dismantling of the reconstructed Pimperne round-house at Butser Experimental Farm in Hampshire. For first millennium AD buildings in Pictland, there is some evidence that such earth-fast uprights were no longer deemed essential. For example, at the Green Castle, Portknockie, the major building recovered has at least one internal post-pad (Ralston 1987, fig 3), and no sign of contemporary post-holes within the structure. Similarly, at Pool, on Sanday, Orkney, excavation evidence led Professor Hunter to posit the former existence of vertical timber members that were no longer always earth-fast in Pictish-Norse interface-period structures. Post-pads have also been recorded in post-Roman buildings further South, in Scotland at the Dod in Roxburghshire, and in the

substantial buildings set at a late stage within Birdoswald Roman fort in northern England (Smith 1991, 277).

At Dundurn, Perthshire, the Glasgow University team revealed evidence that the palisade attributed to Phase 1 (*c*600 AD) was set in horizontal beams, here accommodated in a rock-cut groove; planks with pegged holes belonging to this stockade were also identified (Alcock *et al* 1989, 200–1). In other circumstances, where resistance to hostile attack was not part of the intention and thus anchoring the sill-beams was not essential, it is easy to consider similar constructional methods having been employed in domestic architecture, but without the use of rock-cut or other grooves. The illustration of the Temple in the Book of Kells (redrawn by Reynolds 1980) aside from the wood-working abilities and extensive decoration shown on it, seems to indicate the use of sill-beams for a structure in which buttresses (see also below) are absent.

In the zone of likely destruction, where archaeological evidence has been disturbed by subsequent ploughing and other activities, the detection of non-earth-fast timber architecture is likely to remain archaeologically problematic, and this may be a contributory factor in accounting for recognition problems in some regions of eastern Scotland with regard to Pictish timber-built buildings. As elsewhere, of course, structures in *Blockbau* style (Audouze and Büchsenschütz 1992), essentially built of horizontal timbers and well-suited to the use of softwoods, or those dependant on sleeper beams positioned directly on the ground or on relatively slight stone footings (Greene 1995, 91), pose even more serious challenges to archaeological recovery.

The nature of the record

Overall, concentrating uniquely on secular sites, the major change over the forty years since Wainwright wrote is that if, for him, the problem was what to include as Pictish architecture, the difficulty for the heartland areas of Pictland is now rather the converse. Amongst the settlement types of the 'greater Iron Age' – broadly the first millennia BC and AD – in Scotland north of the Central Belt, few can presently be excluded with confidence as unlikely to have been in use (or individual examples re-used) between the third and ninth centuries AD. Even those categories for which it is currently not possible to point to a securely-dated example within Pictland, include some site types which elsewhere in Scotland are clearly attributable to the first millennium AD, as dendrochronological and radiocarbon determinations demonstrate. Crannogs in south-west Scotland may stand as an instance of this (Barber and Crone 1993), for here they are clearly a first millennium AD site type, as they are across the North Channel in north-east Ireland (Edwards 1990, 37, table 1; Crone 1993). There are no radiocarbon dates for examples north of Loch Tay, but it is possible that here too some may be attributable to the first millennium AD.

General considerations

In this treatment, macro-scale approaches to the identification of Pictish settlement in the heartland that have been used to identify preferred zones for Pictish settlement have been excluded from consideration. Whittington used the distribution of 'pit-' place-names (1975). Other studies have examined the co-occurrence of place-name and symbol stone evidence, as considered by Cottam and Small for Angus (1974) or by Shepherd for north-eastern material culture more generally (1983). So, too, has been any systematic survey of the accumulating cropmark aerial photographic record in relation to known and geographically-fixed elements of Pictish material culture (most notably the Class I and Class II sculpture). Individual instances of the co-occurrence of symbol-stones and cropmark enclosures have already been signalled, as at Barflat, near Rhynie in Aberdeenshire (Shepherd 1983; Ralston and Inglis 1984, 17; Shepherd and Greig 1996 nos 55–56), but as yet none of the associated cropmarks has been tested by the spade, and the definition of their character – whether secular or indeed Pictish at all – remains unconfirmed. Driscoll's study of Strathearn (1991) is a model of what is achievable without excavation through the fuller examination of the aerial photographic data.

Evidence from Early Historic sites

In recent years, the archaeological study of Pictish settlements south of the Moray Firth has been dominated by Emeritus Professor Alcock's sustained reconnaissance campaigns directed at Early Historic sites (as defined by him to comprise those sites with documentary evidence including associated historical dates). The nature of his targeted excavation strategies has meant that, whilst they have thrown considerable light on the fortification history of certain key sites, and, through their recovery of high quality objects, have produced key evidence for the presence of potentates within them, indications of domestic structures – as opposed to domestic and artisanal activities – within these sites remain sparse. This is the case, for example, at Dundurn, where clear evidence – excluding that of the fortifications – was restricted to a wattle floor, other structural elements including traces of floors, stone walling and post-holes being too fragmentary readily to be understood (Alcock *et al* 1989). Of the other sites of this series within Pictland tackled by the Glasgow University expeditions, only Urquhart Castle, above the shore of Loch Ness, provided a few archaeological clues as to the character of its internal buildings. Here, restricted amounts of evidence, primarily in the form of post-pits, inserted into a layer of cobbling, led Alcock and Alcock (1992, 248–60 and illus 26) to reconstruct both a single- and a double-aisled lean-to, backed against the fortification.

Whilst the evidence is necessarily tentative given the small scale of the excavation, it none the less furnishes another hint that timber-built structures in Pictland need not have possessed posts dug into the subsoil, and thus more likely to be recovered in many archaeological circumstances. The limited scale of excavation at Clatchard Craig, Fife, equally precludes extended discussion of the building types it may have held (Close-Brooks 1986), although a rectilinear house may be implied, albeit exceedingly tentatively, by the recovery of a stone-edged hearth of that shape, and a door pivot-stone. Many of the complex round-houses of the Atlantic middle Iron Age, however, contained rectangular hearths. In this instance, however, the attribution of the very Iron-Age-looking multivallate fort at Clatchard Craig wholly to the first millennium AD reminds us that it may be inadvisable to consider surface traces of buildings within other similar examples as forcibly attributable to the pre-Roman Iron Age.

The ring-forts of Perthshire: circular homesteads

In his recent synthesis, Taylor strongly disavows the use of the term 'ring-fort' to describe the series of heavily-walled circular enclosures identified primarily in north-west Perthshire (1990), that have been traditionally so termed. Somewhat similar concerns have been raised about the use of this and related epithets for cognate site types in Ireland (Edwards 1990, 12), where the enclosures surround generally larger areas, up to some 35 m in diameter. In essence, recent excavation evidence points to this series of Perthshire sites having been substantial homesteads, with conical roofs perhaps set on their wall-heads and supported by internal timber uprights, more regularly disposed it would seem in the case of the partially excavated example at Litigan than at Queen's View, Allean Forest (Taylor 1990, figs 2 and 3 respectively). Dating evidence remains scanty (there is a single isotopic determination of 930 AD ± 90 (uncalibrated) for charcoal found above the subsoil at Litigan: Taylor 1990, 17). Taylor nonetheless constructs a reasonable case for seeing them, as Feachem (1955, 72) had earlier hypothesised, as a later first millennium AD phenomenon in Atholl, with a background in the West, and thus as perhaps indicative of Scottic penetration eastward. Since a preferred hypothesis in Ireland is to envisage the upsurge of ring-forts there as a response to technological developments introduced from sub-Roman Britain (Lynn 1983; Edwards 1990, 17–18), and the chronology of dun-houses (Harding 1984; 1997) in western Scotland remains contentious, the case is, however, far from clear-cut. A further distinction is that the 'wholly-roofed' hypothesis does not seem to have found favour even for smaller ring-forts in Ireland (Edwards 1990, 27). Whether it is applicable even to the larger Perthshire examples, some 80 ft (25 m) in diameter (Feachem 1955, 71), or to those with substantial rock outcrops incorporated in their circuits, also remains untested by recent work.

As Taylor readily admits, however, some of the few recovered artefacts from these Perthshire sites could belong distinctly earlier in the first millennium AD, and thus the possibility that these substantial round-houses represent a Pictish-period phenomenon in these uplands cannot meantime be discounted. Perhaps this set of buildings constitutes an instance of the reinvention of first millennium BC traditions of substantial round-house building, as Hingley has proposed for other cases in the Atlantic West (1995, 187). Before leaving these structures,

we may note that their internal diameters are of the order of 14 m (Litigan) to 16 m (Queen's View), giving an internal area close to 200 m² in the case of the larger example.

Above-ground structures associated with souterrains

Wainwright (1955, 92; 1963) had of course drawn attention to the post-souterrain oval drystone houses of Angus sites like Ardestie, examined as a by-product of the rescue excavations on souterrains rendered necessary by their discovery during agricultural operations. It is now clear that at least some, and probably many, of these souterrains, now much more numerous as a result of the successful application of aerial photography (Maxwell 1987, fig 4), were attached to, and indeed entered from within, timber round-houses, as Watkins was able to demonstrate at Newmill in Perthshire (1980a). Watkins (1984, 77) has further proposed that the structures recognised by Wainwright in association with the Ardestie souterrain may have been work-places subsidiary to an unrecognised timber-built round-house located to the southwest of them. It also appears likely that a major function of these below-ground features was for storage, with the implications that some of them, being sizeable constructions, betoken the production of considerable agricultural surpluses. It may be that commodities such as cheeses and meats (rather than cereals) would have been held in their stable environmental conditions. As Maxwell (1987) has pertinently remarked, if there is considerable evidence for the infilling of classic souterrains around the second century AD, this act in itself seems to imply that settlement in their vicinity was intended to continue, as was demonstrated by the Ardestie and Carlungie excavations and, less securely, at Newmill (Watkins 1984).

If an, albeit debatable, case can be made for linking Perthshire ring-forts with their Atlantic Scottish and Irish counterparts, the same does not hold true for eastern Scottish souterrains. Whilst souterrains are very common in Ireland, and were certainly in use (seemingly including amongst their functions those of storage and of refuge) in the last quarter of the first millennium (Edwards 1990, 31–2), there is currently no evidence that the classic series continued to function, still less to be built, in Scotland at this time. No Scottish souterrain of this series is entered, for instance, from a rectangular house, and one main reason for continuing to mention them in the context of Pictish habitation sites, is that they seem, as noted by Watkins (1984) and Maxwell (1987) to be indicative of locations that in several instances did continue in use after the demise of these particular structures later into the first millennium AD.

Now equally becoming clear as a result of excavations and aerial survey is the fact that such classic souterrains may be simply the most recognisable form of below-ground storage associated with first millennium domestic architecture in eastern Scotland. At Hawkhill, Easter Kinnear, in north-east Fife, a cropmark 'blob' – a fairly circular solid mark visible in cropmark aerial photography – was demonstrated to be a first millennium AD round-house, in this case incorporating a semi-sunken interior, interpreted again as a means of creating enhanced internal storage capacity (Watkins 1992, 474). Such features occur widely in the cropmark record of the valleys of eastward-flowing rivers in Scotland north of the Forth, and this may indicate that below-ground storage was much more frequently employed than had been assumed to be the case. This view had formerly been adopted as a result of the scarcity of storage pits on Scottish Iron Age sites, perhaps now more readily explicable as the by-product of a preference for other storage technologies for foodstuffs, rather than indicative of either a predominantly pastoral economy, as Piggott (1958) thought, or the unsuitability of Scottish ground moisture conditions to below-ground storage. This is not, however, the only possible explanation for 'blob' type marks, as opposed to annular or crescentic indications of former house emplacements: they could also result simply from better conditions of preservation, such as intact floor-deposits.

Watkins examination (1980b) of the site at Dalladies 2, near Fettercairn in Kincardineshire, also revealed the existence of a large series of distinctly less formal souterrains, termed by Maxwell (1987, 37) the 'small, irregular, multiple-patterned type', cut into the gravel spreads above the North Esk. A single radiocarbon date from this site points to its continuing use into the middle of the first millennium AD (501 AD ± 65 uncalibrated); the associated houses, like the predominantly stone-footed examples at Ardestie, were small and oval in plan, although in this instance post-built. If this chronological indicator

for the continuation of the aforementioned souterrains is accepted, other similar traces visible in the cropmark record may be suggested as of broadly similar date. A potential instance, at Burnhead of Monboddo near Fordoun in the Howe of the Mearns, has already been published (Ralston 1983; Shepherd and Greig 1996, no 73), and is of particular interest because of its close proximity to, and location on the same fluvioglacial gravel terrace as, a cropmark timber hall set within a circular enclosure at Monboddo. Burnhead of Monboddo shares with other examples identified by the Commission, such as at Arrat's Mill on the South Esk near Brechin, the presence of round-houses in which a radial mark, perhaps representing underground storage capacity, to which access was obtained from within the building, is apparent.

Stone-footed structures in eastern Scotland

Before turning to the possible existence of Pictish timber halls, it would be apposite to consider new evidence for stone-footed buildings of Pictish date from the eastern side of the country. To the set of post-souterrain dry-stone buildings already discussed by Wainwright, relatively few new examples have been examined by the spade. At Northwaterbridge, near Edzell, Small and collaborators (1974) identified an area of paving, not seemingly associated with postholes, adjacent to a souterrain which was argued to have been abandoned in an unfinished state, as a result of the instability of the deposits into which it was cut. Excavation conditions were far from ideal, but the authors felt able to suggest that in this instance the incomplete souterrain was an addition to an already-existing round-house. Mention has already been made of the more substantial structure recovered within the diminutive promontory fort at Green Castle, Portknockie. This consisted for the most part of single course of water-rolled stones defining the inner and outer margins of what may have been a turf-cored wall defining a building some 4 m wide, with rounded corners (Ralston 1987, fig 3). Unfortunately, only one end of the structure survived, but a minimum length of approximately 7 m is indicated. There is no evidence for the door position, and a considerably greater length cannot be excluded. Dr Anna Ritchie has proposed that this building may have been a 'feasting hall appropriate to a warlord's household' (1995, 23), but its relatively modest scale may urge caution in necessarily seeing elite associations for it.

The Pitcarmick series

In numerical terms, the most significant addition to the corpus of likely medieval and potentially Pictish dry-stone structures in the heartland areas has been the identification of a series of buildings in the uplands of north-east Perthshire as part of the RCAHMS (1990, 12–13; Stevenson 1991) survey there. Named after the site of Pitcarmick, they display the following characteristics which distinguish them from the mass of broadly rectilinear post Medieval and pre-Improvement farmsteads: curved, and sometimes bowed, sides; rounded ends; a roughly trapezoidal outline; and, although not universally, the presence of annexes. Some display internal depressions at their narrower ends, suggesting sunken floors, which may again be attributable to storage within these buildings, or could be the by-product of keeping cattle or other livestock within them. The results of excavation at Pitcarmick itself (Barrett and Downes in prep), which indicate that such structures were in use during the last four or so centuries of the first millennium AD, confirm surface observations from sites like that at Lair in Glenshee (RCAHMS 1990, 150–2, no 291). There, a scatter of variants of this style of buildings are distributed amongst other stone-built structures, some of earlier type like hut circles, may be used as tentative support for an earlier, and hence Pictish, attribution. The Commission's Investigators have noted that Pitcarmick buildings tend more frequently to co-occur with hut circles than with pre-Improvement farmsteads, again supporting the proposition that the episodes of upland colonisation of which they are the archaeological witness may belong in the first, rather than the earlier second, millennium. In parentheses, we may remark, at least tentatively, that Wainwright's suggestion of searching for Pictish settlement amongst the deserted remains of other periods may at last have borne fruit on these Perthshire uplands (1955, 89). Measurement of a sample of Pitcarmick-type buildings from the Commission's plans (RCAHMS 1990) suggests that internal floor areas approaching 100 m² probably represents a reasonable order-of-magnitude size for these structures.

Timber halls ?

The existence of substantial timber buildings, normally referred to as halls, is a well-established aspect of post-Roman societies in many parts of Britain. These may occur individually, grouped on unenclosed sites, within palace complexes, as at Yeavering in Northumbria (Hope-Taylor 1977) and in fortified sites, as at South Cadbury, Somerset (Alcock 1972, fig 30). Buildings of this type have been identified as cropmark traces within the former extent of Pictland since the Commission's successful aerial sorties during the drought conditions of 1976. The readier acceptance of the Picts as 'not the mysterious, problematic nation of earlier ideologies' (Alcock 1987, 80), lends credibility to the likelihood that Pictish elites – at least in areas where the necessary timber supplies were available – may well have availed themselves, as did many of their contemporaries, of this kind of prestige structure. The background to the excavations, designed to test this possibility, at Balbridie, on a fluvioglacial terrace across the River Dee from Crathes Castle, in Kincardineshire, is ably sketched by Reynolds (1980). In particular the links, based on the pre-excavation cropmark evidence, with the plan of the sixth century British hall, Doon Hill A, in East Lothian, are rehearsed. This latter example, set above the eastern extremity of the Lothian coastal plain, was excavated in the 1960s by Dr Brian Hope-Taylor, and was demonstrated to precede an Anglian-style hall on the same site, the latter attributable to the advance of the Angles into Lothian in the 630s AD.

Despite the controversies that were raised at the time, there can now be no doubt that the Balbridie building, notwithstanding its initial similarities to Doon Hill A – notably its bowed gable ends and overall size – is much earlier in date, and belongs to the Neolithic period (Fairweather and Ralston 1993). This, however, need not imply either that the Doon Hill structure should be reattributed to an early farming community (in spite of Smith's hypothesis that its plan was laid bare by chance by the much later builders of Hall B at the site: 1991, 267), nor that the other timber halls that have been identified from the air between the Forth and the Moray Firth must forcibly be discounted as candidates for Pictish occupation. Maxwell (1987, 34) has outlined most of the evidence then available: with the exception of the suite of particularly interesting structures at Lathrisk in Fife (Maxwell 1987, fig 2), the examples recognised from air photography are largely unenclosed singletons. In a few cases, two of which are mentioned further below, evidence of a thin circular enveloping ring, probably indicative of a palisaded enclosure, or a more substantial ditch, is evident on the air photography.

As regards such architectural detail within possible halls as can be perceived on the aerial imagery, some tentative comments are possible. Maxwell (1987) has commented on the possible links between the curvilinear annexes attached to one of the shorter ends of at least three of the Lathrisk structures and somewhat similar features at the ends of Doon Hill Hall B and its southern counterparts at Whitekirk, also in East Lothian (illustrated by Smith 1991, illus 9). There are, however, other puzzling features of the set of cropmarks at Lathrisk, notably the strongly marked axial arrangements which seem to be an omnipresent characteristic of them. Some sort of within-structure below-ground storage arrangement might be apposite, although this would conceivably interfere with the satisfactory roofing of these lengthy structures. Certainty as to the interpretation of the remarkable traces within the Lathrisk buildings will almost certainly have to await the spade. A notable distinction between the Balbridie building and many of the post-Roman halls known elsewhere (James *et al* 1984) is that Balbridie lacks any evidence for external buttressing, but unambiguous evidence of external raking timbers is absent in the suggested halls of Pictland, with the possible exception of Monboddo. Indeed, indications of buttresses are missing from some of the major halls of southern Scotland, such as Hall A at Sprouston, Roxburghshire (Smith 1991, 276). The apparent absence of buttressing in the depiction of the Temple in the Book of Kells fol 202v (Reynolds 1980, fig 1) has already been remarked. Large buttressed halls in the north of Britain, it has been suggested, may be a more narrowly Anglian phenomenon (Smith 1991, 284)

Amongst putative candidates in Pictland for the status of hall, some look from the cropmark evidence sufficiently close to Balbridie to be posited as potentially Neolithic: Wester Fintray, near the River Don downstream from Kintore, is a case in point and Smith mentions a further possible example at Auchenlaich near Callander,

Stirlingshire (1991, 267). Such comparisons depend primarily on seeing the structural feature of bowed (or 'open-book', in Smith's felicitous phrase (1991, 267)), narrow ends as chronologically significant, and this may well not be sustainable. Others correspond more closely to the criteria rehearsed by James and his co-authors for first millennium AD halls (1984). The example, set centrally within a circular palisaded enclosure at Monboddo (Ralston 1983), still looks to the present writer from its groundplan one of the likeliest candidates for a Pictish elite residence. Another possible enclosed example is illustrated from Dalpatrick, Perthshire; this appears much more eccentrically placed relative to the enclosure line (Driscoll 1991, pl 5.2). In terms of potential roofed area, at least some of these structures sit relatively close to 200 m²: Maxwell (1987) estimates 25 m by 9 m as the average size represented at Lathrisk, whilst the Monboddo building, rather closer to a length:breadth ratio of 2:1 than those at Lathrisk, seems to be of the same scale order in area terms. The lack to date amongst the important group of cropmarks constituting the royal centre at Forteviot of any indication of a feasting hall (Alcock and Alcock 1992, illus 10) may logically be ascribed either to the vagaries of cropmark formation or to the real absence of such structures in the fields adjacent to the Water of May. In light of the evidence rehearsed above, however, it may very hesitantly be proposed that major buildings in this later first millennium unenclosed centre (Ralston and Armit 1997, 230) may have been built using some of the techniques noted above – such as post-pads, and sill-beams at ground level – such that they may always escape ready aerial detection.

Some preliminary remarks on social context

If the present writer has expressed doubts as to the status of the building, not very different in size from the lesser buildings of Yeavering or Anglian Dunbar, on the Green Castle, Portknockie as a feasting hall, it seems possible that some of the halls of Pictland, such as Monboddo, visible on air photographs, may have held a status not unlike some of the minor *villae* (Alcock 1988; Smith 1991) further South. The admixture of basically circular and more rectilinear forms displayed in 'peripheral' Pictland is also characteristic of what is known of Pictish domestic architecture in at least some areas of eastern Scotland south of the Moray Firth, although here, as in previous periods for which multicellular structures occur in the Far North, this format seems to have been absent. The dating of the transition from round to rectangular structures (or at least the appearance of the latter) in the heartland area is not well established, but the third quarter of the millennium may be posited for the Pitcarmick series, and probably for Green Castle, although that structure has no isotopic determinations.

Considering some of the lesser buildings, it is possible to note distinctions in the 'permeability' of individual buildings and inhabited places. The building described as Buckquoy 4 (Ritchie 1977) (**1.2**), for example, shows some topological depth, if the end-door is employed as the root (the main point of access from the outside world), but rather less if the entrance which gives direct access to the principal room is considered in that capacity. Further, as Brown (1990) cogently argues, the key characteristics of buildings – their shape, size and topology interact; the justified access analysis practised in archaeological contexts by Foster (1989) and others necessarily relegates the scale of the buildings from consideration. And, whilst social, political and ideological factors may well be involved, it is necessary not to disregard the physical constraints of available space in considering the layouts, and the access routes through them, that are eventually accomplished, in assessing their social cohesiveness. This is perhaps particularly the case in certain northern settlements, such as those at Howe and Pool.

None the less, the comparability of layouts and access arrangements within the polyventral buildings is of considerable interest. Several examples, like that at Buckquoy noted above, have two doors. Compared to the single doors of most round-house buildings, this development merits attention; in early Medieval Ireland, two doors into houses seem to have been quite common, and Murray (1979) lists literary accounts pertinent to this. In the Buckquoy 4 type of building, we can perhaps envisage particular oppositions between public and private spaces, as proposed by Hingley (1990) for Iron Age round-houses and the rectilinear architectures of the Romano-British periods. Whether, in due course, further evidence will be forthcoming from distributions of small finds or food waste, or from analytical procedures, remains to be seen.

Were doors locked?

Another concomitant of near-state-level societies on the nearer continent is the first archaeological indication of the locking of house-doors when their inhabitants were absent: iron latch-lifters are frequent finds from continental *oppida* and occur also on some south British forts, such as Danebury (Hampshire). Whilst the bar-checks that are a recurrent feature of the entrance passages of brochs testify to the ability for inhabitants to bar the door when they were in residence, evidence for locking doors remains absent in Pictland, although barbed bolt padlocks, appropriate to chests and the like, are an artefact type widely shared during the first millennium AD in Britain and beyond (Alcock 1987, fig 1). It is arguable that the need to secure smaller personal possessions in chests with padlocks was not matched by the requirement to lock individual dwellings. Some support for this lack may be gleaned from the Irish sources analysed by Murray (1979, 87); references to keys generally refer to churches, or the outer gates of enclosures. Very tentatively, again, this absence may suggest that the communities inhabiting the unenclosed sites of Pictland still retained sufficient kin linkages, real or imagined, and social cohesion, to render this development unnecessary.

Conclusion

In the foregoing discussion, the present author has outlined something of the variability now readily apparent in the domestic architecture found within approximately the latter two-thirds of the first millennium AD in Pictland. It is suggested that the diversity of structural remains encountered, and attributed with lesser or greater certainty to the period under consideration, may be indicative of several developments, and equally embraces the decline of several other traits. For example, the demise of groundplans showing a major chamber with ancillary cells, classically represented at Buckquoy, and for long, if discontinuously, demonstrable in the Far North, seems to occur before the end of the first millennium: such buildings still appear entirely absent in the Pictish heartland. Reference has already been made to the floor areas of some of these buildings, which are relatively substantial; in the accompanying illustration (**1**) the ground floor plan of the two storey Old Gruline House, Salen, Mull (RCAHMS 1980, 232, no 354) (**1**.7), as built in the late eighteenth century, is included as an aid to appreciating the scale of some of the buildings here considered.

Equally, there are intimations of a move to rectilinear structures, more particularly in what seem to be elite residences (to judge solely from their scale) as well as some lesser ones, at least in southern Pictland. In considering the Irish evidence, Lynn (1978) favoured an explication for this change founded on technological innovations in constructional methods. As a possible motivating force, it is impossible to dispute this contention. But the availability of technologies better adapted to the construction of rectangular buildings, is not in itself sufficient to guarantee their social acceptance. The building interpreted as a byre at Pool, which precedes the abandonment of the round-house on the same site, suggests that rectilinear structures were acceptable for specialist structures there at a relatively precocious date, without the living quarters necessarily following immediately suite.

There clearly remains much to learn of the domestic architecture of Pictland. Continuing research at Portmahomack in Easter Ross (Carver 1995), on the islands of the West and North, and elsewhere, will doubtlessly reveal more variants on the forms of architecture discussed above. Perhaps at last some of the grander buildings – the 'elite residences' in contemporary jargon – of the Picts are becoming apparent – suitable settings for the domestic and personal equipment and elaborate furniture depicted on the sculpture, to the study of which Dr Henderson continues to make such a notable contribution.

Acknowledgements
I am indebted to Mr John Barrett, University of Sheffield, and Professor John Hunter, University of Birmingham, for information on Pitcarmick and Pool that has been incorporated in this paper.

References

ALCOCK, L
– 1972 *'By South Cadbury is that Camelot…' Excavations at Cadbury Castle 1966–70.* London.
– 1982 Cadbury-Camelot: a fifteen year perspective. *Proc Brit Acad*, 68, 357–88.
– 1984 A survey of Pictish settlement archaeology. In Friell and Watson (eds), 7–42.
– 1987 Pictish studies: present and future. In Small, 80–92.
– 1988 *Bede, Eddius and the Forts of the North Britons* (Jarrow Lecture). Jarrow.

ALCOCK, L, and ALCOCK, E A 1992 Reconnaissance excavations on Early Historic fortifications and other royal sites in Scotland, 1974–84: A, Excavations and other fieldwork at Forteviot, Perthshire, 1981; B, Excavations at Urquhart Castle, Inverness-shire, 1983; C, Excavations at Dunnottar, Kincardineshire, 1984. *Proc Soc Antiq Scot*, 122, 215–87.

ALCOCK, L, ALCOCK, E A and DRISCOLL, S T 1989 Reconnaissance excavations on Early Historic fortifications and other royal sites in Scotland, 1974–84: 3, Excavations at Dundurn, Strathearn, Perthshire, 1976–77. *Proc Soc Antiq Scot*, 119, 189–226.

ARMIT, I
– 1990 Broch building in northern Scotland: the context of innovation. *World Archaeol*, 21 (1989-90), 435–45.
– (ed) 1990 *Beyond the Brochs: changing perspectives on the Atlantic Scottish Iron Age.* Edinburgh.

AUDOUZE, F and BÜCHSENSCHÜTZ, O E 1992 *Towns, villages and countryside of Celtic Europe.* London.

BALLIN SMITH, B (ed) 1994 *Howe: four millennia of Orkney prehistory* (Soc Antiq Scot Monogr Ser, 9). Edinburgh.

BARBER, J and CRONE, A 1993 Crannogs: a diminishing resource? A survey of the crannogs of South-West Scotland and excavations at Buiston crannog. *Antiquity*, 67, 520–33.

BARRETT, J 1981 Aspects of the Iron Age in Atlantic Scotland: a case study in the problems of archaeological interpretation. *Proc Soc Antiq Scot*, 111, 205–19.

BARRETT, J and DOWNES, J in prep *North Pitcarmick: North East Perthshire: the Early Medieval inhabitation of a prehistoric landscape.*

BATEY, C E, JENSCH, J and MORRIS, C D (eds) 1993 *The Viking Age in Caithness, Orkney and the North Atlantic* (Select papers Proc XI Viking Congress, Thurso and Kirkwall, 1989). Edinburgh.

BROWN, F E 1990 Comment on Chapman: some cautionary notes on the application of spatial measures to prehistoric settlements. In Samson (ed), 93–109.

BRUNSKILL, R W 1982 *Houses.* London.

CARVER, M O H (ed) 1995 *Tarbat Discovery Programme Bulletin,* 1. York.

CLOSE-BROOKS, J
— 1984 Pictish and other burials. In Friell and Watson (eds), 87–114.
— 1986 Excavations at Clatchard Craig, Fife. *Proc Soc Antiq Scot,* 116, 117–84.

COTTAM, M B and SMALL, A 1974 The distribution of settlement in Southern Pictland. *Medieval Archaeol,* 18, 43–65.

CRAWFORD, B E 1987 *Scandinavian Scotland* (Scotland in the Early Middle Ages, 2). Leicester.

CRONE, A
— 1991 Buiston Crannog. *Current Archaeol,* 127, 295–97.
— 1993 Crannogs and chronologies. *Proc Soc Antiq Scot,* 123, 245–54.

DES = *Discovery and Excavation in Scotland.*

DRISCOLL, S 1991 The archaeology of state formation in Scotland. In Hanson and Slater (eds), 81–111.

EDWARDS, K J and Ralston, I B M
— 1978 New dating and environmental evidence from Burghead fort, Moray. *Proc Soc Antiq Scot,* 109 (1977-78), 202–10.
— (eds) 1997 *Scotland: environment and archaeology 8000 BC–AD 1000.* New York and Chichester.

EDWARDS, N 1990 *The Archaeology of Early Medieval Ireland.* London.

FAIRWEATHER, A D and RALSTON, I B M 1993 The Neolithic timber hall at Balbridie, Grampian Region, Scotland: the building, the date, the plant macrofossils. *Antiquity,* 67, 313–23.

FEACHEM, R W 1955 Fortifications. In Wainwright 1955a, 66–86.

FITZPATRICK, A P 1994 Outside in: the structure of an Early Iron Age house at Dunston Park, Thatcham, Berkshire. In Fitzpatrick and Morris (eds), 68–72.

FITZPATRICK, A P and MORRIS, E L (eds) 1994 *The Iron Age in Wessex: Recent Work.* Salisbury.

FOSTER, S M
— 1989 Transformations in social space: Iron Age Orkney and Caithness. *Scot Archaeol Rev,* 6, 34–55.
— 1992 The state of Pictland in the Age of Sutton Hoo. In Carver, M O H *The Age of Sutton Hoo,* 217–34. Woodbridge.
— 1996 *Picts, Gaels and Scots.* London.

FRIELL, J G P and WATSON, W G (eds) 1984 *Pictish Studies: settlement, burial and art in Dark Age northern Britain*

(BAR Brit Ser 125). Oxford.

GORDON, C A 1956 Carving technique on the symbol stones of North-East Scotland. *Proc Soc Antiq Scot,* 88 (1954-56), 40–46.

GREENE, K 1995 *Archaeology: an introduction* (3 edn). London.

HANSON, W S and SLATER, E A (eds) 1991 *Scottish archaeology: new perceptions.* Aberdeen.

HARDING, D W
— 1973 Round and rectangular: Iron Age houses, British and foreign. In Hawkes, C F C and Hawkes, S C (eds) *Celts, Greeks and Romans: studies in venture and resistance,* 43–62. London.
— 1974 *The Iron Age in Lowland Britain.* London.
— 1984 The function and classification of brochs and duns. In Miket, R and Burgess, C B (eds) *Between and beyond the Walls: essays on the prehistory and history of North Britain in honour of George Jobey,* 206–20. Edinburgh.
— 1997 Forts, duns, brochs and crannogs: Iron Age settlements in Argyll. In Ritchie, J N G *The archaeology of Argyll,* 118–40. Edinburgh.

HENDERSON, I B
— 1958 The origin centre of the Pictish symbol stones. *Proc Soc Antiq Scot, 91* (1957-58), 44–60.
— 1972 The Picts of Aberdeenshire and their monuments. *Archaeol Journal,* 129, 166–74.

HILL, J D 1995 How should we understand Iron Age societies and hillforts? A contextual study from southern Britain. In Hill and Cumberpatch (eds), 45–66.

HILL, J D and CUMBERPATCH, C G (eds) 1995 *Different Iron Ages: Studies on the Iron Age in Temperate Europe (BAR Int Ser* 602). Oxford.

HINGLEY, R
— 1990 Domestic organisation and gender relations in Iron Age and Romano-British households. In Samson (ed), 125–47.
— 1995 The Iron Age in Atlantic Scotland: searching for the meaning of the substantial house. In Hill and Cumberpatch (eds), 185–91.

HOPE-TAYLOR, B K 1977 *Yeavering: an Anglo-British centre of early Northumbria* (Dept of the Environment Archaeological Report, 7). London.

HUNTER, J R
— 1986 *Rescue Excavations on the Brough of Birsay 1974–82* (Soc Antiq Scot Monogr Ser, 4). Edinburgh.
— 1990 Pool, Sanday: a Case Study for the late Iron Age and Viking periods. In Armit (ed), 175–93.
— 1997 *A persona for the northern Picts* (Groam House Museum Lecture series). Rosemarkie.

HUNTER, J R, BOND, J M and SMITH, A N 1993 Some aspects of early Viking settlement in Orkney. In Batey *et al* (eds), 272–84.

JAMES, S, MARSHALL, A and MILLETT, M 1984 An Early Medieval building tradition. *Archaeol Journ*, 141, 182–215.

MAXWELL, G S 1987 Settlement in southern Pictland: a new overview. In Small (ed), 31–44.

MURRAY, H 1979 Documentary evidence for domestic buildings in Ireland *c*.400-1200 in the light of archaeology. *Medieval Archaeology*, 23, 81–97.

MUSSON, C R 1970 House-plans and prehistory. *Current Archaeol*, 21, 261–75.

NAISMITH, R J 1985 *Buildings of the Scottish Countryside*. London.

NICOLL, E H (ed) 1995 *A Pictish panorama: the story of the Picts and a Pictish bibliography*. Balgavies, Angus.

PARKER PEARSON, M 1996 Food, fertility and front doors in the first millennium BC. In Champion, T C and Collis, J R (eds) *The Iron Age in Britain: recent trends*, 117–32. Sheffield.

PIGGOTT, S 1958 Native economies and the Roman occupation of Scotland. In Richmond (ed), 127.

POLESKI, J 1992 Datierungsgrundlagen der ältesten Phasen des Frühmittelalters in Kleinpolen. In *Probleme des relativen und absoluten Chronologie ab Latènezeit bis zum Frühmittelalter*, 317–38. Cracow.

OLIVER, B (ed) 1975 Introduction. In idem (ed) *Shelter, Sign and Symbol*. London.

RCAHMS = Royal Commission on the Ancient and Historical Monuments of Scotland

– 1980 *Argyll: An Inventory of the Ancient Monuments, vol 3: Mull, Tiree, Coll, and Northern Argyll*. Edinburgh.

– 1990 *North-East Perth: an archaeological landscape*. Edinburgh.

RALSTON, I B M

– 1983 Notes on the archaeology of Kincardine and Deeside District. *The Deeside Field*, 18, 73–83.

– 1987 Portknockie: promontory forts and Pictish settlement in the North-East. In Small (ed), 15–26.

– 1995 Fortifications and defence. In Green, M (ed) *The Celtic World*, 59–81. London.

RALSTON, I B M and ARMIT, I 1997 The Early Historic Period: an archaeological perspective. In Edwards and Ralston (eds), 217–39.

RALSTON, I B M and INGLIS, J C 1984 *Foul hordes: the Picts in the North-East and their background*. Aberdeen.

REYNOLDS, N M 1980 Dark Age timber halls and the background to excavations at Balbridie. *Scot Archaeol Forum*, 10, 41–60.

REYNOLDS, P 1994 Butser Ancient Farm. In Fitzpatrick and Morris (eds), 11–14.

RICHMOND, I A (ed) 1958 *Roman and Native in North Britain*. Edinburgh.

RITCHIE, A

– 1977 Excavation of Pictish and Viking-age farmsteads at Buckquoy, Orkney. *Proc Soc Antiq Scot*, 108 (1976-77), 174–227.

– 1995 The archaeological evidence for daily life. In Nicoll (ed), 21–5.

SAMSON, R (ed) 1990 *The Social Archaeology of Houses*. Edinburgh.

SCHULDT, E 1989 F 16 Behren-Lübchen. In Herrmann, J (ed) *Archäologie in der Deutschen Demokratischen Republik. Denkmale und Funde: Band 2 Fundorte und Funde*, 603–5. Stuttgart.

SHEPHERD, A N 1994 Howe: a review of the sequence. In Ballin Smith (ed), 267–90.

SHEPHERD, I A G

– 1983 Pictish settlement problems in north-east Scotland. In Chapman, J C and Mytum, H C (eds) *Settlement in North Britain 1000 BC–AD 1000 (BAR Brit Ser* 118), 327–56. Oxford.

– 1993 The Picts in Moray. In Sellar, W D H (ed) *Moray: Province and People*, 75–90. Edinburgh.

SHEPHERD, I A G and GREIG, M K 1996 *Grampian's Past: its archaeology from the air*. Aberdeen.

SMALL, A, COTTAM, M B and DUNBAR, J G 1974 Souterrain and later structures at Northwaterbridge, Kincardineshire. *Proc Soc Antiq Scot*, 105 (1972-74), 293–96.

SMALL, A (ed) 1987 *The Picts: a new look at old problems*. Dundee.

SMITH, I M 1991 Sprouston, Roxburghshire: an early Anglian centre of the eastern Tweed Basin. *Proc Soc Antiq Scot*, 121, 261–94.

STEVENSON, J B

– 1984 Garbeg and Whitebridge: two square-barrow cemeteries in Inverness-shire. In Friell and Watson (eds), 145–50.

– 1991 Pitcarmicks and fermtouns. *Current Archaeol*, 127, 288–91.

TAYLOR, D B 1990 *Circular Homesteads in North-West Perthshire*. Dundee.

VAGINAY, M and GUICHARD, V 1988 *L'habitat gaulois de Feurs (Loire): fouilles récentes* (Documents d'Archéologie française, 14). Paris.

VILLES, A 1983 Quelques exemples nouveaux de maisons protohistoriques circulaires sur le continent. In Collis, J R, Duval, A and Perichon, R (eds) *Le deuxième âge du fer en Auvergne et en Forez et ses relations avec les régions limitrophes,* 153–65. Sheffield / St Etienne.

WAINWRIGHT, F T

– 1955 Houses and Graves. In idem (ed) 1955a, 87–96.

– (ed) 1955a *The Problem of the Picts.* Edinburgh (repr with addenda, Perth, 1980).

– 1963 *The Souterrains of Southern Pictland.* London.

WATKINS, T F

– 1980a Excavation of a settlement and souterrain at Newmill, near Bankfoot, Perthshire. *Proc Soc Antiq Scot,* 110, 165–208.

– 1980b The excavation of an Iron Age open settlement at Dalladies, Kincardineshire. Ibid, 122–64.

– 1984 Where were the Picts? In Friell and Watson (eds), 63–86.

– 1992 Doughnuts and bananas: the Leuchars cropmark project. *Current Archaeol,* 131, 472–4.

WEDDERBURN, L M M and GRIME, D 1984 The cairn cemetery at Garbeg, Drumnadrochit. In Friell and Watson (eds), 151–67.

WHITTINGTON, G 1975 Placenames and the settlement pattern of dark-age Scotland. *Proc Soc Antiq Scot,* 106 (1974-75), 99–110.

ZEUNE, J 1992 *The last Scottish castles. Investigations with particular reference to domestic architecture from the 15th to the 17th century* (Dobiat, C and Leidorf, K (eds) Internationale Archäologie, 12).

The Picts in Shetland

Anna Ritchie

Traces of Early Christian slab-built shrines have been found through eastern Pictland as far north as the Moray Firth area, and there is then a gap in their distribution before reaching Shetland, where there are fragments of at least six such shrines.[1] Isabel Henderson has a long-standing interest in these shrines, most recently demonstrated by her absorbing analysis of the St Andrews Sarcophagus and its wider context (1994). As a mark of my own debt to her scholarship, I should like to offer Dr Henderson an attempt to assess the social and cultural context in which such shrines were adopted in Shetland. Should Shetland be counted as part of the Pictish kingdom in the sixth to ninth centuries or simply as an outpost of the Christian Church?

Wainwright argued that the Northern Isles were part of Pictland on the grounds that the distribution of symbol stones 'marks with precision the known boundaries of Pictland' and that this is supported by the occurrence of ogham inscriptions, for 'despite their Irish-Scottish associations, they are evidence of the presence of Picts' (1962, 95). The latter part of his argument was based on the accepted view of 'Pictish' ogham inscriptions as unintelligible and therefore different from Irish ogham (Jackson 1955), but Katherine Forsyth's work has shown that this view should be abandoned (1995a). The presence in Orkney and Shetland of ogham inscriptions has more to do with the activities of Irish missionaries than with any lost Pictish language. Nevertheless, the ogham inscriptions found in Shetland help to establish the credentials of this island group as part of Pictland. Most of the ogham inscriptions found in Shetland are relatively late in type and post-date the Norse settlement (Forsyth 1996, lxvi), thus supporting Gerald Bigelow's suggestion that the Norse takeover of Shetland may have been somewhat different in date and character to that of Orkney (1992, 14–15).

Although Shetland is generally accepted to have participated in Pictish culture, the archaeological evidence has never been gathered together or its overall significance discussed, and the aim of this paper is to fill that gap (**1**). The Picts were certainly familiar to the Scandinavian-speakers naming the Shetland landscape during the 9th and 10th centuries, for their place-names include several with the element *pettr* meaning Pict (eg Pettadale, valley of the Picts). *Papar*-names indicate that Scandinavian-speakers encountered Christian monks in the islands, and the presence of major Christian stone-carving at St Ninian's

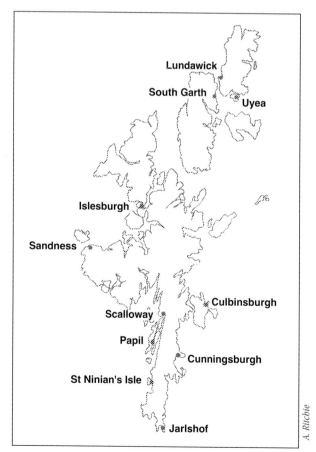

1 *Map of Shetland showing the major places mentioned in the text*

35

Isle, Papil and Cullingsburgh in Bressay underlines the strength of Christianity in the islands by the end of the 8th century. Raymond Lamb has argued that the papar of Shetland were clergy of the Roman Church with an episcopal organization (1995, 21), whereas Ronald Cant envisages the monastic organization of the Celtic Church in place in the islands (1996, 159–60). The story of missionary activity in Shetland, as in Orkney, is likely to have been complex and a mixture of Roman and Celtic. This mixture can be seen in tangible form on the Monks' Stone from Papil (Moar and Stewart 1944; better photograph in Shetland County Museum 1973, centrefold). This is a side-panel from a Pictish type of slab-shrine, and it depicts robed and hooded clerics in procession towards an Irish type of free-standing prayer cross. There are also well-known stylistic links in stone-carving between both Papil and St Ninian's Isle and the Inner Hebridean islands of Iona and Canna with their Irish monasteries.

Overtly Christian sculpture surviving from Shetland is unlikely to be earlier than the late 8th century (Stevenson 1981), but there are two long-accepted instances of the early use of Pictish symbols: a lost stone from Sandness and a stone disc incised with a double disc and Z-rod from Jarlshof. It will be argued here that two fragments from Cunningsburgh and Uyea also belong to symbol stones.

Sandness

The parish of Walls and Sandness, which includes the island of Papa Stour, occupies the most westerly part of the mainland of Shetland. The Sandness symbol stone was seen and sketched by George Low, a skilled draughtsman, in 1774; 'Observed in the wall of the Church a stone, carved with several odd figures, the meaning of which nobody here could give any account of; only they have a sort of superstitious value for it, nor does tradition say for what. The engraving is shallow, nor is any literal inscription' (Low 1879, 121). It is not surprising that 18th-century Shetlanders were unfamiliar with Pictish symbols, since none other was known in the islands at that time, but Low had been born in Edzell in Angus and might be expected to have seen symbol stones in the heart of Pictland, even though the connection between the stones and the historical Picts had yet to be recognized. The present Sandness church was built in 1792–94 at Melby (Gifford

1992, 497), and it seems likely that the church seen by Low almost twenty years earlier was St Ninian's Chapel at Norby, about half a mile to the south-east, the site of which was marked on the 1st edition Ordnance Survey 6-inch map.

The Sandness slab was 3ft 6ins long and 15ins wide (Allen and Anderson 1903, III, fig 2 is correctly scaled, but the accompanying text on p.4 is incorrect as to measurements), and it was incised with a rectangle, an arch and a mirror. Both the arch and the rectangle symbols have an early and predominantly north-eastern distribution, and the decoration on the Sandness rectangle is most closely paralleled on Clynekirkton 1 from Sutherland (ibid, 38, fig 34) (**2**). The arch appears again in Shetland on a stone disc from Jarlshof (discussed below).

The Sandness area is fertile and highly favourable for settlement, with a good harbour giving access both to the sea and to the island of Papa Stour. The Statistical Account records that, in the late 18th century, the parish of Walls and Sandness produced in a good season more than enough corn for local needs and was able to sell grain to other less fortunate parishes. The remains of three horizontal mills at Huxter testify to the arable potential of Sandness. The area also includes the remains of two brochs at Huxter and Bousta (RCAHMS 1946, nos 1605, 1610) and a promontory fort at Ness of Garth (Ritchie 1997, 97, no 50). Fojut suggested that the Ness of Garth fort was re-used as a monastic settlement in Early Christian times, on the grounds that the visible foundations of small sub-rectangular houses appear to be secondary to the fort (1993, 64–5, no 102). This is an attractive idea, although it is equally possible that the fort, if it was re-used, had become a centre of Dark-Age secular power. Some 100m or so from the site of St Ninian's Chapel, a curious underground structure was discovered in 1936, in the garden of a house named *The Skeos* (RCAHMS 1946, no 1612). It consisted of two small cells with a short linking passage, partially cut into solid rock and partially built of drystone masonry; the flat lintels roofing the two cells lay at the level of the surface of the rock, about 1.2m below the modern ground-level, suggesting that a large pit had been dug in which the celled structure was built. This sounds more like the well-cum-cellar of a broch than an earth-house, yet it is unlikely that any broch here had been totally demolished, a major undertaking that has rarely

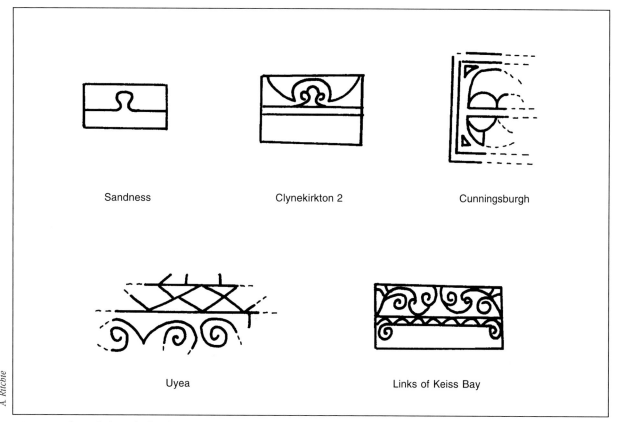

Sandness   Clynekirkton 2   Cunningsburgh

Uyea   Links of Keiss Bay

A. Ritchie

2 *Rectangle symbols in Shetland (Sandness, Cunningsburgh, Uyea), Sutherland (Clynekirkton) and Caithness (Links of Keiss Bay)*

been attempted. A low mound nearby and artefacts suggesting domestic occupation may imply that the underground structure belonged to a non-defensive settlement of some size. Could this have been the original provenance of the symbol stone? Symbol stones have been found in or adjacent to domestic settlements in Orkney, at Gurness, Pool and Brough of Birsay.

Symbol stones and cross-slabs

Two extant fragments of carved stones from Shetland seem likely also to represent rectangle symbols: Cunningsburgh 2 and Uyea (Allen and Anderson 1903, III, 17, fig 11A; 4–5, fig 3A). The Cunningsburgh fragment displays less than half of a rectangle with decorative infilling (**2**) for which there is no close parallel, but among known rectangles there is a wide range of internal decoration. There is part of an ogham inscription on the other side; if this inscription was, as normal, vertical, the proposed rectangle would have been horizontal, like most other rectangles. The Uyea piece includes a cross-hatched band and opposed spirals which are close to the internal decoration on the rectangle on the slab from Links of Keiss Bay (ibid, 28–9, fig 25) (**2**). The other side of the Uyea

fragment bears part of a spiral, suggesting that this may have been part of a two-sided, symbol-bearing cross-slab, as may another fragment with spirals and cross-hatching, the provenance of which within Shetland is unknown (ibid, 3–4, figs 1, 1A).

Charles Thomas suggested that the rectangle symbol might represent some sort of container with a flap (1963, 56). Shetland is unique in possessing carved depictions of ecclesiastical book-satchels (on the cross-slab and shrine panel from Papil), which are shown as rectangles, sometimes with a triangular flap. Perhaps the predominantly northern distribution of the rectangle symbol (Mack 1997, 13) reflects the activities of Irish missionaries. It may be significant that one of the few symbol stones in the Western Isles bears a rectangle (the stone from Benbecula).

Another cross-slab, but this time carved in relief, may be represented by the lost stone from South Garth on the north-east coast of Yell, found during peat-digging a few years before 1859: 'Both sides were completely covered with figures in relief having a border all round carved in zig-zag diamond and spiral lines' (Allen and Anderson 1903, III, 15). The recorded dimensions of this slab, 'a thin slab, between 3 and 4 feet long, about 1¼ inch thick, and about 16 or 17 inches broad at one end and a little broader at the other' (ibid, 15), suggest that it was similar in size to the later cross-slab from Cullingsburgh (Culbinsburgh), Bressay, (3ft 9ins long by 12–16 ins broad by 1⅓ in thick, or 1.1m by 0.3–0.4m by 0.03m, ibid, 5–10).[2]

Contrasting in size, the cross-slab from Papil, part-incised and part-relief, was carved in sandstone on a slab twice as tall (2.1m by 0.45–0.48m by 0.05m, ibid, 10–15). Clearly, the size of sculpture in Shetland was governed to some extent by the available stone, sandstone flags yielding longer slabs than schist or steatite, but choice and the ability to import stone also played a part. The island of Bressay is composed of rocks of Old Red Sandstone age, yet the Cullingsburgh cross-slab was carved of the less tractable schist, imported from the mainland. This must surely reflect the existence in the 9th century of a sculptural centre in southern mainland Shetland, which supplied the market in outlying areas.

The Bressay cross-slab has been accepted as a copy of the Papil cross-slab (Stevenson 1981, 284). The island of Papil consists of schist, which could have produced locally the material for the Bressay slab, yet the earlier Papil cross-slab, and indeed all the early Christian stones from Papil, were made of sandstone imported either overland from the eastern mainland or by sea from the Walls area to the west. Overall in Shetland the choice of stone for carving at this period is interesting. Despite the proximity of steatite to Mail, Cunningsburgh, the wolf-headed human figure found there in 1992 was incised on a fine-grained sandstone (Turner 1994), presumably because it would produce the desired sharp and fine line. But why are there no high-relief sculptures in the easy-to-carve steatite? Were the sources of steatite too far from the major ecclesiastical centres at Papil and St Ninian's Isle? Or had the fashion for high-relief sculpture not reached or not been accepted in Shetland? It may simply have been that large slabs were too difficult to achieve in steatite, which was suited more to carving vessels or small artefacts such as line-sinkers. The 11th-century hogback tombstone from St Ninian's Isle was carved from a block of steatite but it is only 1.19m long and a maximum 0.28m wide (Small et al 1973, vol 1, 37, no 17, vol 2, pl XI; Lang 1974, 231).

The limitations exerted by the geology of Shetland upon stone-carving are reflected in the roofing techniques used in vernacular building. Shetland houses in recent centuries were normally thatched, whereas in Orkney, where large thin flagstones were available, roofs were often of flagstone rather than thatch (Fenton 1978, 175–86).

The small Uyea fragment, incised in steatite, was apparently part of a larger fragment which had been re-used as a cover slab for a steatite urn containing a cremated burial. Steatite was easily available in the neighbouring island of Unst. Such re-use of a symbol stone has also been encountered in Orkney, with the slab carved with an eagle that covered a small cist at Oxtro, Birsay (RCAHMS 1946, no 11). This was part of a cemetery of cremation burials in cists, and one of the cremations was contained within a steatite vessel, as at Uyea. Cremation is rare as a burial rite in the first millennium AD, and these cist-burials are difficult to date. If the Uyea fragment came from a cross-slab, its date is unlikely to be earlier than the 9th century.

Eagles in stone-carving in the Northern Isles
Eagles are a distinctive attribute of artistic taste and symbolism in the Northern Isles. Isabel Henderson has identified the Knowe of Burrian eagle as closest in style to the eagle of St John in the illustrated gospel, Corpus MS 197, in Corpus Christi College, Cambridge (1967, 124–5; Corpus MS 197B,f.1) and it was probably the earliest of the Pictish eagles. This slab was discovered in 1936 at the entrance to a well inside the broch known as Knowe of Burrian in Harray, mainland Orkney (RCAHMS 1946, no 21; verbal information about the precise location from one of the finders, Mrs Anna Hourie).[3] This provenance reinforces both the ritual aspects of such wells and their continuing importance through Pictish times (Ritchie 1995, 113–14). It may not be a coincidence that a Roman intaglio finger-ring from the broch at Howe is carved with an eagle (Smith 1994, 191); dated to the 2nd century AD, this ring may point towards a local interest in eagles that pre-dated but later reinforced the potency of the evangelist symbol. There is also an eagle, albeit a poor stiff version, on the Brough of Birsay stone (Curle, CL 1982, 14). The style and quality of the Oxtro eagle already mentioned is unknown as the slab is lost.

In Shetland, an eagle is pecked on a boulder found near the broch at Islesburgh (now in Shetland Museum; Scott

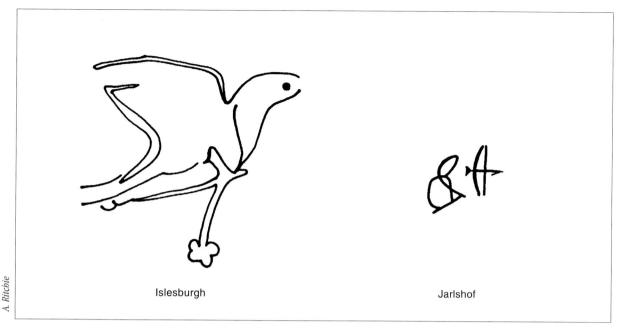

Islesburgh

Jarlshof

3 *The Islesburgh eagle and the Jarlshof archer*

1957, frontispiece) (**3**), but it is an eagle in flight, whereas all other Pictish eagles are shown walking with their wings in repose. The fact that the legs are shown one behind the other, extended on the same axis as the neck, suggests that the bird is either coming in to land or, more probably, taking off. The 1957 illustration (on which fig **3** is based) has added a beak which had in fact weathered away, and the tips of the wings and tail are also missing. Nevertheless, it is clear that this eagle did not possess the fine detail of more formal Pictish carvings. The eye appears to have been a simple circular pit and cannot be compared either with Brough of Birsay, where the head is missing, or Knowe of Burrian where the eye has weathered badly. The foot of the Islesburgh bird is represented by four conjoining pits, which bear a resemblance to the best preserved foot of the Birsay eagle, and the S-scroll at the joint of the wing of the Burrian eagle may be echoed (though anatomically unnecessary) in the slightly curved line rising above the breast of the Islesburgh bird. It is, however, difficult to compare a pecked carving with the detail possible in an incised carving. Even allowing for the blurring caused by weathering, this can have been intended as no more than a sketch, and as such it may be compared with the bird in flight incised, along with a few twig-runes (which need not be contemporary), on a stone found in the chambered tomb at Unstan in Orkney (Davidson and Henshall 1989, 164–5). Although it is definitely not an eagle, a bird carved

in the round from steatite was found in the Northmavine area of Shetland, and Thomas likened its conventional feathering to Pictish eagles (1963, 47, pl II).

There is something of the quality of a graffito about the wolf-headed human figure from Mail already mentioned (even more lightly incised stones have been reported from Cunningsburgh but unfortunately not preserved, Turner 1994). Equally informal but more puzzling is the fish pecked on a slab which was re-used as a lintel over a window in St Olaf's Church at Lunda Wick in Unst; the form of the fish appears to be unlike the normal Pictish salmon, but it is difficult to see in its present location. The church was built in the 12th century, but this particular window (the east window in the south wall) is thought to be a later insertion (Gifford 1992, 496–7) and is therefore of little help in dating the carving.

Mail, Cunningsburgh

Even before the discovery of the wolf-headed figure, this area was known for its several inscriptions in the ogham and runic scripts (RCAHMS 1946, no 1136; Turner 1994). The ogham inscriptions are late and their juxtaposition with runestones and the steatite 'industry' along the Catpund Burn has been interpreted as evidence of continuity of settlement in the area from Pictish into Viking times (Ritchie 1974, 31). Although the evidence from Jarlshof suggests that the native Pictish exploitation of steatite was minimal, this phase of the Jarlshof occupation as recorded was limited, and there has been too little excavation of contemporary sites elsewhere for comparison. While pottery techniques may vary and the inclusion of steatite filler in the clay may fluctuate, it is inherently unlikely that steatite should go out of use for artefacts such as line-sinkers and spindle-whorls.

As a result of the discovery of the Mail figure, attention has been drawn once again to the significance of the place-name, Cunningsburgh, as a Scandinavian name meaning 'king's stronghold' (Robertson 1992, 28). This may well be an instance of the incoming Norse taking over an existing power-centre, the wealth and power here based on control of the essential resource provided by the steatite outcrops in the hinterland. A good Orcadian parallel is the island of Burray, where a concentration of high-status artefacts from late Roman times (Hunter 1993) into the Norse period (Graham-Campbell 1976, 123) can be seen in the context of a fertile island with good peat and lead, silver and copper ores. Cunningsburgh's economic strength included one of the two most secure anchorages on the east coast, Aith Voe, from which the steatite could be exported by boat.

Two hundred years ago, George Low was also aware of the significance of the place-name, when it was known as Coningburg: 'The name tells us that here has been a burgh or castle, and probably the chief in the Isles, as the other component part of the same name would impart' (1879, 180). He also records that the people here in 1774 had a tradition of poor hospitality and that they were 'a stout hardy race, by all accounts the wildest in Schetland'. Hibbert claimed not only that Coningsburghers were physically different, surly and inhospitable but also that they spoke their own dialect (1822, 106–7). It may not be too fanciful to suggest that the Norse overlords may have kept on a Pictish workforce as slaves to quarry the steatite, resulting in a localised concentration of Pictish blood in the population in later times, which could be recognised as somehow different from neighbouring communities.

Cunningsburgh is the name of an area rather than a specific farm or village, and there are several potential candidates for the title of 'king's stronghold'. There were remains of brochs at Mail and at the head of Aith Voe (RCAHMS 1946, nos 1187, 1150), either of which could have had post-broch settlement taking it into historical

Pictish times, and the find-spots of two runestones discovered in the 1870s are marked on the 1st edition 6-inch OS map at North Voxter on the west side of Aith Voe, roughly half-way between the two broch-sites. (The provenances of the various inscribed stones from Cunningsburgh are discussed in Turner 1994.) The fragment, Cunningsburgh 2, with part of a rectangle symbol and part of an ogham inscription, came from Mail, along with another ogham fragment, no 1 (Allen and Anderson 1903, III, 16–17). Katherine Forsyth has made the point that 'the distribution of formal ogham-inscribed monuments appears to be correlated with centres of secular power' (1995b, 237), which, in the context of Cunningsburgh/Mail, underlines the significance of this area of Shetland.

Jarlshof

Jarlshof dominates the archaeological record for Shetland in the first millennium AD simply because it is a multi-period site excavated in the 20th century, not because it has any claim to be a safe gauge of social development in the islands. The fact that it fails to merit a mention in *Orkneyinga Saga* is a warning (whatever its Norse name, it was not of course 'Jarlshof', the name so percipiently invented by Sir Walter Scott in *The Pirate* to identify the ruins of the 17th-century laird's house). Despite the story recorded in the saga of the villagers gathering on the foreshore at Sumburgh Head and sharing in the catch of fish brought in by the disguised Earl Rognvald (ch 85), no name is mentioned for the village. Only six places in Shetland are named in the saga, and of those just one relates to a Norse estate, that of Einar of Gulberwick, on the east coast south of Lerwick (ch 85).

The second element in the name Sumburgh is derived from Old Norse *borg* meaning fort, which could refer to the Jarlshof broch if it were still visible in Viking times (just as the broch of Mousa was given the ON name of Moseyjarborg). Perhaps more likely is that it refers to a fort on Sumburgh Head, which was destroyed in the 1820s when the lighthouse was built (Brian Smith, pers comm). This fort was described by Low in 1774: 'Here the neck of land is cut by a ditch and strong wall, which must in old times have formed a considerable fortification'; there were foundations of a building at the entrance and 'numerous small buildings' inside the fort (Low 1879, 185). Traces of the rampart still survive alongside the modern road (Ritchie 1997, 50, no 4). The building at the entrance may have been a blockhouse similar to those at Ness of Burgi and Scatness on the west side of the West Voe of Sumburgh. It is tempting to speculate whether this fort may have been used in Pictish times. Its precipitous location could be explained in terms of a beacon system, for which the great height of the promontory would be ideal. Such a beacon system existed in Norse times, linking Shetland, Fair Isle and Orkney (*Orkneyinga Saga*, chs 66–7, 69–71), and there is no reason why there should not have been such a system in earlier times.

The archaeological record at Jarlshof appears to show a reduced level of occupation and prosperity in the period immediately preceding the early Norse settlement (Hamilton 1956, 91), and this has been used as evidence for a general recession in Shetland in Pictish times. It is however possible that the focus of Pictish settlement lay to the seaward side of the old broch and has been lost into the sea. There are certainly sufficient traces of Pictish material culture among the artefacts to suggest that the surviving structural evidence is incomplete.

There is great need for excavation on potentially Pictish sites in Shetland. It has long been recognized that brochs with extensive external settlements, such as the broch of Burraland, are likely to include occupation of this period, but less obviously promising sites are also potential candidates. Excavations at the blockhouse fort of Scatness have yielded radiocarbon dates indicating that limited use of the site continued into the late first millennium AD (Carter *et al* 1995, 443–4), and such forts are increasingly seen in terms of ritualized warfare rather than as normal defensive structures (Hingley 1992, 19; Carter *et al* 1995, 476–7). More difficult to identify would be the turf and timber architecture of Pictish Shetland envisaged by Noel Fojut (1996, 110), although a wicker basket preserved in an Eshaness peat bog has been radiocarbon-dated to the period between the mid 4th century and the end of the 6th century AD (National Museums of Scotland).

Decorated stone discs

The clearest evidence for a Pictish presence at Jarlshof is the small stone disc incised with a double-disc and Z-rod symbol (Hamilton 1956, 84, pl XVIIc; Thomas 1963, 45, fig 3, 8), which was unfortunately an unstratified find. This is one of a number of stone discs around 60 mm in diameter and 12–15 mm thick, the incised decoration on which has strong affiliations with Pictish art. They were all found in the Shetland mainland, except for one from Caithness, and they are conveniently illustrated by Thomas (1963, fig 3, 1–8), except for a disc from Jarlshof with a multiple S-scroll design (Hamilton 1956, pl XVIIc) and the ship disc discussed below. The decoration on another of the five discs from Jarlshof was interpreted by Thomas as an arch symbol, infilled with zig-zag (1963, 47, fig 3, 2); on the other side is a deeply cut S-scroll superimposed on a possible snake's head. This is the only disc with a secure context, for it came from the upper floor levels in wheelhouse 1 (Hamilton 1956, 83), but only a broad date in the mid first millennium AD can be inferred. Several discs have decoration on both sides, but one side is more formal in design and usually more carefully executed. These decorated discs could be large playing pieces, but their size suggests that they had another, perhaps ceremonial, function. However they were used, they appear to have been a constituent part of northern Pictish culture, comparable to painted pebbles in date and distribution, except that no decorated discs have yet been found in Orkney.

Painted pebbles

Quartzite pebbles painted with a variety of simple designs, mostly dots and curving lines, have been interpreted as charmstones (Ritchie 1972), and three have been found at Jarlshof, along with one from Clickhimin. Since the recent discovery of five such pebbles at Upper Scalloway (Sharples forthcoming), together with one at Sandsound and one at Balta Isle, Unst (Shetland Museum; Ritchie forthcoming), the total for Shetland has risen to eleven, with another fifteen from Orkney and Caithness. An important feature of the Upper Scalloway examples is the use of S-scrolls, underlining the popularity in Shetland of this motif. The fact that nine pebbles have come from just three excavations in Shetland suggests that a campaign of excavation on Late Iron-Age sites would produce even more.

Sketches on stone

An unusual feature of the Jarlshof assemblage is the number of sketches, mostly on small pieces of slate, from the early Norse levels. In a footnote to his paper on Shetland sculpture, Stevenson suggested that some of them 'were more probably drawn by a native rather than by a Norseman, notably the man's head with a row of curls only paralleled by the chief on the Birsay stone' (1981, 289, n.1). This Pictish attribution was independently recognized by O'Meadhra and extended to include the boat sketches and indeed all the slate-motifs other than one identified as Viking-Age foliage (1987, 78–82; 1993, 427–31, 436). To O'Meadhra's excellent 1993 discussion of the Jarlshof boat-sketches might be added Johnstone's analysis of the boat deeply incised on an earlier sandstone disc from Jarlshof (1980, 153), which is likely to be a Pictish boat similar to the smaller of the two slate-motif boats. Examination of the disc (NMS HSA 791) reveals that the three lines depicting the mast and the outermost rigging are more deeply cut than the intermediate stripes of the sail, and that there is an oblique transverse line between the two outer rigging lines which does not appear on the published photograph in which the visible lines have been enhanced by the use of white ink (Hamilton 1956, pl XXI, 2; NMS HSA 791). The longer boat (ibid, pl XXI,1; NMS HSA 790) shows the mast with a double rather than a single line, the two outer rigging lines, a rudder foreshortened to convey that it is in the raised position ready for landing, and twenty-four oars in the upright position for landing; the mast is somewhat forward of midship, allowing eight oars forward of the mast and sixteen oars behind it.

Another slate fragment in the National Museums of Scotland appears to show the stern of a boat very similar to that shown on the disc: the stern is markedly rounded with multiple lines perhaps indicating a plank-built vessel, with the addition of an L-shaped rudder and six strokes which may represent oars protruding through holes below the gunwale (NMS 1958.1736; unstratified). There is also a large slab of sandstone incised with an impressionist sketch of the prow of a plank-built boat (Hamilton 1956, 145 no 42; NMS HSA 792).[4]

In her study of pre-Norse and Norse sketches and motif-pieces in the Northern Earldoms, O'Meadhra concluded that 'sketching in Scotland might well be a Pictish characteristic' (1993, 425). Perhaps this idea might be taken further to suggest that sketching was a Pictish characteristic specifically of the Northern Isles, and that this was the legacy of the artistic school that produced the superb Burrian eagle. Curle's analysis still stands: 'The representation of a ship, reduced to essentials, and drawn with a sensitive line, is the work of a draughtsman. Many of the other tablets show the most rudimentary attempts at drawing, and might well be the efforts of pupils studying the elements of design. Failing that, they are the meaningless scribbles of an idler produced with the point of his knife on a smooth surface' (Curle, AO 1935, 317).[5]

O'Meadhra drew attention to the sketch of a cross embellished with curls as 'the only possible decorative art motif' on the slates from Jarlshof (1993, 430–1, fig 27.2j). Similar curls may be found on the reverse of a stone disc from Lerwick (Thomas 1963, fig 3,1), and a cross-slab from St Colm's Kirk in Hoy, Orkney, shows the same curls on the foot of the cross (Cursiter 1898). The lost slab with a brief inscription in Latin from St Nicholas Chapel in Papa Stronsay also bears a cross embellished with curls (RCAHMS 1946, no 999). More formal is the S-scroll on the back of the disc with an arch symbol already mentioned from Jarlshof, and this is echoed on a stone fragment from a late pre-Viking context from the same site, on which are incised three S-scrolls (Hamilton 1956, fig 37,8). S-scrolls also appear on the painted pebbles from Upper Scalloway, and curls, spirals and S-scrolls are carved on corner-posts from composite shrines from St Ninian's Isle (Small *et al* 1973, vol 2, fig 12). Double spirals form the base of the figural scene on the shrine-panel from Papil.

Slate is an ideal medium for sketching, for it is relatively soft and can be incised easily with the tip of a knife, and even light incision creates a pleasing colour contrast (although this is lost as the slate weathers). There is an added contrast on one fragment bearing incised interlace (Hamilton 1956, 121, pl XXI, 5; NMS HSA 796), for the slate itself has a light and a dark band which were utilized by an otherwise inept artist for two bands of crude interlace.

Another fragment has a distinctively Pictish motif: the archer with a crossbow. This was illustrated by Curle in 1935 and interpreted by him as a bow and arrow with a cryptic double-circle figure (1935, 310, figs 48,6 and 49,6). If the sketch is seen from a different angle to those already published, it can be identified as a crouched archer with a crossbow, directly comparable to the motifs seen on St Vigeans 1, Meigle 10, Shandwick and Glenferness (3). Crossbows on Pictish cross-slabs have been discussed by Gilbert (1976).

O'Meadhra's concern was with the wider north-west European context for the Jarlshof slate-sketches, but they should also be viewed in the context of earlier graffiti from the pre-Norse settlement and from elsewhere in Shetland. There is a strong pre-Norse tradition of incised sketching on stone not only at Jarlshof but in the Northern Isles generally. The other Shetland evidence has been discussed above, and O'Meadhra discusses the Orcadian evidence from Bridge of Brodgar and Burness (1993, 426–7). The sketch of a bird at Unstan has already been mentioned, and the informally incised symbol stone from Gurness should not be forgotten in this context (Ritchie, J NG 1969).

Outside the Northern Isles, and leaving aside the question of Pictish cave-art, sketches have been found in Pictland only on the lignite pendant from Beauly (Jill Harden, pers comm) and the 'whetstone' from Portsoy (Thomas 1963, 48, pl II), although this may simply reflect the scarcity of excavated Pictish settlements. Nevertheless, the formally incised male figure from Rhynie is clearly related in concept to the Mail figure (Shepherd and Shepherd 1978), although Mail looks altogether more heathen. There may well have been similar figures painted on wood or stone.

If the Mail figure is heathen, it falls into the same category of evidence of ritual beliefs derived from Iron-Age pagan religion as underground well-cum-cellars in the Northern Isles and mythological motifs on Pictish stones throughout Pictland. Hunter has argued that the 'egg' found in Burray and carved of serpentinite from Shetland is also evidence of Iron-Age ritual beliefs (1993, 333).

Conclusions

The corpus of Pictish material from Shetland is impressive. It includes one complete symbol stone from Sandness and a fragment of another from Cunningsburgh. Evidence of Christianity within a Pictish context is provided by complete cross-slabs from Papil, Bressay and probably South Garth in Yell, and by fragments from Uyea, Lerwick and Whiteness, together with parts of slab-built shrines

from St Ninian's Isle and Papil. The cultural implications of the great silver treasure from St Ninian's Isle are still disputed, but there are some basic aspects that most scholars accept and which have a bearing on the character of Pictish society in Shetland. These include the implications that there was in Shetland the wealth and the social status that required expensive jewellery, tableware and weapons. There was access to fine metal-work, whether commissioned in Shetland or imported – the larch box in which the treasure was buried was certainly an import. The artistic links displayed by the silver demonstrate that Shetland was part of an early medieval community of style and tradition stretching far beyond even mainland Pictland to Dalriada, Ireland and Northumbria. Regardless of whether the treasure was ecclesiastic or secular in origin, it exhibits both Christianity and literacy. It also provides the name of a Pictish Shetlander, for the name Resad is included in a Latin inscription on one of the sword chapes. Another Pictish personal name, Nechtan, is written in ogham on a slab from Lunnasting (Forsyth 1996, 418).

Although Pictish symbols occur on silverwork south of the Moray Firth, none of the St Ninian's Isle pieces is so embellished. Symbols on portable artefacts are restricted to small stone discs, the date of which is likely to be two centuries earlier than the treasure. There are strong artistic links between the stone-carving of mainland Pictland and that of Shetland, and the links are echoed on painted pebbles and the slate sketches of Jarlshof.

There is certainly enough material evidence to support the inclusion of Shetland within the cultural area of Pictland, even if its political status can only be a matter of speculation. Its symbol links are with Pictland around and north of the Moray Firth (rectangle, arch and S figure), and, like Orkney, there may have been an early interest in the eagle as a symbol. The earliest datable example of the rectangular burial cairn with stone kerb and corner-pillars was excavated in Unst (Bigelow 1984), again strengthening the impression of a cultural link between Shetland and the Moray Firth area in early Pictish times. By the end of the 8th century, this well-used sea-route was ready to carry from Burghead, Rosemarkie or Tarbat clerics whose cultural luggage included the notion of the slab-built shrine.

Acknowledgements

I am very grateful to Val Turner, Shetland Islands Archaeologist, both for reading this paper and bringing me up to date with relevant discoveries and for allowing me to read her paper on the Mail figure before publication. She also alerted me to the existence of the painted pebbles from Balta Isle and Sandsound. I am grateful to Brian Smith, Shetland Archivist, for drawing to my attention the Low account of the fort on Sumburgh Head, and to Niall Sharples for allowing me to include mention of the painted pebbles from Upper Scalloway. I am indebted to the National Museums of Scotland for access some years ago to the collection of slate-sketches from Jarlshof.

Notes

1 The five shrines from Papil and St Ninian's Isle are discussed by Charles Thomas in Small *et al* 1973; there is now an additional corner-post from Papil (*Discovery and Excavation in Scotland* 1996, 92). A corner-post from a sixth shrine has been recorded from Houss in East Burra (ibid). There is part of another possible corner-post from the island of Noss at Gungstie (ibid, 1994, 93), and a fragment of possibly the first corner-post from Orkney from Papa Westray (RCAHMS 1994, 20).

2 As a child in 1936, Mrs Hourie and her brother Tim Johnston and friend Robert Flett together dug a trench across the broch. Within the broch, they encountered a doorway blocked by a large upright slab with smaller stones filling the gap round about it. With a pick, they levered out the stone and discovered carvings on the other side. The point of the pick made a hollow in the body of the eagle, and the leverage broke the slab into two at a point about two thirds down its length and across the mirror symbol. Charles Calder of RCAHMS visited the site on 25th June 1936, and he recorded in his notebook (no 21) that the trench was dug from the base of the mound through both the natural clay and the superimposed wall of the broch into the interior (no mean feat, but Robert Flett was apparently a strong teenager, who later carried the slab to the house).

The original entry to the well is likely to have been through the floor of the broch, by removing two or three of the cover slabs shown on the plan (RCAHMS 1946, 17). This would create an entry very similar in size to the opening into the well at Gurness. What is puzzling is why later the symbol stone should have been used upright at the back of the entrance passage. Was it inserted as a new back-slab during the use of the well? The symbols were facing inwards and would have been visible from inside the well. Or had the entrance been modified to a vertical opening, which was finally sealed by the symbol stone? Such an opening would have been difficult of access, for the passage was only 0.4 m high at that point, though 0.6 m wide.

The stone is thought to be broadly contemporary in date with the Corpus Christi manuscript (Henderson, G 1987, 76–8), and its re-use in connection with the well is hardly likely before the political disintegration of Pictland in the 9th century. Its provenance is thus an important indication of the continuing use of the well throughout Pictish times.

3 The Bressay cross-slab is reported as having been dug up in waste ground near the ruined church at Culbinsburgh (now Cullingsburgh) on the north-east side of the island. This suggests the existence of an earlier church on a site used at least since Iron-Age times, for there is a large broch-mound on the north-east side of the surviving graveyard. This is a likely candidate for a Pictish settlement, and in chronological terms it echoes the sequence at St Ninian's Isle. The 12th-century chapel on the tiny island of Uyea was presumably also the successor to an earlier church to which the fragment of a 9th-century cross-slab belonged.

4 Another sketch of a possible boat-stern was discovered in April 1995 on a slate knife from Old Scatness broch (Val Turner pers comm).

5 Detailed analysis of a number of the Jarlshof sketches is hampered by the fact that, at some stage after the excavation, the incised lines were infilled with white ink. Detailed stratification of the various pieces is unsatisfactory, but overall most belong to the late pre-Norse and early Viking levels and there may well have been sufficient admixture of midden material to make most of them broadly contemporary. Hamilton faced an almost impossible task in interpreting the results of many seasons of excavation by himself and his predecessors, and the uncertainties are clear from his publication; 'a house floor is an area of minimal growth' because it is constantly cleaned out, yet the finds from Viking house 1 constitute 'a selection of small objects lost or buried in the soft earth floor over three or four centuries' (1956, 97, 128).

References

ALLEN, J R and ANDERSON, J 1903 *The Early Christian Monuments of Scotland*, 3 parts. Edinburgh (repr with an Introduction by Isabel Henderson, 2 vols, Balgavies, Angus, 1993).

BIGELOW, G F
– 1984 Two kerbed cairns from Sandwick, Unst, Shetland. In Friell, JGS and Watson, WG (eds) *Pictish Studies: settlement, burial and art in Dark Age North Britain*, 115–29. Oxford.

– 1992 Issues and prospects in Shetland Norse archaeology. In Morris, C D and Rackham, D J (eds) *Norse and later settlement and subsistence in the North Atlantic*, 9–32. Glasgow.

CANT, R G 1996 The medieval church in Shetland: organisation and buildings. In Waugh 1996, 159–73.

CARTER, S P, McCULLAGH, R P J and MacSWEEN, A 1995 The Iron Age in Shetland: excavations at five sites threatened by coastal erosion. *Proc Soc Antiq Scot*, 125 (1995), 429–82.

CURLE, A O 1935 An account of the excavation of a dwelling of the Viking period at 'Jarlshof', Sumburgh, Shetland, carried out on behalf of H.M. Office of Works. *Proc Soc Antiq Scot*, 49 (1934-35), 265–324.

CURLE, C L 1982 *Pictish and Norse Finds from the Brough of Birsay 1934–74*. Edinburgh. (Society of Antiquaries of Scotland Monograph Series No 1)

CURSITER, J W 1898 Note on a stone bearing an incised cross, from the site of St Colm's Chapel, Walls, Orkney. *Proc Soc Antiq Scot*, 32 (1897-98), 50–2.

DAVIDSON, J M and HENSHALL, A S 1989 *The Chambered Cairns of Orkney*. Edinburgh.

FENTON, A 1978 *The Northern Isles: Orkney and Shetland*. Edinburgh.

FOJUT, N 1994 *A Guide to Prehistoric and Viking Shetland*. Lerwick.

FORSYTH, K
– 1995a Language in Pictland, spoken and written. In Nicoll, E H (ed) *A Pictish Panorama*, 7–10. Balgavies, Angus.

– 1995b The inscriptions on the Dupplin Cross. In Bourke, C (ed) *From the Isles of the North: Early Medieval Art in Ireland and Britain*, 237–44. Belfast.

– 1996 The Ogham Inscriptions of Scotland: an edited corpus. Unpublished PhD thesis, Harvard University.

GILBERT, J M 1976 Crossbows on Pictish stones. *Proc Soc Antiq Scot*, 107 (1975-76), 316–17.

GIFFORD, J 1992 *The Buildings of Scotland: Highland and Islands*. London.

GRAHAM–CAMPBELL, J 1976 The Viking-age silver and gold hoards of Scandinavian character from Scotland. *Proc Soc Antiq Scot*, 107 (1975-76), 114–35.

HAMILTON, J R C 1956 *Excavations at Jarlshof, Shetland*. Edinburgh.

HENDERSON, G 1987 *From Durrow to Kells: the Insular Gospel-books 650–800*. London.

HENDERSON, I
– 1967 *The Picts*. London.

– 1994 The Insular and Continental context of the St Andrews Sarcophagus. In Crawford, B E (ed) *Scotland in Dark Age Europe*, 71–102. St Andrews.

HIBBERT, S 1822 *A Description of the Shetland Islands*. Edinburgh.

HINGLEY, R 1992 Society in Scotland from 700 BC to AD 200. *Proc Soc Antiq Scot*, 122 (1992), 7–53.

HUNTER, F 1993 Four decorated antler mounts and a stone 'egg' amulet from Bu Sands, Burray, Orkney. *Proc Soc Antiq Scot*, 123 (1993), 319–36.

JACKSON, K 1955 The Pictish language. In Wainwright, F T (ed) *The Problem of the Picts*, 129–66. Edinburgh.

JOHNSTONE, P 1980 *The Sea-craft of Prehistory*. London.

LAMB, R G 1995 Papil, Picts and Papar. In Crawford, B E (ed) *Northern Isles Connections*, 9–27. Kirkwall.

LANG, J T 1974 Hogback monuments in Scotland. *Proc Soc Antiq Scot*, 105 (1972-74), 206–35.

LOW, G 1879 *A Tour through the Islands of Orkney and Schetland*. Kirkwall.

MACK, A 1997 *Field Guide to the Pictish Symbol Stones*. Balgavies, Angus.

MOAR, P and STEWART, J 1944 Newly discovered sculptured stones from Papil, Shetland. *Proc Soc Antiq Scot*, 78 (1943-44), 91–9.

O'MEADHRA, U
– 1987 *Early Christian, Viking and Romanesque Art: Motif-pieces from Ireland. 2: A discussion on aspects of find-context and function* (Theses and Papers in North-European Archaeology 17). Stockholm.

– 1993 Viking-age sketches and motif-pieces from the Northern Earldoms. In Batey, C E, Jesch, J and Morris, C D (eds) *The Viking-Age in Caithness, Orkney and the North Atlantic*, 423–40. Edinburgh.

RCAHMS = Royal Commission on the Ancient and Historical Monuments of Scotland
– 1946 *Twelfth Report with an Inventory of the Ancient Monuments of Orkney and Shetland*. Edinburgh.

– 1994 *Pictish Symbol Stones: A handlist 1994*. Edinburgh.

RITCHIE, A
– 1972 Painted pebbles in early Scotland. *Proc Soc Antiq Scot*, 104 (1971-72), 297–301.

– 1974 Pict and Norseman in Northern Scotland. *Scot Archaeol Forum*, 6 (1974), 23–36.

– 1995 *Prehistoric Orkney*. London.

– 1997 *Shetland*. Edinburgh.

– forthcoming Two painted pebbles from Shetland. *Proc Soc Antiq Scot*.

RITCHIE, J N G 1969 Two new Pictish symbols from Orkney. *Proc Soc Antiq Scot*, 101 (1968-69), 130–3.

ROBERTSON, N 1992 The Dog-headed Man of Shetland. *Pictish Arts Soc J*, 2 (1992), 27–8.

SCOTT, L G 1957 The Islesburgh Eagle. *Shetland Folk Book*, 3 (1957), 51–2.

SHARPLES, N forthcoming Excavation of a broch at Upper Scalloway, Shetland.

SHEPHERD, I A G and SHEPHERD, A N 1978 An incised Pictish figure and a new symbol stone from Barflat, Rhynie, Gordon District. *Proc Soc Antiq Scot*, 109 (1977-78), 211–22.

Shetland County Museum 1973 *Catalogue.* Lerwick.

SMALL, A, THOMAS, A C and WILSON, D M 1973 *St Ninian's Isle and its Treasure.* Aberdeen.

SMITH, B BALLIN (ed) 1994 Howe: *Four Millennia of Orkney Prehistory, Excavations 1978–1982* (Society of Antiquaries of Scotland Monograph Series No 9). Edinburgh.

STEVENSON, R B K 1981 Christian sculpture in Norse Shetland. *Frodskaparrit*, 28–9 (1981), 283–92.

THOMAS, A C 1963 The interpretation of the Pictish symbols. *Archaeol J*, 120 (1963), 31–97.

TURNER, V 1994 The Mail Stone: an incised Pictish figure from Mail, Cunningsburgh, Shetland. *Proc Soc Antiq Scot*, 124 (1994), 315–25.

WAINWRIGHT, F T (ed) 1962 *The Northern Isles.* Edinburgh.

WAUGH, D J (ed) 1996 *Shetland's Northern Links: Language and History.* Edinburgh.

Postscript

While this paper was in press, a new Pictish symbol stone came to light in Shetland. I am very grateful to Tommy Watt for informing me of the find and allowing me to mention it here. The surface of the stone has flaked badly, but part of an incised crescent is visible, apparently lacking a V-rod, and beneath it are traces of a probable rectangle symbol. The stone was found at Breck in Dunrossness (southern mainland) and is now in Shetland Museum.

Abernethy and Mugdrum: towards reassessment

Edwina Proudfoot
Photographs by Tom E.Gray

Introduction

The round tower at Abernethy and the tall stone at Mugdrum sit in the landscape as important reminders of both the Picts and the early church in Pictland, yet little attention has been paid to either in context. The known information about the area comprises mainly the carved stones, most of which have been recorded in the past, but not previously collected for study. Increasing information has become available via aerial photography which has revealed groups of sites and individual remains between Abernethy and the Tay to add to existing archaeological data. Although the documentary evidence has been called pseudo-history the archaeological evidence should reflect reality and it might be possible to lead from the slender information contained in the Annals to discover more of the development of Abernethy as a religious site through a closer examination of its archaeology and its wider context.

Archaeological attention has focused on the one Pictish symbol stone, Class I, found at Abernethy, on the later round tower which now stands at the edge of the churchyard, and on the fort on the Castle Law, above the burgh. The Mugdrum Stone, with its surviving scenes of horsemen comfortably fits the repertoire of Pictish Class II stones, but its presence on the boundary of the Mugdrum Estate, and its relationship to the early monastery of Abernethy are unknown. The monastic boundary stones cited in early records, include *Apurfeirc, Caerfuill, that is Lethfoss, and Athan*, none of which sites can be identified with certainty, but the Mugdrum stone, still *in situ*, was not included, presumably because it lay outwith the lands of Abernethy.

For the present preliminary study only the immediate Abernethy area has been considered. However, to develop understanding of Abernethy in context the study should be expanded to include other aspects of Early Historic Scotland. The impetus for this paper was a planned visit to Mugdrum with Isabel Henderson, who had not then seen the stone. We did not make that visit, but I have continued to think about why the stone was erected and what the contemporary environment might have been. I hope Isabel finds food for thought in a different approach to the Picts – and that she might find time to visit Mugdrum someday.

Location

Abernethy is a now small burgh, situated on the north side of the Ochils, overlooking a rich agricultural plain and the confluence of the Rivers Tay and Earn (**1**). It is bounded on the east by the Nethy Burn, which rises on Torduff Hill and on the west by the Ballo Burn, which flows from Abernethy Glen; both flow into the Earn, near its confluence with the Tay. A short distance to the west the River Farg runs through Glen Farg and flows into the Earn. To the south the Ochils rise steeply, with Castle Law at 250m and Pitcairlie Hill, 281m, the highest points locally.

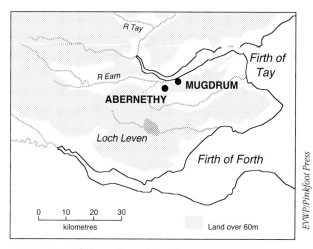

1 *Location of Abernethy and Mugdrum*

The Castle Law fort is sited at 225m OD, on a north-east spur of the hill, above Abernethy Glen and overlooking the modern burgh.

Abernethy lies at 30m OD, on a flat area between the Nethy Burn and the Ballo Burn, and though not at a confluence it is the kind of location favoured for Early Christian sites. It has been described as at the mouth of the Nethy, but a former farm site at Innernethy occupied that location and it is more probable that the name refers to the mouth of the Glen. Similarly Aberargie is not at the mouth of the (F)arg, but at the mouth of the Glen. Mugdrum sits towards the east end of a long ridge at 30m OD, above the Tay, a natural boundary point, from which the ground drops eastwards. From Mugdrum the plain extends westwards between the Ochils and the river Earn, to Forteviot on the Water of May, the site of a later Pictish royal house.

The place names in this area are mixed, with British, Pictish and Gaelic all prominent. Discussion of these names and influences lies outside the scope of the present paper, but a study of all the local names should form part of the wider study of Abernethy. This would expand knowledge of the dates of naming and therefore of both settlement history and any Early Church associations.

The Carved Stones

This section is in two parts, an illustrated Catalogue followed by a Discussion. The Catalogue represents the bulk of the later archaeological information for Abernethy available at present. Although most of the stones have been published previously they have been discussed as individual examples of sculpture, with particular comparisons and not as a source of wider information for Abernethy or the development of the church there. Details of other sites, including the round tower and the church, the earlier Roman fort and the list of sites known from aerial photography, but as yet unexcavated, have been included as basic data in the Catalogue, as they are referred to in the discussion, although not discussed in detail.

The National Monuments Record for Scotland (NMRS) holds archive data and, where available the NMRS reference is given. Several stones are now in the National Museums of Scotland (NMS) and their accession numbers are given. Some stones are in the care of the Abernethy Museum

Trust (AMT) and one is in Perth Museum and Art Gallery (PMAG). Stones in private hands have also been listed.

Catalogue

Tom E. Gray

2 *The Class I carved stone, now placed at the base of the round tower*

1 Abernethy symbol stone; Class I (**2**)
NO 190 164; NMRS: NO11NE19
Allen and Anderson 1903, III, 282, fig 299
On the main face the following symbols have been incised – tuning fork, crescent and V-rod, hammer and anvil. There are no carvings on the reverse. All the symbols have been damaged by trimming of the stone.

The stone is of granite, 838mm high by 559mm wide and has been trimmed for use as a building stone. It was found below the foundations of a house in School Wynd and had probably been used in an earlier structure, perhaps part of the monastic enclosure. It is now built against the south wall of the round tower, adjacent to the entrance to the graveyard.

2 Abernethy graveyard; Class III (**3**)
NMRS: NO11NE20; RMS: IB98
Allen and Anderson 1903, III, 309, fig 323

This stone is carved in relief on one side. Only the lower part of one rear leg of a horse survives clearly, although earlier descriptions suggest there could have been two legs. This possible second leg seems to be a front leg, which could indicate a second horse.

3 *Abernethy 2. Ogham fragment with a horse's rear leg above*

On a raised band below this carved fragment is an incised fragmentary bound-ogham inscription, reading from left to right, I M N or if read from right to left, Q M I (Forsyth, unpublished). Forsyth considers that this stone could derive from a recumbent monument, rather than an upright stone. The lower edge of the stone (or left edge), is broken and measures 63 mm on the left and 108 mm on the right.

The stone is a fragment of a large monument of red sandstone. It now measures 380 mm high by 242 mm wide by 76 mm thick. It was found in the Abernethy graveyard, but mortar still adhering to the surface suggests that it had been reused in a building prior to this. It is now in the NMS.

3 Abernethy; Class III (not illustrated)
NMRS: NO11NE82
Allen and Anderson 1903, III, 310, fig 324
This stone fragment has traces of a panel of diagonal key pattern, carved in relief, but no part of the design is complete.

It is of red sandstone; 220 mm high by 340 mm wide. It is very worn and has been squared off for reuse as building stone. It was found built into the gable wall of a cottage in Abernethy. Its present whereabouts are not known.

4 Abernethy; Class III (**4**)
NMRS: NO11NE83; NMS IB255
Allen and Anderson 1903, III, 310, fig 325
This damaged stone is part of a cross, carved in high relief, with roll mouldings down both edges. This stone is from a free-standing cross and comprises part of the shaft and inward curve of the arms below the central crossing. (The fragment, Abernethy 7 (Butler, pl VII, now lost) is from a cross of similar form). This fragment depicts the lower part of a central crucifixion scene, with Christ standing, his well-formed legs flexed slightly and wearing short trousers to just above the knee. Longinus, the spear bearer, is crouching on the right and Stephanton, the sponge bearer is sitting on the left, with his leg braced against Christ's leg. Both figures are damaged and have been described as having animal heads, but this could be the effect of wear damage. The upper part of the Crucifixion scene would have filled the central area of the cross and extended into the arms.

Below are the damaged heads of three figures wearing hoods and cloaks, with incised decoration, perhaps indicating classical folds or other detail. The hair or a hair

4 *Abernethy 4: fragment of a sculptural cross carved in high relief, with part of crucifixion in the upper register and three hooded figures below*

covering can be seen clearly on the central figure and a faint trace of a similar arrangement can be seen on the figure on the right. The eyes of the central figure have been defaced, but had been deeply set and circular. Very little other detail can be made out. Allen describes these as female figures, but they could be male clerics. The composition of three frontal figures in high relief is not a common one and this group would have been a spectacular example of stone carving.

The fragment is of red sandstone; 590 mm high by 381 mm wide by 152 mm thick and was found recut, built into a cottage as a door jamb and it is now in the NMS.

a   b

National Museums of Scotland

5 *Fragment of defaced stone with surviving carving on both edges:* **a** *plant scroll* **b** *double-bead interlace*

5 Abernethy; Class III (**5**)

NMS: IB176

Allen and Anderson 1903, III, 310, fig 326

This is a severely defaced part of the shaft of a rectangular cross, the carving still visible on both edges, but entirely removed from both faces.

On one edge is a plant scroll (**5a**), the scroll alternating to left and right. The stem and scrolls are heavy and of a double-bead form, seen clearly only on the right of the central scroll, which has a three-berry cluster; the lowest one may also be a cluster, but the upper central element is a small bud or ball end. A strong two-strand binding grips the stems. On the left three round buds have been fitted tightly between the scrolls, while on the right small triangular leaves can be seen on short stalks between the scrolls. There are traces of a beaded edge down both sides of the stone.

The opposite side of the stone (**5b**) has been carved with a panel of broad, flat double-bead interlace, Allen type 568, at least 30 mm wide. There is no indication of heads or tails. The two-bead interlace bands are comparable with the interlace on several stones at Meigle, St Andrews and elsewhere and also with the stone from the Abernethy area, Catalogue no 13. This is a fragment of red sandstone; 431 mm high by 340 mm wide by 152 mm thick, with several patches of damage. It was found in 1896, built into a retaining wall at the side of the road and is now in the NMS.

6 Abernethy; Class III (**6**)

AMT

Allen and Anderson 1903, III, 341; Butler 1897, pl V

This is a roughly tooled stone bearing a crude, undecorated cross with a shaft, carved in relief on one face. The cross is of Allen type 82, with expanded ends (Allen and Anderson 1903, II, 47). Allen recorded that it stood in the churchyard, near the church and he considered that it could have been a gravestone, as are comparable stones in Northumbria. It is an early cross, now broken into two pieces. Chisel marks are clearly visible on the left upper and lower panels. The end of the left arm and the base of the shaft have both been slightly damaged, but the outline around the cross still survives at the broken lower end, showing that little of the shaft has been lost. The stone has broken just below the shaft and on the lower fragment an edge can be made out, as well as recent chisel marks under a coating of mortar from use as a building stone.

The cross is made on a block of red sandstone and as first recorded it measured 660 mm high by 482 mm wide by 120 mm thick. It was inside the church porch in 1985 and recently has been removed to an AMT store.

7 Abernethy; Class III (**7**)

Butler 1897, pl VII

This is a fragment of a heavily carved, but now defaced stone, probably from the shaft of a cross, now lost. It is similar in form to Abernethy 4, with moulded edges and it seems to be from just below the central part of a cross. The left side has a rolled moulding, broken just above the inward curve to the armpit. The right side has been cut for use as a building stone, but a fragment of the edge moulding can be seen. The fragment is broken at the top and bottom, so that no part of the stone is complete.

The carving is severely defaced so that the decoration is almost unrecognisable and in the absence of the stone it is not possible to be certain of the carved figures. There

7 *Abernethy 7: Stone, heavily defaced; now lost (Butler 1897, pl VII)*

appears to be an extremely worn large central figure, with traces of interlace above. What might be two left-facing feet and three right-facing feet can be identified below the central figure. In the lower left corner is a small heavily defaced figure, surviving as an unidentifiable face with pointed chin and plain garment.

Dimensions not known. Whereabouts not known.

8 Abernethy; Class III (**8**)

NO11NE87: NMS: IB 290

Stevenson 1959, no 9, 45, pl VIII, 2

This is a fragment of the face of a cross shaft with a rounded moulding surviving on the left side and the moulding on the right side damaged, but enough survives to show that this is the full width of the stone.

The surviving face is carved in high relief, 25 mm deep. Parts of two rows of figures survive. The upper row shows five clerical figures wearing costly garments with richly trimmed borders reaching almost to their feet. Vertical detail on figures 1, 2 and 5 probably represents the folds of elaborate robes, similar to those in profile on the Papil, Shetland, stone or the frontal figures on the stone from Invergowrie, Angus. The left and right figures have splayed

6 *Abernethy 6: Stone, now in two fragments, with undecorated cross in relief*

Tom E. Gray

8 *Abernethy 8: Fragment of cross, the upper part with five richly robed figures, possibly, two with croziers, one with scales, one with a scourge and the fifth with a harp; below them five defaced, hooded figures.*

to have a scourge and figure 4, possibly a harp.

Immediately below these, without a frame, are five hooded figures, of which only badly defaced heads survive. On heads no 1 and no 4 the hood seems to reach down below the chin in the same manner as on Abernethy 4. Detail is not as clear on the remaining three heads, but the eyes can be made out on all five, and the nose and mouth survive only on figure 1. The distance between the eyes and the hoods is sufficient for there to have been either hair or a hair covering.

The other face of the stone has been completely defaced and the sides have been chiselled off, with faint remains of interlace on one.

This cannot be from the same cross as Abernethy 4 as that is of red sandstone and this fragment is of a cream sandstone. The fragment measures 394mm high by 584mm wide by 253mm thick. It was found built into the window frame of a house in the east of Abernethy and acquired by the NMS in 1957.

feet; no 2 has both feet pointing to the left; the central figure has forward-pointing feet; the fourth figure has one forward and one right facing foot. The hands of all five figures are visible, with figures 1 and 5, left and right, clasping a crozier, figure 2 carrying scales, figure 3 appears

a

b

9 *Abernethy 9:* **a** *fragment of undecorated cross shaft in relief, the return of the base visible* **b** *reverse, with damaged, incised decoration and border*

9 Abernethy; Class III (**9**)

AMT

Butler 1897, pl III (reverse)

This stone is decorated on both faces. On the face, carved in high relief (**9a**) is a cross shaft, the base just visible above the broken edge of the stone (not previously recorded). It is undecorated and has a crudely incised outline, which forms a beading on both edges. At the top the shaft curves to left and right at the start of the arms of the cross. The panels beside the cross fragment are undecorated and faint beaded outer edges can be seen, better preserved on the left side.

The lowest third of the shaft has been trimmed back up to a centimetre and there is a slight horizontal demarcation across the face of the stone and round the sides. The upper two thirds of the stone have been weathered, but the lowest part of the shaft has been defaced.

The reverse of this stone (Butler pl III) (**9b**) is an incised fragment on which the surviving detail is extremely faint. An incised outline surrounds the decoration on all but the left edge. A possible shaft occupies the central area, with a horizontal band of key pattern faintly visible along the lower edge. On the left of the 'shaft' there are traces of key pattern and on the right an indistinct area of interlace. Two incised arcs partly enclose these panels. At the top of the panel are three lines, which continue the line of the shaft and then are turned to the left. A possible frame can be distinguished as a relief border at the top right corner and no more than a suggestion of a similar arrangement at the upper left of the stone. Many cracks and flaked fragments of stone suggest other decorative elements, but no part of the ornament is clear.

This stone is of grey or yellow sandstone and measures 780 mm high, 510 mm wide and 190 mm thick. The cross on the face is 110 mm overall. The reverse has a border 145 mm wide on right side and 110 mm on the bottom.

In 1976 the stone stood behind the porch of the church, but by 1985 it had been moved inside. It is now in store in the care of AMT.

10 Carpow; Class III (**10**)

NMRS: NO21NW1

Allen and Anderson 1903, III, 311, fig 327; Laing 1878, 462, pl XXVIII

This fragment comes from a large cross-slab, split across the arms of the cross and then vertically down one side of the shaft. It is carved on both faces, each of which has a ringed cross sharing pierced circular hollows in the angles. On each face the shaft is carved in high relief, with a shallow, recessed cross behind. The slab was seriously damaged when reused, but sufficient remains to indicate that this was a cross-slab of considerable size with an equal-armed cross enclosed within a ring extending to the edge of the stone. The intact side of the slab has a beaded edge and the right side of the fragment shows the chamfer dressed when the stone was reused. When it was broken, for reuse as a lintel, the chamfer removed all detail on that part of the stone. The fragment probably represents more than one third of the total height of the complete slab.

On the face (**10a**), is part of the right hand side of a ringed cross-slab, comprising the right lower armpit, with traces of the ring, part of the left armpit, the shaft with a shallow recessed shaft and a side panel, all carved in high relief. The ring extends out to the beading down the right edge of the slab; the ring and the recessed shaft merge and both show traces of incised single border spiral decoration. On the lower part of the shaft faint traces of interlace survive, and in the panel at the top right side of the shaft are two entwined creatures, one with a fish tail and the other with an eye, ear and long snout, biting the tail. Their bodies are of broad, double beaded, flat interlace, similar to that on a stone from Coldingham, Berwickshire and on Meigle 4, Perthshire.

The reverse of this fragment (**10b**), comprises, part of the left arm the circular left armpit and lower left quadrant of the ring, and part of the lower right armpit. Part of the shaft survives, carved in high relief, with traces of a recessed shaft and relief decoration on the left panel.

A faint interlace panel on the surviving left arm, traces of another in the central crossing and slight remains of interlace survive on the shaft. The lower left quadrant of the ring has been seriously damaged. A band of interlace runs down the left side of the fragment and forms a division between the two registers, although it is no longer clear

10 *Abernethy 10. Fragment of cross-decorated slab* **a** *Obverse, with incised spirals and beaded interlace animals* **b** *Reverse, with part of interlace ornamented shaft; deer and dog with interlace panel on the side*

whether this was a single chain or if there was a break. In the panels to the left of the shaft two animals have been carved in relief. The upper animal is a deer walking to the left, but with its head turned round, possibly originally with its antlers joining the interlace strip. In the lower register is an animal with bared teeth, perhaps a dog, also facing left. The ears point backwards, the body muscles are emphasised and the surviving part of its drooping tail is well depicted.

When the stone had been broken for reuse the date 1610 had been incised on the outer edge.

This fragment is of red sandstone. It is 736 mm high by 457 mm wide by 152 mm thick. It was found at Old House of Carpow when the well-head was demolished and was moved for safety to the base of the Mugdrum Cross, but it has since been moved to Mugdrum house, where it is in private hands.

11 Mugdrum; Class III (**11,12**)
NO21NW1
Allen and Anderson 1903, III, 367, fig 386; Henderson 1983, 243

This cross shaft stands on a low ridge, on the south side of the Tay. It is *in situ*, set in a rectangular sandstone base. In the late 19th century the stone was leaning and at some time since then it has been returned to an upright position and mortared into place.

The proportions of the shaft are those of a free-standing cross, possibly of similar form to the Dupplin, Perthshire or Camuston, Angus crosses, but taller than these. Wind erosion of the west face and at the base of the stone has been particularly severe. Water percolation damage extends far down the west face and the south side; on the north and east it is severe at the top of the shaft.

A narrow beading runs round each face and side and the individual decorative panels are each set within a narrow frame and are carved in relief. The ornament on the east face survives in four registers, all surrounded by narrow borders some with interlace or key pattern (**11**).

The lowest panel is now faint, but depicts three hounds on the right attacking three deer on the left. The deer are all in crouching positions, with their legs bent back under them, while the dogs are in full forward movement. No detail can be read and the lowest elements are now

11 *Mugdrum cross. East face, showing the weathered condition of the surviving decorated panels*

12 *Mugdrum cross. North side, showing key pattern, vine scroll and damaged upper panels*

almost illegible. A narrow lower border completes the design frame.

The second panel depicts two horsemen moving to the left, the one on the right larger than the one in front. Details are difficult to discern, but the larger rider's left foot can be made out and his head appears to extend into the border between the registers. His horse is well drawn and its long tail can be seen parallel to the panel edge. The rider carries a spear, visible behind him. The smaller horseman also carries a spear, visible beside the front legs of his horse, which has the head tightly reined in, a boldly drawn eye and ears pricked. The rider's left leg and foot are clearly visible but the rest of the figure has been damaged.

The third panel shows a single rider, moving towards the left, filling the panel. He carries a spear, its head pointing downwards beside the horse's front leg. No details

of the rider's upper body can be made out, but his left leg can be seen beside the horse's front leg, while the bridle and possibly a riding blanket, the horse's rump and faint traces of the rear legs as well as a long tail can be discerned. Above the horse's head is a small fragment of interlace, which ends in a triangular terminal.

The fourth panel is also filled by a single horseman, of which mainly the front part and the tail of the horse survive. Like the other figures he is moving towards the left. Details of the horse's head, showing his eye and his ear pricked forward into the border, his bridle and harness are clearly visible. The upper part of the rider cannot be made out, but his lower leg dangles near the front left leg of his mount.

These figures are comparable in arrangement in vertical panels to those on the St Madoes, Perthshire, stone, but the horses are of a less elongated body form, more like the one on Meigle 3, Perthshire, or at Fordoun, Kincardineshire.

The west face has suffered most from erosion and no details can be made out. However, it is possible that traces of a central roundel and of the shaft survive in the differential weathering of the surface.

The north side of the shaft is partly eroded by water running down the stone but much of the decoration is still visible (**12**). The lowest panel has a diagonal key pattern, the bottom of which is eroded. Above this the second panel comprises a three scroll vine. This has been described as inhabited vine scroll, with dragons, (Henderson 1968), but the erosion has caused further damage and details are no longer clear. An animal in the lowest scroll could, however, have been a dragon; above this the creatures seem to sit upright and would thus perhaps have been birds. The vine stem is a double strand and several bindings can be seen in addition to a few clusters of berries and small branches with leaves. The third panel with an interlace lower border appears to contain two creatures, again too eroded for certainty, while the fourth panel is largely defaced, although

two rows of fine interlace survive in the lower left corner.

The south side of the stone has suffered more severely from erosion than the north side and the carving is no longer clear. It has a similar layout to the one on the north side, with key pattern in the lowest register. There are two birds in the second panel and vine scroll above. Above these panels the erosion has destroyed all detail.

The cross is of red sandstone. The shaft is 3355mm high, 736mm wide and 406mm thick. The base measures 1677mm long by 1220mm wide by 458mm high above ground. The cross is situated at Mugdrum, on private land.

12 Abernethy area; Class III (**13–17**)
NO21NW37

This is a small, almost complete stone carved in deep relief with a cross on the face and interlace on the other surfaces. It has broken obliquely so that most of the lower left corner is missing.

The face of the stone has a plain border into which the arms of the equal-armed cross extend (**13**). The cross has an incised border, giving it a beaded edge. It has hollow

Tom E. Gray

13 *Abernethy area, no 12. Undecorated, beaded-edge cross, with quadrilobate ring, slight armpits*

angles and is surrounded by a quadrilobate, beaded, double ring. The outer and inner beads of the ring segments are linked to the cross, but the inner two strands are not. There is a suggestion of a curved beading in the upper left quartile of the central crossing, which could have formed part of a central lozenge filling the centre, but it is too defaced for certainty at this stage.

Details of chisel marks are clearly identifiable on the interlace and on the background. The upper left of the ring appears not to have been completed adjacent to the shaft. Tooling can be clearly identified on the other surfaces, indicating that the stone had not been exposed for a long period. The fresh, unweathered state of the carving supports this suggestion.

Tom E. Gray

16 *Right side, with relief carved vertical key pattern panel*

Tom E. Gray

14 *Reverse, with interlace panel, the upper left corner incomplete*

The back of the stone (**14**) has an interlace panel, but no cross, set within a border similar to the one on the face. The interlace is finely carved in relief to form a double-beaded knot, Allen type 215. The upper right corner of the stone has been damaged, as has the lower part of the panel.

The top of the stone (**15**) has a narrow, incised interlace panel with a knot, Allen type 249. One corner has broken off, but the panel is complete.

Tom E. Gray

Tom E. Gray

17 *Left side, with part of vertical key pattern panel in relief. All carved elements show detail of chisel marks and are unweathered*

15 (opposite) *The top of the stone, with double-bead interlace panel*

Photographs by Tom E. Gray, by courtesy of Perth Museums and Art Galleries

18 *Abernethy Glen, no 14. Stone with seven facets, base with cup-marks (**b**), and three with carved faces in relief (**a,c,d**) and with incised detail*

The two sides of the stone are carved with incised vertical key pattern, within incised borders, executed in the same high quality as the rest of the stone. On the left side (**16**) is key pattern, Allen type 897 and on the right (**17**) is a more elaborate reversing pattern, Allen type 972B.

This stone is of hard red sandstone. It is 310 mm wide, with a maximum surviving height of 255 mm on the right and of 130 mm on the left; it is 140 mm thick.

13 Macduff's Cross (not illustrated)
NO21NW9

The large stone known as Macduff's Cross sits on a mound surrounded by a kerb of stones. The site lies at 126 m OD, on a small triangle of land, formerly part of Newburgh Common. There are cup-marks on the stone and it is alleged to be a cross base, but the slight hollow in the top could not have held a cross.

It is also described as a boundary marker, although it marks neither parish nor regional divisions today. The location is however on a saddle between Ormiston Hill and Pitcairlie Hill, marking a pass between them as well as being a particularly good vantage point. It can be seen clearly from the Mugdrum area and probably from the Tay as well.

This stone measures 990 mm high, 1065 mm wide and it tapers towards the top. The cup-marks vary from 38 mm to 75 mm across and 14 mm to 38 mm in depth.

14 Abernethy Glen (**18**)
NMRS: NO11NE70; PMAG: 1997.432

This stone is crudely rhomboid in shape (**18a**) and has 7 facets – the base, which is almost square, 330 mm by 330 mm in size, four side and two upper facets. On three facets four heads have been carved on prepared bosses. A curving line of short parallel striations runs between some of the heads, perhaps representing hair.

Facet 1 (**18b**), the base, is weathered, but at least 15 cup-marks of approximately 5–10 mm diameter can be identified and there are traces of others along the edges.

Facet 2 (**18c**), on the side, measures 370 mm by 250 mm. The largest head 200 mm from forehead to chin and approximately 30 mm deep, is carved on it. The face is almost round, with incised eyebrows which run smoothly to form the short, stubby nose, with nostrils discernible. The eyes are round, with 10 mm deep sockets or pupils, the left slightly larger than the right. The mouth is 30 mm from the nose, with faint indications of a moustache over the protruding upper lip and the large curving mouth, which has a droop or hollow at the left corner.

Facet 3 (**18a**), the smaller of the two upper surfaces, is carved with one large head, 3/1, and another smaller head, 3/2. The facet measures approximately 310 mm by 180 mm. Head 3/1 (**18d**) measures 175 mm from forehead to chin and is 25 mm proud of the surface. There are eyebrows incised above circular eyes, with circular sockets, the right larger than the left. The nose, formed by an incised line is broad. The small, deeply cut mouth, with a slight droop at the left corner, has a pronounced upper lip and is 28 mm from the nose. Above the forehead is a curved line over which are incised tool marks, perhaps representing hair on the top of the head. Head 3/2 measures 115 mm from forehead to chin, is 15 mm proud of the surface of the stone and is cruder than the others, perhaps unfinished. The eyebrows are uneven, with a thick right eyebrow over small round eyes. The nose has virtually disappeared. The small, deep mouth is 21 mm from the nose. A faint hair line can be seen over the forehead.

Facet 4 measures 330 mm by 230 mm; it bears a featureless or damaged head, measuring 150 mm from forehead to chin which is 25 mm proud of the surface. On the left are striations that might represent hair.

Facets 5 and 6 on the side and Facet 7, on the upper surface, are all blank. Facet 7 measures 230 mm by 150 mm; it is flat and smooth, with a central crack. It has a grey surface, weathered differently from the rest of the stone. Possible graffiti initials (J and W?) have been cut on this facet.

This stone is a fine-grained sandstone, grey-green in colour, but pink and coarser grained below a quartz intrusion running across Facet 2. The sides appear fresher and less weathered than the rest of the stone, perhaps an indication that it has been broken off a larger stone. The stone was found reused in a rubble garden wall near Abernethy. The overall dimensions, viewed from above, are: 230 mm high, 555 mm long, 370 mm wide.

Other remains

15 Abernethy Round Tower

NMRS: NO11NE1

MacGibbon and Ross 1896, 1, 176 (description); Cameron 1994 (date)

The round tower once stood as a free-standing structure at the west end of a church, no longer extant. The symbol stone, Abernethy 1, has been set against the south wall of the tower.

16 Abernethy Church and Monastery

NMRS: NO11NE2 and NO11NE3

The earliest church probably was in the vicinity of that recorded in 1780, but no evidence of it has been recovered. The round tower, Abernethy no 15, stood at the west end of the church.

17 Old House of Carpow

NO 204 174

Demolished, site of former mansion, formerly the house of the priors of Abernethy.

18 Carpow Roman Fort

NO 207 179

Large Severan fort, abandoned in the third century.

19 Castle Law Fort

NO11NE12

Iron Age fort.

20 Crop mark sites, various, including enclosures, souterrains, house platforms and linear features.

21 Quern Stone, upper rotary

NO 1885 1655

PMAG: 1992.651

Discussion

A particular problem in discussion of Abernethy revolves around the significance of the foundation myth, a note inserted at a late date into an early record (Anderson, MO 1980, 92). The brief, unelaborated events recorded in various annals seem impenetrable, but it does appear now that a reassessment of the wider political and social contexts of some of the references could throw light on this other 'Problem of the Picts'.

The chronicles tell of the Pictish king's contact with St Bridget at Kildare (ibid, 92), followed by the building of a church dedicated to her by the 6th century. If this is reconsidered in the light of the strong presence by the 7th and 8th centuries of the Irish church among both Scots and Picts it is possible that this account of the founding of Abernethy could have developed at a late date as a means of explaining the inexplicable, that is, how a church came to be at Abernethy from such an early date as perhaps the 5th century, before the influence of St Columba could have extended as far as the lower reaches of the Tay. The story may well reflect a rationalisation of the situation at Abernethy, in which there was recognition of the extreme antiquity of the foundation without the knowledge of how this could have happened.

Abernethy is described as a Pictish royal centre, before the move to Forteviot, but neither historical records nor archaeology have shown where that royal establishment could have been and it is important now to seek a context that could explain the foundation, the particular location, the church and its carved stones, dates, contacts and influences, and how church and state related to Abernethy at different times. There are implications for early tribal territories, shown by the later existence of a royal estate at Abernethy, and of the neighbouring estate of Mugdrum, and as argued in a study begun by Barrow (1973, 51 fig 12), in his interpretation of 'Abernethyshire'.

Against this background what actual evidence is there for settlement around Abernethy? Aerial photographs show numerous sites, including souterrains, enclosures and square barrows on the ridge between Carpow and Mugdrum, and some at least of these date to the Early Historic period, when Pictish culture was developing in the area. There could have been continuing settlement outside or within the ramparts of the Roman fort of Carpow after its abandonment. The upper stone of a rotary quern (Cat no 21), although not from an excavated context is relevant to any reassessment of the area and perhaps suggests a domestic site site that could survive in the vicinity of Station Road, that is, to the north of Abernethy. Castle Law fort, on the hill above the monastic site has been shown to be of Iron Age date and apparently not in use in the Early Historic period.

It is possible that there was a shrine in the area, perhaps where the later monastery grew up – a suggestion perhaps supported by the finding of the multiple-head stone, Abernethy 14 (**18**), although this was not *in situ* and could have been found anywhere in the area. This stone has not been studied in detail, nor its wider context researched. The individual elements can be paralleled in Celtic contexts, where features such as the drooping moustache, lack of ears, large eyes and mouth are found frequently. Three heads carved on one stone have been found at various sites, but four heads are not common. The arrangement of the faces, two on one facet, one each on two others is not readily comparable with other stones, although several multiple-head stones are discussed and illustrated in Ross (1974, 107). On the basis of the limited available evidence this stone would repay further study as an element of a pre-Christian religious site in the immediate vicinity of Abernethy. Moreover, the existence of a pagan shrine would have attracted the interest of the early Church.

There is abundant evidence for an early Christian presence locally in Fife, as shown by long cist cemeteries, including one on Mare's Craig, a little to the east of Carpow and Abernethy (Proudfoot 1997). It is not inconceivable that Christianity reached the area at an early date through the Roman contact, or through St Ninian, although there is no evidence for this at present. It is still unclear what was the context for these Christian communities, represented in the long cist cemeteries, but the Hallow Hill, St Andrews, had Roman foundation graves and has been interpreted as the location of the early Christian place name *Eglisnamin* (ibid). The Hallow Hill radiocarbon dates show that the cemetery was in use throughout the 7th century, with some earlier graves (ibid). Henshall (1955) collated much of the Early Christian evidence for long cist cemeteries and Thomas (1981) cited evidence for continuing Christianity, in the south west of Scotland, in the Borders and as far as the Catstane, near Edinburgh. Whether this could be the result of a mission by Ninian or a survival from the Roman occupation of the area is still a matter of debate (Thomas 1981, 288), but whatever the origin, the long cist cemeteries from the Hallow Hill through Leuchars to

Mare's Craig are not far from Abernethy and a long cist or long grave cemetery could be expected in that area if any pre-Celtic Church Christian activity had existed.

The carved stones of Abernethy by no means form a coherent collection, but they represent a small and significant element of the history of Early Christian activity at the monastery of Abernethy, their importance being enhanced by their survival at this site, where virtually everything else has disappeared.

The Pictish symbol stone (no 1 (**2**)), now placed beside the round tower is the earliest of the Early Historic stones at Abernethy. It is the only symbol stone from the locality, dating to sometime in the 5th or 6th century, by which time a church or monastic organisation had already existed in Abernethy for many years, since it was visited, not founded, by St Columba. The symbol stone has no direct connection with any others, although the other Abernethy stones all appear to come from the same general area.

The symbol stone at Abernethy is of granite and the sculpture is of extraordinary quality, indicating that the stone must have been of particularly high status in its original context, perhaps in a shrine or in a building in the 'royal enclosure', or it could have been a pagan gravestone (ibid, 288).

None of the stones from the Abernethy area has a direct bearing on the origin of the church there. They show Irish rather than Anglian influence on their art and design. The Carpow stone (no 10 (**10**)), is a fragment of a large slab, with a cross on each face and would have been comparable in proportions perhaps with Dunfallandy or Gask, both in Perthshire. The Carpow stone is Pictish in form and has Pictish style animals surviving on one face, but like the Gask stone shows Irish influence in the perforated hollow angles, resembling a free-standing cross. It is transitional in form, with both incised and relief decoration, of 7th to 8th century date. This stone has been identified as possibly from one of the early monastic boundary stones, recorded in the foundation account of Abernethy as at Caerfuill (Anderson, MO 1980, 92). When the retrospective record was inserted in the Chronicles (ibid, cxxi) boundary stones must have existed and so the date of that record is significant as it suggests a date by which the stone at Caerfuill was already in existence, although this need not be the stone found at Carpow.

Edwina Proudfoot

The Mugdrum stone (no 11 (**11, 12**)), is another significant piece of sculpture, one which has the distinction of still standing where it was erected. This is not a Pictish slab, although the carving on its east face is entirely Pictish in style. The vine scroll on its sides could have reached Mugdrum by various routes, either Irish or Northumbrian (Henderson 1968) and although its head has been lost, this stone was more like an Irish free-standing cross (Henry 1964), similar to the stone from Dupplin, Perthshire, rather than a carved slab. Mugdrum stone although mutilated, still offers opportunity for assessment to place it in its historic as well as its artistic context.

The last of the stones from outside Abernethy (no 12 (**13–17**)), is complex. Its cross head is certainly Pictish in style, with the quadrilobate double-beaded ring extending to the extremities of the arms. One of the few crosses with this type of double beaded, undecorated ring is at Abercromby, Fife, and this also has vertical key pattern on it. Abernethy 12, however, is unlikely to be from a tall monument. Although now damaged it looks virtually complete, apart from the missing lower segment. It could have been a grave marker, a portable altar or part of a shrine. It was too small for a free-standing stone or a boundary marker.

Highly decorated small carved stones of the size and form of this one from near Abernethy have not been recorded or researched in Scotland. They could have been lost easily or regarded as part of a cross arm and not considered separately, but a search of Allen and Anderson (1903) revealed many small fragments of crosses, none of which compared with the one under discussion. Two heavily decorated cross arms, one from Forteviot, no 3 (fig 337), and another from Strathmartine, no 8 (fig 277, now lost), are of different form, since both have armpits. Moreover, it should be noted that the arms of a cross may be decorated, including with scriptural scenes, but the cross is not a decorative element for an arm of a cross. The fragment of recess in the centre of the crossing resembles the upper left part of a small panel, suitable for an inset metal plaque, another feature that would not be placed on a cross arm.

The stones from Abernethy itself were all broken up and dispersed, coming to light reused in more recent buildings, but they still can provide datable and cultural information.

Abernethy stones 4 and 8 are both parts of scriptural crosses, which are of ninth or perhaps tenth century date and of Irish origin (Henry 1964). A study of crucifixions and other scriptural depictions, as opposed to the Old Testament repertoire, on stones in the Pictish areas could certainly improve the general understanding of the early Irish influence seen on these stones. This in turn could help to explain more of the context and influences on Abernethy. One Abernethy stone (no 2 (**3**)), although seriously damaged carries part of an Irish style bound-ogham inscription and a trace of a horse's leg probably of Pictish style (Forsyth, unpublished).

Abernethy 5 (**5**) is defaced on front and back, but both sides of the surviving fragment have been preserved and show carving of high quality. One edge has a spiral, of possibly late eighth – early ninth century date, while the other edge has a double-beaded interlace, broad and flat, Allen type 568, and comparable with the interlace animals on the face of the stone from Carpow, Abernethy 11 (**11,12**).

If these stones were placed in local context and in their wider zone of influence it might establish a framework for the development of Abernethy at different periods, since these fragments are no earlier than the seventh century. A watching brief, if not an excavation programme could result in other fragments of carved stones being recognised, not only at Abernethy but at other local sites, including Carpow, Mugdrum and Aberargie, for example. The Carpow stone was found built into a well-head at Old House of Carpow, but the opportunity to look for further fragments was lost recently when the old building was burned down and later demolished without archaeological supervision. Old House of Carpow is relevant to the story of Abernethy, since the priors of the monastery lived there, although how early this became the practice is not known. As this site is within the Roman fort it is possible that there could be evidence there, too. Additional aerial photography could reveal the outer vallum of the monastery, which it could be expected to have, whether founded through a Kildare connection or through later Columban contacts. A timber hall and a long cist cemetery are among other remains that should be identified in this area.

A renewed examination of the wider documentary and historic context, following Macquarrie (1992),

62

consideration of all the potential influences on Abernethy, together with an archaeological survey and related study would begin to explain the background to this complex and multi-period early monastic site, which had always proved problematic for the Church.

Acknowledgements

I wish to thank Janet Paton who first showed me the stones from the church and Mr and Mrs Macdonald of the Abernethy Museum Trust for access to stones in their care; thanks are due to Mr and Mrs Fenton for allowing regular access to the Mugdrum stone. Particular thanks are due to Katherine Forsyth, for so readily giving access to some of her records. Thanks are also due to Mike Spearman, Fraser Hunter and James Wilson (NMS), to Lesley Ferguson (NMRS) and to Mark Hall (Perth Museum). They have all been generous with their time and access to information and to the stones in their care. I am grateful for the access for photography of the stones at all these institutions. Finally, appreciation is due to David Henry, for his patience.

References

ALLEN, J R and ANDERSON, J 1903 *The Early Christian Monuments of Scotland*. Edinburgh (repr with an Introduction by Isabel Henderson, 2 vols, Balgavies, Angus, 1993).

ANDERSON, M O 1980 *Kings and Kingship in early Scotland*. Edinburgh.

ANDERSON, A O 1922 *Early Sources of Scottish History A.D. 500–1286*, 2 vols. London (new edn 1990, Stamford).

BUTLER, D 1897 *The Ancient Church and Parish of Abernethy*. Edinburgh.

CAMERON, N 1994 St Rule's Church, St Andrews, and early stone-built churches in Scotland. *Proc Soc Antiq Scot,* 124 (1994), 367–78.

HENRY, F 1964 *Irish High Crosses*. Dublin.

HENSHALL, A 1955 The long cist cemetery at Lasswade, Mid Lothian. *Proc Soc Antiq Scot,* 89 (1955-56), 252–83.

LAING, A 1878 Notice of a fragment of an ancient stone cross found at Carpow, in the Parish of Abernethy, Perthshire. *Proc Soc Antiq Scot,* 12 (1874-78), 462–5.

MACGIBBON, D and ROSS, T 1896 *The Ecclesiastical Architecture of Scotland from the Earliest Christian Times to the Seventeenth Century,* vol 1. Edinburgh (repr 1991).

MACQUARRIE, A 1992 Early Christian religious houses in Scotland: foundation and function. In Blair, J and Sharpe, R (eds) *Pastoral Care before the Parish*, 114–18. London.

PROUDFOOT, E and ALIAGA-KELLY, C forthcoming Excavations at the long cist cemetery on the Hallow Hill, St Andrews, 1975–77. *Proc Soc Antiq Scot,* 126 (1997).

STEVENSON, R B K 1959 The Inchyra stone and some other unpublished early Christian monuments. *Proc Soc Antiq Scot,* 92 (1958-59), 33–55.

THOMAS, C 1981 *Christianity in Roman Britain to A.D. 500.* London.

Long Cist Cemeteries in Fife

J.R.F. Burt

Long cists are essentially just stone boxes which were used as coffins. The sides were constructed of one or, more usually, several stone slabs placed upright. Sometimes the floor of the cist was also lined with slabs. Generally the long sides taper inwards at the foot. Some of these cists had a lid made of slabs lying across the top and these are frequently called 'lintel-graves' (Alcock 1992, 125). In cemeteries the cists are arranged in rows.

In her survey of Scottish long cist cemeteries, Audrey Henshall (1956) suggested that although extended inhumation in stone cists was practised from the Bronze Age up to the seventeenth century, most cemeteries (arbitrarily defined as containing six or more cists) date to the Early Historic period – from the fifth to the ninth century AD. Since that publication some sites have been re-examined and others have come to light. Henshall's dates have been confirmed by radiocarbon analysis (Ashmore 1980, 349; Cowie 1978, 199–201; Dalland 1993, 341–3; Proudfoot 1985, 15). In cemeteries most cists are orientated east–west or north-east–south-west, with the head to the west or south-west, and invariably burials are not accompanied by grave goods, implying a deliberate Christian rite.

Most long cist cemeteries are found in south-east Scotland, and Henshall's distribution map shows a concentration in Lothian (1956, fig 6). The discoveries since Henshall's work reinforce this distribution pattern with a concentration on the south side of the Forth (Dalland 1992; 1993). The main long cist and Pictish areas have only a peripheral overlap (Henshall 1956, 270). However, several long cist cemeteries have been identified in Fife, all with a coastal distribution (**1**), and there are others extending across to the northern coast of the Firth of Tay. Professor Charles Thomas has suggested that this series of long cist cemeteries is indicative of the progress in the spread of Christianity reaching into Pictland (1968, 107–8). The Fife examples include Hallow Hill, St Andrews (Stuart 1867, lix; Proudfoot 1976; 1977; 1985), the Isle of May (James and Yeoman 1994), Kilminning Farm/Wormiston, Crail (NSA 1845, 955–56; Primrose 1901, 327), Kingswood, Burntisland (Stevenson 1952, 111), Kirkheugh/Kirkhill of St Andrews (Stuart 1866, 58; Wordsworth 1980), Lundin Links, Largo (Ashmore 1980, 349; Durham 1860; Small and Thoms 1989, 24–5), Old Haaks, Fifeness (McCulloch 1860, 505; Stuart 1867, lxi), Pitmilly Law, Kingsbarns (Skinner 1870), School or Temple Hill, Leuchars (Hooper 1948; Reid 1909) and possibly Mare's Craig Quarry, Newburgh (Stevenson 1952, 111).

Prior to the recent excavations on the Isle of May, the main long cist cemetery in Fife excavated to modern standards and subjected to radiocarbon dating was Hallow Hill on the outskirts of St Andrews which contained over a hundred long cists and several dug graves not in cists. Twenty radiocarbon dates from bone collagen range from AD 460 ± 55 uncalibrated to AD 795 ± 70 uncalibrated (Proudfoot 1985). Some of the graves at Hallow Hill have been interpreted as pagan because of accompanying grave goods (Proudfoot 1976). One, a large short cist, contained a bag with Roman bronzes, horse teeth and quartzite pebbles; another, found in 1860, also in a stone lined cist, had a 'glass bowl and iron knife and other items'. This allows for the possibility that long cist cemeteries were used by non-Christians either before the local advent of Christianity or in a transitional period when pagan burials were also placed in long cists (Dalland 1992, 205). Certainly the Hallow Hill site seems to have been in use before the arrival of Christianity. Here traces of a structure were also found, represented by a number of large post holes located on top of the hill (Proudfoot 1976, 34). Although speculating, this could represent an early chapel or timber church. The place-name *Eglesnamin* has been associated with Hallow Hill. Professor Geoffrey Barrow suggests that Eglesnamin may stand for the 'church of Saint Náemhán' or perhaps simply the 'church of the saint(s)' — which would be closely equivalent to the former name for Hallow Hill, ie 'All Hallows' Hill' (Barrow 1983).

Surprisingly, four other long cist cemeteries in Fife are also associated with early chapels. Stevenson noted that the quarry-master at Mare's Craig Quarry, Newburgh, stated in the late 1920s that cist burials were associated with what he took to be the site of an early chapel (1952, 111). This is in fact the site where a small Celtic bell was found. At the Kirkheugh of St Andrews, Stuart reported 'some long stone cists were recently discovered in and about the ruined chapel, which was the site of an early Culdee settlement there' (1866, 58). And at Leuchars, Reid wrote of '34 cists where once stood an ancient Culdee chapel of St Bonoc or Bonach' (1909). The recent excavations on the Isle of May, where a well laid out long cist cemetery was identified in 1994 (James and Yeoman 1994, 18) and whose earliest

burials have yielded radiocarbon dates spanning the sixth to eleventh centuries AD, have also suggested that there may be an earlier church beneath the 12th/13th century one. Regrettably there is no telling of the temporal relationship between the long cist cemeteries and their associated chapels on many of these sites — it may be that the chapels are no more than later erections.

Whereas the long cist cemeteries *per se* may have been regarded as holy places, and as such could have been used as sites of worship without the need for a church or chapel, it seems that in Fife, contrary to the position in Lothian, it is quite common to find a chapel in association with such a cemetery. This may reflect that long cist cemeteries in Fife are later in date than those in Lothian, in line with Thomas's theory of a northerly spread (1968, 107–8). Edwina Proudfoot's forthcoming *corpus* of long cist cemeteries is eagerly awaited as, indeed, is her full excavation report for the Hallow Hill cemetery. The Fife long cist cemeteries were perhaps accompanied by ecclesiastical buildings by nature of their later date, pointing to a change in religious behaviour whereby the chapel, rather than the burial ground, became the locus of ecclesiastical worship.

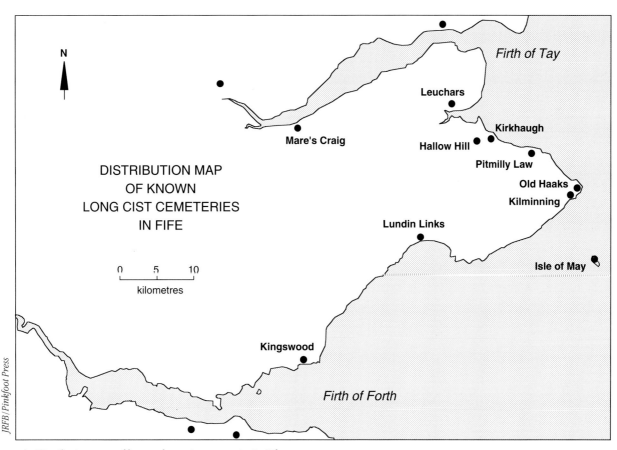

1 *Distribution map of known long cist cemeteries in Fife*

References

ALCOCK, E A 1992 Burials and cemeteries in Scotland. In Edwards, N and Lane, A (eds) *The Early Church in Wales and the West,* 125–9. Oxford.

ASHMORE, P J 1980 Low cairns, long cists and symbol stones. *Proc Soc Antiq Scot,* 110 (1978-80), 346–55.

BARROW, G W S 1983 The childhood of Scottish Christianity: a note on some place-name evidence. *Scottish Studies,* 27 (1983), 1–16.

COWIE, T 1978 Excavations at the Catstane, Midlothian 1977. *Proc Soc Antiq Scot,* 109 (1977-78), 166–201.

DALLAND, M
– 1992 Long cist burials at Four Winds, Longniddry, East Lothian. *Proc Soc Antiq Scot,* 112 (1992), 197–206.

– 1993 The excavation of a group of long cists at Avonmill Road, Linlithgow, West Lothian. *Proc Soc Antiq Scot,* 123 (1993), 337–44.

DURHAM, D 1860 Notice of cists recently discovered on the sea-shore at Lundy in Fife. *Proc Soc Antiq Scot,* 3 (1857-60), 76–7.

HENSHALL, A S 1956 A long cist cemetery at Parkburn sand pit, Lasswade, Midlothian. *Proc Soc Antiq Scot,* 89 (1955-56), 252–83.

HOOPER, J E 1948 Long cist at Leuchars, Fife, *Proc Soc Antiq Scot,* 82 (1947-48), 298–9.

JAMES, H and YEOMAN, P A 1994 Isle of May environmental interpretation project. *Discovery and Excavation in Scotland 1994,* 18–19.

McCULLOCH, W T 1860 Notice of coffins (formed of stone slabs) found on the farm of Milton, Haddingtonshire. *Proc Soc Antiq Scot,* 3 (1857-60), 503–6.

NSA 1845 = *The New Statistical Account of Scotland,* IX, *Fife–Kinross.* Edinburgh and London.

PRIMROSE, J 1901 Ancient graves recently discovered on the farm of Wyndford, in Uphall Parish. *Proc Soc Antiq Scot,* 35 (1900-01), 325–8.

PROUDFOOT, E V W
– 1976 Entry in *Discovery and Excavation in Scotland 1976,* 33–4.

– 1977 Entry in *Discovery and Excavation in Scotland 1977,* 16.

– 1985 Entry in *Discovery and Excavation in Scotland 1985,* 15.

REID, W 1909 Notice of the discovery of a group of full-length stone cists at the School Hill, or Temple Hill, Leuchars. *Proc Soc Antiq Scot,* 43 (1908-09), 170–6.

SMALL, A and THOMS, L M 1989 *The Picts in Tayside.* Dundee.

WORDSWORTH, J 1980 Excavations at Kirkhill, St Andrews. *Urban Archaeology Unit, Interim Report, 1980.*

SKINNER, R 1870 Notices of excavations at Pitmilly Law, and elsewhere on the south-east coast of Fife. *Proc Soc Antiq Scot,* 8 (1868-70), 55–58.

STEVENSON, R B K 1952 Long cist burials, particularly those at Galston (Lewis) and Gairloch (Wester Ross), with a symbol stone at Gairloch. *Proc Soc Antiq Scot,* 86 (1951-52), 106–11.

STUART, J
– 1866 Account of graves recently discovered at Hartlaw, on the farm of Westruther Mains. *Proc Soc Antiq Scot,* 6 (1864-66), 55–60.

– 1867 *Sculptured Stones of Scotland, Volume Second.* Edinburgh.

THOMAS, A C 1968 The evidence from North Britain. In Barley, M W and Hanson, R P C (eds) *Christianity in Early Britain 300–700,* 93–121. Leicester.

Early Medieval Inscriptions in Britain and Ireland and Their Audiences

John Higgitt

Early medieval inscriptions tell us something about the literacy of those who composed them but what of those who read them? Who, if anyone, was meant to read inscriptions? Did they have anything to say to those who could not read? Epigraphy has been defined as 'science de ce qui est écrit, en général sur une matière résistante, en vue d'une publicité universelle et durable' (Favreau 1969, 395; reprinted in Favreau 1995, 5). It is probable that those who ordered texts to be inscribed on materials such as stone or wall plaster were interested in durability; but how wide were the intended audiences of inscriptions in early medieval Britain and Ireland?

The studies of medieval literacy in England published in the 1970s by Clanchy (1979; 2nd edn 1993), Wormald (1977) and Parkes (1973) and the papers in *The Uses of Literacy in Early Medieval Europe* (McKitterick 1990) are evidence of a very productive debate on 'the symbolic function and practical uses of writing' in the early Middle Ages (McKitterick 1990, 319). With a few exceptions (eg Stevenson 1989; Mitchell 1990; Page 1995B) they have concentrated on the evidence of hand-written documents and books. Publicly displayed texts which had a much wider potential audience are a comparatively neglected source of evidence for the debate over the functions of writing in the largely oral society of the early Middle Ages

When considering literacy in Anglo-Saxon England, Wormald (1977, 96) correctly warned against facile assumptions about the readership of inscriptions. 'Inscriptions in sufficient quantity and quality may be symptoms of a literate society, as in the ancient world, but they do not themselves establish its existence.' His suggestion that even long vernacular texts, such as the verses on the Crucifixion inscribed onto the Ruthwell Cross, might have been addressed to God rather than to a secular public provides a salutary challenge (Higgitt 1986, 126; Page 1995B, 297).

In his review of the epigraphic evidence for English runic literacy Page (1995B, 298–9) argues that the Ruthwell verses and most memorial inscriptions were intended for a human readership, whereas this was not necessarily the case for the lightly incised names on St Cuthbert's Coffin. He cautions, however, that 'We know practically nothing of the audience that the inscriptions appealed to, nor indeed whether it was the same sort or size of audience throughout the period.' (Page 1973,15)

In his brief discussion of inscriptions of the years after the Norman Conquest Clanchy (1979, 96; 2nd ed, 1993, 124–5) points to the wide variety of inscribed objects and is surely right to presume that their users 'understood the significance of the Latin inscriptions, even if that were the limit of their literacy.' 'Everyone', he continues, 'would have seen inscriptions, or at least symbolic letters, on vestments and sacred images and utensils in churches. Similarly the Bayeux Tapestry, with its summary captions in Latin (HIC HAROLD REX INTERFECTUS EST, for example), assumes an audience in which someone could read.' I hope to show that the situation was similar, at least some of the time, in the earlier Middle Ages in Britain and Ireland. Inscriptions were not necessarily meaningless or inaccessible to those who could not themselves read them.

In situations of comparatively wide literacy such as a city of the Roman Empire (or of the present day) the potential audience for public written messages is very large. External public lettering has to compete for attention. In the Roman world power and authority were expressed through large and prominently displayed texts.

Petrucci (1980, 5–17; 1993, 1–15) writes very interestingly of the changed character of public lettering in early medieval Italy. The public and external display of inscriptions has come more or less to an end. Inscriptions have become smaller and have retreated into the interiors of churches. The celebratory and symbolic aspects of writing are now more important than its role as a means of communication. These shrunken and retiring inscriptions now often show the influence of books in their script and layout. With the revival of towns from around the 11th century the situation begins to change. Inscriptions come out of the church interiors once more and into the towns with their rising populations of literate citizens; and in some cases they return to antique models and a more monumental scale. The church loses its monopoly of the symbolic language of monumental writing with the growing power and literacy of the laity (Petrucci 1980, 11; 1993, 8). This model may be broadly applicable in Italy, but there were exceptions. Recent work has drawn attention to the Longobard revival of large architectural lettering on a classical Roman scale at San Vincenzo al Volturno and in Salerno in the later 8th and early 9th centuries (Mitchell 1990; Mitchell 1994).

The Petrucci model should not be expected to fit Britain and Ireland exactly. They lacked Italy's urban traditions and comparatively widespread literacy. Furthermore, if inscriptions had largely gone indoors in Italy, there was a strong tradition in early medieval Britain and Ireland of external inscriptions: on standing stones and crosses, if not so much, as far as we know, on buildings. In the Insular world too the clerical monopoly was far from absolute in the early Middle Ages. There are, however, some interesting parallels, such as the small scale of inscriptions and the occasional influences of book-script.

In looking for the audiences of the early medieval inscriptions in Britain and Ireland I would like first to consider the choice of script and language in different areas and at different times (cf Okasha 1990). There is considerable diversity. This may tell us something about differing attitudes to the written word and more particularly to Latin literacy, which was of course foreign to the Irish, Picts and Anglo-Saxons, as well as to the Scandinavian settlers. For Wales and the Celtic west and north of Britain, which could claim some continuity with Roman Britain, Christian Latin literacy was part of the indigenous tradition.

The inscriptions of around the 5th and 6th centuries in the ogham alphabet on the edges of undressed slabs in Ireland and in areas of Irish settlement in Western Britain, where they are often accompanied by a version in Latin, seem to be entirely secular in their concerns (McManus 1991). The ogham alphabet is an adaptation of the system (but not the forms) of the Roman alphabet for texts in Irish. The texts are in the vernacular and mostly take the form of a man's name in the genitive, usually followed by the name of the father and/or a remoter ancestor ('[the stone?] of X son of Y' etc). These inscriptions were surely funerary, whether or not they marked a grave. There are no requests for prayers; nor is there anything else overtly Christian about this type of inscription. Equally there is nothing pagan. The recent tendency has been to see the ogham inscriptions not as exotics but as 'the [Irish] equivalent of the Christian inscriptions of Britain', a view corroborated by the bilingual inscriptions of western Britain (McManus 1991, 59). There is evidence that the Irish ogham stones could come to serve as 'charters of land ownership' (McManus 1991, 163–6; cf Charles-Edwards 1976). Whatever the exact purpose of these monuments, the interest in ancestry and family and the use of the vernacular, and of a script developed for the vernacular, suggest that they would have been of interest to a potentially large and mainly secular audience. Their admissibility as evidence of land ownership must have reinforced that interest. The ogham script may have been devised within the Irish learned class and it is not clear what role, if any, the church had in raising of ogham stones. There is no way of knowing how many and what kind of people could read the script, but the significance of the stones must have been widely understood. As ogham stones were going out of fashion in Ireland grave-slabs with Roman lettering started to appear; these are clearly ecclesiastical in character and distribution (McManus 1991, 128).

The runic alphabets used for many of the inscriptions in Old English and for nearly all those in Norse in the British Isles were non-Christian in origin. They are likely, like inscriptions in ogham, to have been more accessible to more of the laity than Latin inscriptions in Roman lettering. In the Scandinavian world runes were being used freely by the 12th century for ordinary correspondence, to judge from the rune sticks found in Bergen and from graffiti such as those in the prehistoric burial chamber at Maeshowe (Page 1973, 96–100; RCAMS 1946, II, 306–13; Barnes 1993). It is not clear how far runes were used in this kind of informal way in Anglo-Saxon England, but there is a hint of such use in recent finds of runic graffiti of Anglo-Saxon names in Rome and Monte Sant'Angelo (Page 1973, 98–9, 116–17; 1995B, 313; 1995C, 2–3). The clearly Anglo-Saxon runic inscriptions on stone are Christian and most are memorial. In Northern England runes were taken up enthusiastically by the church in the pre-Viking period, as Page has emphasized (eg 1973, 34–5). They were used on the coffin reliquary of St Cuthbert at Lindisfarne, on memorial stones in Northumbrian monasteries such as Lindisfarne and Hartlepool, and on that product of 8th-century monastic learning, the Ruthwell Cross. There are also a number of Christian memorial inscriptions in Old English in Northumbria, most, perhaps all, on crosses, that commemorate individuals outside the context of monastic literacy with texts following the 'X raised this cross in memory of Y' type, sometimes with a request for prayers (listed conveniently in Okasha 1994, 75–6). These can appear in runes or Roman lettering (and on the Falstone monument in both) with no obvious distinction in status or function being drawn between the two scripts (Fell 1994, 130).

There is a comparatively small number of inscriptions in Norse runes in Britain and Ireland, the large group in the culturally mixed Isle of Man being exceptional (Page 1983; reprinted in Page 1995A, 225–44; Barnes 1992; Barnes forthcoming). The Manx crosses and cross-slabs of about the 10th century carry Norse memorial inscriptions in runes (often 'X raised this cross in memory of Y') on a Celtic Christian type of monument. Page (1983, 134; 1995A, 227–8) has suggested that the church 'with its stress on the written record' may well have encouraged, as apparently in northern England, 'any method of recording for Christian purposes'. The choice of language and script would make these displayed texts as accessible as possible.

The early Christian inscriptions of post-Roman Britain in south-west England, Wales and southern Scotland are in Latin, as was appropriate for a church and society conscious of their (real and imagined) Roman past as well as of the contemporary Latin culture of the church on the Continent (Nash-Williams 1950; Okasha 1993; Thomas 1992).

Certain of the epigraphic formulae show that there were continuing contacts with Gaul and perhaps other parts of the Continent, for example the formula *hic iacet*; a pattern of correspondences with Continental monuments suggests in fact that the early Christian Latin inscriptions of these areas were a post-Roman development (Bu'lock 1956; Okasha 1993, 32–7; Thomas 1994, 197–208; Knight 1997). Wales continued to use Latin for its inscriptions almost exclusively right up to the Norman period, the only surviving exception being the perhaps early 8th-century epitaph in Welsh at Tywyn (Towyn) in Merionethshire (Williams 1972).

This contrasts markedly with Ireland in post-ogham period. There, nearly all the inscriptions on stone in Roman lettering resemble the ogham tradition in using the vernacular when the text consists of more than a personal name (Macalister 1949; Harbison 1992, I, 355–66). The handful of exceptions include inscriptions in Latin on the Berechtuine slab at Tullylease (**1**) and on the Tower Cross at Kells, and the Greek doxology on the cross-slab at Fahan Mura (Henderson and Okasha 1992; Harbison 1992, I, 362; Macalister 1949, 36–7, 118–20, pl XLVII). The texts in Irish are generally short requests for prayers or records of patronage. The prominent inscriptions on high crosses at Clonmacnoise, Monasterboice and elsewhere show that there was no inhibition against using Irish for inscriptions even in monasteries. The Irish preference for the vernacular in inscriptions corresponds to the high status accorded to the surviving traditions of native learning and vernacular literature in early medieval Ireland. Such inscriptions with their simple texts in Irish would have presented no problems beyond that of deciphering the plain half uncial lettering.

Anglo-Saxon England uses both Latin and English and uses both in both early and late inscriptions (Okasha 1971; Okasha 1990). Both could appear on the same monument, as on the cross at Ruthwell. Some ecclesiastical centres of the pre-Viking period such as Monkwearmouth/Jarrow and York may have used only Latin for their inscriptions. A number of the vernacular inscriptions come from clearly non-monastic contexts. The use of Old English may owe something to the Irish use of the vernacular. However, extended inscriptions in the vernacular on ambitious Christian monuments seem to survive from earlier in

1 *The Berechtuine slab, Tullylease, Co. Cork*

J. Higgitt

England, for example on the probably 8th-century Bewcastle Cross, than they do in Ireland (Bailey and Cramp 1988, 61–3, 65). The use of Latin in other Anglo-Saxon inscriptions is, however, much more likely to be due to direct Continental influences than to British or Welsh traditions.

The standing stone monuments of Pictish Scotland sometimes carry inscriptions, usually in the later so-called 'scholastic' version of Irish oghams, with the letters carved along an incised line rather than the edge of the stone (Padel 1972; McManus 1991, 45; Forsyth 1995A, 9). These inscriptions are notoriously difficult to interpret but some at least may represent Pictish names and some seem to contain the Irish 'X son of Y' formula. A handful have short texts in Roman lettering, one of which, at St Vigeans, appears to contain three personal names and another, from Tarbat, has a Latin memorial formula (*in commemoratione*) (Higgitt 1982; Okasha 1985; Clancy 1993). Recently it has been noticed that the cross at Dupplin carries very worn inscriptions in both Roman lettering and in ogham (Forsyth 1995B), drawing on two traditions and perhaps addressing two separate audiences. Many of the inscriptions of Pictland seem to have been intended to connect the monuments with individuals – as commemoratees, or perhaps in some cases patrons, or even craftsmen.

Pictish standing stones also generally carry one or more of a limited vocabulary of conventionalized and uniform pictographic symbols of apparently secular significance. It is probable that these symbols somehow identified individuals and families (Henderson 1967, 159) and that they conveyed information broadly comparable to that on Irish ogham stones, or various Insular types of inscriptions that name individuals (Thomas 1963, 66). The Pictish stones arc likely to have been memorial but need not have been. The prominently displayed and easily recognizable Pictish symbols were non-alphabetic inscriptions that conveyed information that was probably much more widely understood than any alphabetic inscription (cf Forsyth in this volume). The rare examples of inscriptions in Roman lettering in Pictland like those of St Vigeans and Tarbat addressed much more limited audiences in and around ecclesiastical centres.

Having briefly surveyed some of the differences in language and script between the main national traditions,

I would like now to turn to other types of evidence for the readerships of various types of inscription. Some inscriptions, but now only a small proportion of the surviving total, look as if they are consciously aimed at a very restricted readership. These may make a conscious display of book-learning, or may try in some other way to be difficult or obscure. They are likely to have been devised by monks or nuns with time on their hands. The clearest examples of deliberate obscurity and exclusiveness are on the 8th-century cross-shaft from Hackness in Yorkshire, where there was a Northumbrian nunnery, or possibly double monastery (Lang 1991, 135–41). In addition to relatively straight-forward Latin texts in Roman lettering and now illegible runes, there are inscriptions in two or more cryptic scripts, one of which is an example of hahal-runes, a system for encoding a runic text, while the other is vaguely ogham-like in appearance. As these cannot be read, we do not know who is being addressed.

The cross-slab at Fahan Mura in Donegal has a version of the doxology in Greek inscribed in a form of Greek uncials down one edge (apparently ΔΟΞΑ ΚΑΙ ΤΙΜΕ ΠΑΤΡΙ ΚΑΙ ΥΙΩ ΚΑΙ ΠΝΕΥΜΑΤΙ ΑΓΙΩ, that is 'Glory and honour to the Father and to the Son and to the Holy Spirit') (Macalister 1949, 118–20, pl XLVII; Berschin 1982, 509–10; Harbison 1992, I, 360). While there was some limited ecclesiastical knowledge of the Greek alphabet and of a few Greek liturgical forms, Greek was not a natural choice for a wide readership in early medieval Ireland. At one level this was a display of recondite knowledge but the text, which is a prayer, was clearly addressed primarily, and perhaps exclusively, to the Trinity.

Latin verse inscriptions in several lines are another type that belonged to the world of ecclesiastical learning. Nothing of this sort survives from early medieval Britain or Ireland, although there are a couple of more modest metrical inscriptions, in two lines, at Cynwul Gaeo and Llanlleonfel in Wales (Nash-Williams 1950, 8, 77, 107–8; Thomas 1994, 104). Longer verse inscriptions are, however, recorded in sources such as Bede's *Ecclesiastical History* or the collection of Italian and English inscriptions compiled in the 8th century by, or for, Milred bishop of Worcester (Wallach 1975; Sims-Williams 1981; Schaller 1977). Bede's lost *Liber Epigrammatum* also included texts for long verse inscriptions (Lapidge 1975; Lapidge 1993).

These could be epitaphs, or dedicatory or pious verses. They were, like surviving or recorded Continental examples, often painted onto the walls of churches rather than carved. (The five red letters on white plaster found in excavations at St Patrick's Chapel at Heysham may possibly be a fragment of an inscription of this sort (Higgitt 1990B).) This kind of epigraphic verse with its imitation of Continental models, preferably from Rome, linked the Anglo-Saxon church consciously with the church on the Continent. Here the audience is learned and, in some cases, could read the text in a manuscript transcription without visiting the monument. Many examples of the genre were in fact probably never executed as genuine inscriptions. The verses written, probably by Bede, for Bishop Cyneberht to celebrate the cathedral that he had built do, however, anticipate a reader ('quisque legis') and ask for prayers for the bishop (Lapidge 1993, 2).

Similarly it is in educated ecclesiastical contexts that we find the most obvious borrowings from books in the appearance and contents of inscriptions, one of the features that Petrucci (1980, 7; 1993, 3) identified in early medieval inscriptions in Italy. There can be very close correspondences between the lettering of inscriptions and the display scripts of books, as for example at Lindisfarne around the year 700 (Higgitt 1990A). There is a striking instance of this kind of influence from the scriptorium in the 8th-century funerary slab at Tullylease in County Cork (Henderson and Okasha 1992).(**1**) The fine detail, the smallish scale (the slab is about three feet high) and the carpet-page-like cross are all reminiscent of contemporary Insular books. The script is a good example of 'Phase II' of Insular half uncial, a direct borrowing from book-script. The text, which reads 'Quicumque hunc titulum legerit orat pro Berechtuine' ('May he who reads this inscription pray for Berechtuine', taking 'orat' as an error for 'oret'; or the literal meaning: 'Whoever reads this inscription prays for Berechtuine'), seems to have been drafted by someone with more experience of books than of inscriptions. The text is modelled on a colophon like that in the Irish Mac Regol Gospels: 'Quicumque legerit et intellegerit istam narrationem orat pro macreguil scriptori'. There are similar borrowings in a number of Welsh inscriptions (Higgitt 1986, 140–1; Henderson and Okasha 1992, 9).

This kind of bookishness implies, in some cases

demands, readers with a fairly advanced clerical education. Such inscriptions were characteristic of religious communities and the insides of churches. The intended readership of these inscriptions and the numbers of those allowed physical access to them may often, therefore, have been very limited.

At the same time there were other much more public uses of inscriptions. In some cases, as in many Continental inscriptions, an audience is not only anticipated but explicitly addressed (cf Favreau 1989, 206–10; reprinted in Favreau 1995, 160–7). A cross on Caldey Island addresses the casual passer-by: 'rogo omnibus ammulantibus' ('I ask all who pass …') (Nash-Williams 1950, 180–2). The reader of the text on the mid 9th-century Pillar of Elise (Eliseg) is expected to read it out aloud: '[quicu]mque recit(a)verit manescrip[tum lapid]em' ('whoever recites this hand-written stone') (Nash-Williams 1950, 123–5; Bartrum 1966, 1–3). A cross-slab at Llanwnnws is addressed to 'q(ui)cunq(ue) explicav(er)it h(oc) no(men)' ('whoever explains this name') (Nash-Williams 1950, 101–2). Here the reader is perhaps being asked to provide a vernacular explanation of the text. These formulae seem to expect that a literate reader will read out or interpret the texts to others. Calling upon the services of such literate intermediaries allows an inscription to address a much wider non-literate public (Higgitt 1986, 125–6). Bede (*Ecclesiastical History*, V.7) implies a similar situation in his account of the death of Cædwalla, King of the West Saxons, in Rome in 689. Pope Sergius I ordered an epitaph to be inscribed on Cædwalla's tomb to keep alive the memory of the king's piety as a religious inspiration for the 'legentes quoque uel audientes' – both for those who read and for those who hear the words. In these circumstances, in a predominantly oral society, it is quite appropriate to talk of the audience of an inscription. This is a good example of what Clanchy has called 'Listening to the Word' (Clanchy 1979, 214–20; 1993, 266–72; cf Crosby 1936). What he says of post-Conquest England seems also to be true of earlier medieval centuries: 'Medieval writing was mediated to the non-literate by the persistence of the habit of reading aloud and the preference, even among the educated, for listening to a statement rather than scrutinizing it in script' (Clanchy 1993, 186).

There was consciousness too of the most obvious

advantage of inscriptions on stone: that they last a long time. Pope Sergius's epitaph for Cædwalla was intended to give the memory of the barbarian king's devotion a more permanent form than oral tradition ('memoria deuotionis ipsius fixa per saecula maneret'; 'so that the memory of his devotion might remain throughout the ages'). The idea is developed in the 12th century by John of Salisbury in his *Policraticus* (Webb 1909, I, 13). In his Prologue he cites two short inscriptions on the Arch of Constantine in Rome to show the power and durability of the written word. He draws the following conclusions from his epigraphic example: 'Triumphal arches only glorify illustrious men effectively when an inscription explains why they were raised and for whom. [...] No man has ever enjoyed permanent fame except through what he or others have written.' The last sentence of course expresses a literary commonplace (eg Curtius 1953, 476–7).

Many of the early medieval inscriptions in Britain and Ireland were intended to be a permanent aide-mémoire of this sort. Some were comparatively private; others were very much public monuments. There were even pale reflexions of the kind of inscription found on public buildings and structures in the Roman world. According to William of Malmesbury there was in his time an inscription taken from an ancient wall at Shaftesbury recording King Alfred's foundation of the town ('fecit hanc urbem') (Hamilton 1870, 186). A fragment from it was found in 1902 and has subsequently been lost (Okasha 1983, 98). If the inscription was of Alfred's time, he may have taken the idea from the inscriptions on the fortifications against the Saracens that were being built by his host Leo IV when he visited Rome as a boy (Gray 1948, 102, 113–14; Keynes and Lapidge 1983, 14, 69, 70, 211, 232, 234). A Latin inscription on a cross-slab at Maughold on the Isle of Man records rather unexpectedly the construction of a sort of early medieval aqueduct – or at least the diversion of a stream (Cubbon 1983, 9). According to Gerald of Wales, Harold of England had a series of triumphal monuments raised to himself after his victorious harrying of Wales (Dimock 1868, 217). They were to be a sign and permanent memorial of his victory ('signum, perpetuamque memoriam') and were raised in accordance with ancient custom ('more antiquo'). Apparently they carried the following Latin text: 'HIC FUIT VICTOR HAROLDUS' ('Here Harold was victorious'). The

principal intended audience in this case was presumably the defeated Welsh, which could be why none of these monuments now survive.

Harold's war-memorials made overtly political statements, if they are not an invention of Gerald. So too did the 9th-century inscribed triumphal Pillar of Elise (Eliseg) (Nash-Williams 1950, 123–5; Bartrum 1966, 1–3). It was raised by Cyngen, king of Powys. The late 17th-century transcription by Edward Lhuyd shows that it commemorated the glories of the dynasty of Powys and in particular Cyngen's great-grandfather, Elise. The damaged Latin text seems also to have claimed descent for the dynasty from the Roman Emperor, Magnus Maximus, and King Vortigern. This is the inscription that invited the reader to recite its contents. Perhaps this is the kind of monument that Gerald of Wales had in mind as the 'ancient custom' which, he said, Harold imitated with his victory monuments – or was he thinking of the triumphal monuments of antiquity?

There is an earlier royal monument with a much shorter, but still grandiloquent, text at Llangadwaldr in Anglesey (Nash-Williams 1950, 55–7). It commemorates Cadfan, king of Gwynedd, who died around 625, simply as 'rex sapientisimus opinatisimus omnium regum' ('the wisest and most renowned of kings'). Perhaps no one except a handful of clergy could read these few words on 7th-century Anglesey but all who saw it would be told that it was Cadfan's tomb and would recognize the voice of authority and power in the writing.

As on the Continent, some realized the potential of an inscription to act as a permanent and public record of an agreement or transaction, to act as what Deloye long ago called a stone charter, a 'charte lapidaire' (Deloye 1846; Favreau 1989, 210–14; reprinted in Favreau 1995, 167–73). A 9th-century inscription in Santa Maria Maggiore in Rome, for example, copied the text of a donation of land in order to guarantee it for future generations ('pro cautela et firmitate temporum futurorum') (Gray 1948, 100–1). We have already seen that Irish ogham stones could serve as evidence in support of claims to land-ownership but a few inscriptions take the idea further and adopt some of the forms of an orthodox charter. Two stone slab-crosses in Glamorgan (Ogmore and Merthyr Mawr) carry damaged Latin texts that seem to have recorded agreements about the tenure or transfer of pieces of land. Nash-Williams thought that they recorded the gifts of property to a church (1950, 154–5, 160). Some of the phrases used are charter formulae in origin (Davies 1982, 259, 268, 270, 276–7). The Merthyr Mawr text refers to itself as a writing ('grefium') and it stresses the perpetuity of the transfer 'usq(ue) in diem iudici(i)' ('until Judgement Day'). These agreements would have been reinforced by being recorded beneath the symbol of the cross. A pillar-stone at Llanllyr (Cardigan) may also have recorded a donation of land (Nash-Williams 1950, 100). The inscription on the early 8th-century standing stone at Kilnasaggart in Armagh probably serves a similar purpose with its record in Irish of a gift of land to the protection of Peter the Apostle (Macalister 1949, 114–15). The crosses on front and back again guarantee the gift. Where these inscriptions publicized donations, one of their purposes might have been to attract further donors who might hope to receive similar publicity.

The Anglo-Saxon church at Breamore in Hampshire has a text in Old English carved, on a comparatively monumental scale, onto the arch opening from the crossing into the south porticus. The text draws attention to an agreement (or covenant) and it may not now be complete. Its wording recalls some secular documents but it is unclear whether the covenant in question is legal or religious (Gameson and Gameson 1993; Tweddle *et al* 1995, 253–5).

Quasi-legal and overtly political texts are rare among surviving inscriptions. There are, however, many that recorded and displayed information which was surely intended to be read. Requests for prayers are a case in point. When Muiredach commissioned a stone cross at Monasterboice and had an inscription carved at its foot asking, in Irish, for a prayer for Muiredach who had the cross made, he must have wanted as many people as possible to read the short text and to offer prayers for him (Harbison 1992, I, 364). Similarly a number of Anglo-Saxon crosses carry requests for prayers either in the vernacular or in Latin, but in this case the prayers are for the soul of the person commemorated (Higgitt 1986, 133). Prayers are also sought on many Irish grave-slabs and on two at Hartlepool (Lionard 1961; Okasha 1971, 77–8).

The positioning of these requests for prayers and

records of patronage on most Irish crosses (but not usually on English and Welsh examples) at the foot of the cross-shaft seems not only to have anticipated an audience; it even anticipates the posture of that audience (Higgitt 1986, 142–3). There is some evidence, including the *Regula Coenobialis* of St Columbanus, for an Irish devotional custom of prostrating oneself in front of a cross. Jonas's Life of St Columbanus tells how Athala, Columbanus's successor as abbot of Bobbio, used to fortify his brow by touching the cross outside his cell as he went in and out. It seems that he knelt before the cross and touched it with his forehead, presumably somewhere near the foot of the cross. The placing of many of the Irish cross inscriptions at the bottom of the cross-shaft can also be taken as a similar act of humility. It brings the inscription down to the level of the prostrate or kneeling worshipper: it also implies that you were not meant to miss the inscription.

It is not clear what audience is addressed, nor why, when grave-markers are inscribed with names but no further text. There are examples from both Irish and Northumbrian monasteries (Lionard 1961, passim; Okasha 1971, eg nos 48–50, 75–7; Page 1973, pl 1–2; Page 1995B, 298–9). The majority were probably tacit requests for prayers, but they might also have served as records of burial rights, or as an indication that a piece of ground is already occupied, or as labels for potential relics, or as helpful information for the angels at the Last Judgement. Whatever the purpose, considerable care was given to providing clear, legible and carefully cut records. As Thomas points out, short texts of this sort (including those of 'Pictish symbols') 'may always have called for a measure of supplementation through orally transmitted data' (1994, 22).

There is another group of inscriptions with a clear practical function in a number of Anglo-Saxon churches: those that preserve and display details of the dedication of the church (Higgitt 1979, esp 346–7, 367–70). The Council of Chelsea in 816 in its decisions on the consecration of churches laid down that the bishop was to make sure that there was an inscription, on the wall, on a 'tabula' (tablet of stone, or perhaps a board), or on the altar, identifying the saints to whom the churches were dedicated (Haddan and Stubbs 1869–78, III, 580). The inscription from the main church of the monastery of Jarrow is a record in Latin of the dedication of 685. It gives the following information: the name of the saint in whose honour the church was dedicated; the day, month and year of the dedication; and the name of the founder. The likely audience for the practical details of the dedication would have been clerical but patronage was a matter of wider interest.

In the late Anglo-Saxon period there was a fashion in Yorkshire for secular patrons of non-monastic churches to record their involvement in an inscription, often in association with a sundial (Lang 1991, 46–7). These are in the vernacular and are primarily records of secular patronage or ownership and do not always give details of the dedication. The well-known inscription at Kirkdale of around 1060 tells us the name of the man who bought and rebuilt the church, the names of the current king and earl, and also the names of two other men, one a priest, who were involved in making something, perhaps the inscription (Lang 1991, 163–6). The church was built in the name of St Gregory but there is no mention of a canonical consecration. This concern with patrons and craftsmen is secular rather than ecclesiastical. Probably few of the laity could read these Old English texts, but all could understand them if they heard them. Wealthy laymen were having their names displayed prominently in inscriptions on stone during their own lifetimes. One function of such inscriptions, as of many of the public inscriptions that name individuals, was as secular status symbols and perhaps also as a way of seeking enduring local fame.

Another of these Yorkshire inscriptions, that at St Mary Castlegate, changes language from vernacular to Latin, almost as if it were starting to address a new audience, when it moves from recording the names of the secular patrons to the details of the consecration, although it is possible that the use of Latin for the list of saints is simply an unthinking reflexion of the written source (Lang 1991, 99–101; Fell 1994, 134–5).

I turn finally to one of the most sophisticated products of the early Northumbrian church, the Ruthwell Cross. Can anything be said of the readership or audience of its complex inscriptions? Unlike the closely related Bewcastle Cross its inscriptions are neither concerned with patronage nor with commemorating the dead. The figure scenes are surrounded by Latin texts which do more than merely identify scenes. Identification of figures and scenes by inscriptions was in fact normally thought unnecessary in Insular sculpture. There are no identificatory inscriptions on stone crosses in Ireland and very few in England. You were either meant to recognize the scenes or someone was meant to tell you what they were. The layout and wording of the Ruthwell inscriptions were carefully composed to accompany their scenes. The texts can be deliberately allusive and can change or enhance the meanings of the images that they accompany (Kitzinger 1993, 8–10). This is clearly the case when Christ standing over the two beasts, an image derived from Psalm 90 (91), is identified as Christ the Judge recognized by, rather than trampling on, the beasts in the desert. The monument and its texts seem to assume an audience, probably a monastic one, at least some of whose members had an informed understanding of the liturgy, of certain monastic texts and of the symbolic approach to the scriptures. The Latin texts at Ruthwell do often identify scenes but they also invite a contemplative reading of the imagery (Ó Carragáin 1987, 123).

The Old English verses of the 'Crucifixion Poem' inscribed in runes on the narrow sides of the cross imply, as Page argues, a human readership rather than the divine one suggested by Wormald, but, as Page has also pointed out, its layout makes it comparatively difficult for a human to read (Page 1973, 150; Wormald 1977, 96; Page 1995B, 297–8). On each side the text starts with a line across the top of the vine panel and then continues down each vertical border in short horizontal lines of two or three runes each. The poem was, however, probably very well-known, to judge from the later and much fuller version in the 'Vercelli Book', and the echo of the poem on the Brussels cross-reliquary. In that case it would only be necessary to recognize what the text was rather than laboriously read each word. The inscription would then have been primarily a mnemonic trigger (Okasha 1971, 57–8; Higgitt 1986, 130–201; Ó Carragáin 1987–88, 10).

The 'Crucifixion Poem' and the Latin inscriptions on the Ruthwell Cross are probably contemporary, although that has been questioned (Page 1973, 50; Meyvaert 1982, 25–6). If so, the cross is probably to be seen as addressing two distinct but overlapping audiences: the one learned and the other familiar with vernacular poetic traditions, although Ó Carragáin (1987–88) has argued a powerful case for the 'Crucifixion Poem' to be read in the same liturgical and iconographic context as the rest of the monument.

Can any general conclusions be drawn from all of this? I hope that I have not fallen for Wormald's 'Fallacy of the Anticipated Audience' in suggesting that, for all the diversity of the national traditions, most early medieval inscriptions in Britain and Ireland had a practical function and some sort of readership in mind (Wormald 1977, 96). Some inscriptions address a very restricted clerical and learned readership; but many more seem to concern a much wider public – in some cases literally an audience – that could be reached through the medieval habit of sharing texts by reading them aloud. I do not mean to argue that all inscriptions were read aloud to everybody. It is on the other hand very likely that those who ordered memorial texts, requests for prayers, or records of patronage to be inscribed often envisaged an audience that went beyond the clergy to include at least those of the laity who mattered.

A number of recent studies of early and high medieval literacy have stressed the role of writing in the exercise of power. In the Carolingian context, for example, literacy has been seen as 'a form of ideology through which power is constructed'; literacy, and especially Latin literacy 'entailed grades of exclusiveness'; 'the written word was a public medium of control imposed externally' (Nelson 1990, 258, 271, 265). The written word in early medieval inscriptions in the Insular world, as elsewhere, no doubt did represent various sorts of divine, ecclesiastical and secular power or status. One could also argue for 'grades of exclusiveness' in the degree of knowledge required to compose and to interpret the inscriptions. The clerical exclusivity of Latin verse inscriptions, the Greek prayer at Fahan Mura and the cryptic texts at Hackness would head such a scale. At the other end of the scale, inscriptions such as the names on ogham stones, runic epitaphs, Pictish symbols, or records of patronage on the inscribed sundial at Kirkdale could have been accessible to much wider audiences. In order to perform their principal functions, including that of status symbol, effectively such inscriptions required an audience not only of 'legentes' but also of 'audientes'.

Dedication and acknowledgement

My first acknowledgement is to the dedicatee of this volume for much stimulating discussion and advice on early medieval monuments, inscribed and otherwise. These discussions have by no means been limited to Pictish art, to the study of which she has contributed so much.

I would also like to thank Katherine Forsyth and Caroline Higgitt for their very helpful comments on an earlier draft of this paper.

References

BAILEY, RN and CRAMP, R 1988 *Corpus of Anglo-Saxon Stone Sculpture*, vol II, *Cumberland, Westmorland and Lancashire North-of-the-Sands*. Oxford.

BARNES, MP
- 1992 Towards an edition of the Scandinavian runic inscriptions of the British Isles: some thoughts. *Northern Studies*, 29, 32–42.
- 1993 The interpretation of the runic inscriptions of Maeshowe. In Batey, C E, Jesch, J and Morris, C D (eds) *The Viking Age in Caithness, Orkney and the North Atlantic*, 349–69. Edinburgh.
- forthcoming Aspects of the Scandinavian runes of the British Isles. In Forsyth, K, Higgitt, J and Parsons, D (eds) *Roman, Runes and Ogham: Medieval Inscriptions in the Insular World and on the Continent*. Stamford.

BARTRUM, PC 1966 *Early Welsh Genealogical Tracts*. Cardiff.

BERSCHIN, W 1982 Griechisches bei den Iren. In Löwe, H (ed) *Die Iren und Europa im früheren Mittelalter*, 2 vols. Stuttgart.

BU'LOCK, J D 1956 Early Christian memorial formulae. *Archaeologia Cambrensis*, 105, 133–41.

CHARLES-EDWARDS, TM 1976 Boundaries in Irish Law. In Sawyer, PH (ed) *Medieval Settlement: Continuity and Change*, 83–7. London.

CLANCHY, M T 1979 *From Memory to Written Record: England 1066–1307* (2nd edn, 1993). London.

CLANCY, T O 1993 The Drosten Stone: a new reading. *Proc Soc Antiq Scot*, 123 (1993), 345–53.

CROSBY, R 1936 Oral delivery in the Middle Ages *Speculum*, 11, 89–110.

CUBBON, AM 1983 *The Art of the Manx Crosses* (3rd edn). Douglas.

CURTIUS, E R 1953 *European Literature and the Latin Middle Ages*. London.

DAVIES, W 1982 The Latin charter tradition in western Britain, Britanny and Ireland in the early medieval period.

In Whitelock, D, McKitterick, R and Dumville, D (eds) *Ireland in Early Medieval Europe: studies in memory of Kathleen Hughes*, 258–80. Cambridge.

DELOYE, A 1846 Des chartes lapidaires en France. *Bibliothèque de l'École des Chartes*, 2nd series, 3, 31–42.

DIMOCK, J F (ed) 1868 *Giraldi Cambrensis Opera*, VI. London. (Rolls Series)

FAVREAU, R
– 1969 L'Épigraphie médievale. *Cahiers de Civilisation Médiévale*, 12, 393–8.

– 1989 Fonctions des inscriptions au moyen âge. *Cahiers de Civilisation Médiévale*, 32, 203–32.

– 1995 *Études d'épigraphie médiévale: recueil d'articles de Robert Favreau rassemblés à l'occasion de son départ à la retraite*, 2 vols. Limoges.

FELL, C E 1994 Anglo–Saxon England: a three-script community? In Knirk, JE (ed) *Proceedings of the Third International Symposium on Runes and Runic Inscriptions, Grindaheim, Norway, 8–12 August 1990* (Institutionen för nordiska språk, Uppsala universitet), 119–37. Uppsala.

FORSYTH, K
– 1995A Language in Pictland, spoken and written. In Nicoll, EH (ed) *A Pictish Panorama: the Story of the Picts and a Pictish Bibliography*, 7–10. Balgavies, Angus.

– 1995B The inscriptions on the Dupplin Cross. In Bourke, C (ed) *From the Isles of the North: Early Medieval Art in Ireland and Britain* (Proceedings of the Third International Conference on Insular Art), 237–44. Belfast.

GAMESON, R and GAMESON, F 1993 The Anglo-Saxon inscription at St Mary's Church, Breamore, Hampshire. *Anglo-Saxon Studies in Archaeology and History*, 6, 1–10.

GRAY, N 1948 The Paleography of Latin inscriptions in the eighth, ninth and tenth centuries in Italy. *Papers of the British School in Rome*, 16, 38–167.

HADDAN, A W and STUBBS, W (eds) 1869–78 *Councils and Ecclesiastical Documents relating to Great Britain and Ireland*, 3 vols. Oxford.

HAMILTON, N E S A (ed) 1870 *Willelmi Malmesbiriensis Monachi De Gestis Pontificum Anglorum Libri Quinque* (Rolls Series). London.

HARBISON, P 1992 *The High Crosses of Ireland: an iconographical and photographic survey*, 3 vols (Römisch-Germanisches Zentralmuseum, Forschungs-institut für Vor- und Frühgeschichte, Monographien, 17). Dublin/Bonn.

HENDERSON, I 1967 *The Picts*. London.

HENDERSON, I and OKASHA, E 1992 The Early Christian inscribed and carved stones of Tullylease, Co. Cork. *Cambridge Medieval Celtic Studies*, 24, 1–36.

HIGGITT, J
– 1979 The dedication inscripiton at Jarrow and its context. *Antiq J*, 54, 343–74.

– 1982 The Pictish Latin inscription at Tarbat in Ross-shire. *Proc Soc Antiq Scot*, 112, 300–21.

– 1986 Words and crosses: the inscribed stone cross in early medieval Britain and Ireland. In idem (ed) *Early Medieval Sculpture in Britain and Ireland* (BAR Brit Ser 152), 125–52. Oxford.

– 1990A The stone-cutter and the scriptorium: early medieval inscriptions in Britain and Ireland. In Koch, W (ed) *Epigraphik 1988: Fachtagung für mittelalterliche und neuzeitliche Epigraphik*, Graz, 10–14. Mai 1988 (Österreichische Akademie der Wissenschaften, Philosophisch-Historische Klasse, Denkschriften, 213. Band), 149–62. Vienna.

– 1990B Anglo-Saxon painted lettering at St Patrick's Chapel, Heysham. In Cather, S, Park, D and Williamson, P (eds) *Early Medieval Wall Painting and Painted Sculpture in England* (BAR Brit Ser 216), 31–40. Oxford.

KEYNES, S and LAPIDGE, M (trans) 1983 *Alfred the Great: Asser's Life of King Alfred and other Contemporary Sources*. Harmondsworth.

KITZINGER, E 1993 Interlace and icons: form and function in early Insular art. In Spearman, RM and Higgitt, J (eds) *The Age of Migrating Ideas, Early Medieval Art in Northern Britain and Ireland* (Proceedings of the Second International Conference on Insular Art held in the National Museums of Scotland in Edinburgh, 3–6 January 1991), 3–15. Edinburgh/Stroud.

KNIGHT, J 1997 Seasoned with salt: Insular-Gallic contacts in the early memorial stones and cross slabs. In Dark, KR (ed) *External Contacts and the Economy of Late Roman and Post Roman Britain*, 109–20. Woodbridge.

LANG, J 1991 *Corpus of Anglo-Saxon Stone Sculpture*, vol III, *York and Eastern Yorkshire*. Oxford.

LAPIDGE, M
– 1975 Some Remnants of Bede's lost Liber Epigrammatum. *English Historical Review*, 90, 798–820.

– 1993 *Bede the Poet* (Jarrow Lecture 1993).

LIONARD, P 1961 Early Irish grave-slabs. *Proceedings of the Royal Irish Academy*, 61 C, 95–169.

MACALISTER, R A S 1949 *Corpus Inscriptionum Insularum Celticarum*, II. Dublin.

McKITTERICK, R 1990 (ed) *The Uses of Literacy in Early Medieval Europe*. Cambridge.

McMANUS, D 1991 *A Guide to Ogam* (Maynooth Monographs, 4). Maynooth.

MEYVAERT, P 1982 An Apocalypse panel on the Ruthwell Cross. In Tirro, F (ed) *Medieval and Renaissance Studies (Proceedings of the Southeastern Institute of Medieval and Renaissance Studies, Summer 1978)* (Medieval and Renaissance Series, 9), 3–32. Durham, N.C.

MITCHELL, J

– 1990 Literacy displayed: the use of inscriptions at the monastery of San Vincenzo al Volturno in the early ninth century. In McKitterick 1990, 186–225.

– 1994 The display of script and the uses of painting in Longobard Italy. In *Testo e Immagine nell'Alto Medioevo* (Settimane di Studio del Centro Italiano di Studi sull'Alto Medioevo, XLI), 887–951. Spoleto.

NASH-WILLIAMS, V E 1950 *The Early Christian Monuments of Wales.* Cardiff.

NELSON, J L 1990 Literacy in Carolingian government. In McKitterick 1990, 258–96.

Ó CARRAGÁIN, É

– 1987 The Ruthwell Cross and Irish high crosses: some points of comparison and contrast. In Ryan, M (ed) *Ireland and Insular Art A.D. 500–1200* (Proceedings of a conference at University College Cork, 31 October – 3 November 1985), 118–28. Dublin.

– 1987–88 The Ruthwell Crucifixion Poem in its iconographic and liturgical contexts. *Peritia*, 6–7, 1–71.

OKASHA, E

– 1971 *Hand-list of Anglo-Saxon of non-runic Inscriptions.* Cambridge.

– 1983 A supplement to *Hand-List of Anglo-Saxon Non-Runic Inscriptions. Anglo-Saxon England*, 11, 83–118.

– 1985 The non-ogam inscriptions of Pictland. *Cambridge Medieval Celtic Studies*, 9, 43–69.

– 1990 Vernacular or Latin? The Languages of Insular inscriptions, AD 500–1100. In Koch, W (ed) *Epigraphik 1988: Fachtagung für mittelalterliche und neuzeitliche Epigraphik,* Graz, 10–14. Mai 1988 (Österreichische Akademie der Wissenschaften, Philosophisch-Historische Klasse, Denkschriften, 213. Band), 139–47. Vienna.

– 1993 *Corpus of Early Christian Inscribed Stones of Southwest Britain.* London and New York.

– 1994 The commissioners, makers and owners of Anglo-Saxon inscriptions. In Filmer-Sankey, W and Griffiths, D (eds) *Anglo-Saxon Studies in Archaeology and History*, 7 (Oxford University Committee for Archaeology), 71–7. Oxford.

PADEL, O 1972 *Inscriptions of Pictland.* Unpublished M Litt thesis, University of Edinburgh.

PAGE, R I

– 1973 *An Introduction to English Runes.* London.

– 1983 The Manx rune-stones. In Fell, C E *et al* (eds) *The Viking Age in the Isle of Man* (Viking Society for Northern Research, University College London), 133–46. London.

– 1995A (Parsons, D (ed)), *Runes and Runic Inscriptions:*

Collected Essays on Anglo-Saxon and Viking Runes. Woodbridge.

– 1995B *Runeukyndige risteres skriblerier:* the English evidence. In Page 1995A, 295–314.

– 1995C Quondam et futurus. In Page 1995A, 1–16.

PARKES, M B 1973 The literacy of the laity. In Daiches, D and Thorlby, A (eds) *Literature and Western Civilization: the Medieval World*, 555–77. London

PETRUCCI, A

– 1980 La scrittura fra ideologia e rappresentazione. In Zeri, F (ed) *Grafica e Immagine, I, Scrittura, Miniatura, Disegno* (Storia dell'Arte Italiana, Parte terza, Situazioni, Momenti, Indagini, II), 5–123. Turin.

– 1993 Public Lettering: Script, Power, and Culture (translation of Petrucci 1980). Chicago and London.

RCAMS = Royal Commission on the Ancient Monuments of Scotland

– 1946 *Inventory of the Ancient Monuments of Orkney and Shetland,* 3 vols. Edinburgh.

SCHALLER, D 1977 Bemerkungen zur Inschriften-Sylloge von Urbana. *Mittellateinisches Jahrbuch*, 12, 9–21.

SIMS-WILLIAMS, P 1981 Milred of Worcester's collection of Latin epigrams and its continental counterparts. *Anglo-Saxon England*, 10, 21–38.

STEVENSON, J 1989 The beginnings of literacy in Ireland. *Proceedings of the Royal Irish Academy*, 89 C, 127–65.

THOMAS, C

– 1963 The interpretation of the Pictish Symbols. *Archaeological Journal*, 120, 31–97.

– 1992 *Whithorn's Christian Beginnings* (First Whithorn Lecture). Whithorn.

– 1994 *And Shall These Mute Stones Speak? Post-Roman Inscriptions in Western Britain.* Cardiff.

TWEDDLE, D, BIDDLE, M and KJØLBYE-BIDDLE, B 1995 *Corpus of Anglo-Saxon Stone Sculpture*, vol IV, *South-East England.* Oxford.

WALLACH, L 1975 The Urbana Anglo-Saxon sylloge of Latin inscriptions. In Kirkwood, G M (ed) *Poetry and Poetics from Ancient Greece to the Renaissance: studies in honor of James Hutton*, 134–51. Ithaca and London.

WEBB, C C I (ed) 1909 *Ioannis Saresberiensis Episcopi Carnotensis Policraticus De Nugis Curialium et Vestigiis Philosophorum Libri VIII.* Oxford.

WILLIAMS, I 1972 The Towyn inscribed stone. In idem (Bromwich, R ed), *The Beginnings of Welsh Poetry …*, 25–40. Cardiff.

WORMALD, C P 1977 The uses of literacy in Anglo-Saxon England and its neighbours. *Transactions of the Royal Historical Society*, 5th series, 27, 95–114.

Anglo-Saxon Architectural Inscriptions

Elisabeth Okasha

One of the most important of Isabel Henderson's contributions to the study of the Picts has been her insistence on the need to view Pictish art not in a vacuum but in the context of contemporary works of art produced in these islands. This paper, discussing some inscribed works of art produced in a neighbouring kingdom to that of the Picts, is offered to her with deep respect.

Anglo-Saxon architectural inscriptions are found only on ecclesiastical stone buildings. Anglo-Saxon secular buildings, and ecclesiastical buildings constructed from material other than stone, may have been ornamented with inscriptions, but it seems unlikely that many were and certainly no such inscriptions have survived. Most of the buildings containing architectural inscriptions date from a period when building in stone had become more common than it had previously been. Only one of the inscriptions discussed here dates from the seventh century and most are considerably later, from the tenth and eleventh centuries. The inscribed stones under discussion, then, are those which formed part of Anglo-Saxon stone churches or other religious buildings and which mainly date from the late Anglo-Saxon period.

There are nineteen such stones where the inscribed texts are reasonably legible. This number could be doubled if every possible example were to be included. It is necessary, however, to exclude from the list those inscribed stones which contain illegible or fragmentary texts, those which are not certainly Anglo-Saxon in date, and those which may not originally have formed part of a building even though they may now do so. These nineteen stones are listed in the Appendix and fall into three main groups.

There is, first, a group of six vertical sundials. Such sundials were only functional if they were fastened on to, or built into, an external south-facing wall. Even then they

were not very accurate, being dependent on factors such as the time of the year, the time of the day and the immediate weather conditions. The texts on these sundials sometimes describe the dial. The sundial from Great Edstone in Yorkshire, for example, has a Latin text probably reading *orlogiu(m via)toris* 'the traveller's clock', as well as an unfinished text in Old English informing us that 'Lo∂an made me' (Okasha 1971, no 41, 73, fig). The well-known sundial from nearby Kirkdale also has a text describing the dial, this time in Old English (ibid, no 64, 87–8, fig): *þis is daeges solmerca aet ilcum tide* 'this is the day's sun-marker at each *tid*' a *tid* being a period of time comparable, but not equal, to an hour. The longer text on this stone names the owner of the church responsible for its rebuilding and dedication to Christ and St Gregory.

The second group of architectural inscriptions are the church dedication stones. Some of these are plain, even utilitarian, as is for example the Jarrow stone (ibid, no 61, 85–6, fig). The text, in Latin, gives the information that the dedication of St Paul's church was on 23 April in the fifteenth year of the reign of King Ecgfri∂ and the fourth year of Ceolfri∂'s abbacy, that is, probably AD 685. There is no decoration or ornamentation, no additional or unnecessary information. By contrast, the dedication stone from St Nicholas' church, Ipswich, probably formed a decorative tympanum and the text is set around the lively carving of a boar (ibid, no 59, 83, fig). The text is now badly worn but begins *in dedicat(ione) e(cl)e(sie) om(n-)*, perhaps 'at the dedication of the church of *or* to all (?saints -)'.

The third group of architectural inscriptions contains what may be termed 'descriptive' texts. The texts in this group are discussed in some detail in order to consider what information they can furnish about the buildings of which they formed part and the people who used these buildings. The texts of the inscriptions in this group are given in the Appendix.

Five of these texts describe the figure carving. The stone from Fletton near Peterborough contains a figure, presumably St Michael, and a rather worn text reading *scs (mich)ae(l)* (Okasha 1983, no 166, 92, figs). The similar carved figure nearby does not seem to be inscribed. The stone from Inglesham in Wiltshire contains a figure of the Virgin and child; its text reads + *maria*, although further text may be lost (Okasha 1971, no 57, 82, fig). Another labelled carving of the Virgin is in York minster, the text reading *scā maria* (ibid, no 149, 132–3, fig).

There are three pieces of stone from St Nicholas' church, Ipswich, each containing a carved figure, probably originally part of a frieze. It seems likely that originally each of the figures was identified by name but all that now remains are two instances of the ending of the Latin word *apostolus* (ibid, no 60, 84, figs). The rest of the titles, along with the personal names, were presumably on pieces of stone now lost. A separate stone in the same church contains a quite legible text in Old English. The carving depicts St Michael fighting an awe-inspiring dragon and the text reads *her scē (m)iha(e)l feht wið ðane draca* 'here St Michael fights (*or* fought) against the dragon' (ibid, no 58, 82–3, fig). In addition the figure of St Michael is labelled and a now illegible text may have identified the dragon also.

The stone from Manchester cathedral contains a carving of an angel holding a scroll (ibid, no 89, 100, fig). The text is set beneath, and partly on top of, the angel but does not describe the carving. It is a biblical text reading *in manus tuas d(mē) commēdo (sp)* 'into thy hands O Lord I commend [my] spirit'. This text is a version of Luke 23, 46 in the Vulgate, or perhaps of Psalm 30, 6 in the Gallican psalter, although it is not an exact quotation from either.

The final stone is in Breamore church, Hampshire (ibid, no 15, 56, fig). The text is cut around the north-facing arch of the doorway to the south porticus and is not associated with any carving. The text is in Old English and is probably incomplete, originally having continued on another part of the church fabric. It reads *her swutelað seo gecwydraednes ðe* and can be translated as 'here the agreement reveals to you -'. Other translations are also possible and this text is discussed in detail below.

These seven texts are all of a similar date, being mainly from the tenth and eleventh centuries, although Fletton may be a little earlier and York a little later. All the texts are inscribed in the script known as 'Anglo-Saxon capitals'. Considered as a group, these stones raise a number of questions. Three are discussed here: first, why are all the stones inscribed in non-runic script and, in particular, in Anglo-Saxon capitals? Second, why do five of these stones label the figure sculpture on them? Third, do these stones imply a literate public?

The first question concerns the script used. None of these stones is inscribed in runic script: is this a function of the ecclesiastical nature of the texts, or of their date, or of their language, or of their geographical location? The possibility that it is due to their association with churches can be dismissed since runic script is well-known in ecclesiastical contexts. There are, for example, several series of small grave-stones, the so-called 'name-stones', from religious sites such as Hartlepool, Lindisfarne and Whitby (See Okasha 1971 and 1992b). Some of these name-stones have texts only in runic script, some only in roman script, some in both. The Anglo-Saxon church in general seems to have had no problem with runic script.

However, the name-stones are all early, mostly datable to the eighth century, as are most rune-stones. There are indeed very few Anglo-Saxon rune-stones dating from later than the ninth century. Anglo-Saxon runic script seems to be mainly associated with the seventh to ninth centuries and, moreover, with texts written in Old English rather than in Latin. Five of the seven stones under discussion here are in Latin and these we would expect to be inscribed in a non-runic script. The distribution of rune-stones is also relevant here. Very few rune-stones are recorded from the midlands or the south of England (Page 1973, 29, fig 7). Five of the stones in this group are from the midlands or the south and these would be unlikely to use runic script. The language, the date and the geographical location of the seven stones under consideration together offer a clear explanation of why they are inscribed in roman rather than in runic script.

We might, however, have expected that some of them would have used a manuscript script since the later Anglo-Saxon church was closely involved with the production of manuscript texts. Inscriptions with texts in manuscript

script are not uncommon, although they occur more frequently on material other than stone. However, instances on stone certainly occur, for example on the cross-shaft from Yarm in Yorkshire (Okasha 1971, no 145, 130, fig). This ninth-century shaft has an Old English text recording the erection of the stone by one brother in memory of another, one brother being described as a priest. There are then some religious texts inscribed on stone in non-capital roman script. However, as with rune-stones, they tend to be located in the northern half of England and to date from the middle centuries of the Anglo-Saxon period. By the tenth century, at least in the midlands and the south, it seems as if Anglo-Saxon capital script was generally preferred for texts inscribed on stone. In the case of the seven texts under discussion, an additional factor could have been that this script was considered fitting for texts on display in public buildings, as opposed to the cursive scripts used in manuscripts.

The second question to be discussed relates to the five stones or series of stones from Fletton, Inglesham, Ipswich and York where the carved figures are identified by written texts. These stones can be related to some free-standing stone crosses, and to some objects on material other than stone, where figures are similarly labelled. An example of a free-standing cross is the one from Bishop Auckland, Co. Durham (ibid, no 11, 53–4, fig). On this cross one sculptured figure is labelled *and* and another *pas*. These labels were presumably intended to be informative and *and* probably identifies St Andrew. It is less clear what or whom *pas* labels. Suggestions have included *paulus*, *paulinus* and *passio* 'passion' referring to the crucifixion of either Christ or St Andrew.

The great majority of Anglo-Saxon stone sculptures associated with buildings, and the vast majority of the sculptured crosses, are uninscribed. Presumably the scenes were usually deemed to be self-explanatory, the figures identifiable, without the need for labels. Why, then, are a few examples given written identifications?

Sometimes such identifications might well have been helpful. The stone from Fletton and the apostle stones from Ipswich are likely to have formed parts of series of stones. It may have been that the individual figures in the series resembled each other and that it was considered useful for the viewers to be able to differentiate between

them. This could have been effected by the use of well-known symbols, St Peter's keys, for example, or by the use of written labels. When we turn to the figures of the Blessed Virgin from Inglesham and York, the texts seem less functional. One would have imagined that the carved figure of the Virgin and child was unmistakeable. The same is true of the Ipswich St Michael stone. Even if the viewers did not immediately recall who was likely to be fighting a dragon and had to read the long text to find out, it does not then seem very likely that they had to read the shorter texts in order to discover which combatant was which. A different explanation seems to be required.

What this explanation might be leads on to the third question: does this group of inscribed stones imply a literate audience, a reading public? Viewed from a twentieth-century literate perspective, this seems a likely hypothesis. Why identify a figure on a stone, why quote (even if inaccurately) the Bible, why note an agreement, unless you are reasonably confident that your text will be read and understood? I have suggested elsewhere that some inscribed stones may have been produced with a divine audience in mind, that a stone requesting prayers for someone's soul could have been addressed to the saints in heaven as much as to a human audience on earth (1995, 69–74). This does not, however, seem to be the case with architectural sculpture. It does not seem likely that anyone in late Anglo-Saxon England would have supposed God or the saints to be in need of a label to identify the Blessed Virgin.

It seems that a human reading public of some size must have been anticipated. The texts on these stones are short and straightforward, either in Old English or in simple and/or biblical Latin. It would hardly require a Latin scholar to translate a text like *sancta maria*. Such texts suggest a literate audience but not a highly educated one, perhaps a predominantly lay rather than a predominantly clerical one. Of course 'audience' may be a misnomer: on occasion a written text might have been intelligible to only one or two people in a congregation who could have read it aloud to others.

It is possible that such texts were also intended as a symbol, as a demonstration of literacy on the part of the carver and/or the commissioner of the stone. Many of those who could not read would nevertheless have been able to recognise the marks as writing. So the York virgin, for example, may have had the figure identified in writing not only, or even primarily, to provide information for the public who entered the church; rather, the written text may have sent a message to the viewer that the person who carved it and the person who commissioned it recognised the status of writing in society. Writing was associated with the powerful in late Anglo-Saxon England, with the upper ranks of society both ecclesiastical and secular (Keynes 1990, 226–57). Through the inscribing of a written text on a piece of architectural sculpture, a clear message was, I suggest, being transmitted about the association of the sculpture, and of its building, with the powerful in society.

One of the seven texts under discussion does, however, seem to have had a different motivation behind its inscription. This is the Breamore text, which is carved not on a piece of architectural sculpture but on the actual fabric of the church. The fact that this text is not associated with any sculpture in itself argues for a literate audience. The content of the text also suggests this. Had the inscriber's intention been primarily to demonstrate literacy, a biblical or liturgical text might well have been deemed appropriate for a church. However this text seems to have been inscribed, mainly at least, in order to impart information.

This inscription has received some recent attention both by Richard and Fiona Gameson (1993, 1–10) and by myself (1992a, 333–45). Interestingly, we reached rather different conclusions about the inscription. However we are in agreement that the Breamore text was intended for a literate audience, that its text was to be read and understood by at least some people. The Gamesons associate the text with the archway on which it is inscribed and suggest that the text refers to the Old Testament story of Noah and the ark (Genesis 9, 8–17). In this biblical story the rainbow is of course explained as a sign of God's covenant or agreement with the human race. The Gamesons suggest that the shape of the archway actually represents the rainbow; they thus see the inscribed archway as a piece of architectural symbolism or iconography.

This suggestion seems to me original and exciting and particularly satisfying in allowing one to consider the text simultaneously as a written message and as a visual symbol. Admittedly, there is cause for concern in that the wording of the text is not closer to the biblical wording. For example, the Latin *signum foederis* 'sign of the covenant' (verses 12, 17) is rendered in the Old English manuscript version of Genesis as *ðaet tacn mines weddes* and in the Old English poem *Genesis* as *andgiettacen* (line 1539) and *waere* (line 1542).[1] In neither Old English version is *seo gecwydraednes*, the word on the Breamore stone, used. Perhaps caution is needed at too readily identifying Genesis 9 as the source of this text; instead the inscription may be better viewed as a reminder or reminiscence of it.

In their interpretation of this inscription, the Gamesons consider that the text is most likely to be complete as it stands. In my view, this must be challenged. As many people before them have done, the Gamesons translate the text as 'Here is made manifest the covenant to you' (1993, 2). They explain that the active verb *swutelað* has here what they call a 'quasi-passive' sense (ibid, 4), that is, that it means 'is shown' rather than 'shows'. The verb *swutelian* can indeed mean 'to be shown', and it habitually has this passive meaning when it is used without an expressed subject. Examination of the instances of this verb with an expressed subject, however, reveals a different picture. The Old English Microfiche Concordance lists 388 examples of this verb with an expressed subject. Of these, 333 are certainly active in that they are followed either by a direct object in the accusative or by a clause beginning with *ðaet, hwaet, hwa* etc. A further 42 are clearly active from their contexts. This leaves 13 instances where the meaning could be active or passive, but in only three cases is a passive meaning at all likely. One of these three, line 32 of the Old English poem Gloria I, is quoted by the Gamesons in support of their translation of the Breamore text (ibid, 4). It is of course possible that the Breamore text is a fourth example of *swutelað* with a subject meaning 'is shown', but statistics and common-sense combine to suggest that this is unlikely.

There is material, as well as linguistic, evidence to support the idea that the Breamore text may be incomplete. In Breamore church there are two other pieces of uncarved stone with inscriptions, both of which are fragmentary. One piece of stone is now built high up into a west-facing interior wall beside the chancel arch. It contains the three letters DE[S] (Okasha 1971, no 16, 56, fig). The other is built into the base of the exterior west wall and contains only the letter G (Okasha 1983, no 160, 88, fig). We cannot be certain that these two fragmentary texts formed a continuation of the long text, but they are at least suggestive. The long text could have continued around another archway or possibly along a straight piece of wall.

The first four words of the Breamore text mean 'Here the agreement reveals…'. If the text is unfinished several sorts of continuation are possible. The fifth word *ðe* could be the accusative of the second person pronoun and mean 'you'; the text could then be interpreted 'Here the agreement reveals you [*for example*, as the son of God / to be the Creator of the world]. Another possibility is that *ðe* is dative and an interpretation could be 'Here the agreement reveals to you [*for example,* that God created the world / that God will save the righteous]. Alternatively, *ðe* could be not a personal but a relative pronoun and the text mean 'Here the agreement which [*for example*, God made] reveals [*for example*, His mercy / Noah's righteousness].

Perhaps we have to accept that we may never be sure of the original significance of the Breamore text. It seems to me that, although there may be a reference to Genesis 9, this cannot be demonstrated conclusively since the inscribed text is probably incomplete and its meaning not fully interpreted. The Gamesons have, however, put forward an attractive idea in seeing the text as an instance of architectural symbolism. They go on to suggest that archways in ecclesiastical buildings might sometimes have been taken as symbolic of key spiritual themes whether or not they ever contained texts (1993, 7). These key themes, they suggest, may well have included the Last Judgement as well as the covenant referred to in the Noah story. They draw a parallel with some later medieval churches where the chancel arch was indeed used to evoke the Last Judgement. These ideas should certainly alert us to the possibility of viewing other pieces of Anglo-Saxon architectural sculpture in a similarly symbolic manner.[2]

Appendix

Sundials	Dedication stones	Descriptive texts
1 Aldbrough*	28 Deerhurst I	15 Breamore I
12 Bishopstone	29 Deerhurst II	57 Inglesham
41 Great Edstone	59 Ipswich II	58 Ipswich I
64 Kirkdale*	61 Jarrow I	60 Ipswich III
99 Orpington	73 Lincoln I	89 Manchester
205 Stow	146 York I	149 York IV
		166 Fletton

* indicates that the sundial also contains a dedication text.

The running numbers refer to the entry numbers in Okasha 1971 (nos 1–158), Okasha 1983 (nos 159–184) and Okasha 1992b (nos 185–211). Each inscription is discussed and illustrated in its appropriate place.

The descriptive texts read as follows. In the transliterations, word-division is inserted and the abbreviations are expanded; brackets indicate damaged letters and a dash marks loss of text.

15 Breamore I: *her swutelað seo gecwydraednes ðe -*, 'here the agreement reveals to you -'. Other translations are also possible.

57 Inglesham: *[+] maria -*, '+ Mary -'.

58 Ipswich I:
(i) *her sancte [m]iha[e]l feht wið ðane draca*, 'here St Michael fights [*or* fought] against the dragon'
(ii) *[sanct]e [m]ihael*, 'St Michael'
(iii) illegible.

60 Ipswich III: (i) *-to[l]us*, '[-] apostle'
(ii) *-ostolus*, '[-] apostle'.

89 Manchester: *in manus tuas do[mine] commendo [spiritum]*, 'into thy hands O Lord I commend [my] spirit'.

149 York IV: *sancta maria*, 'St Mary'.

166 Fletton: *sanctus [mich]ae[l]*, 'St Michael'.

Notes

1 The Old English translation is printed in Crawford 1992, 106–7; the relevant lines of the Old English poem *Genesis* are printed in Krapp 1931, 48.

2 An earlier version of this paper was presented at a conference on *Anglo-Saxon Art and Architecture* held in Romsey, Hampshire, on 22 October 1994. The conference was sponsored by the Hampshire Field Club and Archaeological Society and by the Test Valley Archaeological Trust.

References

CRAWFORD, S J (ed) 1922 *The Old English Version of the Heptateuch…* (EETS Orig Ser 160). London, Oxford.

GAMESON, R and GAMESON, F 1993 The Anglo-Saxon inscription at St Mary's Church, Breamore, Hampshire. *ASSAH* 6, 1–10.

KEYNES, S 1990 Royal government and the written word in late Anglo-Saxon England. In McKitterick, R (ed) *The Uses of Literacy in Early Medieval Europe*, 226–57. Cambridge.

KRAPP, G P (ed) 1931 (repr 1969) *The Junius Manuscript* (ASPR 1). New York, London.

OKASHA, E

– 1971 *Hand-list of Anglo-Saxon Non-runic Inscriptions*. Cambridge.

– 1983 A supplement to *Hand-List of Anglo-Saxon Non-Runic Inscriptions. ASE* 11, 83–118.

– 1992a The English language in the eleventh century: the evidence from inscriptions. In Hicks, C (ed) *England in the Eleventh Century* (Harlaxton Medieval Studies 2), 333–45. Stamford.

– 1992b A second supplement to *Hand-List of Anglo-Saxon Non-Runic Inscriptions. ASE* 21, 37–85.

– 1995 Literacy in Anglo-Saxon England: the evidence from inscriptions. *ASSAH* 8 , 69–74.

PAGE, R I 1973 *An Introduction to English Runes*. London.

Some thoughts on Pictish symbols as a formal Writing System

Katherine Forsyth

Introduction

In recent years the cool breeze of Revisionism has been blowing through Pictish studies. Professional Pictologists, such as Isabel Henderson, Anna Ritchie, Alfred Smyth, Leslie Alcock and his pupils, have been at pains to downplay the exoticness of the Picts and to stress instead their common heritage with other barbarian peoples of northwest Europe. While they certainly haven't ignored the symbols, it would be fair to say that the Revisionists have not dwelt upon them. Their aims are laudable, and their general approach surely correct, but, as our honorand reminds me, it is impossible to get to grips with the Picts without addressing the question of the symbols. They are the one thing unique to the Picts, and without some sense of their significance our understanding of the Picts will never be more than partial.[1]

In addition to their immediate aesthetic appeal, the enigmatic symbols attract those of a romantic or mystic bent, or those with a taste for the exotic. The sense that their code could be cracked **if only the key could be found** draws anyone with a love of problem-solving. Yet, entertaining and enjoyable as it is to approach the symbols as a glorified crossword puzzle, the solution of which is an end in itself, this approach is nothing more than antiquarianism (as argued by Samson 1992). As scholars, our concern must be to understand the symbol-stones not for themselves but for what they tell us about Pictish society. The archaeological analyses of Jim Inglis (1987) and Elizabeth Alcock (1989) have begun to elucidate the position of symbol-carved stones in the social landscape of Pictland, and we must hope for further detailed work in this vein. As Stephen Driscoll has shown (1988), it is possible to gain some understanding of the social function of symbol stones as monuments without attempting to interpret specific carvings. Yet the investigation of meaning can be deferred only so long.

Most writers have been content to make only general statements about meaning. The first major systematic investigation was conducted in the early 1960s by Charles Thomas. He argued that the symbol stones referred to individuals in general terms describing social status and tribal membership (1963). His article incorporated a number of important observations – most notably the identification of different types of 'statement' following 'quasi-grammatical rules' – though certain of his conclusions are open to question (Henderson 1971, Samson 1992). The author himself modified his position when he returned to the topic two decades later (1984). In response to Thomas's original paper, Henderson asserted that 'personal rank of the individual' was not the only possible interpretation and suggested that ownership of land was a valid alternative (1971). The only other large-scale study to date is Anthony Jackson's *The Symbol Stones of Scotland* (1984), an idiosyncratic work with a number of fatal inadequacies (for a sustained critique, see Driscoll 1986). Jackson's interpretation of the stones as recording matrilinear marriage alliances has not found general acceptance.

The most recent contribution on the subject is an important article by Ross Samson (1992). While accepting that each 'statement' (of paired symbols) referred to a specific person, Samson questions two fundamental assumptions of previous writers: namely that each symbol referred to a class of data (the **kind** of person, rather than to a specific person), and that each symbol was self-sufficient in conveying one fact and thus that the syntax of each 'statement' was additive (1+1). He rejects the type of interpretations put forward by Thomas – along the lines of

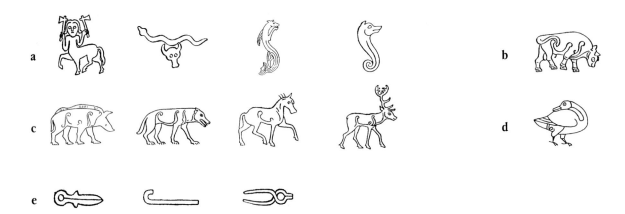

1 **a** *rejected animal designs* **b** *Burghead bull – rejected* **c** *mammals functioning as symbols, though in a limited fashion* **d** *goose symbol* **e** *representational objects – rejected*

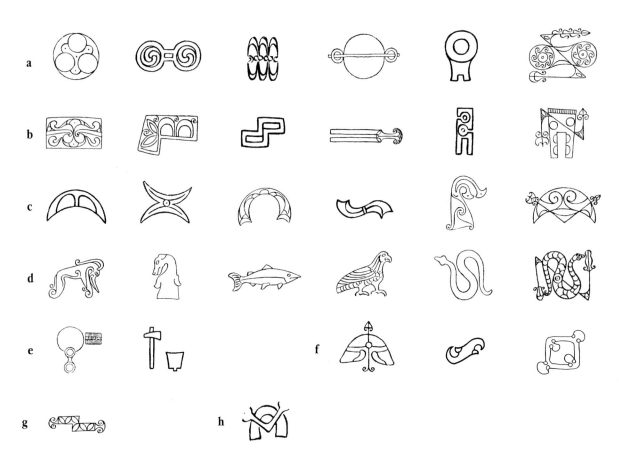

2 *Suggested inventory of genuine symbols – classified according to basic outline and complexity: core symbols (**a–d**), associated symbols (**e**):* **a** *discoid* **b** *rectangular* **c** *crescentic/curvilinear* **d** *animal* **e** *representational* **f,g,h** *uniquely occurring 'core' symbols*

3 **a,b** *symbols modified by a 'notch'*

KF/Pinkfoot Press (after Allen and Anderson 1903, II, figs 117–162) 'an individual who was **a king** and **a poet**', or '**a dead warrior** and **member of the eagle clan** (commemorated by **a woman**)'. Instead Samson argues that there is no reason why the sense need be general (eg a tribe or social status) rather than specific (eg a personal name). Furthermore, he argues that the primary sense unit was not the individual symbol but the symbol pair: the symbols made sense not individually but only in combination (ie 1+2 = 2+1, but 12 is not the same as 21). His ingenious theory of symbols representing the two elements of a di-thematic personal name has much to recommend it, but is impeded, at least for now, by the fact that only a small proportion of the historically-attested Pictish personal names are di-thematic (though, admittedly, our knowledge of Pictish personal names is limited). Samson's hunch that the symbol texts are personal names is very plausible, though to concur with the general hypothesis need not require an acceptance of the specifics of his model. The comparative evidence of contemporary epigraphic practice elsewhere in the British Isles and Scandinavia shows that, with the exception of a small minority of Christian Latin texts of purely liturgical or exegetical significance, the overwhelming majority of monumental inscriptions consists largely or solely of personal names. Surely, then, the burden of proof lies on those who would have the Picts carving anything else, especially since the texts of roman and ogham alphabet monumental inscriptions in Pictland are preponderantly personal names (Okasha 1985, 1996; Forsyth 1996a).

It was reading Samson's article, and realising that it contained a major conceptual innovation in suggesting, apparently for the first time, that the symbols represented **language** rather than **ideas**, which inspired me to look seriously at a problem I had previously ignored. At the time I was working on the ogham inscriptions of Scotland (Forsyth 1996a) and had been struck again and again by the many contextual similarities between the use of ogham and the use of Pictish symbols. Could these similarities, I wondered, provide a clue to the nature of the Pictish symbol system? Specifically, could the formal correspondences I detected between the two schemes be attributable to the fact that, like ogham, the symbols were, a writing system?

For all its unusual appearance, ogham is an alphabetic script which can be shown to depend for its inspiration on the Latin alphabet (for an introduction to ogham, see McManus 1991). Though the form of the letters is novel – each character consists of a bundle of between one and five strokes placed in one of four positions relative to a base-line – the system operates in exactly the same way as our own alphabet. Where it differs from the Latin alphabet is that there **is** a connection between a character's appearance and the sound it represents in the Irish language. Letters are assigned to one of the four groups (and thus four positions relative to the line) on the basis of how they are pronounced. Within each group they are ordered first to fifth. For instance, the vowel group, A O U E I, consists of bundles of short strokes **on** the line, other groups sit **above**, **below** or **across** the line. The formal purity of the original alphabet came to be disrupted when a series of additional characters, or *forfeda*, were invented to cater for later developments in the sound system of Irish (Sims-Williams 1992). These supplementary characters took baroque forms unrelated to the simple parallel lines of the original system. It was the example of the 'mathematically' structured ogham script which caused me to look again at the formal structure of the Pictish symbols.

A Structured System

Agreement has not been reached on exactly how many 'genuine' symbols there really are. The total is frequently stated to be 'about fifty', Elizabeth Alcock put it at between sixty and sixty-five (1989, 11). I believe the symbols to be neither as numerous nor as heterogeneous as is generally maintained. In fact there may be only about thirty 'core' symbols. How are we to decide what is and is not a symbol? Despite the variation in internal decoration, which relates to date and context, all are agreed on the remarkable continuity of individual symbol designs across the country and through time. At least as important, however, is the continuity of syntax. As Diack recognised (1944) and Thomas further explained (1963), the fundamental syntax of extant symbol texts is that of the symbol pair, the elements usually arranged vertically above one another, almost touching.[2] This is the key to defining the members of the system. The conventional style of the designs is a clue, but the acid test is whether or not an example is found in combination with another recognized symbol (the mirror and comb qualify by association).

The geometric symbols are easily identified as such by their common graphic style. More difficult are the various creatures which appear on Pictish sculpture. Most authorities agree that Romilly Allen was mistaken in including among the symbols the centaur, the bull's-head-and-serpent, the hippocamp and sea-horse (**1a**) (Allen and Anderson 1903, II, 58–79). Not only do these occur exclusively on later (Class II) monuments, but, more importantly, they do not combine in pairs to form statements.[3] The key criteria for inclusion in the inventory of 'core' symbols is that the design must appear at least once in paired combination with another recognised 'core' symbol. Straight-off, this excludes the famous Burghead bull plaques (**1b**).[4] Though rendered in the same style as recognised 'core' animal symbols, they never appear in combination with another symbol. They may well be related in meaning to the symbol system but they are not of the same standing as the 'core' symbols and must be set to one side. Also excluded on the same grounds are the lone warrior figures (eg Rhynie Man). More problematic are the boar and the wolf, both of which appear in combination (and therefore must be counted symbols) but also appear singly: boar solo – Dunadd; boar combined – Knocknagael; boar fragment – Dores; wolf solo – Ardross; wolf combined – Newbiggin Leslie, perhaps Keillor. The stag appears only once, in a pair, on the stone from Grantown; the horse appears only once, alone, on a stone from Inverurie. The marked rarity of these mammal symbols (only eight extant examples in total) (**1c**), and their geographical concentration in and around the Great Glen, as noted by Alcock (1989, 15), and the fact that they never appear on Class II monuments, is in marked contrast to the half-dozen remaining animal symbols which are (a) widespread, (b) relatively frequent (occurring at least ten times each), (c) as common on Class II as on Class I and (d) never appear singly. These creatures are: 'the Pictish beast', 'the beast's head', the fish, the eagle and the serpent (**2d**). It is moot to which sub-category the goose belongs (**1d**): it does not appear alone, but neither does it appear on Class II nor is it common. There are only three paired occurrences (Easterton of Roseisle, Gleneagles, and probably Tillytarmont), more than the mammal symbols, but markedly less than the other creatures.

The immediacy and attractiveness of the naturalistic animals may have contributed to the over-emphasis on the animal component of the system. Textbook illustrations of the symbol inventory (eg Jackson 1984 fig 1; Laing and Laing 1993 fig 78) usually show a selection of 'animal symbols' and a selection of 'geometric symbols' giving the impression that the system was equally divided between the two. Yet, as shown above, the animal component of the system is much less prominent than such illustrations suggest. As Hicks notes, they are in a definite minority (1993, 196).

As for the geometric symbols themselves, it is clear to one and all that the 'mirror' and the 'comb' do indeed represent mirrors and combs, literally or metaphorically. So accurate and detailed are the representation of these objects that archaeologists have been able to categorize them using the typology of contemporary combs and mirrors recovered through excavation (Foster 1990, 162–5; Fox 1948; Henry, 1965, 170; Lloyd-Morgan 1980). As for the other symbols, much fun has been had over the years trying to identify which object is represented from which angle, an endeavour reminiscent of the photo-puzzles in children's comics (the greatest exponent being Thomas 1963, but see also Laing and Laing 1984, and many others). Yet, no matter how ingenious the identification, and objectively convincing to its proposer, none can be tested: one man's 'chariot-and-ponies seen from above' is another man's 'Pictish tower'. Surely the very accuracy of the 'mirror' and 'comb' symbols, and of the realistic animals, counts against the other symbols being represent-ational. Noteworthy too, is the fact that, as discussed below, the realistic mirror and comb do not function in the same way as the pair-forming 'core' symbols.

Allen's identification of the crozier on St Vigeans 4 is undoubtedly correct (1903, II, 71; III, 241) but, since this Class II fragment is too small to be sure, there is no compelling reason to regard it as a symbol (rather than say a personal attribute of the hooded figure, analogous to David's attributes of harp, hurley and ball (Henderson 1986)). Another uniquely occurring representation is equally doubtful as a symbol. A pair of shear appears under the left arm of the cross at Migvie (Allen and Anderson 1903, III, 191–2). In the upper quadrants are a symbol pair, but there is no *a priori* reason why the shears must be a symbol since their opposite number to the right (a single horseman) is not. The only other immediately recognizable objects with a claim to be genuine symbols are the 'hammer' and 'anvil' (or more likely 'crucible'?) which occur twice only (Class I, Abernethy; Class II, Dunfallandy). Both times their position on the stone is subordinate and perhaps their role is consciously modelled on the mirror and comb. The tongs appear uniquely on the stone from Dunfallandy. They may be an embellishment of the hammer and crucible or an item in their own right (**1e**).

Henderson recognized that there are three categories of symbol: animals, recognizable objects, and abstract geometric figures (1971, 54). The animals I would divide in two: the 'mammals' and the (non-mammal) 'creatures'. The mammals play only a minor role and for all that the mirror and comb are very frequent, in fact they are the only recognizable objects (other than the very rare hammer and crucible) which occur in 'proper' symbol statements, and then, not in primary combination with another symbol, but always subordinate to a symbol pair (**2e**). With the exception of the five or six 'creatures', the Pictish symbol inventory overwhelmingly comprises abstract geometric designs (**2**). Allen's triquetra is easily ruled out, but exactly how many geometric symbols there are remains subjective: are the 'two discs' (not joined) a variant of the 'double-disc' (joined), or a separate symbol? Accepting, for the sake of argument, these two as variants of a single symbol gives a total of fifteen symbols, three of which may be modified by the addition of V- or Z-rods, to give a total of eighteen (**2 a–c**). Then there are the five unique symbols (**2 f-h**)[5], the five common 'creatures' one of which may be modified by a Z-rod (**2d**), and a further four mammals which do not occur on Class II. To include them all gives a basic inventory of thirty-three 'core' symbols. Added to this is the category of special modifying symbols (**2e**), the mirror and the comb (to be taken separately since the mirror can occur alone) and the hammer and crucible (which only occur together).

The mirror (and comb) appears to qualify the statement as a whole but there are two phenomena – rods and notches – which qualify individual symbols. Four symbols (the crescent, the double-disc, the serpent, and the notched rectangle)[6] appear in two forms, with and without an over-laid 'rod', either in the shape of a V or like a Z or N. The different kinds of rods are applied with

complete consistency, the crescent receives a V, never a Z; the double-disc, serpent and the notched-rectangle receive a Z or N, never a V. With the sole exception of the lone Z-rod on the reverse of the Norrie's Law handpin these rods never occur alone. Thomas (1963) took these rods to be broken arrows and spears and thus to represent death in some way. Anderson adduced comparative evidence that they should be seen as floriated sceptres (1903, I, xxxiv), an interpretation forcefully restated by Stevenson (1993, 16–18). Perhaps they, too, are to be taken as representational, like the mirror and comb.

A further 'modification' is the notch. Two symbols, the crescent and the double-disc very occasionally appear with a small penannular notch, as if a bite had been taken out of them (**3a**). Crescents and double-discs can be modified by both rods and notches, but I know of no examples of a single symbol bearing both. The same phenomenon may be reflected in the square notch at the base of some 'mirror-case' symbols, and perhaps even in the two circular notches sometimes seen on the body of the 'notched-rectangle' (**3b**). The problem is knowing whether the notched and unnotched, rodded and rodless versions were variants of a single symbol or separate symbols in their own right. It is important to note that while modification with the mirror (and comb) was widespread, only certain symbols were modified by rods or notches. This suggests that the significance of these modifiers was restricted rather than pervasive.

As far as I can discern, from the very outset all scholars have assumed the geometric symbols to be stylized representations of actual objects. This may well be, but for the sake of argument I would like to assume, for a moment, that they are **not representational** at all but are purely abstract geometrical figures. As long as they were understood to represent real objects, the symbols have been illustrated (and thought of) in no particular order, and no attention has been given to the formal visual relationships between them. There are, as Romilly Allen tacitly acknowledged in the order in which he set them out (1903, II, 58–79), correspondences between the form of certain symbols. For instance, the 'disc-and-notched-rectangle' could be taken as half a 'double-disc' on its end. The way the two are juxtaposed on Westfield 1, a Class I stone at Falkland Palace (Henderson 1979, 26–7), brings this home most forcefully. Taking this idea a little further, the geometric symbols can be divided into one of three categories depending on whether their fundamental shape is based on complete circles, crescents/curved lines, or rectangles/straight lines (**2 a–c**).

Within each category, the symbols can be viewed as transformations of a single basic shape and arranged loosely in order of increasing complexity. To take the rectilinear group: the simplest outline is that of the rectangle itself, transformed with one move it becomes the L-shaped-figure, once more and it is the stepped-rectangle, bent over it becomes the tuning-fork, and developed even further it becomes the notched-rectangle. A similar mathematical progression may be ascribed to the sequence: single-disc, double-disc, triple-oval, triple-disc-with-bar, disc-and-rectangle.

Of course there is considerable subjectivity in this. Perhaps there are more than four basic categories, perhaps the divisions are to be drawn differently. It scarcely matters at this stage. My aim is merely to suggest an alternative way of conceptualizing the symbols in which the whole series is generated by structured transformations from a number of basic forms. This formal sequence is at least possible, even if how I have chosen to order them here may be contested.[7] I'll stick with the above categories, though, for the moment: discoid (**2a**), rectilinear (**2b**), curvilinear (**2c**) and 'creatures' (**2d**), with the representational symbols in a separate subordinate category of their own (**2e**). Having imputed inter-relationship between the basic forms of the symbols, perhaps we can go on to ascribe correspondences between symbols with the same degree of complexity (ie view the system as a matrix with correspondences down the complexity column as well as along the row of form). Could the third element of the rectilinear group stand in the same relation to the first as the third element of the discoid group does to its first?

A sceptic might argue that such a division is arbitrary and that one could as easily divide our own alphabet into categories of letters comprising solely straight lines (X, T, A), predominantly curves (S, O, C), or a mixture of both (B, Q, R), or draw up progressions along the lines **p q b d** or **I L F E**. We know such patterns to be meaningless (since there is no direct correlation between pronunciation and outline), and could discern as much

from the fact that the combinations in which letters actually appear bears no relation to their shape. Preliminary observations of the Pictish symbol combinations, however, suggest that this division into categories is not arbitrary, but actually operative in the system. Firstly, one member from each category, and only one, also appears in a form modified by a V- or Z-rod (double-disc, notched rectangle, crescent and serpent). Secondly, the category to which a symbol belongs appears to effect the kind of symbols with which it is combined. For instance, symbols more commonly combine with members of other categories and rarely with members of their own category (leaving aside the four or five exceptional cases of symbols combining with versions of themselves). Leading on from this, each of the most common symbols (crescent, double-disc, and beast) occur more commonly with the members of one category than those of the other, eg the double-disc is more commonly found with animal symbols, rarely with rectilinear; the inverse is true of the crescent (based on statistics in Allen and Anderson 1903, II, 110–27; Jackson 1984, 240–6; Samson 1992, 36, 52). Such patterned connections are merely impressions at this stage and need to be tested statistically. They may or may not have bearing on the meaning of the individual symbols but they might well point the way to an understanding of how the system was originally conceived and constructed.

The four sub-categories I discerned immediately brought to mind the four groups or *aicmi* of ogham letters. I'm not suggesting that the discoid Pictish symbols are all 'stop' consonants and the creatures all vowels[8], but I do wonder if the simple transformative structure behind the ogham alphabet might have been an inspiration to the person who invented the Pictish symbol system. The Irish invented ogham when contact with Latin literacy led them to desire a script for their own language (Harvey 1987, Stevenson 1989). This notion that each language should have a script of its own was widespread in Ancient and Medieval Europe and the Mediterranean World (a few of the many examples are: Hebrew, Greek, Latin, Etruscan, Germanic Runes and Rhaetic). Ogham is visually very different from the Latin alphabet which inspired it, even if at a fundamental level they operate in the same way. Perhaps ogham provided the basic concept of groups of 'mathematically' structured forms, and the indigenous art of the period provided the graphic elements from which the Pictish system was constructed.

Several authorities have looked to the art style reflected in the animal and geometric designs for an indication of the symbol system's date of origin. Thomas preferred to see it well back into an Iron Age context, 'scarcely later than the second century AD' (1961, 57). The Laings have restated the debt the symbols owe to late Romano-British art (1984, 262), and for R B K Stevenson comparison with Insular illuminated manuscripts suggested their genesis perhaps as late as the seventh century (1955). Regarding the earliest dating, the recent discovery of the Clonmore Shrine (Bourke 1993, 14–16) underlines the fact that La Tène-style decoration is no longer a guarantee of prehistoric date (Bourke 1995): this Irish reliquary of *c*AD 600 is carved with La Tène spiral ornament which would have been thought at home on a sword scabbard from the last centuries BC ! As for the correspondences with seventh-century manuscript art, we must distinguish between the essential form of each symbol and the various actual expressions of it. To take up the analogy with writing, the distinction is like that between the combinations of lines which makes a T a T, rather than an L or an I , as against the curves, serifs, and variation in relative proportions which distinguish, say, *capitalis*, uncial and minuscule varieties. It is possible that a symbol system, invented in its essentials in the fourth or fifth century, may have been visually recast in contemporary style in the seventh. Stevenson's theory of 'the declining symbol' (1955), further developed by Henderson (1958) and Murray (1986), is a useful tool for the relative dating of individual examples and, perhaps for locating the origin of particular styles of symbol writing (in the way that analysis of Caroline minuscule allows the progress of the canonical form of the script across Europe to be charted (Bischoff 1990, 112–18)). But it does not necessarily tell us about the origin of the **system**. The date of a particular style of script may well be irrelevant to the date of the origin of the alphabet.

If we are looking for a historical context for initial Pictish exposure to ogham then one may be provided by the sixth century Irish Christian *peregrini* who voyaged to the Northern and Western Isles. Two mentioned by Adomnán, Cormac Ua Liatháin and Brendan of Clonfert (*VC* I.6, II.42, III.17), came from areas of Ireland where ogham was

particularly popular at a time when ogham stones were still being erected. Ogham inscriptions of probably fairly early date have been found in North and South Uist, Caithness and at several sites in Orkney (Forsyth 1996a). The earliest datable ogham in Scotland came from the same archaeological context as the earliest datable symbol stone, the sixth-century paved courtyard at the multi-period settlement of Pool, Sanday, Orkney (Hunter 1990, 1997).

Symbols in Use

Even if one rejects the formal, structural correspondences I am proposing between the two systems, the contextual similarities between ogham and symbols are undeniable. As Charles Thomas has already pointed out (1994), from an archaeological point of view the Class I pillars are exactly cognate with the other 'individual inscribed memorials' of the pre-mid-seventh century British Isles: the ogham pillars of Ireland (Macalister 1945) and the unfortunately labelled 'Class I' post-Roman inscribed stones of Wales and western Britain (Nash-Williams 1950). The rise and fall of this monument type reflects social, political and devotional changes in post-Roman Celtic society and the Class I Pictish symbol stones are most naturally seen as the local reflex of a more general phenomenon (Driscoll 1986). The mutually exclusive distribution of the post-Roman British monuments south of the Forth and symbol stones to the north appears to support this conclusion.

The similarities between the use of ogham and the use of symbols extend beyond the monuments, however. Like the symbols, ogham is found casually carved in a cave (at Blackwaterfoot, Jackson 1973) and on small slabs at settlement sites (Birsay and Pool, Forsyth 1996a).[9] Ogham appears on a number of utilitarian domestic objects including knives, combs and a spindle whorl (Holder 1990, Forsyth 1996a, 1996c). The symbol-inscribed objects are less obviously utilitarian, but the sample is small.[10] These domestic and informal examples provide important evidence that knowledge of both systems was not restricted to a narrow group within society. Their wide geographical distribution throughout Pictland is also worthy of note. When it comes to metalwork[11], however, the comparison is with the roman alphabet (Brown 1993, Michelli 1997). The only oghams on metalwork appear to be secondary (McManus 1991:132, Holder 1990).

Returning to the monuments, there is a tendency to regard the Class I stones as the apotheosis of the symbol system with Class II constituting some kind of falling away. In epigraphic terms, however, this is an entirely false impression. Symbols share Class II monuments with a wealth of other carving, which in some cases is given visual priority, but it would be quite wrong to think of them as marginal on these later monuments. Often the symbols are rendered on a massive scale and placed at the very top of the slab (eg Rosemarkie, Hilton of Cadboll, the Maiden Stone, Aberlemno Roadside cross-slab). **As symbols**, Class II examples continue to conform to the basic syntax familiar from Class I monuments: the vertical pair, with or without the qualification of mirror or mirror and comb. At first glance the cross-slabs may appear a confusing jumble of many symbols, but a closer examination reveals that the elements of each symbol statement are carefully differentiated from other pairs by scale and relative placement and, where present, the mirror and comb continue to appear in 'third' position (eg Golspie, Glenferness, Dyce 2, Meigle 1, Dunfallandy). These later texts have the same format as the early ones, the 'rules' continue to apply: the key difference is that some Class II monuments exhibit more than one symbol statement.

Comparison with the roman alphabet-inscribed crosses and cross-slabs of contemporary Ireland and Wales may help explain the differences between the use of symbols on Class I and Class II stones (Macalister 1949, Nash-Williams 1950). Almost without exception, each ogham or roman alphabet-inscribed pillar refers to a single person: 'so-and-so (son of N, of the Y kin-group)'. From the seventh century on, however, the equation 'one monument : one person' does not always hold. Texts on crosses and cross-slabs often name two or three people – the person who caused the monument to be erected, the person whose soul is to benefit from this action, sometimes the saint who is invoked, or the cleric under whose jurisdiction it falls, or the master-craftsman responsible for the work. If each Pictish symbol statement refers to one person then the multiplicity of statements on **some** Class II slabs probably means more than one person is being referred to. This is certainly the conclusion to be drawn from the three human figures on the back of the Dunfallandy cross-slab, each one of whom is 'labelled' by their own symbol statement.

Symbols as writing

To accept the symbol system as some form of writing makes it much easier to relate it to contemporary monumental practice elsewhere. A side-benefit of this paradigm is that with its adoption, apparent conundrums evaporate.

The far-flung geographical distribution of highly standardized symbols has been justly remarked on, but till now explained as the result of a simultaneous imposition of a standard symbolism throughout Pictland by a central authority (see, most recently, Alcock 1996). This in turn has been taken as reflecting a precociously effective political institution (ie kingship). Yet if the symbols are a writing system the standardization of individual characters is no more surprising than the standardization of uncial D or ogham R throughout the British Isles. The sudden appearance of a fully-formed system, without a visible period of experimentation and development also ceases to be a problem.

There has been a tendency to discuss the Pictish symbol system as if it emerged piecemeal from a pool of designs which were only later structured and codified. The implicit model here is surely the fluid language of heraldry in which straightforward personal devices evolved into hereditary symbols and only later were reduced to a system of armorial bearings. Over time one can see the invention of new ways of differentiating between the ever-increasing number of coats-of-arms. To begin with the repertory of charges was small but by now they may be 'anything in heaven, earth or wonderland, from a double-headed eagle to a trivet' (Wagner 1946, 25). This fluidity around a central principle is in marked contrast to the fundamental stability of the Pictish symbol system. To the extant that they can be dated, the extant symbol texts show that all the elements of the system were in place by the first appearance on Class I stones and continued fundamentally unchanged to the last of the Class II cross-slabs. For this reason I think it more likely that the symbol system is like ogham. The individual ogham characters have meaning **only** in relation to the rest of the system, it is impossible to have one without predicating all the others. This shows that ogham was invented at a single point in time, it did not gradually form over a long period. I see no reason for thinking that the Pictish symbol system was any different.

Similarly the comparison with alphabetic script brings to mind the differences between different registers: the simple form of a cursive script need not imply a date any earlier than the baroque forms of a corresponding calligraphic display script. Rather, each style of lettering reflects forms appropriate to the context. Leslie Alcock has recently suggested that the simplest symbol examples, notably those found in caves, are earlier than the rest and stand at a previous stage in an evolutionary progression. These designs, recognisable as 'double-discs', 'Pictish beasts' or whatever, but lacking internal embellishment, he labels 'proto-symbols (1996). Until his hypothesis can be confirmed with datable examples prior to the rest the possibility will remain that these are merely informal, 'cursive' versions of the standard symbols.

To the extent that Pictland may be defined as the non-British, non-Gaelic areas of northern Britain, symbols are found all over Pictland and nowhere else (with only a handful of dubious exceptions). The exclusively 'Pictish' nature of the symbols indicated by their geographical distribution is supported by their chronological range: none appear to post-date the cultural eclipse of the Picts around 900. If the symbols are not writing and represent ideas rather than language *per se* then we must find some feature of Pictish society or culture which was universal and long-lived but exclusive to the Picts (otherwise might not we expect some borrowings by one or more of their neighbours?). If this **was** the case, the fact that the system was used apparently from the start in all the provinces of the Picts, might require us to posit some form of self-conscious 'pan-Pictish' cultural identity. The precociously early date of such sentiments would require no little explanation!

On the other hand, if the symbols do in fact represent the Pictish language then their distribution is easier to explain for it would simply reflect those places where Pictish was spoken. There is no need to postulate a self-consciously shared cultural package, merely a common language. The end of the tradition of carving symbols on public monuments could then be seen to coincide with the decline of Pictish as the language of the ruling elite. The mutually exclusive distribution of, say, Pictish symbols and Anglian runes, would reflect merely the mutually exclusive distribution of the Pictish and English languages. If the symbols do record language, we might be able to explain why symbols are absent from the monuments of certain of the major ecclesiastical centres of Pictland. Their absence at, say St Andrews, may reflect the strong influence of Gaelic there from an early date (Taylor 1996, Clancy 1996).

How might it work?

If the symbols **are** writing, how might the system work? There are three basic varieties among the many different kinds of writing systems of the world: alphabetic script (graphemes represent phonemes), syllabic script (graphemes correspond to syllables, often a consonant-vowel pair), eg Mycenean Greek, and logographic script (graphemes = morphemes, ie words), eg Chinese. Some systems are predominantly of one kind but incorporate aspects of another. The different bases of these different scripts is reflected in their outward appearance. For instance alphabetic scripts tend to have around 20–30 simple characters, syllabic scripts tend to have at least 50 and may have as many as several hundred, and a logographic script needs several thousand to function properly (Crystal 1987, 200–2).

If we had inscriptions consisting of row upon row of Pictish symbols then there would be no problem: we would recognise these as written texts, even if we had no way of reading what they actually said (cf Linear A), though we might live in hope! (cf the now-decoded Maya glyphs, Coe 1992). Furthermore, we would be able to say with reasonable certainty that the number of graphemes (between thirty and forty depending how they are counted) implied an alphabetic script. The brevity of the extant texts, however, all but precludes an alphabetic interpretation for Pictish symbols (unless one is prepared to accept the unlikely scenario that the symbol statements represent pairs of initials). A syllabic script is similarly ruled out since we know the Pictish language did not consist solely of words of two syllables! If there were more elements in the symbol inventory then a logographic script would be a possible explanation. The various modifiers (rods, notches, mirror and comb) would fit very well into such a system, functioning, perhaps, in ways similar to the determinant in Egyptian hieroglyphs, or the radical in Chinese script, a non-phonetic marker indicating the semantic meaning of similarly pronounced words; or alternatively, like diacritics in alphabets and syllabaries, distinguishing between two contrasting phonemes (say, voiced and unvoiced consonants, or long and short vowels). But to cover all the words of the Pictish language would require a hundred times as many symbols as we actually have.

The small number of elements in each statement coupled with the comparatively small number of symbols available means the system cannot have represented the entirety of Pictish language. If we are still to adhere to the theory that the symbol system is writing it must be that its semantic range was in some way limited. Given that symbols appear in a great range of monumental and non-monumental contexts their meaning must be of very broad application, despite its restricted range. It is hard to imagine that it is anything other than a personal identification: '(here lies) A', '(this belongs to) A', '(this was erected by) A', '(pray for) A, A'.

Samson concluded that the symbol pairs represented di-thematic personal names by analysing the frequency of symbols and symbol combinations in comparison with the frequency of personal names and name-elements among the neighbours of the Picts. I would argue towards a similar conclusion on the basis of comparison with the archaeo-logical contexts of the symbols and the contemporary uses of alphabetic writing elsewhere in the British Isles.

Before Samson's 1992 article, the most widespread explanation was that each symbol was the emblem of a tribe or lineage. There are two main reasons why the kin-group badge theory seems a less likely explanation than straightforward personal names. First, inscriptions on cognate monuments always refer to individuals. Often the tribal or kin-group affiliation of such persons is recorded but only as additional information situating that individual in society. I know of no instances of an inscription referring only to a group *per se*. If symbols (either individually or in combination) represent groups ('tribes', lineages, families) it would be impossible to specify a particular individual. Even if a person could be identified as the child of a union of two families it would not be possible to differentiate among siblings, and, in some cases, cousins. Second, perhaps more importantly, if the symbols are hereditary 'badges' of group identity then we would expect to see regional variation in their distribution reflecting the

regional power-bases of the major families. Also we would see fluctuation over the centuries as powerful lineages decline and obscure families rise to prominence – as we see happening so clearly in contemporary Ireland. The group emblem theory stands or falls primarily on a historically credible geographical and chronological distribution of the symbols.

Statistical studies to date have, to my mind, been inconclusive on the question of possible regional variation in the distribution of symbols and symbol combinations. It has been asserted both that there is and that there is not geographical variation but none have rigorously tested the patterns for statistical significance and often the numbers in question are very small. Study of the distribution of symbols over time is hampered by the lack of closely datable examples but it would at least be possible to compare Class I distribution with Class II for a crude 'early' vs. 'late' comparison. Statistical analysis of any variation in distribution from context to context would be problematic because of the small number of non-lapidary examples to have survived in the archaeological record, but a few observations are still possible (eg the absence of the mirror and comb from non-lapidary examples). It is true that names go in and out of fashion and that certain names are favourites of certain families but, in my opinion, given-names better explain the lack of gross regional variation and the apparent stability of the relative frequency of the different symbols through time (ie the symbols most frequent on Class I are also most frequent on Class II, etc.). As Samson's graphs show, the distribution curve of symbol combinations is very close to the distribution curve of individual personal names among the contemporary neighbours of the Picts (1992).

The importance of sound statistical analysis to the future study of the symbols is clear. Though there have in the past been some statistical studies of symbol these have been rudimentary and, in some cases, fatally flawed. Jackson conducted a statistical study (1984), though his calculations are based on contentious views regarding which are the 'genuine' symbols (though some of his tables are useful). Other helpful collections of statistics can be found in articles by Murray (1986), Alcock (1989), and Samson (1992). What is required, however, is something altogether more comprehensive and searching. The total sample is certainly large enough for meaningful statistical analysis, though comparisons within the sample, say of the context or combinations of a particular symbol of even medium frequency, will often be at the margins of statistical meaning. I am nonetheless confident that a comprehensive study of the spatial, chronological and contextual distribution of symbols, individually and in combination, using the techniques of multivariate statistics would produce a number of insights, particularly if the results were combined with analysis of comparative writing systems.

Conclusion

There are several hundred extant symbol 'texts' on a variety of media from a wide geographical area over a very long period of time. From this, the first thing we can deduce about the Pictish symbol system is that it worked! Whatever it was intended to convey, it performed its function sufficiently well that people all over northern Britain found it useful and continued to use it, generation after generation, for perhaps as long as four centuries (from the fifth or sixth century to the ninth or early tenth). This fact is all the more striking when we realise that throughout that period the roman and the ogham alphabets were also in use in Pictland (Forsyth forthcoming 1997). We have yet to discover the special role that only the symbols could perform which meant that the system was able to hold its own against the others for such a long time.

Looking at the way the symbols were used in practice I have highlighted the similarities between the use of symbols and the use of alphabetic writing in the British Isles in the same period. By adopting an essentially synchronic and de-contextualized approach to the system **as a system**, I have attempted to put forward an alternative way of thinking about its structure and, by implication, origins. If I have been unable to go beyond a series of impressionistic statements it is because to do otherwise would require a thorough and comprehensive statistical analysis of the entire body of symbol data – an undertaking currently beyond me. What I have tried to show is that there are new and different ways of approaching the problem and that one of these may lead to the much anticipated breakthrough. Until that happens, however, you may rest assured that the Picts will retain this, their last enigma.

Acknowledgements

An earlier version of this paper was presented at the Tenth International Congress of Celtic Studies, Edinburgh, July 1995. I am grateful to those present for their helpful questions and comments. Stephen Driscoll, Joseph Eska, John Higgitt, and Ross Samson offered many insightful comments on various drafts of this paper, and I am most grateful for their generous assistance. In particular I wish to express my gratitude to Lauran Toorians for sharing with me his knowledge of Mesoamerican writing systems, and for a stimulating discussion on concepts of writing. All errors of fact and judgement are, of course, my own.

Notes

1 At the beginning of my career in Pictish studies our honorand, in her role as undergraduate dissertation supervisor, offered me the following sage advice, 'avoid the symbol stones: there lies madness'. Until now I have conscientiously followed her advice; on reading this she may wish I had heeded it a little longer. I offer the following to her, a continuing source of inspiration, in appreciation of the many pleasurable hours spent discussing a shared enthusiasm.

2 Out of a total corpus of probably over 300 symbol statements there are only a tiny handful of intact objects bearing a single unpaired 'core' symbol. Most of the symbols carved on portable objects stand in pairs and, though possible relationships are often difficult to determine among the jumble of carving in some of the caves, there are unambiguous examples of pairs there too, for instance the 'double-disc and Z-rod' touching the 'beast's head' in the Doo Cave at Wemyss.

3 The Ulbster cross-slab has a hippocamp and a lion paired with two other symbols. Since these motifs occur nowhere else in symbol pairs and are derived ultimately from imported illuminated manuscripts, it can be taken that, at most, Ulbster is a late and isolated example of the one-off co-option of non-symbol designs. It may be that the paired layout of the non-symbols is inspired by the usual symbol statements and the four panels created by the arms of the cross, cf Migvie.

4 Unless otherwise stated, references to individual stones will be found in RCAHMS 1994 and in Allen and Anderson 1903, III.

5 Or is Monymusk's (horizontal) stepped rectangle with curved ends (**2g**) a variant on the (vertical) stepped rectangle?

6 Migvie's V-rod version of the arch is unique (**2h**). It appears in a pair, so qualifies as a 'core' symbol, but

remains rather doubtful in occurring only on this rather unusual Class II stone.

7   I have not included the goose symbol here nor the three uniquely-occurring geometrics (**2f**). The 'bow and arrow' is a bit strained as 'discoid', but the others would fit into the remaining categories easily enough.

8   Though, perhaps some of the rarer Pictish symbols have a status within the symbol system analogous to the baroque supplementary ogham characters, the *forfeda*: eg the three uniquely-occurring (Class I) geometric symbols which are particularly complex in their form – the 'bow and arrow' from Congash (Allen and Anderson 1903, III, 96–7), the double-hook from Mortlach (Simpson 1926, 274–8), and the embellished square on Kintore 4 (Woodham 1974).

9   There are symbols carved in the caves at Covesea, Moray (Allen and Anderson 1903, III, 129–31) and in Fife at Wemyss (Ritchie and Stevenson 1993) and Caiplie (Murray 1961); and on a slab from Gurness, Orkney (Ritchie 1969).

10 An ox-bone, presumably a divination token, from Burrian, Orkney, is carved with two clearly identifiable symbols (Allen and Anderson 1903, III, 25–6); the Portsoy 'whetstone', a ceremonial object of unknown purpose, is carved with what may be symbols (Thomas 1963, 48 pl II); and there are a small handful of incised or painted pebbles from various sites bearing symbols or symbol-like decoration (ibid, 46).

11 There are the seven pieces of symbol-inscribed metalwork extant: the brooch from Carn Liath, Sutherland (Ritchie 1989, 51); the bronze plaque from Monifieth (Laing 1993, 105 no 240); the clasps of two of the massive silver chains (Henderson 1979, Laing 1993, 101–2, nos 221–2); two plaques and a hand-pin from the Norries Law silver hoard (Youngs 1989, 26–8, Laing 1993, 78, 98–9, nos 121, 211–12). I omit for now the more dubious remains of the 'double-disc' plaques from Ballinaby, Islay (Laing and Laing 1993, 116 fig 91).

References

ALCOCK, E 1989 Pictish stones Class I: where and how? *Glasgow Archaeological Journal* 15 (1988-89), 1–21.

ALCOCK, L 1996 *Ur-symbols in the Pictograph-system of the Picts. Pictish Arts Society Journal* 9, 2–5.

ALLEN, J R and ANDERSON, J 1903 *The Early Christian Monuments of Scotland*, 3 parts. Edinburgh (repr with an Introduction by Isabel Henderson, 2 vols, Balgavies, Angus, 1993).

BIRLEY, R 1977 *Vindolanda: A Roman Frontier Post on Hadrian's Wall* (New Aspects of Antiquity). London.

BISCHOFF, B 1991 *Latin Palaeography. Antiquity and the Middle Ages* (trans D Ó Cróinín and D Ganz). Cambridge.

BOURKE, C
– 1993 *Patrick: the Archaeology of a Saint*. Belfast.
– 1995 Further notes on the Clonmore Shrine. *Seanchas Ardmhacha*, 16.2, 27–32.

BROWN, J 1993 St Ninian's Isle silver hoard: the inscriptions. In Bately, J, Brown, M and Roberts, J (eds) *A Palaeographer's View: The Selected Writings of Julian Brown*, 245–51. [Originally published as part of a joint paper with AC O'Dell, R B K Stevenson, H J Penderleith and R L S Bruce-Mitford in *Antiquity* 33 (1959), 250–55.] London.

CLANCY, T 1996 Iona, Scotland and the Céli Dé. In Crawford (ed), 111–30.

CLOSE-BROOKS, J 1984 Pictish and other burials. In Friell and Watson (eds), 87–114.

COE, M D 1992 *Breaking the Maya Code*. New York.

CRYSTAL, D 1987 *The Cambridge Encyclopedia of Language*. Cambridge.

CRAWFORD, B E (ed) 1996 *Scotland in Dark Age Britain*. St Andrews.

DIACK, F C 1944 *The Inscriptions of Pictland: An Essay on the Sculptured and Inscribed Stones of the North-East and North of Scotland: with other writings and collections*. Aberdeen.

DRISCOLL, S T
– 1986 Symbol stones and Pictish ethnography (review of *Symbol Stones of Scotland*). *Scottish Archaeological Review*, 4 pt 1, 59–64.
– 1988 Power and authority in Early Historic Scotland: Pictish symbol stones and other documents. In Gledhill *et al* (eds), 215–35.

FORSYTH, K
– 1996a *The Ogham Inscriptions of Scotland: An Edited Corpus*. PhD dissertation, Harvard University Ann Arbor.
– 1996b The Inscriptions on the Dupplin Cross. In Bourke, C (ed) *From the Isles of the North: Early Medieval Art in Ireland and Britain* (Proceedings of the Third International Conference on Insular Art, Belfast 1994), 237–44. Belfast.
– 1996c The Ogham-inscribed spindle-whorl from Buckquoy: evidence for the Irish language in pre-Viking Orkney? *Proc Soc Antiq Scot*, 125 (1996), 677–96.
– forthcoming 1997 Literacy in Pictland. In Pryce, H (ed) *Literacy in Medieval Celtic Societies*. Cambridge, (in press).

FOSTER, S 1990 Pins, combs and the chronology of Later Atlantic Iron Age settlement. In Armit, I (ed) *Beyond the Brochs: Changing Perspectives on the Later Iron Age in Atlantic Scotland*, 143–74. Edinburgh.

FOX, C 1949 Celtic mirror handles in Britain with special

reference to the Colchester handle. *Archaeologia Cambrensis* 100 (1948-49), 24–44.

FRIELL, J G P and WATSON, W G (eds) 1984 *Pictish Studies: Settlement, Burial and Art in Dark Age Northern Britain.* (*BAR Brit Ser* 125). Oxford.

GLEDHILL, J, BENDER, B and LARSEN, M T (eds) 1988 *State and Society: the emergence and development of social hierarchy and political centralization .* London.

HARVEY, A 1987 Early literacy in Ireland: the evidence from ogam. *Cambridge Medieval Celtic Studies* 14, 1–14.

HENDERSON, I
– 1958 The origin centre of the Pictish symbol stones. *Proc Soc Antiq Scot* 91 (1957-58), 44–60.

– 1971 The meaning of the Pictish symbol stones. In Meldrum, E (ed) *The Dark Ages in the Highlands*, 53–67. Inverness.

– 1979 The silver chain from Whitecleugh, Shieldholm, Crawfordjohn, Lanarkshire. *Transactions of the Dumfries and Galloway Natural History and Antiquarian Society,* Third Series, 54, 20–8.

– 1986 The 'David cycle' in Pictish art. In Higgitt, J (ed) *Early Medieval Sculpture in Britain and Ireland.* (*BAR Brit Ser* 152), 87–123.

HENRY, F 1952 A wooden hut on Inishkea North, Co. Mayo. *Journal of the Royal Society of Antiquaries of Ireland* 82, 163–78.

HICKS, C 1993 The Pictish Class I animals. In Spearman and Higgitt (eds), 196–202.

HOLDER, N 1990 Aspects of ogam with particular reference to the ogam-inscribed portable objects. Unpublished MA dissertation, University of London.

HUNTER, J
– 1990 Pool, Sanday: a case study for the Late Iron Age and Viking Periods. In Armit, I (ed) *Beyond the Brochs: Changing Perspectives on the Later Iron Age in Atlantic Scotland*, 175–9. Edinburgh

– 1997 *A Persona for the Northern Picts* (Groam House Lecture 7). Rosemarkie.

INGLIS, J 1987 Patterns in stone, patterns in population: symbol stones seen from beyond the Mounth. In Small, A (ed) *The Picts – A New Look at Old Problems*, 73–9. Dundee.

JACKSON, A 1984 *The Symbol Stones of Scotland: A social anthropological resolution of the problem of the Picts.* Stromness.

JACKSON, K H 1973 An ogam inscription near Blackwaterfoot. *Antiquity* 47, 53–54, pl ix.

LAING, L R 1993 *A Catalogue of Celtic Ornamental Metalwork in the British Isles c.AD 400–1200* (*BAR Brit Ser* 229). Oxford.

LAING, L R and LAING, J
– 1984 The date and origin of the Pictish symbols. *Proc Soc Antiq Scot* 114 (1984), 261–76.

– 1993 *The Picts and the Scots.* Stroud.

LLOYD-MORGAN, G 1980 Roman mirrors and Pictish symbols: a note on trade and contact. In Hanson, W S and Keppie, L J F (eds) *Roman Frontier Studies: Papers Presented to the Twelfth International Congress of Roman Frontier Studies.* (*BAR Int Ser* 71:1). Oxford.

MACALISTER, R A S 1945, 1949 *Corpus Inscriptionum Insularum Celticarum*, 2 vols. Dublin.

McMANUS, D 1991 *A Guide to Ogam* (*Maynooth Monographs* 4). Maynooth.

MICHELLI, P 1996 The inscriptions on pre-Norman Irish reliquaries. *Proceedings of the Royal Irish Academy* 96C, 1–48.

MURRAY, G 1986 The declining Pictish symbol – a re-appraisal. *Proc Soc Antiq Scot* 116 (1986), 223–53.

MURRAY, J E L 1961 Rock cut symbols in Caiplie Caves. *Proc Soc Antiq Scot,* 94 (1960-61), 324–5, pl 32.

NASH-WILLIAMS, V E 1950 *The Early Christian Monuments of Wales.* Cardiff.

OKASHA, E
– 1985 The non-ogam inscriptions of Pictland. *Cambridge Medieval Celtic Studies* 9, 43–70.

– 1996 The Early Christian carved and inscribed stones of south-west Britain. In Crawford, B E (ed) *Scotland in Dark Age Britain* (St John's House Occasional Papers 6), 21–35. St Andrews.

RCAHMS 1994 Royal Commission on the Ancient and Historic Monuments of Scotland *Pictish Symbol Stones: A handlist 1994.* Edinburgh.

RITCHIE, A 1989 *Picts: an introduction to the life of the picts and the carved stones in the care of the Secretary of State for Scotland.* Edinburgh.

RITCHIE, J N G 1969 Two new Pictish symbol stones from Orkney. *Proc Soc Antiq Scot,* 101 (1968-69), 130–3.

RITCHIE, J N G and STEVENSON, J N 1993 Pictish cave art at East Wemyss, Fife. In Spearman and Higgitt (eds), 203–8.

SAMSON, R 1992 The reinterpretation of the Pictish symbols. *Journal of the British Archaeological Association* 145, 29–65.

SIMS-WILLIAMS, P 1992 The additional letters of the ogam alphabet. *Cambridge Medieval Celtic Studies* 23, 29–75.

SIMPSON, W D 1926 Notes on Lulach's Stone, Kildrummy, Aberdeenshire, a symbol stone recently found in Mortlach Churchyard, Banffshire and other antiquities. *Proc Soc Antiq Scot,* 60 (1925-26), 273–80.

SPEARMAN, R M and HIGGITT, J (eds) 1993 *The Age of Migrating Ideas, Early Medieval Art in Northern Britain and Ireland* (Proceedings of the Second International Conference on Insular Art, Edinburgh 1991). Edinburgh/Stroud.

STEVENSON, J 1989 The beginnings of literacy in Ireland. *Proceedings of the Royal Irish Academy* 89C, 127–65.

STEVENSON, R B K
– 1955 Pictish art. In Wainwright, F T (ed) *The Problem of the Picts*, 97–128. Edinburgh.

– 1993 Further thoughts on some well known problems. In Spearman and Higgitt (eds), 16–26.

SWIFT, C 1997 *Ogam Stones and the Earliest Irish Christians (Maynooth Monographs, series minor* 2). Maynooth.

TAYLOR, S 1996 Place-names and the early church in Eastern Scotland. In Crawford (ed), 93–110.

THOMAS, C
– 1961 Animal art in the Scottish Iron Age. *Archaeological Journal* 118, 14–64.

– 1963 The interpretation of the Pictish symbols. *Archaeological Journal* 120, 31–97.

– 1984 The Pictish Class I symbol stones. In Friell and Watson (eds), 169–87.

– 1994 *And Shall These Mute Stones Speak?: Post-Roman Inscriptions in Western Britain (Dalrymple Archaeological Monographs* 2). Cardiff.

WAGNER, A 1946 *Heraldry in England.* Harmondsworth.

WOODHAM, A A 1974 [Notice of discovery of Kintore 4, Class I symbol stone.] *Discovery and Excavation in Scotland*, 1974. Dundee.

YOUNGS, S (ed) 1989 *'The Work of Angels': Masterpieces of Celtic Metalwork, 6th–9th Centuries AD.* London.

Pictish Fictions

Carola Hicks

Perceptions of the Picts from antiquity to the present day have frequently reflected our views about ourselves and contemporary society just as much as the processes of historical research. In addition to the mythologies, legends and fantasies purporting to be the truth which have flourished from the time of the classical writers onwards (Ritchie 1994) there has also been a role for the Picts in fiction, both historical and general, since novelists even more than archaeologists and historians have used the Picts as a stimulus for their own imaginations; some have selected the Pictish era as a suitable period for a historical novel while others have made more subtle uses of Pictish themes as a source of literary inspiration. Isabel Henderson's lucid studies of the Picts have never involved such fantasy or bias but she has over the years been the courteous recipient of many exotic theories based upon interpretations of allegedly factual evidence. As a tribute to her work and friendship, I describe here some of the ways in which the Picts have been presented in real fiction.

The historical novel (see Buckley and Williams 1912, Sheppard 1930, Marriott 1940, Lukacs 1962) is a genre which developed in the late eighteenth century as part of the Romantic reaction against the Enlightenment. Preoccupations with the post-classical past focused on the Middle Ages, explored in painting and literature, also contributing to a greater sense of a national identity at a time of political upheaval. Sir Walter Scott is frequently hailed as the first major practitioner on the grounds of his deliberate historicism (which in some ways even renounced (Romanticism for Realism); the format was to remain immensely popular throughout the nineteenth century, when the aims of historical novelists were not merely recreational but also patriotic and educational; such motivations carried on well into the twentieth century.

However, we should bear in mind Sir Francis Palgrave's comment that historical novels were mortal enemies to history together with Leslie Stephen's perceptive addition that they were also mortal enemies to fiction.

A recent survey (Collins 1990) defines at least three main types of historical novel; first, that which is ostensibly set in the past but has limited understanding of the period and minimal reference to historical events; second, that with a properly researched background, but with stereotyped or anachronistic characters; thirdly, and the most rare, something authentically researched, with well drawn characters, thus allowing genuine historical issues to be examined. Novels involving the Picts can be fitted into all three categories.

Medieval Scotland was recognised as an entirely appropriate topos for the Gothick novel. Mrs Radcliffe's *Mysteries of Udolpho*, which so thrilled Catherine Morland, had netted the author the sum of £500, a huge fee for 1794; the fact that she could negotiate such a figure resulted from the reputation of her previous novels, the first of which, *The Castles of Athlin and Dunblane* (1789), was set in early medieval, though not specifically Pictish Scotland. While the earliest of Sir Walter Scott's novels is set no earlier than the late eleventh century (*Count Robert of Paris*), he draws upon his own knowledge of the Picts as subject matter in *The Antiquary* (1816). This was partly inspired by Scott's journey around the Western Isles, as reported in his journal of the voyage, *Northern Lights*, where he describes in some detail (Laughlan 1982) the Shetland brochs then attributed to the Picts. Transposed to fiction, his indiscriminate antiquarian, Jonathan Oldbuck, takes advantage of his horse casting a shoe to take a break on his northward journey with his young friend Lovel "aided by his desire of showing his companion a Pict's camp, or Round-about, a subject which he had been elaborately discussing, and of which a specimen 'very curious and perfect indeed', happened to exist about a hundred yards distant". Later on, there is an animated debate about the origins of the Picts, whether Gothic or Celtic, which satirised an issue of extreme concern to contemporary antiquarians and philologists; Oldbuck claims the Picts spoke a Gothic, i.e. Saxon dialect, while his old friend and intellectual adversary, Sir Arthur, cites the king-list as evidence for their Celtic origins: "it was a copious language, and they were a great and powerful people – built two steeples; one at Brechin, one at Abernethy. The Pictish maidens of the blood royal were kept in Edinburgh Castle, thence called Castrum Puellarum." "A childish legend," said Oldbuck, "invented to give consequence to trumpery womankind. It was called the Maiden Castle, *quasi lucus a non lucendo*, because it resisted every attack, and women never do."

The historical novelist has a very wide time span from which to select a particular era as canvas; one popular period is that of the last days of the Roman occupation of Britain, a particular theme being the relationship between Roman and native. The Picts appear here as one of a range of Rome's enemies, not the subjugated recipients of Roman culture but beyond the Wall, and therefore a sinister and mysterious Other.

Herbert Maxwell's *A Duke of Britain: A Romance of the Fourth Century* (1895) is set mainly in Galloway and has for hero Kenneth Maccdairn Coilnaach, the historical Cunedda of Galloway, whose victory over the combined forces of Highland Picts and Irish Scots results in his appointment as a Centurion of the Sixth Legion, in which many Southern Picts serve as auxiliaries. Called to Milan by the Emperor, he meets an old enemy, the Pictish chieftain, Crindal, whose daughter is married to a Roman legionary. As a result of the power struggles between the Emperor Honorius and the various claimants to his position, the legions are withdrawn, and the Britons must defend themselves against the encroaching invaders – Kenneth is appointed Duke of Britain. The Picts are seen here as irredeemably alien, their Druids in conflict with Ninian's mission: "But seriously, Kenneth, do you think these Picts are capable of being made as civilised as the Honorian Brigade?. They seem to me to be so hopelessly savage!" A.J. Church and R. Putnam's *The Count of the Saxon Shore:*

a Tale of the Departure of the Romans from Britain (1887), set also at the end of the fourth century, describes the attempts of Count Aelius to protect the coasts against the resurgent Britons, invading Saxons and raiding Picts who, in a dramatic sequence, besiege the brave Count at Winchester. J. Baxter's *The Meeting of the Ways* (c1890), set in the same period, concentrates on the struggle between Picts and Romans around the Wall. These late Victorian novels express contemporary concerns about the role of Empire, and the seeds of decay then being perceived as innate in the system. They are well-researched, drawing on contemporary historical and archaeological studies, and were seen as approved reading matter for students of history. They contain stirring scenes, emphasising moral values, with noble heroes, passive heroines and strong villains, the Picts generally among the latter.

There are infinitely more shades of light and dark in Rudyard Kipling's interpretation of the same period in *Puck of Pook's Hill* (1908). Una and Dan's excursions into the past include their meeting with Parnesius, a British-born Roman; the three linked stories, *A Centurion of the Thirtieth*, *On the Great Wall*, and *The Winged Hats*, contain Parnesius' unfolding narrative of events at the beginning of the fifth century, incorporating Kipling's own insights into the British in India, the ambitious status of the Anglo-Indian and the power politics of the Great Game.

Parnesius describes Hadrian's Wall: "It was built long ago, across North Britain, to keep out the Painted People – Picts you call them. Father had fought in the great Pict War that lasted more than twenty years." Parnesius' father blames the troubled times on the fact that "Rome has forsaken her gods and must be punished … we may save Britain. To do that, we must keep the Painted People back". Yet Parnesius does not really reward the Picts as enemies. He refers to them as "little beasts", the same words that Stalky & Co use to describe the Lower Third, and, later, the native units of Sikhs and Pathans in the story, *The Slaves of the Lamp*, which describes the adult Stalky's gallant exploits on the frontiers of India. Parnesius reveals the same affectionate yet patronising attitude: "There is never harm in a Pict if you but take the trouble to find out what he wants"; "they are improvident little animals – send them a shipload of corn now and then".

Parnesius serves on the Wall (described as a Siberia for

those soldiers who had blotted their copybooks) where uneasy alliances were forged with 'tame' Picts: "A Pict – there were many such – who speaks a few words of our tongue and slips across the Wall to sell ponies and wolf-hounds". With such Picts, Parnesius learns to 'take Heather': "hunting in the Pict country with a tame Pict. You are quite safe as long as you are his guest, and wear a sprig of heather where it can be seen ... Old Allo, the one-eyed withered little Pict from whom we bought our ponies, was our special friend ... The Roman-born officers rather looked down on us for doing this but we preferred the heather to their amusements". Allo was tattooed "blue, green and red from his forehead to his ankles. He said it was part of his religion".

The animosity between Pict and Roman is defined by Allo: "You shoot us Picts when we come to borrow a little iron from the Iron Ditch; you burn our heather, which is all our crop; you trouble us with your catapults. Then you hide behind the Wall and scorch us with Greek fire."

It is from Allo and the Picts' more efficient channels of communication that Parnesius learns of General Maximus' depletion of the British legions in his attempts to become Emperor; on a hunting expedition with Allo they spot the Winged Hats, the invading Saxons, who terrify the Picts far more than the tired legions. The Picts' main concern is to avoid being crushed in the struggle between the two greater powers. Maximus offers Parnesius control over the Picts "to keep the North quiet till I win Gaul" but Allo says that it is too late; the Picts need to be on the side of the Winged Hats, the power of the future. He offers Maximus a further three years' peace, and the Winged Hats are temporarily kept at bay; but the news of Maximus' defeat and execution by Theodosius "runs through the heather like fire", the Winged Hats invade, and the Picts reluctantly throw in their lot with the Saxons, although Parnesius describes how "they were as much our spies as our enemies, for the Winged Hats oppressed them and took their winter stores. Ah, foolish Little People."

Details of Pictish life include their passion for hunting, their long-distance smoke signals, and the role of honey in their economy, to make their "holy heather-wine"; this is Kipling's reworking of the old legend of the Pictish heather ale, the subject of a ballad by Robert Louis Stevenson. The sequence of stories ends with the poem, *A Pict Song*:

We are the Little Folk – we!
Too little to love or to hate.
Leave us alone and you'll see
How we can drag down the Great!
We are the worm in the wood!
We are the rot at the root!
We are the germ in the blood!
We are the thorn in the foot!

This stress on their small stature reflects the deep-rooted belief, being challenged at the beginning of the century, in the indigenous nature of the Picts.

Another imaginative recreation of the Saxon settlements with a specifically Pictish accent is *Ninny's Boat* by Clive King (1980), which echoes the 'otherness' of the Picts proposed by Kipling, but also addresses the topic of an adolescent's search for self-identity (a theme for a novel only appropriate after the invention of teenagers in the 1980s). Ninny, short for Ninian, was the son of a converted Pictish king, but was kidnapped as a small child by pirates and sold as a slave to Angles on Jutland, with whom he emigrates back to Britain in a fleet of longships as a result of the increasing flooding of their homelands. He travels from East Anglia to Whithorn, his sense of alienation finally dissolved when his Pictish nationality is rediscovered – he is short and dark, and called 'black beetle' by his tall, fair-haired Saxon masters. In East Anglia, Ninny meets the mysterious and cat-like Mab, and for the first time recognises someone of his own kin, dark haired, black-eyed, with pointed ears and pointed chin; Picts are here presented as the ancient inhabitants of the north, the little people who lurk underground and travel at night to hide from the many waves of subsequent invaders. Ninny and Mab are identified as "the little people who don't exist" by a young Roman Briton, and other Picts in the story are shown in a permanent secret underworld, watching the battles between Roman and Saxon.

As popular as the early fifth-century end of Roman Britain is the late sixth-century coming of Columba to Iona and his conversion of the Picts. This topic also belongs to a wider format, very popular from the late Victorian period, dealing with the general theme of the conversion of the Anglo-Saxons and Britons to Christianity. There was the very clear moral lesson that the invading Saxon or Viking was pagan, therefore evil, and threatening the beliefs of virtuous Celts and Picts already converted to Christianity.

The personality of Columba himself has been a major attraction; the nature of his mission, the relationship with the Pictish king Brude and his magicians, or Druids, as described in Adomnan's biography have proved an irresistible stimulus to novelists. Their tales range from Mary Outram's exciting *Branan the Pict: A Story of the Days of St Columba* (1890), to short stories by GF Elliott ('St Columba' in *The Romance of Early British Life from the Earliest Times to the Coming of the Danes* (c1905), Mrs Andrew Lang ('St Columba' in *The Book of Saints and Heroes* ed. Andrew Lang, 1912), Dorothy King ('St Columba' in *Stories of Scotland in Days of Old*, c1930), and Patricia Lynch ('Columcille, Dove of the Church' in *Knights of God: Tales and Legends of the Irish Saints* (1945). The most recent novel is Nigel Tranter's *Columba* (1987).

This combines Tranter's unrivalled knowledge of the geography of Scotland, including meticulously detailed descriptions of the route from the Western Isles to Inverness, with some solid research. Tranter does not treat the Picts as exotic aliens but as Celts, not so different from the Dal Riatans, with whom they have intermarried in the west, with a high level of culture, art and political organisation, but dominated by their Druid-led religion; Columba is presented as a roving ambassador for peace as much as a missionary, who tries to stress the elements in common between the warring factions as a means of conversion. For Tranter, Pictish symbols have a rather flexible function; they have already been sanctified by a cross in the neglected chapel which Columba finds on his arrival on Iona. He and his colleagues inspect the Dunadd boar, and deconsecrate a Druid shrine in a cave by Loch Caolisport; the altar is surmounted by carvings of V-rod and crescent, Z-rod and double-disc, and Pictish beast; other carvings in the cave include the mirror and comb, and 'cauldron'. As they travel inland, they are increasingly impressed by Pictish carving on standing stones, both the symbols and portraits of warriors, druids and huntsmen – all present by c570, so Tranter clearly supports an early chronology for Class I. On Skye, the hostile Pictish King Cathal wears a silver chain as his badge of office and his druids use carved stone balls ceremonially; his guards are women warriors. Another novel by Tranter shows his continuing interest in early Scotland and the conflict

between pagan Picts and early Christians; *Druid Sacrifice* (1993) is set in the sixth century and is the story of Thanea, the mother of St Kentigern (who appears briefly in *Columba*). Thanea is the niece of King Arthur, and daughter of Loth, King of the Southern Picts, or Gododdin; allowed by her father to be educated in a Christian convent, she is cast out when she refuses to marry the pagan Owen of Rheged. In her travels through Scotland, she visits Forteviot and meets Nechtan, the Mormaer of Fortrenn. Tranter here describes the matrilineal succession of the Picts, but again emphasises their essential Celticness. As in *Columba*, there is fear of the invading Saxons, and the need for Picts and Britons to make alliances to defeat them, as well as graphic accounts of Druid ceremonies.

Iona is used more as a focus for an Ossianic invocation of a Highland twilight by William Sharp, a supporter of the Celtic Revival movement at the end of the nineteenth century, whose nom-de-plume for his most romantically Celtic writings was the more convincing-sounding Fiona MacLeod. *The Divine Adventurer* (1900) is a series of reminiscences about Iona, which is described as "the Mecca of the Gael", with Columba the epitome of the Celt, facing the antagonism of the Picts and their Druids, with their more ancient tongue. The Picts are treated here as definitely non-Celtic.

The later and slightly better documented history of the Picts has also inspired novelists, concerned both with known historical individuals and imaginary characters. Tranter's third dark-age story, *Kenneth* (1990), is set in the ninth century and is a study of Kenneth MacAlpin, and his reconciliation of Picts and Scots to create a new nation. E. Kellett's *The Conflict, A Saga of the Seventh Century* (1930) is about King Ecgfrith and his campaigns against the Picts, while in M. Macbride's *King Penda's Captain, A Romance of Fighting in the Days of the Anglo-Saxons* (1909), the hero is the young Pict who serves the King of Mercia; it is set in Mercia and in Pictland. Henry Treece wrote several adventure stories about the Viking period; his *Viking's Dawn* (1955), the first part of a trilogy, is set in the late eighth century, and tells of the raiding voyages of the *Nameless* and her crew to north-east Scotland and then via the Orkneys to Ireland. One of the main characters is the Pictish seafarer Wolf, who has left his own country to live with the Vikings. Wolf joins in the vicious fights against the

Picts, whom Treece, unusually for novelists on the Picts, describes as tall, with red hair, and woad-painted faces; they do drink the familiar heather-honey ale. One of their leaders is a Druid, who wears a cap of catskin. The Picts are shown here more honourable than the Vikings, who steal their gold treasure.

In the majority of novels, women generally play minor or supporting roles but in Dorothy MacNab Ramsay's 1990s trilogy, three strong women are at the very centre of events, appropriate feminist exemplars of the allegedly matrilinear system of the Picts. The first, set in the sixth century is *Honey in the Mead* (1991), recounting the adventures of Caterin, daughter of King Brude of Inverness (she also appears in Tranter's *Columba*, where she is called Nessa), who, the author suggests, is depicted as the lady rider on the Hilton of Cadboll slab. *The Flame Within* (1993) is set against the background of the Anglian advance into the North in the late seventh century; Pictish princess Tansen married Eanfrith of Northumbria, becomes Queen of Pictland after his murder by Ecgfrith, and contributes to the defeat of the Angles in the battle of Dunnichen. In *The Harps are Hushed* (1995), Alma, Queen of Picts, confronts the disintegration of her kingdom in the ninth century.

A far more oblique approach to the Picts is that of Arthur Ransome, whose knowledge was undoubtedly derived from the conversation and writing of his old friend W.G. Collingwood, archaeologist, authority on Scandinavian sagas, companion and biographer of Ruskin, and historical novelist himself, using his beloved Lake District as the setting. Collingwood's *Thorstein of The Mere* (1895) is a tenth-century saga, describing how Norse, Gaels and Scots attempt to withstand the encroaching Saxons; *The Likeness of King Elfwald: A Study of Northumbria and Iona at the Beginning of the Viking Age* (1917) is set at the beginning of the ninth century, and includes a graphic account of the sacking of Iona by the first Viking invaders.

Ransome stayed many times with Collingwood and his wife at their home in the Lake District, adopting them as an honorary aunt and uncle who provided the warmth and stability lacking in his own first marriage. He was also a close friend of their son, R.G. Collingwood, distinguished Roman archaeologist and philosopher. Lakes Windermere and Coniston were the background for many of the Swallows' and Amazons' adventures, one of which,

The Picts and the Martyrs (1943) is about the summer when the brainy Dick and Dorothea, whose father is a professor of archaeology, are hidden by the Amazon Nancy from the dreaded Great-Aunt who has unexpectedly come to stay.

The romantic and literary Dorothea compares their position with that of the Picts, whom she defines as "Ancient Britons ... Prehistorics. Original inhabitants. They had to hide from the invaders and went on living secretly in caves and in the end people thought they were fairies and used to leave milk outside the door for them. Something like that. I heard Father talking about it." And later "Picts were the people who went on living secretly when everybody thought they were extinct. At least I think so. I've asked Mother to find out from Father. He'll know."

Like all Ransome's fictional parents, Mother turns up trumps and writes –

> "now about your Picts. Your father says that in a way you are right and in a way you are wrong. There used to be a theory among folklorists that the origin of the belief in fairies and such was the half secret presence in remote places of the original inhabitants of the country who had been for the most part driven out by conquering tribes. I think I have remembered his exact words. He says it is an exploded theory, but he also says that most theories get exploded sooner or later."

> "what does it mean when a theory's exploded?" said Dorothea. "Just that someone's invented another" said Dick... "So the Picts are all right."

Ransome is here referring to the changing theories about the indigenous nature of the Picts, incorporating their legendary small stature, with which Collingwood would have been more than familiar. There is also a reflection of this in Ransome's *Great Northern* (1947), set in the Hebrides; his characters find the remains of a broch, which is firmly associated with the Picts, although Dorothea reveals a lamentable imprecision in chronology for one who aspires to write historical novels):

> "They could all see it now, a green, turf-covered mound on the top of the hill, and, as Titty came breathlessly up to it, Roger came scrambling out.
> "What about this?" he said.
> "It's a Pict-house," said Dorothea. A real one. Prehistoric, like that one they showed us on Skye."
> ... Dick had just glanced at the tunnel, and then climbed

the steep side of the mound.

"I thought so" he said. "The roof's fallen in. It's just like that one on Skye. A room in the middle and a tunnel for getting in and out".

Dick makes a plan of the Pict-house in his note-book — drawn by Ransome, who did his own illustrations for all his stories, it shows a circular mound, marked 'about 7ft high' and 30 paces round outside, and is clearly based on direct observation, Ransome having also sailed around the northern coasts. The ruined broch plays quite an important role as look-out and meeting place in this story of the Swallows and Amazons' attempts to foil an illicit egg collector.

A modern genre is that of fantasy, or science fiction — Picts have actually appeared in *Conan the Barbarian*. But the most sinister evocation of the Picts was that created at the beginning of the century by John Buchan in his horror story 'No Man's Land' (first published in *The Watcher by the Threshold and Other Tales*, 1902) It is the tale of Oxford Fellow and the Deputy Professor of Northern Antiquities, Mr Graves, whose main interests are "the ancient life of the North, of the Celts and the Northmen and the unknown Pictish tribes". On a walking holiday in Galloway, he discovers, to alarming effect, that the Picts still survive in the hills. Buchan was exploring the then still current topic of controversy already tackled by Scott in *The Antiquary* that the Picts were quite separate from the Celts, of far earlier and indigenous origin. "I reflected on the older and stranger race who were said to have held the hilltops. The Picts, the Picti — what in the name of goodness were they? They had troubled me in all my studies, a sort of blank wall to put an end to speculation". Another area of archaeological concern addressed in this story was the nature and extent of the Pictish occupation of south-west Scotland.

Graves at first mocks the views of an academic colleague who suggests that the legend of the Brownie, "the little swart man of uncommon strength and cleverness who does good and ill indiscriminately and then disappears", recorded in Galloway as recently as 1756, was evidence of the survival of an ancient race of Picts in the hills. Gradually, a nightmare develops; one evening, lost on the moors, with night falling, Graves spots a figure "little and squat and dark; naked apparently, but so rough with hair that it bore the appearance of a skin-covered being." He is pursued and captured by a group of these creatures, is able to communicate with them in an ancient form of Gaelic, and learns that they are indeed Picts. He is allowed to drink their Galloway heather ale before managing to escape from his imminent sacrifice. He returns, shaken, to Oxford but is drawn back irresistibly to the same spot, is tracked down again by the Picts while rescuing a woman they have captured, and again escapes but finds that the world will not believe his story: "an article on Primitive Peoples of the North, … was unanimously rejected by every responsible journal in Europe." He is a ruined and broken man.

The special fascination of this story lies in Buchan's combination of familiarity — a hill-walking hero is a conventionally Buchanesque character, set in the much loved Galloway terrain that featured so frequently in his writings as in his life — with the evocation of fear and revulsion through his reworking of Pict as Neanderthal monster; "I felt that beast-like clutch at my throat; those red eyes seemed to be staring at me from the mist; I heard ever behind and before and on all sides the patter of those inhuman feet". Their leader "was like some foul grey badger, his real eyes sightless and his hands trembling on a stump of bog oak." These original inhabitants of Scotland, forced into refuge in the hills but the many subsequent waves of invaders and settlers, have been replenishing their race by the "ghoulish carrying away of little girls" — child abduction and rape.

This survey has been brief and partial. Novelists dealing with the Picts have inevitably reflected the problems of interpretation faced by antiquarians and modern archaeologists. The debate over the language and origins of the Picts is still unresolved, while conventional views are frequently reinforced, sometimes harnessed to more immediate preoccupations. It is through the imaginative creation of fine writers like Kipling, Ransome and Buchan that we can gain genuine insights into their various and very personal concepts of the Picts; the solid historical research of other novelists certainly contributes to our knowledge of the past, but does not put much flesh on the bones. I would therefore add a fourth category to the three types of historical fiction defined at the beginning of this piece: and that is one in which the imagination is given full rein.

Acknowledgement

I am most grateful to Shaun Tyas of Paul Watkins Publishing Ltd., for providing me with references to Picts in fiction, drawn from some of the hundreds of novels in his remarkable Anglo-Saxon Library.

Bibliography

BUCKLEY, J and WILLIAMS, W 1912 *A Guide to British Historical Fiction.* London.

COLLINS, I (ed) n.d. [*c*1990] *Recent Historical Novels.* Historical Association, London.

LAUGHLAN, W (ed) 1982 *Northern Lights by Sir Walter Scott.* Hawick.

LUKACS, G 1962 *The Historical Novel.* London.

MARRIOT, J 1940 *English History in English Fiction.* London.

RITCHIE, A 1994 *Perceptions of the Picts: from Eumenius to John Buchan* (Groam House Lecture Series 4). Rosemarkie.

SHEPPARD, AT 1930 *The Art & Practice of Historical Fiction.* London.

pictish arts society

The Pictish Arts Society was founded in 1988 to affirm the importance of Pictish culture in Scotland's past. The illustration above is of the 'Pictish beast' carved on a stone found last century at Linlathen near Dundee. This fragment has since been lost and it has been chosen as an emblem of the Pictish Arts Society to symbolise the Society's commitment to preserving Pictish culture and heritage.

The Society encourages a broad approach to the study of the Picts, providing a focus for research and discussion by promoting a wide range of activities – lectures, conferences, field-trips, exhibitions and craft-fairs. Its publications include field-guides, conference proceedings, occasional papers, a lively newsletter, and an influential journal, which has become the forum for new ideas and information. The major publication to date is *A Pictish Panorama*, incorporating an innovative *Pictish Bibliography* compiled by J.R.F. Burt and *The Story of the Picts*, essays on history, language, place-names, secular and Early Christian archaeology, and one on Pictish art, written by Isabel Henderson.

In recognition of Isabel Henderson's outstanding contribution to Pictish studies and in gratitude for her much-valued support and participation in the Society's programme of events over the years, the Pictish Arts Society has supported production of this *Festschrift*.

The following contribution is from the President of the Society.

The Wee Dark Fowk o' Scotland:
The role of oral transmission in Pictish studies

Stuart McHardy

'Within the oral tradition of Scotland there are many references to the Picts and… we might strive to learn more about them from that tradition' (Burt *et al* 1994, preface)

History is primarily concerned with written sources. When dealing with recent history the role of eye-witnesses and commentators is accepted as relevant. In dealing with the far past our understanding is based on the analysis of written historical resources in conjunction with archaeological investigation. The situation regarding the Picts is complicated by the fact that the vast majority of written material comes from furth of Scotland. However there is a body of evidence that is indigenous but that has been virtually ignored in our search to gain greater understanding of post-Roman pre-medieval Scotland. That evidence comes from the fields of folklore, legend and even mythology. Again because of the paucity of indigenous sources we are much more informed of the legendary and mythological material of both Ireland and Wales. It is generally accepted that there is no indigenous Scottish mythology as such and that the great Irish sagas are the basis of the oral traditions of the Q-Celtic speaking people of Scotland. Similarly the P-Celtic people of Wales have a body of legendary material from the far past in the Mabinogion but nothing similar is believed to have survived in Scotland. Because of this we are in the position that in attempting to increase our understanding the nature of the life and society of the P-Celtic, tribal peoples of Scotland within the period under consideration there has been a reliance on external annals and archaeological investigation. This I believe ignores a great deal of potentially useful information which has in fact been transmitted orally in Scotland over the past two millennia.

The problem can be understood when one looks at the classic texts on 'Celtic Studies' in the British Isles. In Anne Ross's *Pagan Celtic Britain*, Rees and Rees's *Celtic Heritage* and Dillon and Chadwick's *The Celtic Realms* there is very little reference to Scotland (and even less to the Picts). This despite the fact that the longest lived Celtic-speaking warrior society was that of the Scottish Highlanders which lasted well into the 18th century though it was by then in the throes of terminal decline. In fact there is a great deal of material that can shed light not only on Highland society but also on their distant ancestors the Picts. In Wilkie's *The History of Fife* we find the following, 'the Pechs [were] short wee men wi red hair and long arms and broad feet… They stood a in a row from the quarry to the building stance, and ilka ane handed forrit the stanes to his neebour till a was biggit' (1926, 21). This belief Wilkie tells us was from Wemyss, whose caves are of such importance. The point here is that the name the locals use is 'Pechs' and not Picts, the term based on Ammianus Marcellinus' first reference in 296 AD. There are other references to Pechs, Peghs and Pechts in Scottish folklore (Mackenzie 1935, 265–6) and this term has support as a more likely name for the ancient tribal people of eastern and northern Scotland.

In Rivet and Smith's *Place names of Roman Britain*, we find the following treatment of an entry in the sixth century Ravenna Cosmography,

> 'It is possible that Ravenna's PEXA at 107 53 is for Pecti, or even more interestingly Pectia – Pictland. The Cosmographer lists the name as that of an Antonine Wall fort, but we already know that this section contains several names that are nothing of the sort, including two that are probably tribal names misread from a map as though they were forts (Volitario=Votadini,

Credigone=Creones). Pexa could well come into this category…'

After making the point that this name probably comes from the Severan campaign of the early 3rd century and thus is anterior to Ammianus Marcellinus's Picti they go on,

'there is support for it in the fact that the people was known in Old Norse as PETTR, in Anglo-Saxon as Peohtas, in Old Scots as PECHT, and in Middle-Welsh as PEITH-WYR, all forms which demand original PECT-'.

This position is supported by Nicolaisen who writes,

'The Roman Picti corresponds to the Old Norse Pettar or Pettir… and to the old English Pehtas, Pihtas, Pyhtas, Pehtas and Piohtas of the Anglo-Saxon Chronicle (as well as to the first elements of the personal names Peohthelm, Peohtred, Peohtwald, Peohtwine, Peohtwulf, etc.) and there is little doubt that these linguistic variants do not derive from each other but from a common source – probably a native name.' (1976, 151)

It is worth noting that Ammianus Marcellinus uses Picti twice and Pecti once, at xxvi, 4 and that Rivet and Smith think the use of the term Picti is due to the influence of Virgil's *picti Agathyrsi* (*Aeniad* iv.146) and *pictosque Gelonos* (*Georgics* ii, 115) and had an overpowering influence. The point here is that the survival of Pech, Paich (Dalyell 1924, 532) and other variants within the oral tradition can be seen to have support from more conventional sources.

Recent research in Australia is beginning to stress that the capacity of oral transmission to communicate accurate information has been much underestimated. In talking of Australian aboriginal oral tradition, Jennifer Isaacs has the following,

'The legends when distilled create a story of the origins of man in Australia and of the Australian landscape as it is today of which much can be substantiated by scientific investigation.' (1980, 11)

Isaacs writes of aboriginal legends of living side by side with Diprotodons, rhinoceros like creatures, and giant kangaroos which have generally been treated as fantasy but which can now be dated from physical evidence to over 20,000 years ago (ibid, 14). In Scottish terms we should always remember that though there have been written records for many hundreds of years, general literacy among the population is relatively recent. It is here that the works of J.F. Campbell have, I believe, a particular importance.

In the introduction to *Popular Tales of the West Highlands* he says of the people he visited to collect tales,

'Many, I know not how many "have no English" at all, and have never been taught to read.' (1994, 13).

This was in the 1850s and the importance and centrality of these tales to social life is underlined when he writes

'Men and women of all ages could and did tell me stories, children of all sizes listened to them; and it was self-evident that people generally knew and enjoyed them. Elsewhere I had been told, that thirty or forty years ago, men used to congregate and tell stories; here, I was told, that they now spend whole winter nights about the fire listening to these old world tales.' (ibid, 14)

It is difficult to overestimate the importance of such activity in pre-literate societies as the tales, and poems, that are handed from one generation to another contain a vast amount of the living culture of the community. Such stories underpin and reinforce the community and give moral precepts and knowledge of the world across a very broad base. The idea that they are simply entertainment for long winters' nights is simply preposterous. Even just a couple of hundred years ago literacy was mainly the prerogative of the privileged and, just as importantly, most people lived for most of their lives close to where they were born. Unless involved in an occupation that involved travelling, e.g. fisherman, peripatetic craftsman, trader etc. most individuals lived close to their birthplace in communities which were in the main self-sufficient. Such close communities were probably much more like tribal societies than modern communities and it is noteworthy that tales that were common over wide areas like that of Finn McCoul among Q-Celtic speakers or Arthur among P-Celtic speakers are generally found told in the local landscape – the environment that the audience understood (Buchan 1984, 7)

The combination of the innate conservatism of oral transmission, easily seen in the nearly identical stories of Dairmaid and Grainne found hundreds of miles apart (Rees and Rees 1990, 68, 288; Swire 1964, 87), and the localised setting for such tales raises the possibility that such stories can give us tantalising glimpses of the far past. As has been said elsewhere, 'Folk-lore custom and beliefs were no idle play, but earnest attempts to safeguard vital human interests' (Bennett 1992, xv). While there is a vast amount of material collected from oral transmission much of it as regards the Picts has not come about as a result of organised projects like Campbell's or the important collections made since the 40s of this century by Dr Hamish Henderson and others at the School of Scottish Studies. Much relevant material is contained in 19th century guidebooks and local histories but it must be treated with caution. All over Scotland there are antiquities which have been referred to as Pictish. One example should suffice to illustrate the problem. Near Butterstone in Perthshire there is an extensive earthwork known locally as the Pict's Dyke. It is in fact a 15th century Deer Dyke but perhaps due to an upsurge of antiquarian interest among the gentry the late 18th and 19th century it seems to have been given this name. This is not an isolated case and it is almost as if in many places the term Pict took on a generic meaning of 'the ancestor people'. Another limitation on such material is that it is often incidentally collected from local sources to whom, or which, no reference is given. However this incidental material has a value of its own particularly if it can be corroborated from archaeological or historical sources. The instance of Norrie's Law in Fife is well enough known to serve as an exemplar in that one local tale told of a warrior called Norroway buried in silver armour inside the 'law'. This was eventually proved to be correct in a complicated fashion but points to the tenacity of oral tradition. This incidental material is also of interest as it was not deliberately 'collected' which means that although we have no references to source, it also has not been subjected to any particular interpretation, leaving it a fruitful area for further study.

There are other examples of legendary and mythological material that can be seen to have direct relevance in the study of the Picts. Elsewhere I have written about the relationship between Class I animal symbols and legendary material from both Wales and Ireland (1991, 33-8). Given the proximity of the historical Picts to their fellow P-Celtic speaking cousins in Manau Guotodin and Strathclyde and to the Q-Celtic tribal peoples in western Scotland such resonances should not be a surprise. Such material from the Mabinogion and the Irish sagas is usually seen as being essentially literary and much of such material seems to hold very few, if any, of the markers, such as alliteration, assonance and other mnemonic tricks that would represent orally transmitted materials. That such

material does seem to be primarily literary is indisputable but the tales they are based on continued to be orally transmitted in both Ireland and Scotland. In the past decade Dr Sheila Douglas collected a tale that is of interest in this respect. Called 'Jack and the Seven Magic Islands' (Douglas 1987, 55-61) it is clearly a previously unrecorded version of the Imram of Maelduin (Dillon and Chadwick 1967, 188, 256). The storyteller, James Stewart, told the tale in Scots, a clear example of the capacity of such stories to cross linguistic boundaries, as well as to survive in oral form for centuries, if, as is generally accepted, the original was in Irish Gaelic. A further point of interest is that this version, unlike that in the Book of Leinster has no Christian glossing on the ending. In the Christianised version Jack forgives his enemies where in James Stewart's version he kills them. This raises the intriguing, though unproveable possibility that the oral version might be truer to the original form than the early medieval manuscript version from Ireland. It is a fact that many motifs occur in different linguistic communities, a point I will return to later.

Surviving material in both Gaelic and Scots traditions points to very ancient tales indeed particularly regarding the *Cailleach*. This mythological being is known extensively in the West of Scotland in particular and is generally presented as the Winter Hag. Her counterpart in the East, in the Scots tradition is the *Carlin* (Mackenzie 1935, 149). The *Cailleach* is a complicated figure who in different tales is seen as extremely ancient (ibid, 163) the creator of the Hebrides (Macnab 1984, 208), many of Scotland's mountains (Mackenzie 1935, 164) and is associated particularly with Ben Nevis and the Whirlpool of the Corryvreckan (McNeill 1957, 2, 20). Given the relationship between the *Cailleach* and Bride it is particularly interesting that the *Cailleach* is seen as the creator of the Hebrides and in popular etymology the name Hebrides comes from *I-Bride* islands of Bride. Such material is the faint remnants of foundation myths and clearly points to the *Cailleach* as being a mother goddess figure, whether of the Celtic-speaking peoples or inherited by them from a earlier stratum of peoples being impossible to stay. Recent work by Dr Emily Lyle (1990, 119) has pointed to an ancient duality within indigenous cosmology and this is of particular interest with the *Cailleach*. In some versions of the *Cailleach* story she is portrayed as the enemy of Bride, the Goddess of Summer (McNeill 1957, 2, 21) while in others she is said to change into Bride by drinking from a well on Beltain (ibid). This is a clear correspondence with the division of the year into the time of the Big Sun and the Little Sun as noted by McNeill (ibid, 2, 20), and that division was marked by the major festivals of Beltain and Samhain (ibid, 1, 18; 2, 20). It is in the figure of Bride, later euhemerised into St. Bridget that the most remarkable ideas are associated. Scholarship has long relied on the notion that most concepts within Gaelic culture originally emanated from Ireland. The fact that there are many more *Cailleach* stories and place-names associated with this figure in Scotland would suggest that she is not necessarily an import following the generally accepted arrival of the Scots *c*500 AD. The possibility exists that such stories and their associated beliefs are from an older pre-Celtic time.

There are in Angus alone several Bride place-names that are not associated with Christian sites which is what we would expect if the idea of St Bridget came in with Gaelic-speaking priests subsequent to either the Synod of Whitby in 664 or the merging of the Scottish and Pictish nations in the 9th century. Perhaps we have been misinterpreting the evidence. Chadwick is said to have believed that Bride originated in Scotland (1949, xii) and Small (1823, 171) mentions that Bride originated in Glen Esk in Angus. This belief finds interesting corroboration in Leslie's *Historie of Scotland* where it is said, of St Bridget,

> 'The Irland men contendes that her haly body that have with thame in that toune quhilke thay cal Dun, in quhilke place the body of thair Apostle S. Patrik is keipit. our cuntrey men ascryues the same Glore unto thame, quha thinkes, that hitherto that have honouret it, in the Chanrie of Abernethie, and rychtlie have done thay think.' (1888, 229)

Small's statement about Glen Esk is corroborated by a place-name, Bride's Bed, attached to a strange circular excavation at the foot of Craig Maskeldie at the head of Glenesk, and the neighbouring glen, Glen Clova too has an interesting Bride placename, Bride's Coggie (Marnie 1966, 22).

While this an interesting area for further study, St Bridget is associated with a particularly Pictish group at Abernethy. These are the Nine Maidens who are variously said to have come to Abernethy from Glen Ogilvy, a few miles north of Dundee (Jervise 1861, 334-5) and to have arrived with St Bridget from Ireland. These Nine Maidens, unusually, crop up as a group of Pictish saints in Forbes' Breviary (1872, 420-1) but I have found no reference to them as such in Irish sources though Bridget's sacred fire at Kildare is variously said to have been tended by nine or nineteen maidens (Ross 1992, 454; McNeill 1959, 2, 22). Mackinlay (1906, 255) drew attention to dedication to this group of Pictish saints and suggested that the common place-name Ninewells suggests dedications to them all over Scotland. Be that as it may there can be little doubt of their Pictish provenance. Martin's Stane, a broken Class II symbol stone, north of Dundee, has a tale of Nine Maidens slain by a dragon before being killed by the eponymous Martin (Jervise 1875, 1, 206) – a motif echoed by the foundation myth of the Forbes' family in Aberdeenshire where the Pictish warrior Ochonochar is said to have slain a wild boar that had slain Nine Maidens there (MacFarlane, 1, 34). In fact these Nine Maidens are associated with a wide range of localities throughout Scotland and beyond in the Celtic and Germanic speaking worlds. What is interesting here is not just that we have a series of locations and stories that suggest this group to be pagan priestesses (McHardy 1991, 35-7) but that the cult of the Nine Maidens with its associated wells lasted until a century ago when the farmer at Pittempton, just outside Dundee covered up the Nine Maidens Well in the late 1870s because too many people were visiting it (Warden 1884, 1, 297). Here we seem to have a survival of the cult that Mackinlay wrote of (Mackinlay 1905, 255) almost into the twentieth century. This, I suggest, is proof of the tenacity of the oral tradition and of its potential for study. Given that these Nine Maidens seem very like the 'Druidesses' reported by Pomponius Mela off the Breton coast in Roman times (Dillon and Chadwick 1967, 129f; Leslie 1866, 90) and that a variety of sources say Avalon was inhabited by Morgan and her 8 sisters (Markale 1986, 19; Paton 1960, 43; Loomis 1927, 191) what we are seeing is not only a widespread cult, as Mackinlay stated, but one which lasted a thousand years at least. Most of the material relating to this group comes originally from oral tradition, and the point should be stressed that although there are some instances of Nine Maidens in Irish sources such as the attendants of Bride's Fire at Kildare, as mentioned above, and others, who seem to be associated with Norse tradition (Edward 1903, II, 27), there are far more in Scotland. Similar groups existed throughout the pagan Scandinavian world and they crop up elsewhere in Europe and beyond. I intend to publish an extensive account of Nine Maidens groups, the existence of which I was made aware of by the story of Martins' Stane mentioned above.

The point is that by paying attention to what has survived within oral tradition we can access material that might otherwise have disappeared. The cliché that history is written by winners has some relevance when we try to study the Picts. Here is a people who were at the very least culturally subsumed by Q-Celtic speakers and who have left us few written records worthy of note. The Picts themselves must have been in the main pre-literate which does not mean they were ignorant, savage or even illiterate, in the sense that they must have had a large corpus of oral literature. The capacity of the human memory as noted in all oral societies is remarkable and even if there were written Pictish records in the court and in a few monasteries when Kenneth mac Alpin triumphed, most of the population would have learnt their own history and tradition through storytelling or recitation.

Craig Cessford, in a recent article (1996, 7), makes the interesting suggestion that the famous battle-scene on the cross-slab in Aberlemno Kirkyard (Aberlemno 2) was designed after the detail of a poem that had been composed to celebrate the Battle of Dunnichen of 685. The suggested model for such a poem is *The Gododdin*, Britain's oldest indigenous language written text and the survival of praise poetry within all the Celtic-speaking peoples of Britain makes this a viable suggestion. As Cessford points out, there are mentions of specific Pictish warriors in *The Gododdin* showing their close relationship with the Welsh-speaking tribes who supplied most of the warriors in the battle described therein. That oral tradition changed with changing circumstances is undeniable but I hope I have here shown that by paying attention to the surviving corpus of material referring to the Picts and comparing what we find with material from other sources such as written history and the archaeological record, we can begin to have a clearer idea of who the Picts were and how they lived. After all, although Schlieman was ridiculed for trying to locate Troy by studying Homer – he was in the end right and we might indeed strive to learn more about the Picts from their folklore.

References

BENNETT, M 1992 *Scottish Customs from the Cradle to the Grave*. Edinburgh.

BUCHAN, D 1984 *Scottish Tradition*. London.

BURT, J R F, BOWMAN, E O and ROBERTSON, N M (eds) 1991 *Symbols, Stones and Stories, Aspects of Pictish studies*. Edinburgh.

CAMPBELL, J F 1994 *Popular Tales of the West Highlands*. Edinburgh (repr of 1860 edn).

CESSFORD, C 1996 A Lost Pictish Poem? *Scottish Literary Journal*, Nov 1996, V23 N 2.

DALYELL, J G 1924 *The Darker Superstitions of Scotland*. Edinburgh.

CHADWICK, H M 1949 *Early Scotland*. Cambridge.

DILLON, M and CHADWICK, N K 1967 *The Celtic Realms*. London.

DOUGLAS, S 1987 *The King o' the Black Art*. Aberdeen.

EDWARD, G 1903 *The Metrical Dinsenchas*. Dublin.

FORBES, A F 1872 *Kalendars of Scottish Saints*. Edinburgh.

HUTTON, R 1991 *The Pagan Religions of Prehistoric British Isles*. Oxford/London.

ISAACS, J 1980 *Australian Dreaming: 40,000 years of Aboriginal history*. Willoughby NSW, Australia.

JERVISE, A
– 1875 *Epitaphs and Inscriptions*. Edinburgh.
– 1882 *The Land of the Lindsays*. Edinburgh.
– 1861 *Memorials of Angus and the Mearns*. Edinburgh.

LESLIE, Forbes 1866 *The Early Races of Scotland*. Edinburgh.

LESLIE, Jhone 1888 *The Historie of Scotland* (repr of 1830 edn). Edinburgh .

LOOMIS, R 1927 *Celtic Myth and Arthurian Romance* (repr of New York, 1927 edn). London.

LYLE, E 1990 *Archaic Cosmos*. Edinburgh.

MACKENZIE, D A 1938 *Scottish Folk Lore and Folk Life*. London and Glasgow.

MACFARLANE, W 1906-08 *Geographical Collections*. Edinburgh.

MCHARDY, S A 1991 The folklore of the Picts. In Burt *et al*, 33–8.

MACKINLAY, J M 1905 Traces of the cultus of the Nine Maidens in Scotland. *Proc Soc Antiq Scot*, 40 (1905-06), 255–65.

MACNAB, P 1984 *Tall Tales From an Island.* Barr.

MCNEILL, F Marian 1959 *The Silver Bough,* 4 vols. Glasgow.

MARKALE, J 1986 *Women of the Celts* (trans of *La Femme Celte*, Paris, 1972). Vermont.

MARNIE, E J 1966 Place names in Glen Clova. In Wilson, E M (ed) *Aspects of Antiquity*. Dundee.

NICOLAISEN, W F H 1976 *Scottish Place-Names: Their Study and Significance.* London.

PATON, L 1960 *Studies in the Fairy Mythology of Arthurian Romance* (repr of 1902 edn). Boston.

ROSS, A 1992 *Pagan Celtic Britain* (repr of 1967 edn). London.

SMALL, A 1823 *Some Interesting Roman Antiquities: Discovered in Fife.* Edinburgh.

SWIRE, O 1964 *The Inner Hebrides and Their Legends.* Glasgow.

WARDEN, A 1884 *Angus or Forfarshire*, 4 vols. Edinburgh.

On Pictish Rivers and Their Confluences

W.F.H. Nicolaisen

In the study of Pictish place-names in Scotland, the element *Pit-* (from an earlier *pett*) has, quite rightly, received the most attention (Fraser 1942; Jackson 1955, 146–8; Nicolaisen 1972; 1975; 1976, 151–8; 1995; Watson 1926, 407–14; Whittington and Soulsby 1968). The main reason for this preoccupation with names like *Pitlochry, Pittenweem, Pitgaveny, Pitliver, Pittencrieff,* etc., is probably the fact that this generic which apparently referred to a 'piece, portion, or share' of land, when plotted on a map in its toponymic usage provides us with a convincing visual impression of what the settlement area of the p-Celtic Picts once must have been. There is no other place-name element which has the same persuasive distribution, both in quantity — there are more than 300 known examples of names in this category — and in its exclusive restriction to what might be termed, from a linguistic/toponymic point of view, 'Pictland'. Ever since Kenneth Jackson produced his well-known map of the distribution of *Pit-*names forty years ago (Jackson 1955, 147), the mapping of such names has, therefore, in one form or another, been the basic evidence in the study of Pictish toponymy, especially as an aid to the isolation of a Pictish settlement area and stratum in Scotland. The investigation of other place-name elements which might be termed 'Pictish' has had comparatively much less emphasis.

Not that the study of *Pit-*names has not had its potential pit-falls. The fact that in the great majority of all identifiable and etymologisable instances (all the examples quoted above belong to this category) the second element or specific is demonstrably Gaelic has caused more than one eyebrow to be raised, leading some scholars to the conclusion that *pett* is itself Gaelic. Such a position is, as is to be expected, especially taken by those for whom Pictish is simply a form of Gaelic, i.e. q-Celtic rather than p-Celtic

(for example, Skene 1836; Fraser 1942). Although this point of view has never been completely abandoned by a minority of scholars, it is difficult to defend when all factors are taken into account, and it is sounder and, in general, more acceptable to envisage a situation in which the Pictish toponymic generic *pett* was adopted, perhaps for administrative reasons, by speakers of Gaelic when they encountered it in Pictish territory in the ninth century; it subsequently became part of their place-name vocabulary and was therefore productively used by them even after the demise of Pictish.

Because of their circumscribed spatial distribution, roughly from the Firth of Forth in the south to the Moray Firth and a little beyond in the north, and to Perthshire and Badenoch in the west, *Pit-*names can undoubtedly be regarded as reliable evidence for what at one time was p-Celtic 'Pictland', even though most of the names in question are likely to have been given by speakers of Gaelic. They have also deserved the attention they have had not only from linguists but also from geographers who have, through their own techniques and application of their own criteria, been remarkably successful in fleshing out the rather skeletal, two-dimensional image of the toponymic distribution maps, coming to the conclusion that, at least in Fife, 'the sites with *pit* place-names' show 'a distinct preference for loamy soils and for well-sheltered and well-drained positions. Inland rather than coastal locations are preferred and these are often associated with the easiest lines of land movement available at the time' (Whittington and Soulsby 1968, 124). Avoiding the floors of the river valleys and the coast, *pit-*names occur primarily at an altitude of between 50 and 650 feet; they are obviously associated with farming communities the members of which were very selective in their choice of sites.

As already hinted, it is probably the numerical strength of the *Pit*-names as well as their apparently exclusively 'Pictish' distribution that makes them such attractive evidence for students of the 'Pictish Question' or of what used to be called 'The Problem of the Picts' (Wainwright 1955). In contrast, none of the other toponymical elements usually associated with the Picts — *carden, lanerc, pert, pevr, aber* — either matches *pett* in numbers or occurs exclusively in 'Pictland'. For these reasons, none of them has been subjected to the same kind of scrutiny as *pett* although they have, of course, been taken into account in attempts to reconstruct the extent of Pictish territory in terms of the toponymic evidence which has survived. In particular *aber* 'confluence, river-mouth, estuary' deserves a better fate as *Aber*-names complement *Pit*-names in several respects: *Aber* is to be found outside the *Pit*-area, not only in Scotland south of the Forth-Clyde line (*Abercarf, Aberlosk, Abermilk*; also *Aberlady* in East Lothian) but also in Wales (*Abergavenny, Aberystwyth, Aberdare*), though not in Cornwall; it is therefore an important link between Pictish and the other p-Celtic languages, like Cumbric and Welsh. *Aber* not only differs in its distribution from *Pit*, however, but also insofar as it does not seem to have been absorbed into Gaelic as a productive toponymic element, like *pett*, as its replacement by Gaelic *inbhear* in *Inverbervie* KCD[1] (*Haberberui* 1290) shows. Whereas, for some reason, Pictish *pett* appears to have filled a gap in the Gaelic lexicon, *aber* would simply have duplicated its Gaelic equivalent. There may, in fact, be other *Inver*-names within the *Pit*-area in which *inbhear* (*inbhir*) has replaced an earlier *aber* (like *Inverpeffer* ANG and *Innerpeffray* PER, for example) but we have no means of knowing of how frequently, if at all, this may have happened (Watson 1926, 459). Despite some claims to the contrary (Diack 1926), *aber* should not be regarded as a Gaelic term but as firmly anchored in insular p-Celtic.

There is a third obvious aspect in which *aber*-names differ from *pit*-names — the location of the sites which they designate. Instead of avoiding 'the floors of the river valleys' like the namers of those places which Whittington and Soulsby examined, the namers of *aber*-sites positively sought them, with a special preference for river-mouths and confluences. While in some instances this may also point to communities engaged in agricultural and pastoral activities, the chief conclusion surely must be that there were also Picts who made a living from rivers, whether through fishing or through using them for travel or other kinds of routes of communication, as far as the watercourses were navigable. This would naturally also involve coastal travel by boat from river-mouth to river-mouth and perhaps even longer voyages. Dwellers at *Pit*-sites and inhabitants of *Aber*-sites may have had different needs, interests, habits and predelections but their presence at both these locations gives us a larger picture of Pictish activities and habitats. Linguistically the Picts involved will not have differed from each other. River people will have known what a *pett* was and those pursuing farming activities at an altitude between 50 and 650 feet will have been able to refer to a river-mouth as *aber*. *Aber*-names, while serving as evidence for strong linguistic connections between 'Pictland' and the regions to the south at least as far as Wales, are consequently as significant within the Pictish borders as *Pit*-names and, for that reason alone, deserve to be rescued from their relative neglect. In fact, the argument will be made in the following that they may be, in certain respects, of greater significance than the *Pit*-names, even if they do not prove Pictish linguistic autonomy or, in their general spatial distribution, are equally capable of delineating discernible dialect boundaries.

It is reasonable to assume that the river names which form the specifics in many *Aber*-names either already existed when their confluences or mouths were named or, at the latest, that the water-courses were given names simultaneously with the latter. Taking Beveridge's inventory of *Aber*-names as our starting point (Beveridge 1923) and augmenting it by Watson's proposed etymologies (Watson 1926, 459–69 *et passim*), we can with a great degree of certainty compile the following list of Pictish river names:[2]

*BERBA, in *Aberbervie, now *Inverbervie* KCD (*Haberberui* 1290); River Bervie, cf Irish *berbaim* 'I boil', Welsh *berwi* — 'the boiling one'.

*BODERIA, in *Aberbothrie* PER (*Abbyrbothry*, etc. 1375); tributary of the Isla, identical with Ptolemy's name for the Forth, cf Gaelic *boidhre* 'deafness' — 'deaf one, noiseless one'.

*BRUTACA,-OS, in *Arbroath* ANG, Gaelic *Obar-brothaig* (*Aberbrudoc* 1189–98, *Abirbrothoc* 1199); Brothock Burn, cf Gaelic *bruth* 'heat', and Welsh *-awc*, now *-og*, which in Gaelic has become *-ág* — 'little boiling one'. Compare also Burn of Brown BNF, Gaelic *Allt Bruthain(n)*, from *BRUTONA.

BUADHNAT (Gaelic), in *Arbuthnott* KCD (*Aberbothenoth* 1242); tributary of Bervie, cf Gaelic *buadh* 'virtue', with the diminutive suffix *-n-ant-* added — 'little one of virtue, i.e. healing'.

*CAT-, in *Abercattie* ABD (*Abircawte* 1473); ? South Cattie Burn; the upper reaches are called Glencat. The settlement name has been replaced by Whitehouse. Meaning unclear.

*CRUMB-, in (1) *Abercrombie* FIF (*Abercrumbin* 1153–66), and (2) *Abercrombie* FIF (*Abercrumbin* 1227); Gaelic *Aber-chrombaidh*; cf Welsh *crwm*, Gaelic *crom*, Old Irish *cromb* 'bent' — 'the bent one'.

*DELG-, in *Aberdalgie* PER (*Aberdalgin* 1215–21); tributary of Earn, cf Cornish *delc* 'necklace', Gaelic *dealg*, Old Irish *delg* 'thorny pin' — 'pin-shaped one'.

*DEVONA, *Aberdeen* ABD, Gaelic *Obar-dheathan* (*Aberdon* 1150); River Don (*Devana* c150 AD Ptolemy), from *devos* 'god', cf River Dee (*Deva*) — 'goddess'.

*DUBRON and derivatives, in *Aberdour* ABD (Aberdouer 1178–99) and *Aberdour* FIF (*Abirdouer* 1329); Dour Burn, cf Welsh *dwfr*, *dwr*, Gaelic *dobhar* 'water' — '(flowing) water'. *Aberarder* ABD (*Abirardoure* 1451); Feardar Burn. *Aberarder* INV (Twa *Aberardoris* 1458); tributary of River Nairn. *Aberarder* INV (*Oberarder* 1696); tributary of Loch Laggan — 'high water'. *CALETO-DUBRON, in *Aberchalder* INV (*Abbircaledour* 1238), Gaelic *Obar-Chaladair*; Calder Burn — 'hard water'. CIAR-DOBHAR, in *Aberchirder* BNF (*Abirkerdour* c1204); tributary of River Deveron — 'black water'.

*GELIDIOS/-A, in *Abergeldie* ABD (*Aberyedly* 1438), Gaelic *Obar-Gheallaidh*; Geldie, cf Old Irish *gel* 'white', also Irish and Welsh *glan* 'pure' — 'the white or pure one'.

*LABARA,-OS, in *Aberlour* BNF (*Abyrlouer* 1224–42); Burn of Aberlour, cf Gaelic *labhar*, Welsh *llafar* 'loud' — 'the loud one'.

*LEMONACA, in *Aberlemno* ANG (*Aberlimenach* 1242) *Aberlevinach* 1250); Lemno Burn, cf Gaelic *lemnach*,

adjective from *leam(h)ain*, Irish *lem* 'elm tree' — 'elm river'.

LIDNÁIG (Gaelic), in *Aberlednock* PER (*Abbirlednoch* 1444), Gaelic *Obar-Lidnáig*; Lednock Burn. Obscure.

LUATHNAT (Gaelic), in *Aberluthnot* KCD (*Aberluthenoth* 1242); tributary of North Esk, cf Irish *luath* 'fast' + *-n-ant-* — 'little swift one'.

*NECTONA, in *Abernethy* INV (*Abyrnythy* 1187–1203), Gaelic *Obar-neithich*; River Nethy; and *Abernethy* PER (*Aburnethiga* 10c); tributary of Earn, Pictish *Neithon* > Gaelic *Nethech* — 'pure one'.

-NYTE, in *Abernyte* PER (*Abernyde* 1296); Abernyte Burn — Obscure.

*TARVOS, in *Abertarff* INV (*Abirtarf* 1208–15), Gaelic *Obar-thairbh*; River Tarff, cf Welsh *tarw*, Gaelic *tarbh* 'bull' — 'bull (river)'.

*TURTHAID (Gaelic), in *Aberturret* PER (no early forms); Turret Burn, cf Gaelic *tur* 'dry' + *-that* — 'little dry one'.

*VERG0, in *Aberargie* PER (*Apurfeirt* = *-feirc* 10th cent.); twa tounis of *Aberargyis* 1492); River Farg, also Glenfarg, cf Old Welsh *guerg* 'effective', Gaelic *fearg*, gen *feirge* 'wrath' — 'effective or wrathful one'.

This is obviously not a complete list of the river names which the Picts knew and used in their own territory. As already indicated, there may have been other names of confluences in which Pictish *aber* was replaced by Gaelic *inbhir* but the earlier *aber*-name has not survived in the record. There may also be the occasional 'Pictish' river name which never formed the specific of either an *aber* or an *inver*-name. The following names might therefore, among others, be justifiably added to an inventory of Pictish names of water-courses: *Abona* (*Water of Aven* ABD/KCD), *Bremava* (*Braan* PER), *Brivara* (*Bruar* PER), *Brutona* (*Burn of Brown* BNF, see under *Brutaca* above), *Caleto-dubron* (*Calder* PER, *Callander* PER, *Callater* ABD, ANG, etc.), *Catona* (*Inverhadden Burn* PER), *Dubona* (*Devon* PER/CLA/STL, and *Black Devon* CLA), *Iektona* (*Ythan* ABD), *Isca* (*Esk* ANG, KCD), *Lemona* (*Leven* FIF), *Limenti* (*Livet* BNF), *Limona* (*Lyon* PER). It is also more than likely that major pre-Pictish river names (Nicolaisen 1976, 180–91) like the *(Find)horn*, the *(Dev)eron*, the *Nairn*, the *Earn*, probably also the *Tay* and the *Spey*, were adopted by the Picts and widely used in reference to the rivers in question. Even though the list of names in these two categories is not complete, they nevertheless provide an indication of a substantial corpus of Pictish river names, whether ever incorporated in an *aber*-name or not.[3]

On the other hand, one also has to bear in mind that the confluence is usually named after the influx of the smaller tributary which explains why, for instance, the *Earn* which is a major river flowing through the heart of 'Pictland' has five recorded *aber*-confluences, the *Spey* has three, and the *Dee* and the *Forth* have two.' There are single *aber*-names on the rivers *Nairn, Isla, Deveron, Black Devon, Tay*, the *South Esk*, the *Don*, and (outside Pictland) the *Annan. Aber*-sites are also located on Loch Laggan, Loch Oich, and Loch Ness (2), and there are identifiable *aber*-names on the east coast (6), including the Firth of Forth. *Applecross* is the lonely example on the west coast.

What is striking, although not surprising, about those stream names that are Pictish in both origin and usage is that they are without exception morphologically complex, i.e. formed with a suffix, and, except for the river name contained in *Aberlemno* and the *Bruar*, refer to qualities of the water-courses themselves and not to their surroundings as becomes the custom later when compound names come into vogue (Nicolaisen 1957). The attempted reconstructions are, of course, not recorded as such and offer an added degree of difficulty because they have come down to us in their Gaelic form or in Anglicisations which have passed through Gaelic. Watson comments, for example, in connection with the *Boderia*, the stream name that forms the specific of *Aberbothrie*: "This is one of the many instances in which a British name has either been taken over direct into Gaelic or translated during the period of transition from British to Gaelic" (Watson 1926, 436). He also points out that name formations like the *Geldie* of *Abergeldie* 'came into vogue during the period of linguistic transition, and that the practice started as a method of inducing and incidentally gaelicizing old compound names' (Watson 1926, 440). The *lemnach* of *Aberlemno* he regards as 'most probably a Gaelic adaptation of a British name or stream name' (Watson 1926, 464), and *Abertarff* is to him 'a British name preserved in full, for Gaelic *tarbh* and W. *tarw* are identical' (Watson 1926, 453). It is also possible that the two

recorded spellings quoted for *Arbroath* above (*Aberbrudoc* and *Abirbrothock*) have preserved the Pictish and the Gaelic forms, respectively, of the river name for us. Because of the problems involved I have therefore sometimes let the Gaelic(ised) form stand or listed an abbreviated name.

Although '*aber*+river name' is the most common pattern in the formation of Pictish designations of confluences, there are exceptions to this model. *Aberfoyle* PER, Gaelic *Obarphuill*, for instance, is simply 'confluence of the poll', an unnamed sluggish stream. *Aberfeldie* PER, Gaelic *Obarpheallaidh*, contains the name of *Peallaidh*, an old water demon; the second element in *Abercairney* PER and *Abergairn* ABD is Pictish *carden* 'a copse'; *Abercorn* WLO (*Aebbercurnig c*720) is the 'horned confluence'; the obsolete *Aberdolo* FIF (*Aberdolloche* 1630) is compounded with *dolach*, the old genitive of *dol* 'meadow'; *Aberlady* ELO is etymologically related to Gaelic *lobh* 'putrify'; *Aber(r)uchill* PER (*Abbirruchil* 1461, *Aberurquill* 1594) probably has as its second component the adverbial phrase 'on-wood'; and the specific in *Aber(r)uthven* PER (*Aberruadeuien c*1198, *Abruthven* 1198–1609) refers to a 'red place'. It is possible that some of these place names may originally have contained a stream name which was later superseded by an alternative description but it is not easy to make that assumption without an actual example of a doubling of this kind.

There cannot be any doubt that the basic meaning of *aber* is 'confluence, river-mouth', or the like. Such a meaning is not put in question by the fact that some of the settlements which now bear *Aber*-names are not located at the confluence or mouth itself. The transfer of a topographical *Aber*-name to a nearby village or farm has numerous parallels elsewhere, involving other terms for natural features in the landscape. After all, a site close to the confluence itself may not be suitable for human habitation. There is, however, another reason why the location of the natural feature and the site of the settlement named after it may not be the same, for this discrepancy may also stem from an extended use of the word *aber*. It is, after all, not self-evident why so many Pictish place names associated with water-courses designate sites at or near confluences and not other locations along the banks of the rivers concerned. There may be practical reasons why these situations are particularly attractive but somehow practicality may not furnish sufficient grounds for the overwhelming choice of these locations. I would therefore like to argue that river-mouths and confluences also frequently had cultic significance.

Perhaps the most convincing example is the name *Aberdeen* 'Don-mouth' since we know that the name of the river was, in Pictish times, *Devana* or *Devona*, meaning 'goddess' and that it must have shared its divine qualities with its sister river *Deva*, the *Dee* (Nicolaisen, forthcoming). As their names indicate, both these water-courses were at the same time rivers and goddesses. What form Pictish river worship took is difficult to say but it may well have included the offering of votive objects. It is also not clear whether the whole river from source to mouth was regarded as 'divine'. The worship of springs as sources of life is well known but this does not mean that the whole river was worshipped. Similarly, it is more than likely that Pictish 'river-worship' was concentrated on locations at which a smaller tributary joined a larger water-course or at which a river flowed into the sea, and that the flowing water turned into a goddess at that particular point or in its vicinity. *Abers* could, therefore, have been regarded as holy ground, a notion which is reinforced not only by references to the 'purity' of a river as in *Abernethy*, or its healing powers as in *Arbuthnott*, but also by references to a water demon, as in *Aberfeldy*, or its identification with a bull, as in *Abertarff*. If, indeed, confluences were cultic places for the Picts who had their 'nemeta' nearby, then it is not surprising that Christian establishments and places of worship were created close to such pagan locations, and that at least twenty-two of the Scottish *Aber*-names designated, or are still applied to, parishes. In three instances in which the original *Aber*-name has been replaced as a parish name (*Abercrombie* FIF, *Aberluthnot* KCD, and *Abermilk* DMF), the replacement has distinctive Christian connotations: St Monance, Marykirk, and St Mungo. This special status of *Aber*-names contrasts strongly with that of *Pit*-names of which only two (*Pitsligo* ABD and *Pittenweem* FIF) have become parish names whereas most of the others are described in gazetteers by terms such as 'village, hamlet, house, estate'.

It is probably not necessary to stress that it would be

unwise to think of *Aber*-names — or *Pit*-names, for that matter — in isolation or solely as a separate name type. It is, however, gratifying to see that such caution is not just theoretical or hypothetical but finds support in the landscape, as in the 1227 reference in the Register of Dunfermline to 'the water that runs between the land of Petliuer and the land of Gelland on the one part and the land of Abercrumbin on the other' (Watson 1926, 462), or in the fact that 'the stream at Aberlady is the Peffer' (Watson 1926, 461). In another coupling, *Abergairn* in Aberdeenshire contains as its specific Pictish *carden* (*Abergardin* 1468), while *Abercairney* PER, if it can be shown to have the same etymology, would link *aber, carden*, and *pefr* because it stands on a burn which joins the *Peffray* (Watson 1926, 463); *pett, aber, carden*, and *pefr* can therefore be seen as a small semantic field in the toponymic sector of the Pictish lexicon, and *lanerc* and *pert* can undoubtedly be related to it, too.

Although it would be rash to claim that every *aber*-site has cultic origins or unspecified connections with 'river-worship', several of them can confidently be placed in that category. It is for this additional reason as much as for this name-type's close links with a corpus of Pictish river names and its complementary sitings to those of the *Pit*-names, that *Aber*-names are arguably of considerable importance in the inventory of Pictish place names in general. They throw, it seems to me, much more light on a number of aspects of Pictish language and culture than they have so far been given credit for, and they are certainly worth examining in much greater detail. The place-name scholar will also look with anticipation to the results of archaeological investigations at or near *aber*-sites, for only the material evidence of excavations will either confirm or disprove the theory put forward in this paper.

Notes

1 The county abbreviations employed are those used by the Scottish Place-Name Survey in the School of Scottish Studies. For a complete list see Nicolaisen 1976, xxvii–xxviii.

2 Despite Diack's very harsh review of Beveridge's compilation (Diack 1926), this constitutes a very useful collection of the Scottish *aber*-names, their locations and some of their early spellings. Diack's low opinion was greatly influenced by his dogmatic belief that *aber* was not

p-Celtic, did not mean 'confluence' and should therefore not have been twinned with *inver*.

3　It is worth noting that none of the apparently pre-Pictish river names just listed has produced any *Aber*-names, and it is therefore possible that some of the Pictish stream names, at least at their mouths, were created simultaneously with the names of the confluences.

References

BEVERIDGE, ERSKINE 1923 *The 'Abers' and 'Invers' of Scotland*. Edinburgh.

DIACK, F C 1926 Aber and Inver in Scotland. *Scottish Gaelic Studies* 1 (1926), 83–98.

FRASER, J 1942 Pet(t) in place names. *Scottish Gaelic Studies* 5 (1942), 67–71.

JACKSON, K H 1955 The Pictish language. In Wainwright, F T (ed) *The Problem of the Picts*, 129–60, and appendix 161–8. Edinburgh.

NICOLAISEN, W F H

– 1957 The semantic structure of Scottish hydronymy. *Scottish Studies* 1 (1957), 211–40.

– 1972 P-Celtic place-names in Scotland: a reappraisal. *Studia Celtica,* 7 (1972), l–ll.

– 1975 Pictish and British (Cumbric) place-names. In McNeill, P and Nicholson R (eds) *An Historical Atlas of Scotland c.400–c.1600,* 3–4. St Andrews.

– 1976 *Scottish Place-names: Their Study and Significance.* London.

– 1995 Pictish place names. In Nicoll, E H (ed) *A Pictish Panorama: the Story of the Picts and a Pictish Bibliography,* 11–13. Balgavies, Angus.

– forthcoming The Dee at Chester and Aberdeen: thoughts on rivers and divinities. In Rumble, A R and Mills, A D *Names, Places and People. An Onomastic Miscellany in Memory of John McNeal Dodgson*, 250–5. Stamford.

SKENE, WF 1836 *The Highlanders of Scotland*, 2 vols. London.

WAINWRIGHT, F T 1955 *The Problem of the Picts.* Edinburgh.

WATSON, W J 1926 *The History of the Celtic Place-names of Scotland*. Edinburgh and London.

WHITTINGTON, G and SOULSBY, J A 1968 A preliminary report on an investigation into pit place-names. *Scottish Geographical Magazine,* 84 (1968) 117–25.

Recording Early Christian Monuments in Scotland

J. N. Graham Ritchie

The illustration of the Early Christian monuments of Scotland forms one of the most important aspects of the record of their decoration. Structured verbal descriptions came late to the presentation of the information recorded in the field, or in nature, as was the phrase of the early nineteenth-century illustrator. This paper explores some of the ways in which carved stones have been recorded in the past and is intended to complement Ian Scott's paper on how such evidence is presented today. It may be that how an illustration is to be published will affect how the original observation is made in the field; it may be that the skills and approach of the illustrator may dictate whether a linear or a textured style is preferred. Such a dichotomy of approach is also evident in the illustration of early rock carvings in Scotland; do you draw the stone and let the art show through, or do you outline the carvings as black linear markings on a white surface?

Aspects of early recording have been explored in the Introduction to the Handlist of Pictish Stones first prepared in 1985 and reissued in 1994 (RCAHMS 1994a), and by Dr Henderson in the new Introduction to the reprinted *The Early Christian Monuments of Scotland* by J R Allen and J Anderson, published by the Pinkfoot Press in 1993. Nevertheless an exploration of one stone through the observation of different illustrators may be instructive. It may be unwise to choose such a contentious stone as Meigle 10, Perthshire, but, as it no longer exists, interpretation of the earlier illustrations focuses crucially on how such depictions were created. The stone was a slab of sandstone, three edges of which had been broken off, and which had come to measure 3 feet in length by 1 foot 6 inches in height.

Alexander Gordon, the author of the first account, sets the scene; Gordon himself was a member of the circle of Sir John Clerk of Penicuik and was Secretary to the Society of Antiquaries of London from 1736 to 1741, when he emigrated to America to become Secretary to the Governor of South Carolina (Piggott 1976, 142–3; Piggott and Robertson 1977, nos 21, 22, 25).

> 'At a Village called Miggle, about four Miles from Cowper, several stones are erected in the Church-yard, on one of which... are three small Crosses, with many Animals above and below. On another... is a fair Carpentum, or Chariot, drawn by two Horses, and some persons within it, and behind the Carpentum is a Human Figure devoured by a Wild Beast.' (Gordon 1726, 162, with spelling modernised)

Gordon's illustration is of interest as the earliest showing this stone, and it is a representative example of a style of illustration that sets Pictish and Anglian sculpture alongside Roman altars and inscriptions. The style sees figural art as secondary to the inscription on the representations of Roman pieces; the figures are shadowy on Pictish monuments when compared to the linearity of the cross. Nevertheless the depiction is clear: a pair of horses pulls a wheeled vehicle with a driver and two tentative figures in an enclosed part set on the body of the vehicle; a squatting figure and an animal are in the foreground; to the left the hind portion of an animal is set above another animal, also partial, which appears to be devouring a two legged figure, possibly a person (**1a**).

Of particular interest is the way the pair of horses is so clearly shown with a double line indicating that there is one behind the other and the way in which the thickness of the stone is indicated (in a manner comparable to the illustrations of Roman altars). Thus it is made clear that the right side has been sheared. Gordon's care in measuring and recording is not to be doubted, his plans show scale lines in paces, and the sculptured stones are for each part

a

b

c

1 **a** *Meigle 10, Gordon 1726* **b** *Meigle 10, Pennant 1772* **c** *Antiquaries in action, Gordon 1726*

a

b

c

2 *Meigle 10:* **a** *Chalmers 1842* **b** *Stuart 1856* **c** *Allen and Anderson 1903*

of the volume provided with a scale in feet (not for each plate). This interest in the provision of illustrations to consistent scales was perhaps not always successful, but it was a laudable aim that is not always apparent from the plates.

Gordon appears to have sketched on site, musing at one point 'while I was copying the Monuments at Glames…', and these drawings were then transcribed by others on to copper plates. Other hands too were involved, for the charming scene on the plate of Brechin round tower, which illustrates antiquaries in the field, is in an altogether more assured style (**1c**). Gordon concludes his Preface:

> 'I confess, I have not spared any Pains in tracing the Foot-steps of the Romans, and in drawing and measuring all the Figures in the following Sheets from the Originals; having made a pretty laborious Progress through almost every Part of Scotland for Three Years successively.' (spelling modernised)

Pictish studies are fortunate that his eye caught so many more later monuments than was his original intention.

Some years later Thomas Pennant was to illustrate the stone rather differently (**1b**). 'A Welsh squire with interests in natural history, antiquities, and topography' (Piggott and Robertson 1977, no 35), Pennant was accompanied by his Artist, Moses Griffith (Holloway and Errington 1978, 57, 59). The illustration (Pennant 1772, ii, pl xvii) is interesting in that it is a spirited representation of several activities, but there is no impression of the pair of horses, successfully evoked by Gordon. There is a clear impression of the damaged right hand side of the stone and of the relief nature of the sculpture, with the basal moulding clearly shown; the depth is intended to be less than that indicated for no 4 depicted immediately above on Pennant's illustration. The driver of the vehicle is confidently shown, and the reins have a circular feature halfway between horse and driver, which is difficult to explain in practical terms, and which is seen again on Stuart's illustration many years later. The disposition of the figures on the vehicle and the irregular nature of the upper part of the vehicle accord with the tentative illustration by Gordon. The figure beneath the vehicle is interpreted as an archer and a small animal is detected below the horse. The tail of the upper animal on the right hand side is set between its legs, and the toothiness of the devouring monster below is crisply depicted. The more sensitive use of the medium of engraving gives a far greater sense of the relief nature of the carving than does Gordon's earlier attempt.

These writers make no mention of how the monument related to the other stones at Meigle, but the author of the parish entry in the *Statistical Account* at the end of the eighteenth century was very specific and the stone was seen as one element of the 'grand sepulchural monument of Vanora… wife of Arthur' of ancient fable (Playfair 1791, 506–7). The monument, with Meigle 2 at its centre, and its traditions are discussed in Ritchie 1995. But that the stones were moved around or sometimes covered up seems clear, as Jervise writing in 1859 recorded its discovery, or rediscovery, in 1805 when the road was made on the north side of the churchyard, when at least two rude stone coffins were found near the base of no 2, as well as the curious stone bearing 'ane goddes in ane cairt' (no 10) (Jervise 1859, 245, using in fact the phrase used to describe a scene on a lost stone from Newtyle).

A sketch by James Skene of Rubislaw, an eminent antiquary and friend of Sir Walter Scott, so closely follows the irregular shape of the stone given by Pennant that it may confidently be said to be derived from it; however Skene has observed the pair of horses and adds the additional line with the note, 'there are two horses, indicated by a double line'. He also adds that the stone is in 'the wall of Stable court at Meigle' (sketch book in the Society of Antiquaries of Scotland papers deposited in the National Monuments Record of Scotland). Rather tetchily, however, in 1814, John Pinkerton dismisses the work that has gone before, and, as quoted by Patrick Chalmers in 1848 (Preface, x), opines

> 'It is much to be wished, that a general collection of these curious Monuments was published in Plates of a just size, those of Mr. Pennant being too diminutive, as well as those of Mr. Cordiner, whose representations cannot be trusted, his imagination being strangely perverted by some fantastic ideas of the picturesque, while those of Mr. Gordon are too rude and inaccurate.'

Cordiner, described as the first Pictomaniac, was not involved in recording work at Meigle (RCAHMS 1994a, 3).

Patrick Chalmers of Aldbar took up the task and commissioned the recording of the stones of Angus in a volume which was published in 1848, but in choosing the artist he must also have known that the style of publication would have been by the now popular medium of lithography. He felt that

> 'it is necessary that accurate Drawings should be collected, of sufficient size to exhibit all the details of the Sculpture; and it is with a view to lay the foundations of such a collection, that the present work has been undertaken. It is merely an attempt to delineate with strict accuracy, all the Ancient Sculptured Stones now extant in Angus.' (1848, iii)

His remarks about the relationship of the antiquarian or archaeologist to the artist are very percipient.

> 'In conclusion, it may be permitted to remark, how hard it is to persuade an Artist, that in Antiquarian Drawings, extreme accuracy in delineation is far preferable to picturesque effect; and how difficult to restrain the imagination, when tempted by dim lights and uncertain lines. In drawing from old and weather-worn stones, such as are the subject of this volume, it is often necessary to watch the lights; – to draw one side of the Stone in the morning, the other in the afternoon; and above all, the sense of touch is, in some cases, to be more surely relied on, than that of sight. Those rules and precautions have been observed in the present instance; and it is hoped that the result is as near an approach to accuracy as is possible; the work has this advantage, that the Artist who made the original drawings transferred them himself to stone.' (ibid, v)

The lithographic process, which had been chosen for the publication, had been invented in Germany by Aloys Senefelder in 1798 and became popular in Britain in the 1820s as a publishing medium for a variety of illustrations. The principle involves the preparation on the surface of a polished stone of grease-receptive and grease-resistant areas which will form the printing and non-printing areas respectively. The advantage of transfer lithography over other forms of illustration was that the image did not have to be created in reverse as on an engraver's plate. The transfer paper was coated and the artist could use the range of strokes offered by the lithographic 'chalk' to create a range of textures and shadows. The prepared paper was pressed on to the stone; the paper and coating were then washed off, and the prepared stone was ready for printing (Twyman 1970; Gascoigne 1986). Scotland's particular role in the development of commercial lithography has been acknowledged (Pennell and Pennell 1915, 121–2).

Chalmers' artist was P A Jastresbski [*recte* Jastrzçbski] a Polish painter and draughtsman, based in Aberdeen (McEwan 1994, 299). For Meigle 10, he has shown a spirited

horse, with the rather tentative outline of a second around it, pulling a carefully delineated vehicle with a driver and two passengers (**2a**). The form of the vehicle is clear, with a platform and side rail supported on uprights with central ball-shaped decoration; the lower line of figures, the archer, animal, and the man being devoured by a beast are all positioned along the basal moulding. The small animal beneath the horse is not recorded.

John Stuart's compendious volumes for the Spalding Club of Aberdeen were designed to widen the scope of Chalmers' pioneering study. Stuart felt that 'in various cases' it was necessary to see the stones himself, implying that this was not always the case. He entrusted the execution of the drawings for his great enterprise to P A Jastresbski, by whom the Sculptured Stones in Angus had been drawn, but following 'his removal to Australia', a phrase redolent of one of the unsolved mysteries of Sherlock Holmes, the work was taken up by A Gibb, of the lithographic firm Keith and Gibb in Aberdeen, for whom Jastresbski was also working. Stuart is at pains to explain the methods used – the drawings made by Jastresbski and Gibb were transferred to the stone by the illustrators themselves thereby avoiding 'one considerable source of mistake'. A degree of rivalry can be detected in that 'Jaztresbski's drawings having been found, on comparison, to be deficient in minute accuracy, apparently from this hasty execution, the figures have again been drawn by Mr Gibb.' (Stuart 1856, xvi). Rather more, however, can be discovered from recent work on the biography of Sir George Reid, or more strictly autobiography, as it appears that it was dictated by Reid to his wife in 1882, and kindly made available to the present writer by Jennifer Melville, Aberdeen Art Gallery. Reid (1841–1913) was to become a distinguished portrait and landscape painter, but his early training was in lithography, being apprenticed to Keith and Gibb at the age of thirteen in 1854 (McEwan 1994, 479–80).

> 'Another piece of work which was in progress during the whole seven years G. [George Reid] was in Keith & Gibbs was the Sculptured Stones of Scotland, for the Spalding Club, the work was in two Vols. Many of the earliest plates in the first Vol. had been done before G. went to K&G's. They were drawn on stone by Jaztresbski, a Polish Refugee, but after a time some one, report whispered Mr Gibb, discovered inaccuracies in

the drawings the consequence was, that a good many of the plates, of which four hundred each had been printed off, were condemned as worth less, and the work was taken out of Jaztrebski's hands and entrusted to Mr Gibb – Jaztresbski shortly after emigrating to Australia, and died in a poors house there. It was the third or fourth year of his apprenticeship before G. was entrusted with any of the Sculptured Stones to draw; several of those in the latter part of the 1st Vol. were drawn by him on stone from Mr. Gibb's sketches. He, Mr. Gibb, going away every summer for some weeks, and visiting the different localities to make drawing[s], and measurements from the originals; these drawings he afterwards carefully reduced, and finished and they were then handed over to his apprentices to put on stone. A considerable portion of the earlier plates in the 2nd Vol. were drawn on stone by G. St Martin's Cross, Iona. Maclean's Cross, and many others among the number. G. spent much of his time in the last years of his apprenticeship on this work, indeed long before his apprenticeship had expired he was doing all the principal draughtsmans work in the establishment and being paid with eight or nine shillings a week.'

This insight into the behind the scenes activities involved in the preparation of Stuart's two volumes is of interest not only in the present context, but also in identifying the hand of the illustration of St Martin's Cross (1886, pls xl and xli), which, unusually for the presentation of the material, has a view of the Abbey behind the cross and the Sound of Mull beyond, rather in the manner of Gordon's background scenery on his Brechin plate and linking the scientific illustration to the tradition of topographic lithography popular at the time.

But to return to Meigle 10, Stuart described it thus: 'The oblong Stone in the upper part of Plate lxxvi, is placed on a mound in the churchyard.' The depiction offered by Gibb (**2b**) is very specific: the two horses are carefully shown both with plaited tails and the pole of the cart passing between the tails; the driver is given a seat with a pair of legs and the cart is provided with ball decoration on its corner uprights and further upright rails visible behind the wheel, which has very definite spindle shaped spokes. The figure with the bow is clear and the animal at which he is aiming is given rather lion-like paws. The devouring animal is shown with snout and toothed jaws. The figure is stabbing the throat of the animal and the man's hair and arms are clearly depicted. By comparing Gibb's drawing of

surviving stones with present illustrations his customary accuracy is not in doubt. The shadows and highlights are characteristic of lithographic work. Very specific aspects seem to have been over-emphasised: the horses' tails, the spokes, and the teeth and muzzle of the devouring beast. A knowledge of what a decorated stone was supposed to look like ensured that the driver and the man about to be devoured were given very definite Pictish looks.

The essential rapport between illustrator and antiquary is nowhere clearer than in the Preface to Stuart's second volume:

'I have reserved to the last my acknowledgement of the services of my friend Mr. Gibb, the artist by whom the drawings from the stones have been made and lithographed, and to whose intelligent interest in the subject I have been greatly indebted in the arrangement of the volume. The beauty and artistic finish of the Plates assert their own excellence; but I desire to record my testimony to his care and patience in copying the weather-worn and faded monuments there represented, which have secured for Mr. Gibb's drawings the more valuable character of scrupulous accuracy in detail.' (1886, 47–8)

By the 1880s the new medium of photography was becoming more common in archaeological recording, and its potential as a method of illustration is nowhere more firmly stated than in the Prefatory Note to Joseph Anderson's Second Series of Rhind Lectures (1881, vi).

'I have thought it necessary that some examples should be represented with that absolute truthfulness which is only obtained by Photography, and have therefore preferred the rugged realism of these reproductions to illustrations more picturesque in character.'

Anderson's publisher tipped in specially printed pages. The slow, and initially expensive, introduction of photography into affordable publications with large print-runs has been charted by Gernsheim (1969, 539–52). Anderson also illustrates Meigle 10 with a rough tracing from Stuart (**2c**) and records that the stone had 'perished in the burning of the church in 1869'; some of the areas of shading on the lithograph have been overemphasised, the hunter particularly being given either a shoulder garment or very long hair. Anderson interprets the scene with confidence as the Ascension of Elijah and the bear tearing the Children that mocked Elisha (1881, 158, fig 103), but it is fair to say that the main scene is so calm that the sense of Elijah's whirlwind into heaven is missing (Harbison 1992, 223–4).

A S Aglen, Rector of Alyth and Meigle and Archdeacon of St Andrews, who wrote the first guide book to the stones at Meigle, not dated (but the present author's copy is inscribed 1895), used a sketch of Meigle 10 for the front cover decoration based on Stuart, and thus the iconic nature of the stone as representing the Meigle collection, although it had already been lost, was enshrined. Aglen was aware of, though not altogether in accord with, Anderson's interpretation; interestingly he draws attention to the vehicle's 'tilt or covering' (Aglen n.d., fn p.7).

The culmination of over a century of illustration and cataloguing of the Early Christian monuments of Scotland is Romilly Allen's magisterial catalogue in Allen and Anderson 1903. Analysis and written description take precedence for the first time over illustration. The structured description of each stone and the painstaking analysis of the decoration are often of greater importance than the illustration. The Council of the Society of Antiquaries of Scotland, who initiated the survey, resolved that photography should be used for illustration as far as possible, together with detailed drawings, and rubbings or squeezes, when these were desirable (Allen and Anderson 1903, I, Preface vi). The possibilities of the new medium proved to be less satisfactory than were hoped, indeed 'most tantalising' (ibid). Allen goes on to explain that 'photography from the stones themselves, in cases where the stone is unfavourably situated, or much weathered, or overgrown by lichen, is frequently unsuitable'. The possibility of casting stones and photographing the casts, as had been undertaken at Govan by J Stirling Maxwell in 1899, was considered, but was rejected on grounds of cost. 'Still a sufficient number of photographs were obtained to afford a representative set of plates of the monuments carved in relief, while the method adopted for the unshaped stones with incised sculptures was to make outline-drawings from rubbings reduced by photography.' Allen himself prepared the drawings up to page 212 (part III) of the published volume, but from that point on they were mostly prepared by F R Coles, Anderson's assistant at the Society's Museum and himself an accomplished draughtsman.

The original intention to rely on photography rather than to commission new drawings of the stones as an integral part of the survey may seem odd at this remove, but it may be that the sort of draughting skills required were not available; there are no obvious candidates among the contemporary illustrators in the *Proceedings of the Society of Antiquaries of Scotland*. Allen and Anderson were themselves of literary and analytical bent, rather than questioning the nuance of line. But perhaps more importantly is the impression that the volume is intended to be used with copies of Stuart and Chalmers to hand for illustrations, and that the published line drawings are in the nature of aides-memoire. This can be evoked in visual form by examining the depiction of the back of Meigle 23. The illustration in Stuart (pl v, no 2) is carefully executed and makes full use of the range of texture offered by lithography (**3a**); that in Allen and Anderson (1903, III, 337, fig 351b) is a rapid sketch from a photograph (**3b**), but there is a clear prompt to Stuart for fuller description and illustration. The drawing by the Royal Commission strives for the same degree of nuance as Stuart by using a stipple technique (**3c**). Equally Meigle 23 can be used to illustrate advances in photographic techniques available today, with greater flexibility in lighting permitting the overall clarity of decoration, for which Allen and Anderson had clearly hoped (Quick 1975) (**3d**).

The outline drawing of Meigle 10 in Allen and Anderson (1903, III, 331, fig 344) is a linear interpretation by Coles of the illustration created by Gibb; it is a faithful enough translation, except in the depiction of the wheel of the vehicle and the tip of the pole between the pair of horses, which may be taken from Chalmers. But it is ironic that it is the most optimistically interpreted version of the stone from which Coles's linear drawing is taken. The spindle-shaped spokes lose their distinctiveness in the redrawing, and the hunted animal poses rather jauntily on the border moulding. Perhaps the most frequently consulted illustration of the stone is at some remove from the earlier illustrations taken from the stone itself. Such a situation can be compared to the various retracings of the plan of Dunadd, which progressively lost the sophistication of Thomas Ross's original (the various stages are shown in RCAHMS 1988, 150); such considerations are important when comparing drawings or tracings from different sources, and offer a contemporary parallel to notions of the 'declining symbol' in the study of Pictish art.

3 *Meigle 23:* **a** *Stuart 1867* **b** *Allen and Anderson 1903* **c** and **d** *RCAHMS 1994b in drawn and photographic record*

This unique carving is known only through a series of independent illustrations, for the stone was destroyed in a fire that consumed the church in 1869, and it thus offers one of the most telling demonstrations of the importance of accurate recording. The most important of these are the observations of Jastresbski and Gibb, the latter specifically improving on his predecessor. That a stone of this shape existed, with carved figures laid out in the general disposition, is surely undisputed. It is ironic that the only local parallel, a stone from Newtyle, is also lost; the description of the figures around the cart does not match that for Meigle, and there is every reason to think that two stones bearing the comparable scene formerly existed (Ritchie 1995, 9 n 1). There are no other parallels in Scotland, and it may be constructive, after our rigorous examination of the history of recording of Meigle 10, to look to Ireland. The base of the North Cross Ahenny, Co. Tipperary, shows a wheeled vehicle (eight-spoked wheel) moving from right to left, with two figures, but no indication of the framework of the vehicle, nor of spindle-shaped spokes (Harbison 1992, 13). The vehicles depicted on the worn base of the Cross of the Scriptures, Clonmacnois, Co. Offaly, are shown moving from right to left, and have large eight-spoked wheels, very comparable in proportion to those of Ahenny in relation to the horse, but again there is no indication of the structure of the vehicle itself. There is the suspicion that they may be drawn by two horses apiece (ibid, 48). The base of the Cross of Saints Patrick and Columba from Kells, Co. Meath, has a rather weathered representation of a vehicle moving from right to left, the proportion of wheel to horse being very comparable to the other two Irish examples (ibid, 110), and thus the figures are interpreted as passenger and charioteer. The depictions on Killamery, Co. Kilkenney and Muiredach's Cross, Monasterboice, Co. Louth, are too indistinct to be helpful (ibid, 123, 142). Laing and Laing have noted the differences between the Meigle stone and the Irish examples, the smaller wheels and open sides with baluster shafts of the former, and have concluded that it is an illustration of a native style of vehicle (1984, 278). Reconstruction of what an earlier Irish cart might have looked like, based on literary sources, suggests a simple two-wheeled vehicle with low solid sides, and possible fragments have been found in wetland sites in Ireland, but

so far there is nothing to confirm the balustered railed sides of Meigle 10. However, it says much for the scholarship of two of the earlier writers on the subject that they have drawn attention to aspects of the depiction of Meigle 10 that have otherwise largely been passed over: Gordon describes the vehicle as a *carpentum* and Aglen underlines in his footnote that the 'vehicle had a tilt or covering'. Piggott acknowledges *carpentum* as a 'tricky word', but describes it as 'a covered civil vehicle used especially for women and on priestly occasions in the Roman world, and usually drawn by mules and asses, not horses' (1992, 34). Such a tilt cart accords better with the representation of the external driver and enclosed passengers of Meigle 10 in the baluster decorated vehicle, than does the 'chariot' of Elijah's ascension; he would have gone through the roof! It seems rather more likely that the scene derives from a classical source rather than representing any native vehicle.

This brief consideration of the ways that monuments have been illustrated in the past has not intended to demonstrate a preferred style or draw attention to 'unreliable' execution, for in most cases the style and approach have been appropriate for the day, and indeed Pictish studies have been fortunate in the approaches of its researchers. The survey of the stones at Meigle by the Royal Commission on the Ancient and Historical Monuments of Scotland (RCAHMS 1994b) demonstrated that Patrick Chalmers' views of the importance of light and touch, as well as checking the accuracy of the depiction with the stone, remain paramount. Thus today the possibilities of publication and dissemination remain important constraints, for only a limited number of photographs or detailed drawings can be published in book format; gone are the days of what Dr Henderson has described as the 'magnificent, if impractical, imperial volume' prepared by Chalmers and Jastresbskl, but the possibilities of text, drawings and photographs being available in the near future in manipulable form in interactive digital formats mean that the study of Early Christian monuments may never be quite the same again.

Acknowledgements

This contribution has depended on the assistance and advice of friends and colleagues from associated fields, but any remaining errors or misinterpretations are my own;

Dr Mungo Campbell, National Galleries of Scotland, Mr G B Quick, Royal Commission on the Ancient and Historical Monuments of Scotland, Miss J Mitchell, City of Aberdeen Art Gallery, Miss Sara Stevenson, Scottish National Portrait Gallery, have all provided information and references from which this note has benefitted. Dr Anna Ritchie as well as colleagues within the Royal Commission on the Ancient and Historical Monuments of Scotland have all assisted during the preparation.

References

AGLEN, A S n.d. [1893] *The Sculptured Stones at Meigle*. Dundee.

ALLEN, J R and ANDERSON, J 1903 *The Early Christian Monuments of Scotland*, 3 parts. Edinburgh (repr with an Introduction by Isabel Henderson, 2 vols, Balgavies, Angus, 1993).

ANDERSON, J 1881 *Scotland in Early Christian Times* (Second Series, the Rhind Lectures in Archaeology for 1880). Edinburgh.

CHALMERS, P 1848 *The Ancient Sculptured Monuments of the County of Angus*. Aberdeen.

GASCOIGNE, B 1986 *How to Identify Prints*. London.

GERNSHEIM, H and A 1969 *The History of Photography from the camera obscura to the beginning of the modern era*. London.

GORDON, A 1726 *Itinerarium Septentrionale: or, a Journey through most of the Counties of Scotland and those in the north of England*. London.

HARBISON, P 1992 *The High Crosses of Ireland: an iconographic and photographic survey*. Bonn.

HOLLOWAY, J and ERRINGTON, L 1978 *The Discovery of Scotland*. Edinburgh.

JERVISE, A 1859 Notices descriptive of the localities of certain sculptured stone monuments in Forfarshire, etc. *Proc Soc Antiq Scot*, 2 (1854-57), 242–51.

LAING, L and LAING, J 1984 Archaeological notes on some Scottish Early Christian sculptures. *Proc Soc Antiq Scot*, 114 (1984), 277–87.

McEWAN, P J M 1994 *Dictionary of Scottish Art and Architecture*. Woodbridge.

PENNANT, T 1772 *A Tour of Scotland 1772*. London.

PENNELL, J and PENNELL, E R 1915 *Lithography and lithographers, some chapters on the history of the art*. London.

PIGGOTT, S

– 1976 *Ruins in a Landscape*. Edinburgh.

– 1992 *Wagon, Chariot and Carriage*. London.

PIGGOTT, S and ROBERTSON, M 1977 *Three Centuries of Scottish Archaeology*. Edinburgh.

PLAYFAIR, Dr 1791 Parish of Meigle. In Sinclair, J (ed) *The Statistical Account of Scotland*, vol 1, 505–8. Edinburgh.

QUICK, G 1975 The photography of relief carvings. *Photographic J*, 115 (1975), 272–7.

RITCHIE, A 1995 Meigle and lay patronage in Tayside in the 9th and 10th centuries AD. *Tayside and Fife Archaeological Journal*, 1 (1995), 1–10.

RCAHMS = Royal Commission on the Ancient and Historical Monuments of Scotland

– 1988 *Argyll: An Inventory of the Ancient Monuments*, vol 6, *Mid Argyll and Cowal: Prehistoric and Early Historic Monuments*. Edinburgh.

– 1994a *Pictish Symbol Stones: a handlist 1994*. Edinburgh.

– 1994b *South-East Perth: an Archaeological Landscape*. Edinburgh.

STUART, J 1856 and 1867 *Sculptured Stones of Scotland*. Aberdeen and Edinburgh.

TWYMAN, M 1970 *Lithography 1800–1850*. Oxford.

Illustrating Early Medieval Carved Stones

Ian G. Scott

The possibility of contributing to this volume was a temptation I could not resist. For some time I have wanted to explain why I draw carved stones in the way I do and why I believe this process should be continued, despite the valuable contributions of photography and the amazing developments in computer technology.

My work in illustrating St John's Cross from Iona offers an appropriate example: this is not because I am particularly proud of my drawings of it, but, in describing what I did, I hope to provoke discussion of the neglected subject of the methods and standards which are appropriate to the illustration of carved stones. I offer this effort in celebration of Isabel Henderson's interest in all aspects of the study of early medieval sculpture in Scotland and her long association with Iona in particular.

It is only comparatively recently that I have been engaged in the study of carved stones outside Argyll and the west of Scotland. I should explain that this bias follows directly from my work with the Royal Commission on the Ancient and Historical Monuments of Scotland (Scott 1996) and the production of the Argyll volumes from 1960–1991 (RCAHMS 1971; 1974; 1980; 1982; 1984; 1988; 1992) only slightly extended in scope by the volume *Late Medieval Monumental Sculpture in the West Highlands* (RCAHMS 1977).

My methods of recording medieval sculpture follow a long tradition, adapted for the examples published within these volumes so that comparisons could easily be made within the series. While Historic Scotland and the museums are concerned primarily with conservation and preservation, it falls to the Royal Commission to record what can be observed and to the National Monuments Record to archive what has been found out. There is much active interest in stone preservation but I have heard very little

discussion about methods of recording carved stones which are, sadly, vulnerable to many risks. The bibliography of archaeological illustrating is meagre enough, even if you include cognate subjects, and examination in any detail of the methods most suited to carved stones, is almost non-existent. The usual assumption is that only photography is objective enough, and cheap enough, to be considered.

My plea for the necessity of drawing does not argue against photography, but rather insists that we should not accept any photograph, however good, as enough to record a stone. My impression is that when confronted with the study of a particular stone everyone agrees that photography alone is not adequate, yet economic pressures are such that the principle is lost. Because of this, not even photographs are presented for study but only their reproduction in halftone, printed by lithography with a consequent loss of tonal range and sharpness. I have drawn much from photographs and inevitably made terrible mistakes in the interpretation of detail and in emphasis; from printed halftones, it is even more difficult to arrive at a reasonable version of the truth.

As I find it so difficult to interpret the photographic record it will be readily understood why I seriously question the advisability of founding our record on photographs, and the value of presenting a photograph in demonstration of an argument. The onus of identification and interpretation of what can be seen is passed to the beholder who will almost certainly see things differently, and probably with difficulty, even when following a written description. A considered, studied drawing will present ambiguities, but these can be assumed to be intentional. In my opinion the presentation of a subjective image is the more direct and quickly understood method of publication. This version can then be checked either against the reality

130

in stone or its representation in various lights and from several directions by photography. Further, drawing should be fundamental to our methods of archive: a necessary counter to the inevitable omissions of two-dimensional photography, limited as it is to a chosen pattern of lighting. Stereo-photography would be the only reasonable alternative, but poses too many problems in handling.

Illustrating St John's Cross, Iona

When I went to Iona to draw its carved stones for volume four of the Argyll Inventory (RCAHMS 1982) I was looking at High Crosses for the first time. Only one, St Martin's Cross, was still complete and standing; the others were lying about in pieces. The many fragments of the so-called St John's Cross were in crates for their own safety when Dr Steer, Secretary to the Royal Commission and the author who had taken responsibility for recording medieval carved stones, and I arrived to inspect them. They had been erected at least twice and blown down as recently as 1957. From photographs of the latest reconstruction we managed to identify the stones in earlier photographs. To avoid the stresses caused by making rubbings of the delicate minute detail, each side of each stone now had to be photographed, and prints made to a uniform scale. From these I prepared a montage omitting the concrete in-fills of the reconstruction, which were at that time confusingly still in place.

I had also recorded a decorated boss in the Nunnery Museum of Iona at the same scale. The montage of the St John's Cross fragments allowed me to show that space existed for this boss to be the central feature of the front and to propose that a slight ledge at the back suggested the existence of an otherwise unnoticed mortice. The concrete replica, now much photographed, outside the abbey was unfortunately prepared before this work, but the actual fragments of the original can now be seen in the Iona Museum's reconstruction of this, over five metres high, cross.

The montage reconstruction was printed in 'halftone' by lithography in a sample printing arranged by our publisher Her Majesty's Stationery Office. The result, however, was considered unacceptable as the principal

record and I was, therefore, asked to draw the High Crosses in addition to the smaller cross-marked stones of early-medieval date. The existing montage of both sides was photographed and printed at 1:10. On the introduction of standardisation, this scale for recording had been adopted for early medieval stones because of the small size required for reproduction (1:15). On a polyester overlay, John Stevenson, who had just been appointed to an additional-illustrator post, and I developed a pencil drawing of as much as we could interpret from the fragments, which, thankfully, were now in the care of Historic Scotland awaiting reconstruction at Newbattle near Edinburgh. Back at the office, I traced a more considered version of this pencil drawing using a steel pen and 'Indian' ink on polyester. This drawing was returned to the stones for checking and correcting until both I and Ian Fisher, the officer responsible and now the author of the relevant text, were satisfied.

We were drawing only what we could see and under-stand (**1A**). If we thought that we could be sure of the form which had once existed, I used a very light, fairly even, stipple in contrast to a more emphatic style used for existing detail, as sharply defined as we felt was reasonable; if we wanted to suggest that something had continued, I used a broken (dashed) line; for a worn surface, interpretation went from slightly misty to positively hazy; if form was lacking, all became shaded – not white.

I adopted the technique of stipple for what I would have thought were obvious reasons, but perhaps it might be as well to recite some of them. Of first importance was the comparative lack of an individual 'handwriting' character (usually detectable in other styles of drawing), thereby allowing a more uniform repetition of the style by others in the drawing-office and indeed, hopefully, by future generations. It is also the most natural way to convey the modelling of the third dimension without giving it an affected texture when you are obliged to use only black ink for the sake of clarity in reproduction and longevity in the archive. The technique also allows additions and corrections to be made to an extent not so easily achieved with, for instance, a 'hatched' style.

Drawing from the montage provoked a controversial

1 (opposite) *St John's Cross, Iona:* A *East face, 1:20* B–F *enlarged details* G *photo-montage showing existing surfaces* H *exploded section showing constructional detail (RCAHMS 1982, 198)* suggestion that I put to Ian Fisher and R.B.K. Stevenson, ex-Director of the National Museum of Antiquities. We had been puzzled by the use of a different kind of stone for the top capping and for a fragment of the ring found by Mr Fisher. Also the drawing was now showing a seemingly impractical sequence of mortices and tenons connecting several stones and suggesting a very precarious cross. This led, after much consideration, to the tentative theory of collapse and remaking in antiquity, proposed in the Inventory (RCAHMS 1982, 201). Drawings can, and should, stimulate such questioning and not simply be an inert record of the bits and pieces: they should provide the means for a paper reconstruction and analysis. (Even with individual drawings completed it is perhaps obvious, but should be noted, that advantage should then be taken to arrange sets and combinations to suggest sensible connections and conclusions.)

There were some areas which we felt were not as fully interpreted at 1:10 as we could manage. These areas we drew at twice the scale (1:5) (**1B–F**). Also, we demonstrated at a smaller scale and in outline how we thought the cross had been constructed (**1H**). The montaged photographs were used to show existing surfaces (**1G**).

For the 1982 publication the two faces of the cross were mounted on opposed pages (198–9), surrounded by their details and separated by their small montaged versions. Supporting photographs of detail, and diagrams, follow. It was a disappointment that the size of the cross obliged us to reproduce at 1:20 instead of 1:15, which had been adopted as standard for this material throughout the Argyll series.

The experience of drawing Argyll's stones, such as St John's Cross, encourages me to propose the creation of an archive of drawings in elevational view, which would be subject to continuous revision, at a scale making comparison immediately possible.

The Argyll Inventory (RCAHMS 1971; 1974; 1980; 1982; 1984; 1988; 1992) and a current survey of early sculpture elsewhere in the West Highlands are creating a visual index which could be expanded to include the rest of Scotland. The Pictish stones from Meigle have already been added (RCAHMS 1994). The outstanding advantage of this form of basic archive is the quality, speed and cheapness of its reproduction by photocopier. This should in turn encourage much wider distribution and a more comprehensive base for our studies.

As a strange footnote, the pieces of St John's Cross were finally restored and prepared for their return to Iona in the very building which has been reconstructed as the new headquarters for the Royal Commission.

Acknowledgements
I must express my thanks; to Historic Scotland for access to the fragments of St John's Cross; to Dr Kenneth Steer who ordered the work; to John Dunbar and Roger Mercer, his successors as Secretary, and the present staff of the Royal Commission for permission and encouragement to publish this story from 'below stairs'; to Ian Fisher, my long-standing (-suffering) colleague for ever-helpful direction; to Alastair MacLaren and John Higgitt who both read an earlier version of this paper and made me think again; to David Henry of the Pinkfoot Press who persuaded me to write for the first time; and to Isabel Henderson for providing an excuse for this unusual exercise, in addition to her more usual inspiration.

References
RCAHMS = Royal Commission on the Ancient and Historical Monuments of Scotland
– 1971 *Argyll: An Inventory of the Ancient Monuments*, vol 1, *Kintyre*. Edinburgh.
– 1974 *Argyll: An Inventory of the Ancient Monuments*, vol 2, *Lorn*. Edinburgh.
– 1977 Steer and Bannerman, *Late Medieval Monumental Sculpture in the West Highlands*. Edinburgh.
– 1980 *Argyll: An Inventory of the Monuments*, vol 3, *Mull, Tiree, Coll and Northern Argyll*. Edinburgh.
– 1982 *Argyll: An Inventory of the Monuments*, vol 4, *Iona*. Edinburgh.
– 1984 *Argyll: An Inventory of the Monuments*, vol 5, *Islay, Jura, Colonsay and Oronsay*. Edinburgh.
– 1988 *Argyll: An Inventory of the Monuments*, vol 6, *Mid Argyll and Cowal: Prehistoric and Early Historic Monuments*. Edinburgh.
– 1992 *Argyll: An Inventory of the Monuments*, vol 7, *Mid Argyll and Cowal: Medieval and Later Monuments*. Edinburgh.
– 1994 *South-East Perth, an archaeological landscape*. Edinburgh.
SCOTT, IG 1996 Archaeological illustration: personal experience and the drawing of carved stones for publication. *Graphic Archaeology 1996* (Journal of the Association of Archaeological Illustrators and Surveyors), 1–13 .

The Early Medieval Carved Stones of Fortingall

56°35.1 N
4° 40 W

N N 737 465

Niall M. Robertson
Photographs by Tom E. Gray

Historical Background

As is the case with many of Scotland's churches, the parish church of Fortingall in Glen Lyon (**1**), in the mountainous north-west of the former county of Perthshire (NN 742 470) lacks early documentation, but has evidence for an ancient origin in the form of carved stones of the early medieval period. This collection has been little studied since the cross-slab fragments were first published in J. Romilly Allen and Joseph Anderson's *The Early Christian Monuments of Scotland* (hereafter ECMS) in 1903. Since then several new fragments and complete undescribed cross-slabs have come to light. The collection now comes to eight pieces, one of the more notable assemblages in the country, and the presence of these sculptured stones, several of them finely carved, or of unusual form, bespeaks the existence of an early medieval ecclesiastical establishment at Fortingall. Several other strands of evidence strongly suggest the presence of an early church here, and hint that it may have been one of considerable importance.

The place-name Fortingall is first recorded (as the title of a thane/thanage) in the form *Forterkil* in the *Scone Liber*, 1214 x 49.[1] It appears to be derived from the Gaelic *fortir* 'upper land' or, more appropriately given Fortingall's situation at the foot of a steep rise, 'projecting land' (Simon Taylor pers comm).[2] The element -kil, < Gaelic *cill*, 'church, churchyard', more commonly found as the initial syllable in place-names elsewhere in Scotland and Ireland, and usually followed by the name of a saint[3], in itself points to an early date. It has been proposed that, because of the distribution of the place-name element *cill* in Scotland, and other reasons, names containing *cill* 'are in general not likely to be much younger than 800' (Nicolaisen 1976, 142–4; cf Taylor 1996, 99).

Fortingall is set in a fertile mountain valley, bordered to the south and west by the river Lyon which emerges from the mountains 1.5 kilometres west of the church and surrounding village. Despite its setting at the heart of the Highlands, almost equidistant from the sea east and west, the flat bottom of the Vale of Fortingall is only some 120m above sea level, but high hills rise abruptly round it on all sides. To the south, beyond the Lyon, Drummond Hill rises to 455m before dropping down to the shores of Loch Tay, while to the west, Creag a' Mhadaidh, rising to 601m, and Beinn Dearg and Creag Mhòr, rearing to 630m and 822m respectively, spectacularly frame the narrow entrance to the western part of Glen Lyon.

Fortingall is situated at the heart of a network of glens which must always have allowed relatively easy communications in most directions. Some 2.5 kilometres north-east down the valley of the Lyon, the Keltney Burn feeds into the river, and the Pass of Keltney can be traversed northwards to Foss and Loch Tummel-side. A little further to the south-east the Lyon meets the Tay which then tends eastward along Strathtay to Logierait, then southwards to Dunkeld and the lowlands beyond.

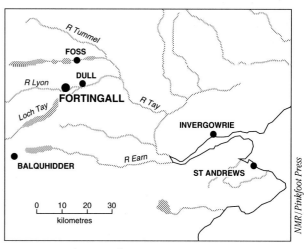

1 *Location of Fortingall*

To the south of Fortingall a short unnamed glen links its valley with Loch Tay-side at Fearnan. From here the far west of Scotland can be reached using the route Loch Tay – Glendochart –Strathfillan– Glen Lochy – Loch Awe. Long and narrow Glen Lyon, immediately west of Fortingall, also allows communication to or from the west by more mountainous roads[4], though the traveller in early times might have preferred the first named corridor, with its possibility of using water transport for a large part of the route.

In the Dark Ages Fortingall lay in the region of *Fotla* or *Athfothla*, one of the seven traditional provinces of the Pictish kingdom (Watson 1926, 107–8, 111, 228-9; Anderson 1973, 79–83, 139–40, 143). The name appears to mean 'new [or second] Ireland' (Watson 1926, 229), though this is open to question. The modern district-name Atholl derives from it. The area seems to have been something of an independent entity within the larger Pictish kingdom, and conflicts between kings of Atholl and the overkings of the Picts are recorded in the Irish annals (Henderson 1967, 61, 63). The name Athfothla, if it did mean 'new Ireland', may imply an early folk-movement into what is now highland Perthshire from the Gaelic-speaking areas of the west.[5] The likely influx of missionaries from Iona (and possibly other Irish monasteries) must in itself have Gaelicised the culture of the area to some extent (Taylor 1996, 103; 1997, 48–9).

The area surrounding Fortingall is extraordinarily rich in archaeological sites of all periods. Of prehistoric antiquities, cup-marked stones are particularly numerous, and a large stone carved with fourteen cup-marks was unearthed in the churchyard itself in 1903.[6] Single standing stones and stone settings are also common. A field about 300 m east of the church contains three settings of standing stones in a triangular arrangement. About the same distance westward of the church within Fortingall village is a monolith known as Clach Mo-Lucháig, a name possibly of Early Christian origins.[7] Early defensive or domestic sites occur near Fortingall in the form of two hill-forts[8], and several of the massively-walled circular homesteads or 'ring-forts' whose heaviest concentration is in Highland Perthshire.[9]

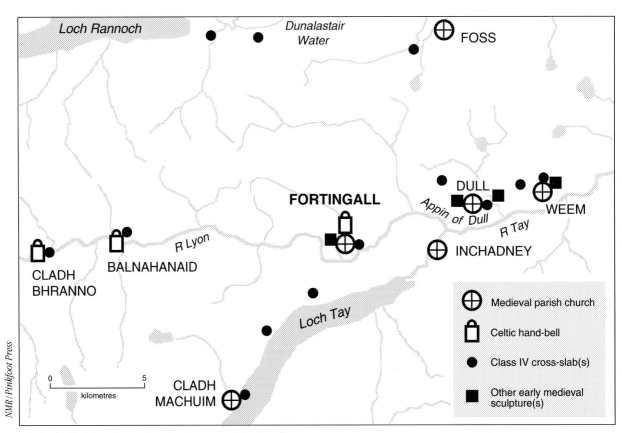

2 *Early Christian sites and antiquities around Fortingall*

other structures connected to the putative monastery. It would be fascinating to learn what excavation of these features would tell us about the ancient community here.

It may be that the religious settlement at Fortingall was relatively short lived. It seems to have left no trace in the oral traditions of the area, except for the vague memory of an early saint being buried in the village (see n17). It may have been eclipsed in importance by nearby Dull[25], as the cult of Coeti was perhaps eclipsed by that of Adomnán.[26] If the two churches were founded from Iona about the same time, as their dedications suggest, their resources may have been too slender to support two communities so close to each other in a mountainous area with restricted good land. The two monastic communities might have been amalgamated, with Fortingall's status being reduced to that of an outlying church serving the spiritual needs of the lay population in the Vale of Fortingall, a function that survived into the Middle Ages and beyond, with the creation of an organised network of parishes in the twelfth and thirteenth centuries. That the early church of Fortingall may have received substantial patronage in its day, whether lay or ecclesiastical or both, is suggested by the good quality of its surviving early medieval sculpture.

The Carved Stones

This description of the carved stones Fortingall 1–4 follows the numbering used in ECMS (III, 508–10), with the cross-slabs 5–8, found subsequently, identified by the order of their discovery. The discovery of the former is described

as follows:

> 'Three stones belonging to Class III were recently found here during the demolition of the old Parish Church, for the erection of a new church on the same site, and one was found a few years previously in the wall of an old thatched cottage in the neighbourhood of the church. The church demolished was a pre-Reformation building, and the stones were found in its walls.' (Allen and Anderson 1903, III, 508)

Fortingall 1–3 were the stones found in the church. Only the largest surviving fragment of Fortingall 4 is figured in ECMS, and the writer has been unable to ascertain when and where the other three pieces of this stone were discovered. It is likely that they came to light with the recorded fragment, but that they were not brought to Allen's attention when he was cataloguing the Fortingall cross-slabs. Allen's description of the stones implies that he had not been to Fortingall himself, and had only seen a rubbing of Fortingall 4 (op cit).

Fortingall 1–4 are at present preserved in the parish church, within the window alcoves at the east end of the building. The fragmentary state of these cross-slabs is no doubt to be attributed to their being shattered into conveniently sized fragments for re-use as building rubble.

Fortingall 1 Class III (**5–7**)

L 340 mm (max); B 435 mm; W 50 mm

Allen and Anderson 1903, III, 508, fig 553

An upright cross-slab of fine-grained grey sandstone of

Tom E. Gray

a　　　　　　　　　　**b**

5 *Fortingall 1:* **a** *cross-face* **b** *reverse*

which only two fragments of its middle part survive. In ECMS, three fragments are described and figured, but the piece which included part of the rounded upper edge of the stone, is no longer to be seen in the church (**6**).

6 *Fortingall 1: drawing published in 1903 showing the now-missing top fragment (top left) (Allen and Anderson 1903, III, fig 553, p508)*

Front (**5a**) Part of the lower half of an outlined cross with round hollow angles, decorated with double-strand interlace. The outlines defining the arms of the cross connect with a wider margin running round the edge of the stone. The semicircular outlines at the angles of the cross are elongated into spirals within the hollows. A circular outlined ring connects the shaft and arms of the cross. It is decorated with a running pattern of S-shaped spirals interspersed with triangular hollows. The panels on either side of the shaft are filled with a symmetrical key-pattern made up of triangular elements. Most of this panel has flaked off at the left side. Where it survives, the carving is little weathered, and is of a high standard of workmanship. The carving gives an impression of relief, but only the hollows at the angles of the cross are sunk below the surface. Much of the decoration is incised. The drawing of the missing upper fragment shows that the cross-slab was originally round-topped, with its shape echoing that of the ring. The ECMS illustration appears, uncharacter-istically, to be rather out of drawing.[27]

Back (**5b**) This face is much less well preserved. The remains of an edge-margin can be seen, and the outlines of what is presumably the shaft of a second cross, flanked by fragmentary robed figures. Parallels to this arrangement on other cross-slabs (eg Aldbar, Monifieth 1, St Andrews 26, St Vigeans 11 and 17) would suggest that they are ecclesiastics. This may give another hint as to the status of the early church at Fortingall. The figures' 'corrugated' garments are particularly reminiscent of those on cross-

slabs from Invergowrie (Allen and Anderson 1903, III, 255, fig 266B) and Tower of Lethendy (Fisher and Greenhill 1972, 238–40, pl 36a). The figures on the latter stone are musicians rather than ecclesiastics or saints. It is unfortunate that the Fortingall I ecclesiastics are not more complete as they represent the only surviving figural carving at the site.

Right Edge (**7**) An incised band of stepped key-pattern.
Left Edge An incised band of stepped key-pattern.

7 *Fortingall 1: stepped key-pattern along the right edge*

Fortingall 2 Class III (**8**)
L 260 mm; B 240 mm; W 40 mm
Allen and Anderson 1903, III, 508–9, fig 554
A fragment of the centre of an upright cross-slab of fine-grained grey sandstone, which is carved with crosses on both faces. No part of the edges of this stone survives.

Front (**8a**) A fragment of the shaft or arm of an undecorated outlined cross with round hollow angles. The stone has spirals in the quadrants at the intersections, as on the front of Fortingall 1, but on this slab the outline of the arm of shaft also continues into the hollows of the cross, and makes a right angle to connect with the outline of the adjacent arm. The cross is surrounded by an outlined ring decorated with double strand interlace.

Back (**8b**) A cross of almost identical form and dimensions, but ornamented on its ring by what is presumably a running spiral pattern interspersed with triangular hollows, as on Fortingall 1.

It is impossible to say whether this cross-slab originally had decoration on its edges, but it is perhaps likely that it did not, as it is only 40mm wide. Where the hollow angles of the crosses on both sides coincide the stone is a mere 20mm thick – possibly the thinnest surviving early medieval sculptured stone in Scotland carved on both sides. Though only a small fragment, it can be seen to have

Tom E. Gray

a

b

*8 Fortingall 2: **a** front **b** back*

been worked with care, and the surviving surfaces are in fairly good condition. Individual tool-marks are still obvious, especially on the front.

Fortingall 3 Class III (**9**)

L 255 mm; B 230 mm; W 60 mm

Allen and Anderson 1903, III, 509–10, fig 555

Four fragments survive of this upright cross-slab of fine-grained grey sandstone carved on one face and on one edge.

In 1903, what remained of the slab was in two fragments; it has since suffered further damage, and is now in four pieces, with a wedge-shaped fragment of the upper edge missing.

Tom E. Gray

a   **b**

*9 Fortingall 3: **a** cross-face **b** left edge with stepped key-pattern*

Front (**9a**) The upper part of an undecorated outlined cross with round hollow angles, with a compass mark at the centre of the cross. A circular outlined ring connects the shaft and arms of the cross. The hollows at the angles are slightly 'keyhole-shaped', *contra* Allen's drawing (Allen and Anderson 1903, III, fig 555), which shows the ring springing directly from the angle of the arm and hollow. It is decorated with a running key-pattern of outlined T-shaped elements. The rounded edges of the cross-slab were outlined by a raised margin incised with interconnecting spirals above a cable moulding. Damage to the top edge of the stone has made it unclear what this margin looked like above the upper arm of the cross. It may perhaps have terminated in confronting beast heads, as on several other cross-slabs.[28] The spirals on the broader part of the margin would presumably represent the animals' mane.

Back Neatly dressed by stugging but otherwise uncarved.

Left Edge (**9b**) An incised band of stepped key pattern, as on both edges of Fortingall 1 (**7**). The pattern does not run over the flat top edge of the stone.

Fortingall 3 is more truly in relief than the other cross-slabs described here: the cross, the ring and the plain background are all carved at different depths.

Fortingall 4 Class III (**10**)

L c111 mm; B 550 mm; W 50–70 mm (surviving fragments assembled)

Allen and Anderson 1903, III, 510, fig 556

An incomplete recumbent cross-slab of fine-grained grey

Tom E. Gray

10 *Fortingall 4: four surviving fragments of a recumbent cross-slab showing three conjoined equal-armed ringed crosses*

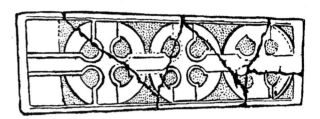

12 *Saint Andrews 43: recumbent cross-slab with three crosses (Fleming 1931, fig 60, p38)*

sandstone in four fragments with carving on one face.

In ECMS only the largest surviving fragment of this unusual recumbent cross-slab was recorded. Three more pieces of the same slab are now known, allowing a much better idea to be formed of its original appearance. It is described in ECMS as 'the upper part of an upright cross-slab' (op cit), but has clearly been a recumbent slab, and of unusual form.

Upper Face Within an edge-margin, parts of three adjacent outlined equal-armed crosses with round hollow angles enclosed by plain rings, and circular outlined rings connecting the ends of their arms. The upper and lower crosses are decorated with two-strand interlace, while the middle cross is undecorated, except for a second narrower outline around its edge. The rings of the crosses are decorated with simple two-strand interlace, and the spaces between the rings are filled by two-strand triquetra knots. The undecorated upper (and presumably once the lower) corners, and the hollows at the cross angles are sunk deeper than the surface of the rest of the slab, which is thus carved in false relief. The area between the edge moulding and the upper edge of the slab is undecorated. The slab appears to have been more or less rectangular originally. The sides are undecorated, and the back uncarved. This stone is more weathered than Fortingall 1–3.

This recumbent cross-slab has been a monument of

N.M. Robertson

11 *Fortingall 4: reconstruction of the possible original appearance*

ambitious scale, carved with a complex and elegant design. If it was entirely symmetrical, its original length would have been about 1580 mm. The only other monument in Scotland of this form is a recumbent slab preserved in St Andrews Cathedral Museum, which is also carved with three conjoined equal-armed ringed crosses in false relief (**12**). This 1500 mm long stone differs from Fortingall 4 in being tapered and lacking decoration within and between its crosses, which are also conjoined lengthwise across their rings (Fleming 1931, no 43, 37–9, fig 60). Despite these points, the two stones are in many ways very similar, and it is tempting to speculate that there might have been some kind of artistic contact between these two early church sites, especially as there are other points of comparison between their collections of Dark Age sculpture. A somewhat similar cross-slab to Fortingall 4 is preserved in St Serf's Church, Dunning, but it only has two crosses (Allen and Anderson 1903, III, fig 333).

Fortingall 5 Class IV (**13**)

L 1150 mm; B across top edge 340 mm; B at broadest point 450 mm

Lines, M 1992, 42; Robertson, NM 1988, 27

A recumbent (? originally upright) cross-slab of brown schist carved on (?) one face.

Currently lying north-south in re-use as the threshold of the kirkyard gate, with one of its iron gateposts riveted to the upper end. A flat wedge-shaped slab incised towards the narrower end with a broad shallow cross. The cross is very worn, and the surface of the slab has been 'polished' by the passage of countless feet. The cross has upper and lower arms of equal length and shorter side arms. It appears to measure c380 x c320 mm. The maximum breadth of the incision is 35 mm.

The slab's tapering shape, and the fact that the incised cross is in the narrower upper half, might suggest that it originally stood upright with the broader edge set in the ground. This could be confirmed if there were carving on the other face, but the back of the slab is at present inaccessible. There are comparable upright cross-slabs within a few kilometres of Fortingall at Fearnan, Loch Tayside (NN 702 428), Tombreck, Foss (NN 774 569) and Craig Fhiannaidh, Glen Lyon (NN 625 477). The wide shallowly incised crosses on both faces of the first named monument are particularly similar to that on the present stone, although Fearnan has straight sides. Such cross-slabs are widely paralleled in Scotland, Ireland, Man and Wales, although Fortingall 5's tapered shape is uncommon. It is possible that part of the upper right side of the slab has split off, and that it was originally more nearly rectangular. The stone is rather larger than the majority of Scotland's simple upright cross-slabs. A cross-slab incorporated into the monument known as St Patrick's Chair at Marown on Man is particularly similar to it (Kermode, 1907, 102–3, pl VI, 5, fig 46).

Tom E. Gray

13 *Fortingall 5: now used as the threshold of the kirkyard gate*

This cross-slab is perhaps the earliest stylistically surviving at Fortingall, and could date from as early as the seventh century AD. Its present position is therefore unfortunate, as the cross will inevitably continue to be degraded until it is completely worn away.

Fortingall 6 Class IV (14)

L 1410 mm (max); B 410 mm (max)
Robertson, NM 1991, 72

A recumbent cross-slab of flakey brown-grey schist carved on one face. Though broken in two, the slab is still complete.

This slab lies east-west 6.5 m west of the east end of the church, and 3.5 m south of it. It has roughly shaped, parallel sides but rather irregular ends. About a quarter of its length

has become detached at the eastern end, but the stone is otherwise complete. At roughly the centre of the slab a cross has been incised. It consists of a stem line 300 mm long crossed by three transoms about 120 mm long. The cross is 680 mm from the western end of the slab as it presently lies, and 430 mm from the other end. The slab perhaps originally lay the other way round, with the cross nearer the west end.

Tom E. Gray

14 *Fortingall 6*

The initials DMG have been added to the west end of the stone at some point, probably in the eighteenth century. A headstone to a Donald McGrigor (*sic*) who died in 1783 stands at the west end of the slab. It is possible that Fortingall 6 was re-used as a temporary marker over this man's grave before the headstone was erected.

The cross is now rather difficult to see because of weathering – unlike the better-preserved Fortingall 7 and 8, the slab was not grassed over when first recorded. The triple-transomed cross is of rare form: its nearest parallel in Scotland appears to be a slab recorded in 1985 at a chapel site at Lochead in Knapdale (NR 777 780) (RCAHMS, 1992, no 85, fig A(1), 190–1). A roughly rectangular slab of chlorite-schist at this site, 1190 mm long, has a cross with three bars incised in its centre, but in this case the shaft of the cross does not extend beyond the upper and lower transverse bars. Both these crosses might conceivably represent in very stylised form Christ's cross with its *titulus* board and foot-rest. The foot-rest at least seems to be occasionally represented elsewhere in Scottish early medieval stones, for instance on two recumbent slabs incised with outline crosses on Isle Maree in Loch Maree (NG 931 724), and in relief on a cross-slab at Hougharry on North Uist (NF 708 706). There might be some relationship too with certain other recumbent slabs in Highland Perthshire, which have three incised crosses in a row.[29] An incised cross with two transoms is recorded at Balquhidder (see n32).

Fortingall 7 Class IV (**15**)

L 1520 mm; B across top edge 470 mm; B at lower cross 430 mm

Robertson, NM 1991, 72

A recumbent cross-slab of local blue-grey schist which is probably complete and carved on one face.

The slab lies east-west in the kirkyard and is usually turfed over. It lies 9m west of the eastern end of the church, and 14m south of it, by a table tomb. The sides are roughly tapered and the surface is somewhat rounded. The upper (western) edge is crudely cut straight across, but the lower edge is irregular. The position of the upper cross might suggest that some of the west end of the stone has been lost, but it is of good length as it lies at present and there is no proof of this. The carvings are clear and well preserved, consisting of an outline representation of an axe or hatchet between two equal-armed crosses, all neatly incised by pecking. The dimensions of the carvings are: upper cross – 125 x 125 mm; lower cross – 135 x 120 mm; axe: L 405 mm, B across blade 215 mm. The upper cross is 60 mm from the edge of the slab, and the lower 400 mm from the other end.

15 *Fortingall 7*

There is no great difference in technique between the three motifs that would lead one to suppose that they are not contemporary, though this is not impossible. If, however, it is accepted that the carvings on the stone are of one date, the combination of two crosses and a hatchet would appear to be otherwise unknown in Scotland. The short-handled implement represented is presumably a woodworking tool rather than a weapon, suggesting that the slab may represent a memorial to a wright or similar craftsman. The carving of representations of tools symbolising the trade of the deceased on grave memorials was a very common custom in Scotland from the late Middle Ages up to the early nineteenth century (Willsher and Hunter 1978, 62).[30] It was not unknown in the early medieval period, but appears to have been rare.[31] The appearance of this tool on a slab which bears two

simple crosses is therefore remarkable. The crosses are identical in appearance and carving technique to any number throughout the British Isles which are taken to be broadly early medieval in date. One does not have to go further than the churchyard the slab lies in to find a parallel to the crosses in the simple equal-armed cross incised on Fortingall 8. That stone is close to 7 also in being recumbent and having two crosses, though in this case of differing type.

Fortingall 7 seems to belong to a small class of recumbent monuments occasionally found in Scotland which appear to combine simple crosses of Early Christian type with other motifs which would generally be taken to be later in date.[32] The dating of these stones is enigmatic, but the writer at least would prefer to see Fortingall 7 as being early rather than late medieval in date.

Fortingall 8 Class IV (**16**)

L *c* 1630 mm; B 530 mm

A recumbent cross-slab of blue-grey schist, which is broken in two but still complete. It is carved on one face.

The slab lies east-west in the kirkyard to the west of the church, near the enclosure containing the Fortingall Yew; it is usually turfed over. This stone has been more carefully shaped than the other three Class IVs. It is nearly rectangular, and the carving is particularly well preserved, though the upper (western) quarter of the slab has become detached, and the crack passes through the edge of the upper cross. About three quarters of the surface of the slab has been carefully dressed by stugging. This area of the stone includes both the crosses. The lower 400 mm is apparently unworked, though very smooth.

The carvings consist of a ringed cross measuring 120 x 120 mm, incised 370 mm from the upper edge of the slab, and an equal-armed cross 165 x 170 mm incised 490 mm in from the other edge. Both neatly pecked crosses are almost as clear as the day they were carved. The equal-armed cross is markedly more deeply incised. The incision is also

16 *Fortingall 8*

broader, a maximum of 20mm as compared to the ringed cross' 10mm.

Both forms of cross are readily paralleled elsewhere, but their inclusion on one stone is very unusual. The only parallel known to the writer is at Dull (NN 806 492), 6.5 kilometres east from Fortingall. A recumbent slab in the kirkyard at Dull is so similar to Fortingall 8 that it would be hard to believe there was no contemporary connection between them, especially given the proximity of the sites.[33]

Discussion

Fortingall 1–4 are sufficiently close to each other stylistically to have been in all likelihood the products of a definite 'school' of masons. This can occasionally be discerned elsewhere in Scotland's early medieval sculpture: the high crosses of Iona, with outliers at Kildalton, Islay and Keills, Knapdale, and groups of related Pictish or Picto-Scottish cross-slabs at St Andrews, Kirriemuir and Portmahomack. Fortingall 1 and 2, for example, have the same pattern of running S-scrolls interspersed with triangular hollows on their crosses' rings on one face, as well as spirals in the hollows of their angles, while 1 and 3 have an identical stepped key-pattern incised along their edges.

All the cross-slabs are thin, neatly carved, and made of the same fine-grained grey sandstone. This stone was presumably brought to Fortingall from elsewhere, perhaps Strathmore, where very similar sandstone was used to carve many of the Pictish cross-slabs of Perthshire and Angus. The simple Class IV slabs in the churchyard are incised on pieces of the local schist.

The closest parallels to the Fortingall cross-slabs seem to be stones that would generally be reckoned to be relatively late in the evolution of Picto-Scottish sculpture. Pictish symbols are absent from the surviving pieces (the nearest Class II Pictish cross-slabs are at Dunfallandy and Logierait).

The Fortingall stones are rather similar to the large collection of cross-slabs at St Andrews, although the stones at that site are thicker, and the local Fife sandstone is softer and more liable to weathering.

The similarity of Fortingall 4 to a St Andrews recumbent was mentioned above, and there are other close points of comparison: for instance the angle spirals of Fortingall 1 and 2 appear also on St Andrews 30 and 64 (Fleming 1931,

30–1, fig 47; 51–2, fig 83). Like Fortingall 1 and 3, the St Andrews cross-slabs frequently have decoration on their edges, often incised key-pattern, and figural scenes are almost absent.

The cross-slab Invergowrie 1 is also reminiscent of the Fortingall stones, with its four sculptured faces (also its top edge), its strict, space-filling geometric patterns, and its figures with 'corrugated' robes (Allen and Anderson 1903, III, 255–6, fig 266).

All these slabs bear comparison with the Dupplin Cross and the Benvie cross-slab (ibid, 319–21, fig 334; 247–8, fig 260).[34] The Dupplin Cross has been dated around the early ninth century by the transliteration of a recently discovered Latin inscription on its west face mentioning Constantin son of Fergus, King of the Picts (d 820) (Forsyth 1995, 240–3). This is the first secure date for any early medieval carved stone in Scotland. The writer would prefer to see the Fortingall cross-slabs as dating a little before Dupplin and the majority of the St Andrews cross-slabs, with their rather stereotyped and repetitive ornament. The finer finish of Fortingall 1–4 might suggest an earlier date, perhaps in the last decades of the eighth century.

The Class IV cross-slabs are even more difficult to date with any confidence. Simple crosses can be incised on slabs at any date, but the writer would prefer to see these stones as preceding the upright cross-slabs and the elaborate recumbent, and to regard them as the earliest Christian monuments remaining at Fortingall, dating to perhaps as early as the seventh or early eighth centuries.

Acknowledgements

The writer would like to thank Rev John T. Mann for granting permission to study the stones preserved at Fortingall; Mrs Jenny Kininmonth, for her help at the site, and Tom E. Gray for producing the splendid photographs. I would also like to thank David Henry, Dr Simon Taylor, and my mother, Irene Robertson, for their help in preparing this paper.

Notes

1 *Liber Ecclesie de Scon* (Bannatyne and Maitland Clubs, 1843), no 65. Note also the form *Forthirkill* in 1465 (RMS II, no 986). The modern Gaelic form is *Fartairchill* (Watson 1926, 69).

2 Personal communication from Dr Simon Taylor, August 1997. Compare the parish name Kirkforthar in Fife (NO 298 048): Taylor lists such early forms as *Forthir*, *Fortyr* (both *c*1250); the Scots prefix *Kirk-* was added by the first half of the fifteenth century. Forthar 'is probably from G[aelic] *for thìr* 'projecting land, upper land', with *for* used either as a preposition or an intensifying prefix. It would refer to the relatively sudden rising of the land beside the most southerly corner of the flat Howe of Fife, which is around 40m above sea level: within 2km the land has risen to the 157m high Hill of Forthar'. (Taylor 1995, 266–7)
Watson (1930, 283) put forward a tentative comparison with Welsh *gwerthyr* 'fortress'. The place-name would thus mean 'fortress church', and refer to the nearby 'ring-fort' known as Dùn Geal (see n8). Taylor's etymology is perhaps more convincing.

3 For an ancient church-name formed in the same way, but with a different prefix, compare Bunkle, in the Scottish Borders (formerly Berwickshire) (NT 809 596). This 'seems to derive from Gaelic *bun chill* ... probably meaning something like 'bottom church, church at the foot', which well describes its position ...' (Taylor 1997, 51). Interestingly, this church may have been a Columban foundation (ibid, 51–2).

4 Via the head of Glenlyon, southwards through Auch Gleann to Tyndrum in Strathfillan and hence to the west. That this route may have been used by early churchmen is suggested by the place-names Beinn Mhanach 'monk's peak' a mountain rising above the presumed route at the head of Glenlyon (highest point NN 374 412) (Watson 1939-30, 296), and by Allt na h-Annait in Auch Gleann: 'stream of the (old, or former) church' (the exact meaning of Gaelic *annaid* in Scottish place-names is uncertain) (MacDonald 1973, 138–9). An old burial ground at NN 346 380 by the stream is presumably the site of the *annaid* (ibid, no 40, 138, 142).

5 Archaeological evidence for influence from the west exists in the form of the numerous homesteads or 'ring-forts' of Atholl (see n9).

6 '...in 1903, when some alterations were being made to that portion of the burying-ground belonging to the late Sir Donald Currie of Garth, the workmen came upon this Stone lying at a depth of 8 feet [2.5 m], at a point not many feet distant from the stem of the famous Yew-tree. Noticing the cup-marks on the Stone, the workmen raised it and set it up erect on the site it now occupies, close to the western wall of the Garth burial-ground – about 25 feet [7.6 m] from the spot where it was unearthed.' (Coles 1910, 120–1, fig 2). The stone is still in the same place.

7 'Clach Mo-Lucháig', a large boulder in a garden by the roadside at Fortingall, may contain the affectionate form of a name such as Luchar or Luchta or Lochein, all names of saints; but Luch, 'mouse', was itself a woman's name. At one time, as I was informed, scolds were fastened to this stone; part of the irons used for fastening them remain on it.' (Watson 1926, 325). Coles (1910, 124) calls the monolith St Moloch's Stone, and writes that it is 'said to be cup-marked'. Neither iron fastenings nor cup-marks are at present to be seen on the stone.

8 On Creag a' Ghiubhais (NN 751 478), a little over a kilometre north-east of the church, and on Drummond Hill further eastwards on the other side of the Lyon (NN 779 477). The latter fort is known as Dùn Mac Tuathail.

9 Ably discussed by D.B. Taylor (1990). The nearest examples to Fortingall are Dùn Geal (NN 746 476) and the partly excavated one at Litigan (NN 766 496). There are ten others along Glenlyon (ibid, 75–7), and a heavy concentration north-east of Fortingall around Foss and Loch Tummel (ibid, fig 9, 53). Taylor suggests that this type of monument may relate to an early movement of Gaelic-speaking people into the Pictish province of Atholl, and notes an apparent correspondence between the homesteads and Early Christian sites and cross-slabs (ibid, 62–4). 'The evidence for function, dating and origin... suggests a Gaelic-speaking pastoral people with origins ultimately in Ireland, forming one element at least of the people we call Scots and moving north-eastwards between 500 and 800 AD. Once established in Atholl, they formed part of what is called the Pictish kingdom. The close association of homesteads with... the early Christian movement, especially in Glen Lyon... require[s] further investigation' (ibid, 64) (cf n14).

10 One might speculate that it could have been the dwelling of the 'thane of Fortingall' mentioned above; it has never been scientifically excavated. In the nineteenth century it was assumed to be the 'praetorium' of a Roman camp, presumably because of its square shape, and to be linked in some way to the unaccountable local legend that Fortingall was the birthplace of Pontius Pilate (Fraser 1973, 22).

11 Fortingall's bell is preserved in a niche inside the present church. Cladh Bhranno (NN 582 468), now a burying ground, was the site of a chapel of probable early medieval origins. A primitive font of early type remains in the enclosure, and several recumbent graveslabs of Dark Age or medieval date. When first recorded the Cladh Bhranno bell, known as St Adomnán's, stood in the open in the graveyard; it was later kept in a recess in the inner face of

its east wall, and is now preserved in a grilled niche in Innerwick church (NN 588 475). A third bell was discovered in 1870 between the wall and eaves of an old cart shed on the farm of Balnahanaid (Anderson 1881, 181–2). It was in poor condition and has since been lost. The name Balnahanaid (Gaelic *Bàile na h-Annaide*, 'farm or township of the *annaid*'), implies the former existence of a church. The farm buildings are on the site of its graveyard (NN 623 472). For the meaning of *annaid*, see note 4 above. The possible former existence of a fourth bell in Glen Lyon may be implied by the place-name Radhar a' Chluig 'outfield of the bell' behind the ancient burial ground of Cladh Chunna at Invervar (NN 670 484) (Watson 1930, 287).

12 'The use of hand-bells in Scotland can reasonably be attributed to the influence of the Irish church. Bells were central to Irish ecclesiastical tradition, and the surviving total of 75 examples far exceeds the totals of 7 and 19 known from Wales and Scotland respectively'. (Bourke 1983, 465). It is striking that a total of seven hand-bells are recorded from the former county of Perthshire, more than in any other Scottish county (ibid, 467 (complete list)).

13 Boulders, pillar-stones and slabs bearing simple crosses (usually, though not always, incised) but no other ornament (Henderson 1987, 46).

14 Specifically in northern and western Perthshire in the valleys of the Tay and its tributaries the Tummel, Garry, Lyon and Earn. There is a complete lack of recorded examples in the former county east of the valley of the Tay, and a comparatively meagre number in lowland Perthshire. The distribution map of Class IV cross-slabs in highland Perthshire is so strikingly similar to that of the massively-walled homesteads or 'ring-forts' that it is difficult to believe that the two classes of monument were not in some way connected (cf n9). For distribution maps of the homesteads and simple cross-slabs, see: Taylor 1990, 53, fig 9, and 59, fig 11, and MacNeill and MacQueen 1996, 56, 'Stones with incised crosses'. The latter map was prepared by Isabel Henderson and the author some years ago and is now well out of date. The under-reporting of examples is so severe as to make the map almost misleading. It is, however, the only published plan of the distribution of these monuments in Scotland.

15 Negative evidence for the simple cross-slabs' Irish origin is their almost complete absence in the regions of what is now Scotland settled by the Angles of Northumbria. The concentration of examples in Argyll and its islands, with lesser numbers elsewhere in the area of the Pictish kingdom, clearly implies a western origin. The heavy concentration in Atholl – at the end of the passes directly eastward through Druim Alban from Dál Riada – would

seem to bespeak an early and sustained penetration of this province of Pictland by Irish churchmen.

16 For example, the two places near Fortingall called Balnahanaid (NN 669 380 and NN 623 472), on Loch Tay-side and in Glen Lyon. See note 11 for the latter and note 4 for a discussion of the place-name element *annaid*. There is also Annet on the north shore of Loch Rannoch (NN 635 594). All three are now farms (MacDonald 1973, 141).

17 Recorded by W.J. Watson (1930, *Erratum* on Contents page):

'I have met the following note by the late Mr Alexander Campbell of Boreland, in regard to Saint Mo Choide's grave:– "He died and was buried at Tigh na Sràide (just east of Fortingall Manse), where the stone slab that covers his grave is still pointed out. None is allowed to meddle with it, for '*am fear a chairicheas leac Mo Choide, cha tig an latha bhios mac air a leac-tighe fein* [the one who moves Mo Choide's slab, the day will not come when he will have a son on his house floor (slab)]'."'

A version of this tradition appears in Campbell (1888, 80), but the saint is there identified as the Northumbrian ecclesiastic Cedd. This is a good example of the vagaries of oral tradition uncorrected by documentary sources: by the second half of the nineteenth century, the true identity of Mo-Choide had been long forgotten, and he was assumed to be Cedd (well-known from Bede's *Ecclesiastical History*), it would seem for no better reason than the superficial similarity of the names. The rediscovery of the early Irish sources allowed the more plausible (and more historically interesting) dedication to Coeti of Iona, first mooted by Watson (1926, 314), to re-emerge.

18 They are much more common in Atholl than commemorations of Columba himself (Taylor 1997, 48), despite the assertion in the *Amra Choluimb Chille*, an Old Irish elegy on the saint composed within a few years of his death in 597, that he taught 'the tribes of the Tay', and that 'his blessing turned them, the mouths of the fierce ones who lived on the Tay, to the will of the King' (Clancy and Márkus 1995, 104–5, i.15, 112–3, viii.5–6).

19 The place-name evidence has been listed by Nollaig Ó Muráile (1997, 217–8, map 10, 228), and Simon Taylor (1997, 67–8, fig 2, 70).

20 Cormac Bourke has recently suggested the possible existence of Columban monasteries in the same area, with particular reference to the impressive number of recorded Celtic hand-bells (cf n11): '... it is tempting to speculate that monks from Iona were active in Glen Lyon, and that dependant monasteries were founded here, among the

southern Picts, in the lifetime of Adomnán if not of Columba himself.' (1997a, 162–3).

21 The massive, irregularly-shaped font at Fortingall is set on a pedestal by the east wall of the church porch. Its maximum dimensions are 1140 x 850 x 360 mm, with a rounded bowl 500 mm across and a depth of *c*200 mm. The font at Dull, also preserved in the open air (it lies by the west door of the church), is very similar in appearance. Examples of primitive fonts at sites in highland Perthshire that have come to the author's attention are: Balquhidder (NN 536 209); Chapelton, Glen Fincastle (NN 869 615 – original site: now preserved at Chapelton Farm, not the nearby burial ground); Cill Mo-Charmaig, Ardeonaig (NN 672 355); Cladh Bhranno, Glen Lyon (NN 582 468); Cladh Machuim, Loch Tay-side (NN 685 396); Dail Chiarain, Fearnan (NN 721 447); Foss, Loch Tummel-side (NN 790 582); Killin (NN 574 334 – original site: now preserved in the parish church); St Fillans Priory, Strathfillan (NN 358 284); Weem, Aberfeldy (NN 843 500). A font is said to have been removed from Dull to Blarmore, Loch Tay-side (NN 652 370) (MacKenzie 1901, 310). It seems to have been lost sight of, and MacKenzie does not describe it.

The fonts listed above vary widely in size and finish, but are all fairly substantial, and undecorated, except for the example at the chapel site of Dail Chiarain in Fearnan village, which has a crude cross incised across its bowl (Gillies 1938, 49–51). Some primitive hollowed stones on a much smaller scale survive at certain probable early church sites which are perhaps stoups or holy water stones rather than fonts. Examples in Highland Perthshire are: Killichonan, Loch Rannoch-side (NN 544 582); St Blane's Chapel, Lassintullich (NN 695 577); St Fillan's Chapel, Dundurn (NN 704 236 – original site: now preserved in St Fillan's parish church). Such smaller stones are perhaps more likely to have disappeared over the centuries than the often massive primitive fonts. Both fonts and stoups are often almost identical in appearance to the stones hollowed out at all periods for mundane use as knocking stones or troughs, which are so common throughout Scotland. Their ecclesiastical origin is chiefly indicated by their survival at church or chapel sites.

The distribution of 'Celtic' fonts is by no means limited to Highland Perthshire; examples known to the author elsewhere in Scotland include: in Angus, Kingoldrum (NO 334 551). In Aberdeenshire, Tullich (NO 391 975), a particularly massive example in red granite preserved at a site with one of the largest collections of Class IV cross-slabs in the country. In the central Highlands: Kincardine, Strathspey (NH 938 155), and Castle Roy (NJ 005 218). They are not unknown south of the Forth, for instance at Ecclesmachan, West Lothian (NT 058 736). There are no doubt many other examples. The main discussion of Scottish dark age and medieval fonts is by

J. Russell Walker (1887), who described several of the above.

22 Gaelic *Tulach a' Bhile* (NN 784 492) and *Cois a' Bhile* (NN 777 493), 'hill of the sacred tree' and 'hard by (or 'at the foot of') the sacred tree'. Compare Cladh a' Bhile, Ellary, in Argyll (NR 733 756) 'burial ground of the sacred tree', a site which, as so often in Scotland, lacks documentation, but whose importance in Early Christian times is shown by one of the largest collections of early cross-slabs in Scotland (twenty-nine) (RCAHMS 1992, no 20, 53–61). The element *bile* is not uncommon in Ireland: eg Moville 'plain of the sacred tree'. It should be pointed out that Watson (1930, 278) suggests meanings for Tullichville and Coshieville derived from Gaelic *bil* 'brae-edge'.

23 '… the present Gaelic is *Tigh-neimh*' (for -*neimhidh*); the plural form is due to there being two farms, Duneaves proper and *Tigh-neimh' Ghearr*, 'short (ie little) Duneaves', anglicized Tynayere. The name means 'house of the nemed'… A field on the farm is called *Dail mo-Choid*, 'St. Coedi's dale.' The Yew tree at Fortingall is well known; it was reported by Penant that its ruins measured fifty-six feet in circumference in 1772. This yew may well have been a sacred tree connected with the Nemeton…' (Watson 1926, 247–8).

Another possible translation of Duneaves, without pre-Christian connotations, might be 'house of the church-land'.

24 See n6 and Coles 1910, 121.

The Fortingall example is not the only cup-marked stone to come to light in a churchyard in Highland Perthshire. The author has found other specimens at Kilmaveonaig (NN 879 657) (Robertson 1991, 71) and Old Blair (NN 867 665) (unpublished), both by Blair Atholl. Cf two examples recorded at Convinth, Inverness-shire (Wallace 1911, 310–11, figs 4 and 5).

25 Early Christian remains discovered at Dull include five simple cross-slabs, a massive 'Celtic' font (cf n20), a cross-base and a probable shrine panel carved with warriors and horsemen reminiscent of those on Pictish Class II cross-slabs (Allen and Anderson 1903, III, 315, fig 329). Three free-standing crosses of uncertain date are said to have formerly marked a girth or area of sanctuary around the site. One remains in the village, two are now in Weem Old Church (ibid, 342). There are no obvious remains of the enclosure that would be expected round an early monastery on the ground at Dull, but the place-name Appin (Gaelic *Apuinn,* < Old Irish *apdaine* 'abbey land' (Watson 1926, 124), applied to the surrounding strath, is a reminder that a religious house once stood there.

26 Cf the legend of St Eonan narrated in Gaelic by an old man of Glen Lyon, recorded and translated by Campbell (1886,

317–8), which includes the death of the saint in Glen Lyon, and the burial of his body at Dull. The church of Fortingall receives no mention, though lying between the two places. The historical Adomnán is known to have been buried on Iona, but a vague tradition of relics of the saint being kept at Dull might lie behind the legend.

27 The upper arm of the cross does not line up properly with the shaft, as it surely must have done given the careful layout of the surviving part of the cross-slab.

28 For example: Aberlemno 2, Cossans, Dunfallandy, Meigle 4, Farnell, Monifeith 2. All these cross-slabs are in Angus or Perth and Kinross.

29 Two recumbent slabs at Kirkton of Strathfillan (NN 358 284), and one within the roofless old church at Old Faskally in the pass of Killiecrankie (NN 918 631), are incised with three simple crosses in a row. This motif is very rare elsewhere in Scotland, the only parallel the writer is aware of being a slab preserved at the old church of Tullich, on Deeside in Aberdeenshire (NO 391 975)

30 A close parallel to the axe is to be seen on a late medieval recumbent slab at Lochgoilhead, Argyll (RCAHMS 1992, no 87 (7), fig D(7), 197). On this monument the implement is of similar proportions, but the lower edge of the head is rounded rather than square. An incised axe also occurs on a slab in Cladh Bhranno graveyard in Glenlyon (NN 582 468), but it is unclear whether this represents a tool or a weapon.

31 A smith's hammer and anvil are carved on the Abernethy symbol stone (ECMS 1903, III, 282, fig 299), and a hammer, anvil and tongs on the back of the Dunfallandy cross-slab (ibid, 288–9, fig 305B).

32 In the kirkyard of Balquhidder (NN 536 209), formerly in Perthshire, are three recumbent slabs (two of them not fully published) where a simple cross is combined with a pair of shears, the latter a common motif on late medieval grave monuments, where it appears to symbolise the commemoration of a woman (Stuart 1867, pl LXVIII, no 7; the illustrated slab is not at present visible at Balquhidder – probably grassed over). In Aberdeenshire is an originally recumbent slab at Birse near Aboyne (NO 555 973) described by F.C. Eeles in 1912. It shows a sword of medieval appearance along with two Early Christian-looking outline Latin crosses with expanded arms carved at opposite ends of the stone (1912, 365–6, fig 1). Closer to Fortingall 7 in style are certain slabs at St Medan's Kirkyard, Fintray, also in Aberdeenshire (NJ 872 156), published by James Ritchie. Ritchie's slabs nos 3 and 4 show incised crosses of Early Christian appearance at both ends and motifs one might assume to be later in date in the middle (3 shows a pair of shears and a rectangular motif; 4 a sword) (1911, 339–43, figs 5 and 6).

33 The Dull stone is also a Class IV recumbent cross-slab of blue-grey schist, and it also has a ringed cross and an approximately equal armed cross. The ringed cross is again less deeply incised than the other cross. The slab is 1550 mm long and is still complete. The ringed cross measures 125 x 125mm, and the other cross 190 x 210mm. The two crosses are somewhat closer together on the Dull stone (Robertson 1989, 64).

34 Such characteristics as the tendency for cross-slabs to be carved on all four sides, the rather mechanical and repetitive panels of interlace, scroll-work or key-pattern, which tend to take up much or all of the space around the cross, and the increasingly rigid and stylised figure sculpture, more anatomically distorted than on the best Class II Pictish stones, seem to be marks of later sculpture, particularly in the southern half of Pictland (though not unknown in the north, eg at Kinneddar, Moray).

References

ALLEN, JR and ANDERSON, J 1903 *The Early Christian Monuments of Scotland*, 3 parts. Edinburgh (repr with an Introduction by Isabel Henderson, 2 vols, Balgavies, Angus, 1993).

ANDERSON, J 1881 *Scotland in Early Christian Times.* Edinburgh.

ANDERSON, MO 1973 *Kings and Kingship in Early Scotland.* Edinburgh.

BOURKE, C

– 1983 The hand-bells of the early Scottish church. *Proc Soc Antiq Scot*, 113, 464–8.

– (ed) 1997 *Studies in the Cult of Saint Columba*, 162–83. Dublin.

– 1997a Insigniae Columbae II. In idem (ed).

CAMPBELL, D

– 1886 *The Lairds of Glenlyon.* Perth.

– 1888 *The Book of Garth and Fortingall.* Inverness.

CLANCY, TO and MÁRKUS, G 1995 *Iona: The Earliest Poetry of a Celtic Monastery.* Edinburgh.

COLES, FR 1910 Report on stone circles surveyed in Perthshire (Aberfeldy district)....*Proc Soc Antiq Scot*, 44, 117–68.

EELES, FC 1912 Note on a sculptured stone at the parish church of Birse, Aberdeenshire. *Proc Soc Antiq Scot, 46*, 365–7.

FISHER, I and GREENHILL, FA 1971 Two unrecorded carved stones at Tower of Lethendy, Perthshire. *Proc Soc Antiq Scot, 104* (1971-72), 238–41.

FLEMING, D HAY 1931 *St Andrews Cathedral Museum.* Edinburgh.

FORSYTH, K 1995 The inscriptions on the Dupplin Cross. In Bourke, C (ed) *From the Isles of the North,* 237–44. Belfast.

FRASER, D 1973 *Highland Perthshire.* Montrose.

GILLIES, W A 1938 *In Famed Breadalbane.* Perth.

HENDERSON, I B
– 1967 *The Picts.* London.
– 1987 Early Christian monuments of Scotland displaying crosses but no other ornament. In Small, A (ed) *The Picts: A New Look at Old Problems,* 45–58. Dundee.

LINES, M 1992 *Sacred Stones, Sacred Places.* Edinburgh.

MACDONALD, A D S 1973 'Annat' in Scotland: a provisional review. *Scottish Studies* 17, 135–46.

MACDONALD, A D S and LAING, L R 1970 Early ecclesiastical sites in Scotland: a field survey, Part II. *Proc Soc Antiq Scot,* 102 (1969-70), 129–45.

MACKENZIE, J B 1901 Notice of two stone axes... found at Balnahannait, Loch Tay. *Proc Soc Antiq Scot,* 35, 310–2.

MACNEILL, P G B and MACQUEEN, H L 1996 *Atlas of Scottish history to 1707.* Edinburgh.

NICOLAISEN, W F H 1976 *Scottish Place-Names.* London.

Ó MURÁILE, N 1997 The Columban onomastic legacy. In Bourke, C (ed), 193–228.

RCAHMS = Royal Commission on the Ancient and Historical Monuments of Scotland
– 1982 *Argyll: An Inventory of the Monuments,* vol 4, *Iona.* Edinburgh.
– 1992 *Argyll: An Inventory of the Monuments,* vol 7, *Mid Argyll and Cowal: Medieval and Later Monuments.* Edinburgh.

RITCHIE, J 1911 Some old crosses and unlettered sepulchral monuments in Aberdeenshire. *Proc Soc Antiq Scot,* 45, 333–53.

ROBERTSON, N M
– 1989 Dull Kirkyard (Dull parish), Early Christian cross-slabs and an incised stone. *Discovery and Excavation in Scotland,* 64.
– 1991 Kilmaveonaig Kirkyard (Blair Atholl parish), cup-marked stone. *Discovery and Excavation in Scotland,* 71.

ROSS, A 1967 *Pagan Celtic Britain.* London.

RMS 1882–1914 *Registrum Magni Sigilli Regum Scottorum.* Thompson J M *et al* (eds).

SHARPE, R (trans) 1995 *Adomnán of Iona: Life of St Columba.* St Ives.

SMITH, I 1995 The origins and development of Christianity in North Britain and Southern Pictland. In Blair, J and Pyrah, C *Church Archaeology: Research Directions for the Future* (CBA Research Report 104).

STUART, J 1867 *Sculptured Stones of Scotland, Volume Second.* Edinburgh.

TAYLOR, D B 1990 *Circular Homesteads in North West Perthshire.* Dundee.

TAYLOR, S
– 1995 Settlement-names in Fife. Unpublished PhD thesis, University of Edinburgh.
– 1996 Place-names and the Early Church in Eastern Scotland. In Crawford, B E (ed) *Scotland in Dark Age Britain,* 93–110. St Andrews.
– 1997 Seventh-century Iona abbots in Scottish place-names. *Innes Review* 48 no 1, 45–72.

WALKER, J R 1887 Scottish baptismal fonts. *Proc Soc Antiq Scot,* 21 (1886–87), 346–498.

WALLACE, T 1910 Notes on some sculptured slabs and headstones in the churchyards of Glenconvinth and Kirkhill, Inverness-shire. *Proc Soc Antiq Scot,* 45, 309–14.

WATSON, W J
– 1926 *The History of the Celtic Place-Names of Scotland.* Edinburgh.
– 1930 Place-names of Perthshire: the Lyon Basin. *Trans Gaelic Soc Inverness* 35 (1929-30), 277–96.

WILLSHER, B and HUNTER, D 1978 *Stones: A Guide to Some Remarkable Eighteenth Century Gravestones.* Edinburgh.

Old Testament Heroes:
Iconographies of Insular Sculpture

Jane Hawkes

In discussions of insular art, much has been written on the political, ecclesiastical, cultural and artistic influences of the various areas of Britain and Ireland upon each other; it is a debate in which Isabel Henderson has played a seminal role. And, with regard to the iconography of insular art, she has been one of the few scholars to examine iconographic schemes across modern regional boundaries. As a contribution to this particular approach to insular iconography it is my intention to examine the use of Old Testament imagery on stone carvings, with special reference to the iconography of the Old Testament strong-man, Samson.

Old Testament Iconographies of the Insular World
Perhaps the most noticeable aspect of the carved insular Old Testament images is their very varied use in the different geographical regions of the area. In the material which has survived from pre-Viking England, for instance, only five or six Old Testament scenes can be counted: portrayals of Adam and Eve, at Newent in Gloucestershire (Heighway 1987, 132), Abraham and Isaac, at Reculver, Kent (Tweddle 1983, fig 6c), David the Psalmist and David Slaying the Lion, at Masham in North Yorkshire (Henderson 1986, pls 5.8a-b), and two examples of Samson Bearing the Gates of Gaza, at Masham and Cundall, also in Yorkshire (**1, 2**).[1]

The extremely limited nature of this corpus becomes even more apparent when it is realised that of these scenes, no less than four emerged from a single centre of production; the workshop responsible for the Masham column, also produced the cross-shaft fragment at Cundall (Lang 1983, 185).

On these two monuments the Samson figures are mirror images of each other; where Samson walks to the right steadying the 'gates' with his right hand at Cundall, he walks to the left, holding them with his left hand at Masham. Apart from this difference, however, which is probably best explained in 'template' terms (Bailey and Lang, p.comm.), both scenes show Samson wearing a knee-length tunic, his body awkwardly turned, and the 'gates' represented as an arch set on his shoulder.

If the scope of the Anglo-Saxon material is extended to include Viking-age sculpture, the picture of a restricted interest in Old Testament imagery remains largely unchanged. The number of monuments carved with Old Testament scenes increases (approximately eleven can be identified), but the range of events illustrated is still rather limited. Depictions of harpists, usually interpreted as David the Psalmist, continue to be produced, at Sockburn in Northumberland (no 6) and Tynemouth, Tyne and Wear (Cramp 1984, pl 132.720; Trench-Jellicoe 1991, fig 1), and images of Adam and Eve survive at Breedon-on-the-Hill (Leicestershire), Dacre (Cumbria), Elwick Hall (Co. Durham) and Pickhill in North Yorkshire (Bailey 1988, fig 5; Bailey and Cramp 1988, pl 245; Cramp 1984, pl 52.254; Collingwood 1907, fig 381d). At Breedon and Dacre these scenes are further accompanied by depictions of Abraham's abortive attempt to sacrifice Isaac, which may also have featured at Bilton in Yorkshire (Collingwood 1915, fig 140d). But, apart from these images, and isolated portrayals of the Three Hebrew Children, also from Bilton (Collingwood 1915, fig 140h), and the Martyrdom of Isaiah, at Winwick, Cheshire (Bailey 1980, fig 39), Old Testament subjects do not feature in Anglo-Saxon sculpture.

This apparent paucity of Old Testament iconography, is of course, very different from the situation elsewhere in the insular world. In Ireland, for instance, one study has identified up to thirty-seven different Old Testament scenes

J. Hawkes

J. Hawkes

1 *Samson Bearing the Gates of Gaza, Masham*

2 *Samson Bearing the Gates of Gaza, Cundall*

still extant on the sculpture (Harbison 1992, 187–229). They include the episodic illustration of single events, as well as the depiction of episodes not found at all in Anglo-Saxon sculpture. The Fall of Humanity, for instance, is illustrated by up to three episodes: Adam and Eve eating the Forbidden Fruit, Adam and Eve Knowing their Nakedness, and (possibly) the Lord reproving Adam (ibid, 189–93). In some cases these episodes are further extended by illustrations of the First Murder, Cain killing Abel (ibid, 190–5), while other Old Testament events such as the Flood (illustrated by Noah's Ark), and the Exodus of the Israelites from Egypt are also depicted (ibid, 197–8, 200–8). What is more, not only is the range of material surviving in Ireland far greater than that in England, individual scenes are repeated more frequently. Thirteen examples of Adam and Eve with the Forbidden Fruit, for instance, and a similar number of carvings illustrating David killing the lion, have been identified (ibid, 214–15).

In Scotland the use of Old Testament iconography is also quite distinctive. Of the images which have been clearly identified, Davidic scenes feature most prominently: depictions of David and the Lion appear on eight or nine

different monuments (Henderson 1986, 88–9, 93–4), and the Psalmist on at least seven (Allen and Anderson 1903, III, 245, 377; Henderson 1986, 90-92; RCAHMS 1982, fig 205), while other Davidic scenes, of the Anointing and Enthronement, may also have been illustrated (RCAHMS 1982, fig 205). Images of Adam and Eve similarly seem to have enjoyed some popularity, having survived on four or five pieces (Allen and Anderson 1903, III, 219–21, 266–7; RCAHMS 1982, fig 208d; RCAHMS 1956, pls 47c, e), but other scenes portraying Old Testament figures, such as Abraham and Isaac, Daniel, Jonah, Samson and the Hebrew Children, can only be identified with any certainty in one or two instances (RCAHMS 1982, fig 211a; Allen and Anderson 1903, III, 391, 242, 286, 317–19, 297–8).[2]

While this total is a fraction of the material found in Ireland, it clearly exceeds the number of Anglo-Saxon Old Testament images, but it is interesting to notice that the range of scenes illustrated on the Scottish stones is broadly comparable to that represented by the Anglo-Saxon sculpture: of the eight different Old Testament scenes clearly identifiable in Scotland, only carvings of Jonah and Daniel cannot be paralleled in England. Furthermore, the two regions seem to share a common iconographic interest in images of David and Adam and Eve who are by far the most commonly illustrated of the Old Testament figures.

Of course, such similarities (and differences) may be more apparent than real. The accidental survival of so much of the sculpture strongly affects the current distribution and occurrence of the sculptured images from the pre-Norman period. It is worth remembering that if Squire Lawson had not interrupted road menders breaking up the Cundall cross-shaft outside his front door at the turn of this century, the second Anglo-Saxon image of Samson with the Gates of Gaza would have been lost with no record of it ever having existed (Brown 1937, 207).

Nevertheless, even if accidental survival is taken into account, Old Testament imagery was probably always a rare phenomenon on Anglo-Saxon sculpture. Such scenes form a very small percentage of the overall corpus of extant figural sculpture, itself a small proportion of the total amount of sculpture which has survived from the pre-Norman period. Of the 159 stone monuments documented in Northumberland, for instance, only sixteen use human figures in their decoration, one of which may be associated with the Old Testament. Even where such iconographic subject-matter is clearly identifiable, as for example, in County Durham, it features on only one of the forty-seven monuments decorated with figural scenes, a number representing less than a quarter of the 271 pieces of sculpture in the area.

In fact, viewed proportionally, it would seem that Old Testament iconography was always rare on Anglo-Saxon sculpture, and moreover, it would appear that in this respect, as well as in the range of subjects illustrated, the Scottish carvings demonstrate a general correspondence to the Anglo-Saxon. The seventeen stones from pre-Norman England thought to depict Old Testament images represent just 3% of the number of extant pieces (over 390) featuring figural subject-matter. In Scotland, although more monuments survive decorated with Old Testament scenes than are found in England, the thirty-odd stones clearly featuring such images form barely 17% of the total number of monuments (approximately 190) displaying figural ornament in the area. By contrast, forty-five (nearly half) of the 92 monuments carved with figural scenes in Ireland include Old Testament scenes in their decoration. Against

this distribution, the occurrence of Old Testament images on the pre-Norman sculpture of Scotland and England is, and probably always was, a comparatively rare phenomenon.

The question of iconographic models

Another distinctive feature of the stone-carved insular Old Testament images, albeit one less immediately apparent than their regionally diverse occurrence, is their iconographic sources. Of course, the fragmentary condition, the crudeness of the carving and the influence of local styles mean it is not always possible to identify the original models lying behind the images. On the Viking-age pieces at Elwick Hall and Pickhill, for instance, it is only the stylised representation of a tree and fruit, or the arrangement of the figures to hide their nakedness (an action which is, in any case, not entirely understood at Elwick Hall where both figures hide their breasts), which enables these images to be potentially identified as depicting the Fall. Such carvings suggest, at best, access to a model which had been current in Anglo-Saxon England for some time, but one which had lost its coherence in the process of multiple copying.

Nevertheless, where specific source material can be identified, it would seem that, for the production of certain images, the different regions of Britain and Ireland did have access to very different iconographic sources.

In Ireland, for instance, it has been argued, by Harbison (1977; 1984; 1987; 1992), that Carolingian models played a significant role in the iconography of the sculpture, and certainly, for the image identified as Samson Destroying the Temple on the West (Tall) Cross at Monasterboice (Harbison 1992, fig 707), this hypothesis would seem to be valid. The details of the image include three rows of seated onlookers confronting Samson (identified by his long hair) who pushes a long thin object (presumed to be a column). These features suggest the scene derives from an iconographic version current in Western Europe by the tenth century (Bologne, Bibl. Mun. MS 20, fol 63v: Harbison 1992, fig 708). They certainly distinguish the scheme from the iconographic type found in Eastern contexts, such as that illustrated in the ninth-century Byzantine *Homilies of Gregory Nazianzus*, itself apparently based on earlier, sixth-century

3 *Inchbrayock 1, Front*

4 *Inchbrayock 1, Back*

3a *Delilah cutting Samson's hair, Inchbrayock*

4a *Samson slaying the Philistine, Inchbrayock*

Photographs by Tom E. Gray, courtesy of Angus Council

sources (Paris, Bibl. Nat. MS gr. 510, fol 347v: Der Nersessian 1962, pl 14).

But if such Eastern model-types did not influence the iconography of the Irish Samson scene, they clearly played a part in the production of Samson scenes elsewhere in Britain. Henderson, for instance, has long argued for their influence on the scene identified as Delilah cutting Samson's hair found on Stone 1 from Inchbrayock, Angus (Henderson 1967, 146–7). Here, Samson is shown as a diminutive figure standing before Delilah who grasps the lock of hair trailing over his forehead (**3**). The image probably derives from an iconographic type depicting Delilah cropping Samson's hair while he lies with his head in her lap; the type occurs in the Byzantine *Homilies* (Der Nersessian 1962, pl 14), where it is juxtaposed with scenes of Samson Slaying the Philistine(s), an episode also featured at Inchbrayock (**4**).

The likely derivation of these carved images from earlier Eastern iconographic traditions is underlined by the appearance of the (apparently veiled) female figure seated next to Samson and the Philistine on the Inchbrayock Stone. This figure is awkwardly displayed, with the lower part of the body (wearing a long robe) being shown in profile, and the upper part (with the head) facing forwards. The upper portion is further distinguished by a series of concentric curved mouldings which circle round the general area of the chest. These details suggest that the figure probably evolved from a type of seated figure similar to that carved on the late eighth-century Anglo-Saxon sarcophagus cover at Wirksworth in Derbyshire (Hawkes 1994, pl 10). In this image (of the Annunciation) the Virgin sits in an awkward, half-turned, pose, with one hand grasping and pulling her robe over her stomach in such a way that the parallel folds of the garment curve round the area in a very stylised and patterned manner. The pose, the figural style, and the depiction of the robe are all details demonstrating the close dependence of this Mercian image on an earlier Eastern version of (probably) sixth-century date (ibid, 259–60). Derivation from a similar source for the figure on the Inchbrayock Stone, perhaps transmitted through Anglo-Saxon channels, while suggesting that she might be identified as the Virgin, would also explain the curious pose of the figure and the method of rendering the garments, and would be consistent with the (Eastern)

sources of influence claimed by Henderson for the Samson scenes.

Certainly, Eastern sources lie behind the iconography of the Anglo-Saxon images of Samson (Bearing the Gates of Gaza) at Masham and Cundall in North Yorkshire. In the Byzantine manuscript version of Samson Destroying the Temple (Der Nersessian 1962, pl 14), he stands, wearing a short tunic, facing forwards, his arms outstretched on either side to grasp the columns of an arch which surrounds him. The similarity between this and the carved images is marked, but it does not necessarily follow that the Masham-Cundall scene should be re-interpreted as actually depicting the Destruction of the Temple. Although the manuscript shows Samson under an arch, the position of his arms is very different from that adopted by the carved figure, whose arm crosses his body awkwardly to steady the arch. Moreover, the arch rests on the shoulder of the Masham-Cundall figure, passing behind his head; he does not stand **under** the arch as he does in the manuscript. Furthermore, in the Byzantine miniature, Samson faces forwards under the arch; on the sculpture, by contrast, whilst the lower half of the figure is also forward-facing, the feet are turned to the side and the upper half of his body is twisted so that the arm can reach the arch. The awkwardness of the pose is striking, both in comparison with the manuscript, and with the other figures on the Masham column which are competently positioned in full- and semi-profile.

The iconographic details of the carved scenes thus suggest they are correctly identified as Samson with the Gates of Gaza, and, although they do not illustrate Samson Destroying the Temple, they were, nevertheless, based on a model depicting that event. This model, probably closely related to the sixth-century Eastern original lying behind the later, Byzantine manuscript scene, was adapted to create the new, Anglo-Saxon, scene by half-turning the figure to the side and moving the arch down behind his head.

It would seem, therefore, that in some cases the various regions of the insular world did make use of different iconograhic model-types. In Ireland, those responsible for the Samson scene, appear to have had access to Western European source material, while those producing the earlier images of Samson in Anglo-Saxon England and the (possibly) later carvings of Scotland, employed a different, ultimately early Eastern, iconographic source-group.

The question of iconograhic function

A third factor distinguishing the Old Testament imagery on the carved insular monuments is their iconograhic function. Again, the fragmentary and poorly executed nature of some of the Old Testament scenes means it is not always possible to recover their significance; the condition of the Elwick Hall stone, is such that the overall context and any tell-tale iconograhic details of this image of the Fall have been irretrievably lost.

Furthermore, even where the images have survived in relatively good condition with their associated decoration intact, it is not always clear that a specifically Old Testament iconographic significance was necessarily intended. Depictions of harpists, for instance, may not always have portrayed David the Psalmist. At Ardchattan, Argyll, the harpist shares a panel with two beasts, at least one (but probably two) other musicians, and a warrior brandishing a shield and spear (Allen and Anderson 1903, III, fig 393). The beasts cannot be identified as a lion, bear or sheep, creatures which might be expected to accompany depictions of David, and so help to identify the harpist as the composer of the Psalms. Nevertheless, they may owe their ultimate derivation to iconographic material associated with pictures of David; the shield held by the warrior bears a close resemblance to one depicted on the St Andrews Sarcophagus, Fife, where the figure in question survives in a demonstrably Davidic context. All this implies, however, is that those responsible for the Ardchattan stone may have drawn on images at one time associated with Davidic iconography; it does not mean the harpist can be identified as David the Psalmist.

Similarly, the image of a figure set between two beasts found on a stone from Inchinnan (no 3), Renfrewshire, sometimes identified as Daniel in the Lions' Den, is unlikely to actually depict that event, although in this instance, it may function iconographically as a Daniel scene. Nominally, the scheme bears some resemblance to schemes found on stones from Meigle (no 2) and Dunkeld (no 2), Perthshire, where Daniel stands in prayer flanked by four lion-like creatures which, on the Meigle stone raise their forepaws in adoration (ibid, figs 311B, 332A). At Inchinnan,

however, the central standing figure does not stand in the *orant* position, and the two flanking beasts almost encircle his head with their open jaws (ibid, fig 478A). This arrangement has more in common with the general motif of a figure threatened by beasts found frequently in insular art, than with images of Daniel and the Lions.

Nevertheless, the associated decoration on the monument may imply that it was intended to function iconographically as a Daniel image, which, in early Christian contexts could have signified both the fortitude of the faithful Christian and Christ's redemptive death (Grabar 1968, 8–17; cf Augustine, De Baptismo. IV, ii, 3: *P.L.* 43, 155). On the Inchinnan stone the figures are set below a cross, and immediately above both the cross and the man-and-beasts are pairs of confronting creatures with their heads deeply bowed. This overall arrangement suggests the man-between-the-beasts is being presented as a direct parallel to the cross; as such it may well have been intended to refer (as a Daniel image might in a similar context) to Christ's redemptive death.

However, this context and the more general nature of the scheme (compared with other, 'orthodox', Daniel images), also means the group is open to alternative interpretations, such as Christ Recognised between the Beasts, a Eucharistic scheme which Ó Carragáin (1986, 379–90) has argued was circulating in the insular world from the eighth century onwards. If this explanation is relevant at Inchinnan, as the overall context and the generalised appearance of the scheme would suggest it is, it would imply that a decorative motif was employed which may have functioned as a Daniel image, but which could equally have functioned as a Eucharistic scheme.

With the carved insular images of Samson such iconographic ambiguities are less apparent. On the Irish, Scottish and Anglo-Saxon monuments these scenes illustrate the Old Testament hero unequivocally, and they function as an integral part of the larger iconographic programmes decorating the monuments. The themes conveyed by these programmes, however, do vary.

In Ireland, for instance, it has long been argued that the Old Testament images generally functioned as part of iconographic programmes presenting the intervention of God in the affairs of Humanity (eg Henry 1967, 144–6; 1979, 40), and the image of Samson Destroying the Temple on the east face of the West (Tall) Cross at Monasterboice, Co. Louth, does seem to conform to this explanation. At the base of the shaft, and below the Samson scene, David, as God's Anointed on earth, slays the lion and the Philistine giant, Goliath. Between these panels are images recording the moments when God saved the unfortunate Isaac from being sacrificed by his father, and provided the Israelites (through Moses) with water in the desert. Above, the Hebrew Children are saved from a fiery death, and the prophet Elijah is rewarded with corporeal ascension into heaven, a privilege enjoyed by only two others: Enoch and Christ.

Samson is not mentioned often in early Christian exegesis, and where he is, the destruction of the temple is not commonly invoked, probably because of the pyrrhic nature of this particular victory. However, in the few instances where the episode is referred to, it is presented as proof of the power of the Holy Spirit to overcome adversity, proof of what the true Christian can achieve through faith (eg Ambrose, De Spiritu Sancto II, prolog.12: *P.L.* 16, 776). On the (West) Monasterboice Cross, therefore, it would seem that the Samson scene functions, as one of a number of Old Testament scenes, to demonstrate the power of God to aid, save and reward Humanity.

On the Inchbrayock Stone, it is Delilah cutting Samson's hair, and Samson slaying one of the Philistines which are portrayed, but here the scenes do not seem to function primarily as examples of God's almighty power. On this monument they are (on the main face) depicted with the central cross and two beasts curled round each other, and (on the reverse), with the seated figure of the Virgin and a hunt scene. Associated with this selection of images the Samson scenes appear to refer, more generally, to faith in the Church and its sacraments.

In Ambrose's Treatise on the Holy Spirit, for instance (De Spiritu Sancto II, prolog.12: *P.L.* 16, 776), the loss of Samson's hair signifies the loss of the power of the Holy Spirit which results from loss of faith, while the smiting of the Philistine develops into a paean for the Christian victory over death:

> Invictus ergo Samson, atque ita insuperabilis, ut in maxilla asini viros mille percuteret; ita plenus gratiae coelestis, ut etiam aquam in maxilla asini sitiens reperiret: sive hoc ad miraculum conferas, sive ad mysterium vertas... Per hanc enim injuriarum patientiam, quam erudiunt sacramenta baptismatis, de quibusdam stimulis iracundiae triumphamus: ut morte obita, resurrectionis requiem consequamur.[3]

Viewed in association with the elevated cross and the Virgin, who can usually be understood to refer, at some level, to the incarnation of Christ and the salvation afforded by that event (Clayton 1990, 140–70; Belting 1994, 30–4), the Inchbrayock Samson scenes may well have been intended as part of an iconographic programme demonstrating the salvation attainable through faith in Christ and the sacraments of his Church.

This thematic programme may also have extended to include the other images on the Stone. The secular hunt scene, may serve to widen the frame of reference by portraying (more generally) those for whom salvation is available: the audience and/or those commemorated by the monument (if such was its function). Even the two beasts on the main face of the Stone may have been part of the overall iconography, although doubts surrounding their identification do make any conclusions concerning them uncertain.

While these creatures may have been simply part of a general repertoire of animal ornament, it is not unlikely that they illustrate a more specific iconograhic point (having been drawn from a store of locally-available animal motifs). If this is so, and if the larger beast can be identified as a lion (an explanation which is not entirely certain), it is possible they represent the lioness and her cub described in early medieval bestiary traditions as symbolic of the resurrection; it was believed that the cub, born dead, had life breathed into it by the third day (Hicks 1994, 108).[4]

This significance would certainly be consistent with the general iconographic programme implied by the Samson scenes, and would suggest that those responsible for the production of the monument intended to present a series of iconographic references to the nature of Christ's salvation and his Church. Here it may be that the Old Testament images were chosen because they were deemed most appropriate to illustrate the triumph of Christianity and its institutions.

On the Masham column, many of the figural scenes accompanying the Samson image are too worn and damaged to be identified, but, alongside the depictions of David the Psalmist and David Slaying the Lion a Eucharistic image of two peacocks confronting a vine emerging from a chalice (Hawkes 1989, pl 7), and a composite scheme of the twelve apostles flanking Christ, can still be identified. Here the Samson scene appears to function as a Type of Christ's redemptive death and resurrection, described most vividly in Gregory the Great's Sermon for Easter Sunday, the Day of the Resurrection (Homil. in Evang. II, Hom. xxi.7: *P.L.* 76, 1173):

> Quem... hoc in facto, quem nisi Redemptorum nostrum Samson ille significat? Quid Gaza civitas nisi infernum designat? Quid per Philisthaeos nisi Judaeorum perfidia demonstratur? Qui cum mortuum Dominum viderent, eiusque corpus in sepulcro iam positum, custodes illico deputaverunt, et eum qui auctor vitae claruerat, in inferni claustris retentum, quasi Samsonem in Gaza se deprehendisse laetati sunt. Samson vero media nocte non solum exiit, sed etiam portas tulit, quia videlicet Redemptor noster ante lucem resurgens, non solum liber de inferno exiit, sed et ipsa etiam inferni claustra destruxit. Portas tulit, et montis verticem subiit, quia resurgendo claustra inferni abstulit, et ascendendo coelorum regna penetravit.[5]

The carved scene thus depicts, not simply the Old Testament story, but Samson as a Type of Christ the Redeemer. His actions at Gaza foreshadow those of Christ in hell, an event foretold by David in Psalm 23/24, and recited by the denizens of hell in the Apocryphal account of the Harrowing preserved in the Gospel of Nicodemus, known to have been circulating in the insular world from the eighth century onwards (James 1924, 130–2).

In this way the Samson scene at Masham also relates to the other Old Testament scenes depicted on the monument: David Dictating the Psalms and Slaying the Lion. Inspired by Augustine's Commentary on the Psalms (In Psalmum VII, 2: *P.L.* 36, 98), this latter event was commonly understood to signify the deliverance of Christians from the power of evil through Christ's redeeming death: as David, the psalmist-prophet and ancestor of Christ, took the sheep from the lion, so Christ in his death, descent and resurrection, took all the faithful into his fellowship, having overcome Death (and the devil).

The significance of these events is corroborated by the iconography of the other images surviving on the column. The Eucharistic scheme, depicts the result of Christ's actions (revealed through Samson and David); it represents both the bread and wine of the Eucharist, and the immortality available through the sacraments of the Church, the institution founded on Christ, this being the general notion expressed by the composite image of Christ and his apostles. On this monument, therefore, the Samson scene, and indeed the Davidic scenes, function at a typological level in an overall iconographic programme dedicated to the central Christian doctrines of salvation, redemption and resurrection.

Not many of the other Anglo-Saxon carved Old Testament scenes have survived with any of their associated ornament intact, but the few that have also seem to have functioned typologically. The Breedon and Dacre depictions of the Fall, for instance, together with the portrayals of Abraham and Isaac, have been shown by Bailey to have served as Types of Christ's Sacrifice on the Cross (Bailey 1977; 1988, 11). Absolute conclusions cannot be drawn from such meagre evidence, but these examples (widely separated from each other in time and place) do suggest that at least some Old Testament images were viewed by those producing the Anglo-Saxon sculpture as having a primarily typological function. It is a relatively narrow perception of the material which may explain, in part, the restricted use of Old Testament imagery on the Anglo-Saxon monuments. Certainly such notions cannot have been the deciding factor; other considerations, such as the availability of models, must also have played a part in the selection of scenes for the carvings.

Nevertheless, whatever the reason for the apparent disinterest in Old Testament imagery on Anglo-Saxon stone carvings, and indeed on the Scottish stones, it would appear that those producing the early Medieval carvings of both these areas were less likely to use Old Testament images on their monuments than other figural scenes. Moreover, they seem to have shared an interest in the same limited range of Old Testament events, and, in some instances, had access to similar iconographic source material. The use to which they put their images, however, could, and did, differ, a fact which raises further questions about the perceived roles and audiences of the monuments in the various regions of the insular world during the pre-Norman period.

Notes

1 The date of the Reculver fragment is uncertain, but current estimates place it within the ninth century, a period which embraces the so-called Anglian and Viking ages of Anglo-Saxon England (Backhouse, Turner and Webster 1984, 41). However, being of southern English manufacture, such divisions are of limited relevance to this stone. Adam and Eve may also have been depicted on a fragment from Eccleshall (Pape 1946–47, 32–3, pl III), but although two figures flanking a central moulding can still be discerned on this stone, the carving is too worn for the scene to be identified with any certainty.

2 Potential Old Testament scenes surviving in Scotland:

Abraham and Isaac: Iona 83 (St Martin's Cross) and possibly Kildalton, Argyll.

Adam and Eve: Iona 84 (St Matthew's Cross), Argyll; Farnell, Angus; Jedburgh 1, Jedburgh 2, Roxburghshire; Strathmartine 8, Angus.

Daniel in the Lions' Den: Dunkeld 2, Meigle 2, Perthshire. Identification of the schemes featuring a figure between beasts as Daniel on stones from Hamilton, Inchinnan 3, Renfrewshire; Iona 83 (St Martin's Cross) and Keills, Argyll, is uncertain.

David, the Psalmist: Aldbar, Angus; Dupplin, Perthshire; Iona 80 (St Oran's Cross), Iona 83 (St Martin's Cross) Argyll; Nigg, Easter Ross. The identity of the figures at Invergowrie, Perthshire; Kirriemuir 1 and Kingoldrum, Angus, is not clear as the existence of a 'harp' is uncertain. cf the harpists at Aberlemno 3, Monifieth 4, Angus; Ardchattan, Argyll; Hilton of Cadboll, Easter Ross; Lethendy, Perthshire , where the figures exist within a potentially secular scene including other musicians.

David, Slaying the Lion: Aberlemno 3, Aldbar, Angus; Dupplin, Perthshire; Iona 80 (St Oran's Cross), Argyll; Kinnedar, Moray; Nigg, Easter Ross; St Andrews 1 (sarcophagus), Fife, and on a now-lost piece from Tannadice, Angus. It is uncertain whether this scene was also featured at Kildalton, Argyll.

David, Anointing and Enthronement: possibly illustrated on Iona 83 (St Martin's Cross), Argyll. As Henderson (1994) has recently suggested, it is unlikely that the figures commonly identified as David the Warrior and David on Horseback actually depict the Old Testament hero.

The Hebrew Children: Iona 89 (Abbey Museum 21), Argyll.

Jonah: Dunfallandy, Perthshire; Woodrae, Angus.

Samson, and Delilah and *Slaying the Philistine*: Inchbrayock 1, Angus.

The Martyrdom of Isaiah: was possibly illustrated on St Vigeans 7, Angus, which shows the lower half of two standing figures flanking a central figure set upside-down on a block.

3 Translation: "Samson then, was unconquered, and so invincible as to be able to smite a thousand men with the jawbone of an ass; so full of heavenly grace that when thirsty he found even water in the jawbone of an ass, whether you consider this as a miracle or turn it into a mystery... For, by this endurance of injuries, which the sacrament of baptism teaches, we triumph over the stings of anger, that having passed through death we may attain to the rest of the resurrection." (Trans, Schaff and Wace 1957, 117)

4 Although one of Samson's heroic exploits involved the slaying of a lion, it is unlikely the two beasts illustrate this event. They bear no resemblance to the known iconography of such scenes, and this interpretation does not explain the presence of the smaller creature.

5 Translation: "Whom does Samson symbolise... if not our Redeemer? What does Gaza symbolise, if not the gates of Hell? and what the Philistines, if not the perfidy of the Jews, who seeing the Lord dead and his body in the sepulchre, placed guards before it, rejoicing that they had him in their power, and that he whom the Author of Life had glorified was now enclosed in the gates of hell, as they had rejoiced when they thought they had captured Samson in Gaza. But in the middle of the night Samson not only went forth from the city, but also bore off its gates, as our Redeemer, rising before day, not only went forth free from hell, but also destroyed the very gates of hell. He took away the gates, and mounted with them to the top of a hill; for by his resurrection he bore off the gates of hell, and by his ascension he mounted to the kingdom of heaven." (Trans, Toal 1958, 244–5)

References

ALLEN, J R and ANDERSON, J 1903 *The Early Christian Monuments of Scotland*. Edinburgh (repr with an Introduction by Isabel Henderson, 2 vols, Balgavies, Angus, 1993).

BACKHOUSE, J, TURNER, M and WEBSTER, L (eds) 1984 *The Golden Age of Anglo-Saxon Art: 966–1066*. London.

BAILEY, R N

– 1977 The meaning of the Viking-Age shaft at Dacre. *Trans Cumberland Westmorland Antiq Archaeol Soc*, 2 Ser, 77, 61–74.

– 1980 *Viking-Age Sculpture in Northern England*. London.

– 1988 *The Meaning of Mercian Sculpture* (Brixworth Lecture No 6).

BAILEY, R N and CRAMP, R J 1988 *Cumberland. Westmorland and Lancashire North-of-the-Sands* (*Corpus of Anglo-Saxon Stone Sculpture*, II). Oxford.

BELTING, H 1994 *Likeness and Presence: A History of the Image Before the Era of Art.* Chicago.

BROWN, G B 1937 *Anglo-Saxon Sculpture* (The Arts of Early England, VI.ii). London.

CLAYTON, M 1990 *The Cult of the Virgin Mary in Anglo-Saxon England.* Cambridge.

COLLINGWOOD, W G
– 1907 Anglian and Anglo-Danish sculpture in the North Riding of Yorkshire. *Yorks Archaeol J*, 20, 149–213.

– 1915 Anglian and Anglo-Danish sculpture in the West Riding, with addenda to the North and East Ridings and York, and a general review of the Early Christian monuments of Yorkshire. *Yorks Archaeol J*, 23, 129–299.

CRAMP, R J 1984 *County Durham and Northumberland (Corpus of Anglo-Saxon Stone Sculpture,* I). Oxford.

DER NERSESSIAN, S 1962 The illustrations of the Homilies of Gregory of Nazianzus, Paris Gr. 510: a study of the connections between text and images. *Dumbarton Oaks Papers*, 16, 195–228.

GRABAR, A 1968 *Christian Iconography: A Study of its Origins.* Princeton.

HARBISON, P
– 1977 On some possible sources of Irish high cross decoration. *Festschrift zum 50 Jahringgen Bestehen des Vorgeschichtlichen Seminars,* I, 283–97. Gladenbach.

– 1984 Earlier Carolingian narrative iconography: ivories, manuscripts, frescoes and Irish high crosses. *Romisch-Germanisches Zentral Museum Jahrbuch*, 31, 455–71. Mainz.

– 1987 The Carolingian contribution to Irish sculpture. In Ryan, M (ed) *Ireland and Insular Art A.D. 500–1200,* 105–10. Dublin.

– 1992 *The High Crosses of Ireland,* 3 vols. Dublin/Bonn.

HAWKES, A J
– 1989 *The Non-Crucifixion Iconography of the Pre-Viking Sculpture in the North of England.* Unpublished PhD thesis, 2 vols, University of Newcastle, Newcastle upon Tyne.

– 1994 The Wirksworth slab: an iconography of female humilitas. *Peritia*, 9, 246–89.

HEIGHWAY, C M 1987 *Anglo-Saxon Gloucestershire.* Gloucester.

HENDERSON, I B
– 1967 *The Picts.* London.

– 1986 The 'David cycle' in Pictish art. In Higgitt, J (ed) *Early Medieval Sculpture in Britain and Ireland*, 87–123. Oxford. (*BAR Brit Ser* 152)

– 1994 The Insular and Continental context of the St Andrews sarcophagus. In Crawford, BE (ed) *Scotland in Dark-Age Europe,* 71–102. St Andrews.

HENRY, F
– 1967 *Irish Art During the Viking Invasions.* London.

– 1979 *Early Christian Irish Art.* Cork.

HICKS, C 1994 *Animals in Early Medieval Art.* Edinburgh.

JAMES, M R 1924 *The Apocryphal New Testament.* Oxford.

LANG, J 1983 Recent studies in the pre-Conquest sculpture of Northumbria. In Thompson, F H (ed) *Studies in Medieval Sculpture*, 177–89. London.

Ó CARRAGÁIN, É 1986 Christ over the Beasts and the Agnus Dei: two multivalent panels on the Ruthwell and Bewcastle crosses. In Szarmach, P (ed) *Sources of Anglo-Saxon Culture*, 377–403. Kalamazoo.

RCAHMS = Royal Commission on the Ancient and Historical Monuments of Scotland
– 1956 *An Inventory of the Ancient and Historical Monuments of Roxburghshire with the 14th Report of the Commission,* vol 1. Edinburgh.

– 1982 *Argyll: An Inventory of the Monuments,* vol 4, *Iona.* Edinburgh.

TRENCH-JELLICOE, R M C 1991 A recent Viking-Age sculpture find from Tynemouth Priory. *Archaeologia Aeliana*, 19, 71–8.

TOAL, M F 1958 *The Sunday Sermons of the Great Fathers,* vol 2. London.

TWEDDLE, D 1983 Anglo-Saxon sculpture in South East England before *c*950. In Thompson, F H (ed) *Studies in Medieval Sculpture*, 18–40. London.

Pictish and Related Harps:
Their form and decoration

Ross Trench-Jellicoe

Isabel Henderson's formative article on Pictish Davidic iconography (1986, 84–124), firmly signposted attention towards an important and hitherto neglected area of study. In her overview, she placed these images within the context not only of Insular parallels on stone and in manuscript but, where relevant, drew in material from much further afield. From her study it can be appreciated that, while the presence of the harp is an integral part of some aspects of Davidic iconography, in Pictland its use was extended, through the use of a harp as a symbol, into other Davidic contexts where David's role as a musician was irrelevant. In such circumstances the harp was added to resolve possible ambiguity. Furthermore, the portrayal of harps over a period of time potentially permits a study of the instrument *per se.*

Five Pictish scenes (**1**) have a harp inappropriately added and arbitrarily placed so that it functions almost like a so-called 'Pictish symbol', as an attribute or means of identification.[1] An example of this phenomenon is the instrument which lies on its back in the lower right panel of Aberlemno 3C, Angus (ibid, pl 5, 4a; Allen and Anderson 1903, III, fig 228B), where it appears in a context with David, the Lion-killer and one of the sheep he protects. It was added in this instance to ensure that the viewer would identify the scene as Davidic rather than one depicting Samson slaying a lion (Alcock 1995). A second example occurs in a hitherto undescribed scene in the penultimate register of the lower right-hand quadrant (LR2) of Gask 1A, Perthshire (Appendix 1) (**4**). That version seems to share the same basic model as the Aberlemno scene and occupies a similar position in the design of the slab face. The Gask harp also acts as a means to identify David. It is significant that neither of these harps is archetypical, both are distinguished by a tendency towards rhomboidality.

Another scene, carved on Nigg 1C, Easter Ross, (Henderson 1986, pl 5, 5a), includes what is probably the earliest preserved Pictish representation of a true harp (perhaps around AD 800), although Nigg is by no means the earliest Pictish example of Davidic imagery.[2] This isolate harp, unlike the Aberlemno and Gask versions is carved in the vertical plain, nevertheless it stands within an overall Davidic tableau, juxtaposed with a David the Lion-killer motif. Thus it too seems to function as a Davidic attribute and perhaps operates in a similar manner to the 'Pictish symbols' at the top of the slab. Linked to the Nigg scene is another hitherto unidentified David, the Lion-killer, carved onto the long edge of a recumbent grave slab (middle panel, middle register) Kincardine 1D, Easter Ross, overlooking the upper reaches of the Dornoch Firth. Both Stuart (1856, 12, pl 36) and Allen (Allen and Anderson 1903, III, 85) failed to recognise this badly worn scene as Davidic, despite its overall similarity in the use of a Gilgamesh type of lion-killer model to that at Nigg. At Kincardine the vertically portrayed harp appears to the upper right of David's head, this being the only available space remaining in the design. The sculptural evidence on this monument is severely limited through the virtual total abrasion of three of the five faces and no evidence remains for the presence of Pictish symbols (**5**).

A fifth example of this signifying type of harp appears on the reverse of a slab from Aldbar (1C), Angus, where the third register includes: a David breaking the lion's jaw, a staff, probably representing his shepherd's crook, a sheep positioned vertically and a vertical solo harp (Allen and Anderson 1903, III, fig 269B). From its location it is clear that the harp is included within the scene and its presence is used to confirm the identification of David. Although 'Pictish symbols' are lacking at Aldbar, the selection of images is closely similar to those found on the other four solo harp examples in Pictland.[3] Each of the five scenes observes a similar formula: David interacts with a lion, breaking its jaw, one or more sheep is present and each vignette includes a harp functioning symbolically as an attribute to confirm the identity of David. It perhaps also served to remind the audience of David's more important signification in the paradigm of the 'Cycle of David' as the Psalmist.

In addition to these solo harps, three further examples occur in southern Pictland and each is played by a harper.[4] One, carved on side D of the Dupplin Cross, Perthshire (Allen and Anderson 1903, III, fig 334B), is probably subsumed within a Davidic context because David the Lion-killer appears on another face. A harper, plucking the strings with both hands, sits on a high-backed chair topped with zoomorphic terminals. A panel containing a harper also decorates a shaft fragment on Monifieth 4A, Angus (ibid, fig 275). Stylistically the scene bears a close resemblance to that at Dupplin; parallelling chair, figure, harp and their orientation. The angle of the two main harp members is more acute than Dupplin's representation but this compression occurs because of a lack of vertical space within the scene. Monifieth contrasts with Dupplin in preserving no other Davidic iconography but both examples share the fashion of framing the figure in isolation, nonetheless they probably represent David the Psalmist (Henderson 1986).

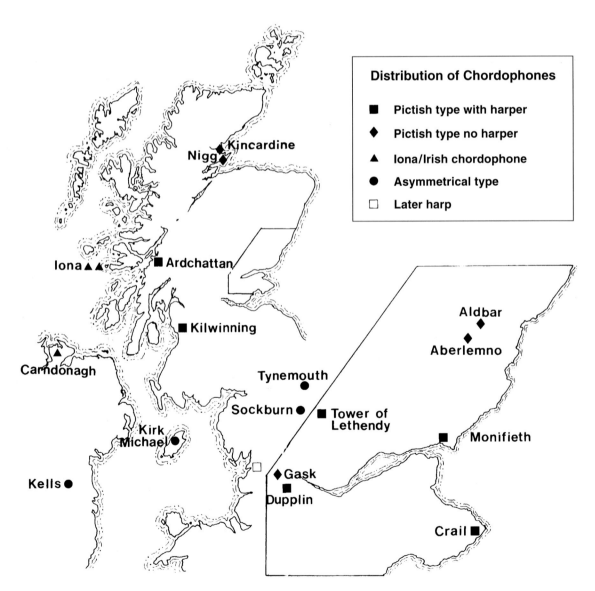

1 *Distribution of chordophones*

A novel scene appears on a fragment at Tower of Lethendy, Perthshire (Fisher, Greenhill 1971-72, 238–40, pl 36a; RCAHMS 1994, fig 97) which includes two confronted instrumentalists; the figure to the left plays a harp while the right hand figure holds a triple pipe. Between them lies an elongated vertical feature comprising three elements bound, top and bottom, like a barrel. This seems to represent a tabor[5], a drum probably suspended from the piper's neck. Beneath is a dog-like animal considered by Fisher (ibid, 340) to represent a Davidic sheep, and thus to be an attribute of him. This scene most probably represents another version of the *Choir of David*. The panels from Dupplin, Monifieth and Tower of Lethendy, together with the relevant register from Aldbar, all seem to post-date the initial group of Nigg, Kincardine, Aberlemno and Gask and belong to the 9th or 10th century. Another complex scene on a slab at Crail 1A, Fife (Allen and Anderson 1903, III, fig 381), has at different times incorrectly been claimed to contain either a *Virgin and Child* or a harper and should be excluded from this group.

Related to, but distinct from Pictish harp represent-ations is a group of four examples in the west of Scotland. Two scenes of seated instrumentalists occur on Iona, one on St Oran's Cross and another on St Martin's Cross (RCAHMS 1984, figs 195A, 196B, 205ii, 207A). These instruments are not the three-sided harp of Pictland, rather they comprise four elements with variously curved corners. The presence of parallel sides indicates a similarity to chordophones found in Ireland, particularly that on the north pillar at Carndonagh, Donegal (Roe 1949; Buckley 1990; Lacy 1983, 251, pl 30). A harper carved in the neck of the cross arm on St Oran's Cross sits on the ground. By contrast the musicians' panel of St Martin's Cross is carved in the middle of the shaft. The composition of this scene, although carrying a different form of harp, is similar to that from Tower of Lethendy, above, including a harper on the left and a triple-piper to the right, who frame a barrel-like drum. Differences between Iona and Lethendy scenes are minor; the harper sits on a low stool, the piper kneels, the drum lies horizontally rather than vertically but such variations are attributable to a lack of vertical space on the Iona shaft. The 8th-century date attached to St Martin's cross suggests that, in any perceived relationship between Iona and Perthshire scenes, the

model travelled from west to east.

A third example from the same cultural zone is Ardchattan 1A, Argyll (RCAHMS 1975, 110–11, fig 99). The incomplete slab now preserved at the site of the medieval priory includes, in the lower right quadrant, a vertical sequence of three hooded musicians, seated in profile. The largest and uppermost of the three is a harper whose hands pluck the strings of a damaged instrument, approximately 20% is lost along the outer edge. The lower figures include a triple-piper and a horn player (not a figure carrying a crown or rattle, *pace* RCAHMS 1975; Allen and Anderson 1903, III, 378; Lang 1995, 6). The harp, slightly more rounded in form than the Pictish examples, is a three-sided instrument, a fact confirmed by the direction of the remains of harp strings revealed beneath the harper's hands. This 10th-century version of the Davidic choir is perhaps in part derived from St Martin's Cross, Iona, but the image has undergone reformation and displays evidence of harping practice borrowed ultimately from Pictish models.

Of similar date is another slab recently rediscovered at Kilwinning, Ayrshire (Craig 1994, 77–8, 81–2, fig 44). A three-sided harp is juxtaposed with a profiled male figure; they are clearly intended to be bracketed together but the relative positions of the two make it impossible for the harper to strike the harp with his hands.[6] It cannot be certainly demonstrated that this iconography is Davidic and the presence around the figure of snake-like monsters suggests it may be a mythological representation of *Ragnar in the Snake Pit* in which the figure plays the harp with his feet. The style of the figure suggests it falls within the same ambit as contemporary Manx carvings (Kermode 1907, pl XXV, no 66A) but the harp representation is quite unlike the single Manx example of an asymmetrical harp (Trench-Jellicoe 1991, 74, fig 4; Kermode 1907, pl LIV).

Amongst the harps with a western distribution, those from Iona are early and perhaps pre-date the Nigg and Kincardine versions by half a century (ie they are roughly contemporary with the earliest evidence for Davidic iconography in Pictland), while those from Ardchattan and Kilwinning are contemporary with or slightly later than the Picto-Scottish group. It is significant that those chordophones found in Pictland and Dalriadic Scotland enter the northern Insular sphere at about the same time. This contemporaneity of the advent of innovative liturgical

2 *Pictish and Scottish chordophones:* **a** *Iona, St Oran's Cross* **b** *Iona, St Martin's Cross* **c** *Aberlemno 3C* **d** *Gask 1A*
e *Nigg 1C* **f** *Kincardine 1D* **g** *Monifieth 4A* **h** *Tower of Lethendy 1A* **j** *Dupplin 1D* **k** *Ardchattan 1A* **l** *Aldbar 1C*
m *Kilwinning 1A*
* *Denotes reversed image to aid comparison*

concerns may have derived from the Continent or from the Anglo-Saxon Midlands (Henderson 1986) but no evidence remains to confirm a Mercian source was used to provide models for instruments adopted into either northern location (Lawson 1981).

This suggests that of the twelve harps (**2**) from the area of modern Scotland, those deriving from Pictland, including examples drawn from the earlier group, linked to specifically Pictish iconography and the later representations of Picto-Scottish type from the same region, comprise a distinctive collection marked by their triangular form; only the two earliest harp examples from Iona stand apart. Other later western British examples conform to the Pictish model but these remain distinctive from other types of chordophone such as the Manx example from Kirk Michael (MIC 1:130(104)A), Tynemouth 8A (Trench-Jellicoe 1991, 71–8), Sockburn 6A, Co Durham (Cramp 1984, illus 720) and contemporary Irish types (Roe 1949; Rensch 1989, 40–5; Buckley 1990; Trench-Jellicoe 1991; Buckley 1992; Sanger and Kinnaird 1992, 11–30).

The Decoration of Picto-Scottish Harps

A significant aspect of two Picto-Scottish harps which has not hitherto received comment, is the decoration they carry. The relief-carved Dupplin harp (**3**; Allen and Anderson 1903, III, fig 334B) is played by a figure with a nose guard on his helmet, resembling warriors in other panels of the Dupplin monument. The harp's upper member (string carrier) and deep soundbox below are straight and set slightly more than a right-angle apart. The identification of a forepillar poses a problem. Is it present or is it not? On balance it seems that the straight outer line is thicker than the inner strings and can thus be taken to represent the outer line of a forepillar. Moreover, eight remaining vertical lines indicate the harp strings within the frame, one more than the usual number expected on Pictish harps. It seems probable that the outermost of these lines represents the inner edge of the forepillar, a detail that would have been obvious when the scene was painted. This arrangement would regularize the Dupplin harp's design as seven strings and a stout forepillar.

The harp's structure is of great interest but it is the decoration of the terminals of the string-carrier and soundbox which is most impressive. The identification of

the presence of decorated terminals is not new, they appear in Jastrzębski's lithograph for Stuart (1856, pl LVIII). The upper terminal comprises the profiled head of a creature, probably a bird with long curving beak and tear-shaped eye within a prominent brow, reminiscent of the slab framing, bird-headed beasts on Monifieth 2C (Allen and Anderson 1903, III, fig 242B; Trench-Jellicoe, forthcoming) and also of the decorated terminal of a fragment of stone furniture recently recovered during excavation at Heysham, Lancs (Cramp 1995, 106–11) and its analogues. The lower terminal of the broad soundbox is similarly decorated although the line of the upper curving beak (seen upside down) is interrupted by the characteristically crossed foot of the harper, a significant feature which may be paralleled in the harp scene of Monifieth 4A (ibid, fig 275A). No other Pictish harp approaches in detail the proportions, arm length and angularity of the Dupplin design.

A second decorated harp appears on the Aldbar slab (ibid, fig 269B), a Picto-Scottish scene harking back to Pictish models. The worn instrument was carved near the

3 *Dupplin 1N: seated harper with decorated harp*

R. Trench-Jellicoe

right edge of the slab within a border which has partially protected it from damage. The harp, of handsome design, expands slightly in the deep soundbox and curves at a right-angle into an upper string carrier, two-thirds the thickness of the soundbox. It tapers before thickening a little towards the terminal. As at Dupplin, the main members are quite straight but at Aldbar both terminals are joined by a bowed forepillar of uniform thickness, half the width of the string-carrier. Oblique lighting reveals seven strings within the harp frame. Its outline is similar to those of the Nigg, Kincardine, Tower of Lethendy, Ardchattan and Kilwinning harps, indicating it conforms to the mainstream development of Picto-Scottish harp design.

Aldbar's harp differs from other examples in the swelling of the outer third of the string-post whose upper line undulates before terminating in a tight rising curl. The outline forms the head of a dragonesque beast whose curved brow frames a faint almond-shaped eye. The spiral represents a pronounced curled snout positioned above an open mouth containing what appear to be shield-shaped teeth. A curving line defines brow from snout. The shape of the Aldbar terminal differs markedly from the Dupplin heads and is not repeated at the lower corner of the instrument. Useful parallels for this type of beast-head in Picto-Scottish sculpture are limited, although those beasts which adorn the high backs of chairs show some similarities, as on Kirriemuir 1C (ibid, fig 239B) or the nose scrolls of the interlaced serpents of Meigle 4C (ibid, fig 313B). Curl-snouted dragonesque beasts are more readily paralleled on metalwork. Examples appear in the terminals of the Hunterston brooch (Youngs 1989, 91–2, pl opp 74), on a penannular brooch of the 8th to 9th century, probably from Perthshire (ibid, 94–5, no 72), and on an 8th-century brooch recovered during excavation at St Ninian's Isle, Shetland (ibid, 112, no 107).[7] It is reasonable to look to metalwork as a source for this decoration particularly if the model for the Aldbar harp representation were taken from an actual contemporary harp. Despite close scrutiny of other harps no decorated examples have been identified, however, the presence of two roughly contemporary instruments of independent design, occurring 69km apart, suggests that the decoration of high-status harps was not uncommon.

Although the iconography of David with a harp was first depicted on Iona displaying a slightly different type of chordophone from that found in Pictland, it seems that it was the Pictish form of instrument that became adopted by the Scots after the take-over of Pictland. This became in time the dominant type. From the 9th century, these sophisticated examples appear on monuments associated with high-status sites at Dupplin, close to the royal seat of power at Forteviot, and Brechin an important centre of lay and ecclesiastical patronage. Sculptors at both sites perhaps reproduced, in carved form, locally available high-status models, thus reflecting a change in emphasis from an earlier, often esoteric, monastic significance of the message embodied in the sculptural programmes to develop into a statement suggestive of lay prestige.

The Pictish harp form became dominant iconographically in the Picto-Scottish phase, suggesting it may also have been technically superior and replaced other types of chordophone. The spread of its imagery south and westward may reflect the adoption of this type of harp as a high-status instrument in new areas. This harp type also spread to Ireland, where it appears, *inter alia,* on the Breac Maodhog shrine (Henry 1970, pl 31) and to England where it occurs before the millennium in manuscripts such as Caedmon's *Metrical Paraphrase of the Scriptures:* Oxford, Bodley, Junius 11(Rensch 1989, fig 40) and although its representation is rare in sculpture, it is carved on a recumbent grave-marker at Heysham, Lancashire, dating to the 12th or 13th century.

Acknowledgements
Grateful thanks to Richard Bailey and Jane Hawkes for their comments and to David Henry for fruitful discussions.

Appendix 1: Gask 1A, Perthshire, and a newly-recognised example of David the lion-killer identified by a harp

The obverse of the damaged slab from Gask, 1A, Perthshire (Allen and Anderson 1903, III, 290–1), has only (as far as is known) been illustrated by Gibb in Stuart (1856, pl CIV). Allen was unable to provide an illustration for his curtailed discussion of this 'much defaced' side. 20% of the slab is lost at the top, removing upper left and a small section of the right cross arms, together with the contingent ring. The arm pits are pierced. Today, the slab is erected on the front lawn of Moncreiffe House, by Bridge of Earn, so that 15% more of the slab is visible at the base than was revealed in Stuart's day.

Face A includes the remains of a circular crossing panel and a cross-shaft panel[8] containing four types of interlaced ornament. Quadrant panels flank the shaft. They are plain bordered along the outer edges but lack formal internal divisions. The upper registers are filled with realistic animals and fantastical monsters, similar to those mythical creatures recorded in *Physiologus*-type bestiaries, while lower registers contain various figural scenes drawn from biblical or related sources. At the point where the cross member and ring abut a spiral erupts from each corner, intruding into the quadrant panels.

The Lower Quadrant Panels

The upper section of the left panel is substantially as drawn by Gibb (ibid, pl CIV). The uppermost quadruped faces L, its head (**4**, LL6) is turned to look over its back. A boar, facing R, in register LL5 has a typically curled tail and large bristles on its neck. Scene LL4 contains a left-facing quadruped with lowered equine head, the body tapers and spirals, interweaving with the hind quarters and looping tail. Beneath, in LL3, the tail of a supine left-facing quadruped performs a double twist above the hind quarters while its head is thrown back across its shoulder. The head develops a large lappet which twists downwards twice to terminate in a bulbous knot on the shoulder. Register LL2 contains two figural scenes: to the left, a seated

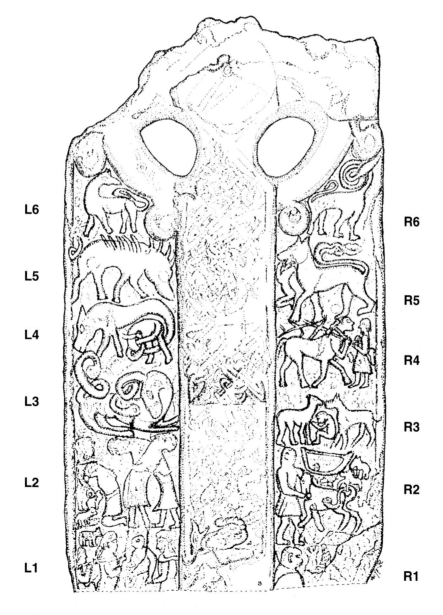

L6
L5
L4
L3
L2
L1

R6
R5
R4
R3
R2
R1

4 *Gask 1A: working sketch*

R. Trench-Jellicoe

figure embraces a second figure who kneels before him, head bent forward. To the right, two standing figures bend forward, holding each other, as if wrestling or embracing. The lower section of LL1 lies buried. Above, at the centre, two figures confront each other, that to the left has a raised hand of acknowledgement. The figure to the left appears to have a damaged figure seated on the ground behind him, while the figure to the right is supported by the arms of another figure standing behind him on the right of the scene.

The upper scenes of the right panel (LR4-6) are designed to balance the upper left registers. A walking quadruped (LR6) facing R, has a long coiled neck which interlaces with itself to terminate in the upper R corner. The long snout of a left-facing, pacing quadruped in LR5 holds a pendent human figure in its mouth. The beast's prominent tail weaves a double loop above its back to terminate in a plait. LR4, below, contains a right-facing quadruped with a human head and torso: a centaur who holds axes and a branching rod across his shoulder. A male figure in a short tunic and with his legs braced stands before it. Scene LR3 depicts confronted quadrupeds whose noses touch. Between them squats a left-facing human whose arms reach forward to touch the beast on the left. To the left of LR2 stands a profiled figure with stout legs and wearing a short tunic. Facing right he grips the jaws of a straining quadruped. In the upper right corner of the scene and at the bottom appear two left-facing quadrupeds. Carved centrally at the top of the register is a dished curving line. The right half of LR1 is lost in damage but the left contains the upper half of a right-facing figure whose facial features are well preserved.

Discussion

Both faces of the Gask slab have a similar layout but a comparison reveals that the emphasis of the decoration differs markedly. Side C is carved overall with mythical beasts (LL–all; LR4–6) except for the 'Pictish symbols' of *Snake and Z-rod* (LR3) and what has been claimed as a *Flower* (LR2r) but is more probably a tree forming an integral part of the rest of register LR2. Registers LR2 and LR1, which ought probably to be considered together as one unit, contain two riders and a hound, travelling to the left, extrapolated from a hunt scene.[9]

Side A, by contrast, includes more figural decoration so that a total of seven out of the twelve registers contain ten figures, which compares with a count of two riders only on C. Subject matter, too, differs as the hunt scene of face C contrasts with the figural and probably biblical vignettes of face A. It was clearly intended that a different message be understood from each face. Structurally Face A is designed to highlight paralleled and mirrored motifs almost exclusively. Animals in opposing registers of the shaft panels are deliberately placed so that they are either adorsed or face each other. Even below, in the figural scenes, there is a strong element of repetition and mirroring of motifs.

Parallels occur for nearly all motifs of face A. For the four upper registers (LL3–6, LR3–6), parallels of realistic animal or mythical bestiary type occur mainly within a restricted area including Perthshire and Angus. Each scene except for LR3 may be paralleled elsewhere and sometimes several examples occur together, particularly on monuments found at Meigle, Perthshire. This should be expected given its proximity to Gask, the large number of monuments recovered from the site and their rich iconography. However, only one potential parallel for LR6 has been identified at another richly endowed site, on St Vigeans 1A, Angus.[10] In fact, almost all parallels for Gask 1A seem to radiate from Meigle and Gask itself should perhaps be considered as another outlier of Meigle influence.[11]

Registers LL6 and LL5 can both be paralleled at Meigle and three examples of the beast with a curled back (LL4) are found there too. The latter form is more common in metalwork, for example, on the St Ninian's Isle bowls, nos 2 and 3, a sword pommel and a mount also from that site (Small *et al* 1973, figs 21–2, 31–2, pls XVIII–XIX). It has not been possible to parallel the double curl of the tail or lappet of LL3 in sculpture. Examples of a quadruped with long curled tail and neck (LR6) are widespread although a specific parallel for the coiled form of the neck seems unavailable. A figure hanging from a quadruped's mouth (LR5) appears in the lower right panel of Aberlemno 3A, Woodrae (Aberlemno) 1A, Rossie Priory 1A, Perthshire (RCAHMS 1994, 103, fig J) and a related scene is found on Fowlis Wester 2A, Perthshire (Henderson 1967, pl 44), but the latter is not an apposite parallel iconographically, as the scene probably represents 'Jonah and the Whale'. A closer parallel still appears on another Fowlis Wester monument, 1C (Allen and Anderson 1903, III, fig 306B; Henderson 1997, ill VIIb) where a quadruped also holds a figure hanging from its mouth. Other possible examples appear on Meigle 9c and 11C. The centaur of LR4 is most closely paralleled on Meigle 2C although it also occurs on the base of Aberlemno 3C. The scene perhaps represents the desert meeting of St Anthony and a Centaur in Jerome's hagiographical tale *The Life of St Paul* (Jerome 1936, 45) in which the creature guides St Anthony towards St Paul's cell. Significantly the disposition of the figures in the scene does not infer the portrayal of the evil centaur of the *Physiologus* tradition, a subtle nuance which Henderson (1997, 20–3) has recently discussed. This version of the scene, which includes a human figure, is unique in Pictish sculptural art and, if the identification is correct, is its most complete representation and may, therefore, lie closest to the model. Register LR3's unique, crouching figure between two quadrupeds may be an attempt to represent the Old Testament statement in the Old Latin version from Habbakuk 3, "Between two beasts ye shall know Him" (Ó Carragáin 1988, 20–31), equally it perhaps portrays another element in the Saints Paul and Anthony legend in representing the benign lions who help the weakened St Anthony bury St Paul (Jerome 1936, 51–2), however, there are difficulties in parallelling this iconographically. An attempt to interpret the scene as *Daniel in the Lion's Den* would meet similar objections of the use of an aberrant model.

In the lower four registers, LL1–2, LR1–2, too little contextual evidence remains of LR1 to permit any identification of the remaining bust. The problematic scene, LL2–left, a kneeling figure before one enthroned, may represent *David's penitence before Nathan* (2 Samuel 12: 5–6) as portrayed in Gibb's lithograph of Meigle 9A (Stuart 1856, pl LXXII). The scene type found in LL2–right, has in the past been identified as *Jacob wrestling with the Angel* (Genesis 32: 24–30). A potential parallel scene occurs at Glenferness, Nairn (Stuart 1856, pl XXIV) but a clearer example appears on a fragmentary slab from Eilean Mor, Argyll (Allen and Anderson 1903, III, fig 396A). An Irish parallel is present on the north face of the Durrow Cross, Co Offaly (Harbison 1992, fig 748). In register LL1, at Gask, the left figure appears to salute the approaching linked

figures to the right, suggesting an explanation of the scene as the *Presentation of Christ to Simeon in the Temple,* recorded in Luke 2: 25–35 (Harbison 1992, 224–5). A similar scene is carved on a small edge panel, Govan 29D, Lanarkshire (Allen and Anderson 1903, III, fig 488B; Fisher 1994, figs 23A, 24A)[12], and another version appears on a later 10th-century, north Italian manuscript, fol 88r of the *Sacramentary of Warmundus* (= Cod.31, Biblioteca Capitolare, Ivrea (Harbison 1992, fig 787)). The small squatting figure carved to the left of the seated figure can also be found on Meigle 27C (Allen and Anderson 1903, III, fig 353).

The final scene, LR2, contains the necessary elements to identify it as *David, the Lion-Killer.* To the left David breaks the lion's jaw (1 Samuel 17: 34–6). Two other quadrupeds, standing nearby either represent the sheep flock guarded by David or both the sheep and a bear who is also mentioned in the Old Testament text. Above, a harp has been inserted horizontally to ensure recognition of the scene as Davidic. This form of the scene is closely similar to that on Aberlemno 3C and both occur on the lower right of the decoration. Other lion-killing scenes at St Andrews, Kinneddar, Nigg, Kincardine and Dupplin, although interrelated more closely to each other than to Anglo-Saxon or Irish models, are nevertheless distinguished iconographically from those examples from Aberlemno and Gask because of the orientation of the harp.

A discussion of the significance of the iconography is hampered because the formation of a visual programme created from a mixture of realistic animals and mythical beasts juxtaposed with biblical and related imagery is yet little understood. The function of the Gask animals in LL3-6 and LR6, which seem to operate in isolation, is obscure. Isabel Henderson's suggestion (1997, 46–7) that the beast holding the figure in its mouth (LR5) represents Hell or Hell's mouth in a parallel scene on Fowlis Wester 1C, seems difficult to reconcile with context of the Gask programme.

The figure, in this context is juxtaposed with the cross, as if being sacrificially offered to Christ so perhaps a martyrological implication lies behind the image. Likewise, it is difficult to see the image in terms, say, of the *Physiologus* lion breathing life into its cubs on the third day (Curley 1979, 8–9). The benign and helpful centaur guiding

Anthony on his quest to find Paul should be understood in terms of the legend as a pilgrimage for 'it seemed to him that he saw Christ in Paul' (Jerome 1936, 50). The scene below, although the specific reference is elusive, indicates some form of protection for the central figure by the beasts and probably in this context implies heavenly intervention. David-the-Lion-Killer is well documented as an Old Testament salvational icon. In the two lowermost registers of the left panel, the burden of *David before Nathan* is that David admits his sin and in so doing is remitted the penalty of death so that he may ultimately be forgiven and achieve salvation. *Jacob wrestling with the Angel* recalls the linked biblical phrase 'he who has been seen by God' indicating that he had gained sufficient purity to be worthy of achieving salvation. The scene of the *Presentation of Christ* focuses on Simeon's acclaimed recognition of Christ 'in action and faith' as deliverer of Israel (and the gentiles). The selection of biblical icons, therefore, appears to signify: repentance, purification, recognition of God's ability to intervene in the human predicament and offer protection and salvation in terms of the Old Testament together with an acknowledgement of Christ (prefigured as David in the Old Testament) as the instrument of mankind's salvation. All the individual images are subsumed beneath the great cross, Christian symbol of salvation, dominating the face of the slab.

Appendix 2: The programme of Kincardine 1D, Easter Ross, another David the Lion-killer with a harp

The neglected recumbent monument at Kincardine, Easter Ross, retains two relief-carved faces together with vestiges of decoration on a third, long side. All decoration is extensively abraded which is a barrier to clear identification of the representations. The top of the monument, face A, is completely lost while B, the long edge to the left, is so worn that little is visible beyond the suggestion of a beast leaping to the left in the central section and a small scene, perhaps a separate panel containing two confronting human figures at the left end. On the base, C, no carving remains.

The right edge, D (**5**), is the most extensively decorated, being bordered at the top and divided formally by a plain border into three panels; a larger central section and two smaller panels at the ends. An incomplete description indicates that the left panel contains a mounted rider, hair hanging behind, travelling to the right. The rider is under attack from at least one hound above the horse's back, while two hounds run beneath the horse, one biting the belly and a second at the front turning back and rising to grip the chest or neck in its jaws. The central and largest panel is sub-divided into three registers. The left area includes two confronted seated asymmetrical beasts flanking a tree which branches and carries leaves of lentoid form and perhaps also bears fruit. The beasts, hind limbs with knees tucked up, have their forelimbs resting on the base of the tree. The beasts' long necks are interwoven and bound to the tree branches but whether the source of the strand is floral or faunal is unclear. The beast head to the left, seemingly with long ears, feeds on the top of the tree's main stem while the head of that to the right is inverted towards the bulbous head of the right branch of the tree. Standing in the central register is a fronted figure wearing a calf-length tunic and cloak, who grips a quadruped in the Gilgamesh pose, by both jaws, pulling them apart. The beast's tail curves across the body to terminate in a brush. To the left above is a sheep, facing right, whose head turns backwards while beneath this is a pacing quadruped with sharp claws and its head bearing large rounded ears. The beast is positioned at an angle, descending unnaturally across the panel so that its muzzle touches the arm of the main figure. Above, to the right of the figure, is a small space left by the sub-scene to the right. This contains a badly worn triangular shape with a quadruped carved leaping to the left, superimposed across it. The beast's forepaws rest on the figure's shoulder and its head with jaws a little apart also touches him. Above appears another apparently benign beast's head. On the right, the third register comprises a large quadruped travelling to the right with a figure standing behind the hind quarters, the feet visible below. Seated on the beast's back are two figures, one upright and frontal, while a second, slightly smaller figure, positioned before, is seated in profile on the other's lap with raised legs resting on the horse's neck. The arm of the smaller figure reaches forward grasping the beast's mane. The animal's long ears, abraded but present, suggest this is a donkey rather than a horse. The right panel contains two fronted figures standing on the lower frame.

R. Trench-Jellicoe

5 *Kincardine 1D (side): salvational programme*

They have hanging wings and large rectangular objects across their chests held by their right arms across and left hand beneath. Each figure also holds an insignia of office, diagonally across the chest. The figure to the viewer's left appears to have a circular terminal on his right shoulder and sports a large object perhaps identifiable as a penannular brooch on his left shoulder. His companion holds a wand with lozenge-shaped terminal on his left shoulder. The figure to the right has one, perhaps two rectangular objects hanging from his belt. Each figure has a large item crossing the lower body. These appear to be two confronting beasts but they are too badly worn to be identified with certainty. The flared hems of their tunics are visible, cut at calf length. Finally the end panel E also carries a complex image. Two confronting profiled monstrous beasts, with human bodies and beast-heads, frame a scene wherein their beaks flank a fronted bust, probably human, in a manner similar to that on the slab from Dunfallandy 1C, Perthshire (Allen and Anderson 1903, III, fig 305B). Within the frame half a dozen or so balanced pairs of variously-sized, monstrous beasts interact to create a restless scene above a fronted bovine. This centrally-positioned beast faces forward with its forelimbs splayed beneath.

Discussion

The panel sequence seems to have been carefully constructed and makes most sense if read from left to right. The left panel's rider is clearly under attack from all sides by hounds and his rightward direction of travel points the viewer towards the middle panel which contains scenes with biblical references. The left register shows two beasts receiving sustenance from a fruit tree. These beasts derive

from a similar model to the 'wood woses' of the St Andrews shrine, main panel and also those in the small panel along its side (Allen and Anderson 1903, III, fig 365) whose Mercian parallels are discussed by Henderson (1994). The middle register contains an extended version of a David the Lion-killer scene, very similar is design to that from Nigg (ibid, figs 72A, 81). The sheep with inverted head is to the upper left, also closely similar to the Nigg representation, while the harp has been repositioned to the upper right to make room for this unique Pictish introduction of a bear which, indicated by its draped, splayed position, has already been killed by David. This is a visual representation of 1 Samuel 17: 34–6, "Thy servant kept his father's sheep and there came a lion and a bear and took a lion out of the flock: And I went out after him, and smote him and delivered it out of his mouth: and he rose against me, I caught him by his beard, and smote him and slew him. Thy servant slew both the lion and the bear...". The scene can be generally paralleled in the early 9th-century *Khludov Psalter*, fol 147v (Henderson 1986, pl 5.2a), illustrating Psalms 149–50. To upper right, the lion, lying across the harp does not appear to attack David and seems to function benignly, its benevolent nature characteristic of Christ. It behaves in a similar manner to the lion on the base of Tarbat 1A, Easter Ross (Allen and Anderson 1903, III, fig 71), who intervenes with a hound (one of at least three in the badly damaged register) intent on attacking a mounted horse, a thematic variation of the meaning intended in the left panel at Kincardine. This lion, a Christ-type, acts in a manner very different from the malevolent lion symbolising sin, attacking 'His sheep'. The register to the right seems most satisfactorily identified as carrying the New Testament story of the Flight into Egypt, Matthew 2:

13–4. Joseph walks behind on the far side of the donkey which bears Mary who holds' the Christ-child seated before her. The direction of travel and the burden in this register echo the horse and rider of the left panel, subtly paralleling their condition. The right panel contains two angels carrying books which are most probably intended to represent the Old and New Testaments. The figures' wings are particularly reminiscent of the angels of Aberlemno 3A who adore the cross, the representation of Christ.

Sculptured scenes were unlikely to have been intended as individual items, rather they combine into a programme, forming a message for the viewer to read and understand. So what does this face tell us? Here, if the message is read from left to right, the sculptor shows us a rider, harried by alien forces. The scene is probably intended to represent 'mankind in middle earth', surrounded by and eternally under siege from the evil forces of sin. In the second panel we are offered three examples of God's intervention in the human predicament. Firstly, He provides sustenance to his creatures, a message carried in Psalm 144 (AV.145), verses 16 and 19 where He "satisfiest the desire of every living beast" and "will fulfil the desire of them that fear him, he also will hear their cry and will save them". This message is intended to be comprehended not merely on the literal level but also at the spiritual, whereby the substantial food symbolises the salvational message, the 'bread of heaven'. In the second register, God is again seen to intervene in man's predicament. David, the Old Testament ancestor and precursor of Christ in the New Testament, confronts and destroys evil in the form of lion and bear. He acts to save his sheep who are intended to be understood symbolically as Christ's sheep, the witnessing mankind, of the New Testament. In the third register He intervenes yet again, this time in a scene directly from the New Testament where, by sending warning dreams to Joseph, he intervenes, to protect the Christ-child, the Saviour, together with His mother, Mary, from the Massacre of the Innocents, so saving, mankind. The final panel represents the third level, the culmination of the message of the other two panels. Angels, the harbingers of heaven, address the viewer directly. They bear the books which embody and summarize the message of salvation in both Old and New Law, examples of which have been taught and illustrated in the scenes appearing to the left. The monstrous scene

on face E is probably intended to represent hell, into which the viewer gazes at ranked monsters who confront each other. It offers an alternative to the juxtaposed scene of heaven at the top of the previous side but it may also represent Christ symbolically portrayed at the top of the scene as a head between two beasts, as in Habbakuk 3 of the Old Latin Bible "Between two beasts ye shall know him" (Ó Carragáin 1988, 20–31) – that is Christ, *sotor,* or at the base of the scene symbolising the sacrificial beast who descended for our salvation. The beast's head is reminiscent of fronted metalwork heads.

It seems reasonable to interpret the overall message of the Kincardine slab's faces D and E as salvational, wherein the viewer is urged to recognise the power of God through His Son in both Old and New Testaments.

Notes

1   This extension of the use of one motif into other related but inappropriate scenes is not unique in Christian iconography. Mathews (1993, 54–91) cites a similar expansion of Christ's contextualization with his wand which is used to denote miracle-working in Late Antique scenes.

2   Davidic iconography was probably introduced into Pictland in the third quarter of the 8th century (Henderson 1986). The initial manifestation perhaps appeared on the St Andrews shrine, Fife (Allen and Anderson 1903, III, fig 365), which draws heavily on Late Antique or Byzantine models (Henderson 1994). This version was adopted as a model for other examples amongst the first of which was the fragment from Kinneddar, Moray (Ferguson 1956, 225; Henderson 1986, pl 5.3B)), now preserved in Elgin Museum. Neither of these examples which precede the Nigg Davidic tableau, preserves any harp iconography (Henderson 1986).

3   In the context of Pictish and other symbols, David Henry has drawn my attention to the ecclesiastic accompanied by a crozier and degenerate Pictish double-disc on the fragment, St Vigeans 4C, Angus (Allen and Anderson 1903, III, 240–1, fig 255B). This 9th century piece seems to use both attributes to qualify the figure much in the way that the triquetra knot is used to qualify the cross on the opposite face. Whatever value the 'Pictish symbols' retained at this date, their placement alongside ecclesiastical symbols seems fully accepted.

4   Robertson's identification of a harp on a small shrine fragment from St Andrews (1977, 259–61) has been excluded on the grounds that it is too uncertain (Henderson 1994, 92, fig 5.10).

5 The pipe and tabor as such appear after the crusaders brought that particular combination back from the Middle East but the ensemble probably existed in some form prior to that time in an Insular context.

6 The Kilwinning sculptor unimaginatively re-used the same template to construct the harper and the carved rider below him, consequently the harper is in a seated position but no evidence for a chair is present.

7 The large number of curl-snouted parallels of Irish provenance (Youngs 1989) suggests that this may be primarily an Irish style adopted into Pictland.

8 The form of the Gask cross is BAC A10 and the ring is Type A (Cramp 1991, figs 2–3).

9 Isabel Henderson (1997, 29–33) has recently discussed the elements of Gask 1A and analysed their significance.

10 A selection of parallels might also have been expected at St Vigeans. Their absence may be explained if the foundation became active, as stylistic aspects of the monuments imply, in the 9th century (see Henderson 1978, 55).

11 Relevant Meigle parallels for Gask 1A also appear at sites along Strathmore: Cossins (1), Glamis (1), Aberlemno (1), Woodrae (3), Aldbar (1), Inchbrayock (1) and also up the Earn (2) and Tummel (2) valleys. St Madoes provides one example of the popular back-biting motif and Monifieth (3) like Woodrae is rich in monster-beast iconography.

12 The Gask scene is a preferable parallel for Govan 29D than Fisher's citation of the Castlebernard (Kinitty) Cross, Co Offaly (1994, 49–50), which may represent 'Samuel anointing David' (but see Harbison 1992).

References

ALCOCK, L 1995 What is David doing to a lion? *Pictish Arts Society Journal* 7, 1–2.

ALEXANDER, J J G 1978 *Insular Manuscripts 6th to 9th Century* (Survey of Insular Manuscripts Illuminated in the British Isles, I). London.

ALLEN, J R and ANDERSON, J 1903 *The Early Christian Monuments of Scotland*, 3 parts. Edinburgh (repr with an Introduction by Isabel Henderson, 2 vols, Balgavies, Angus, 1993).

BAILEY, R N 1980 *Viking Age Sculpture in Northern England*. London.

BUCKLEY, A
– 1990 Musical instruments in Ireland from the ninth to the fourteenth centuries: a review of the organological evidence. In Gillen, G and White, H (eds) *Musicology in Ireland* (Irish Musical Studies, I), 13–57. Dublin.

– 1991 Music related imagery on early Christian sculpture: identification, context, function. *Imago Musicae* 8, 135–99.

– 1992 Harps and lyres on early medieval monuments of Great Britain and Ireland. *Harpa*, 7, 15–21.

CRAIG, D 1994 The early medieval sculpture of the Glasgow area. In Ritchie, A (ed) *Govan and its Early Medieval Sculpture*, 73–91. Stroud.

CRAMP, R J
– 1984 *County Durham and Northumberland,* 2 parts (*Corpus of Anglo-Saxon Stone Sculpture*, I). Oxford.

– 1991 *Grammar of Anglo-Saxon Ornament (Corpus of Anglo-Saxon Stone Sculpture*, General Introduction). Oxford.

– 1995 The sculpture. In Potter, T W and Andrews, R D, Excavation and survey at St Patrick's Chapel and St Peter's Church, Heysham, Lancashire, 1977-78. *Antiquaries Journal* 74, 55–134.

CURLEY, M J 1979 *Physiologus.* Austin, Texas.

FERGUSON, W 1956 Note on a fragment of sculptured stone in Elgin Museum. *Proc Soc Antiq Scot*, 88 (1954-56), 225.

FISHER, I and GREENHILL, F A 1971 Two unrecorded carved stones at Tower of Lethendy, Perthshire. *Proc Soc Antiq Scot*, 104 (1971-72), 238–41.

HARBISON, P 1992 *The High Crosses of Ireland: an Iconoraphical and Photographic Survey*, 3 vols. Dublin and Bonn

HENDERSON, IB
– 1967 *The Picts*. London

– 1978 Sculpture north of the Forth after the take-over by the Scots. In Lang, J T (ed) *Anglo-Saxon and Viking-Age Sculpture in its context (BAR Brit Ser* 49), 47–74. Oxford.

– 1986 The 'David cycle' in Pictish art. In Higgitt, J (ed) *Early Medieval Sculpture in Britain and Ireland (BAR Brit Ser* 152), 87–123. Oxford.

– 1994 The Insular and Continental context of the St Andrew's Sarcophagus. In Crawford, B E (ed) *Scotland in Dark Age Europe* (St John's House Papers 5), 71–102. St Andrews.

– 1997 *Pictish Monsters:symbol, text and image* (H M Chadwick Memorial Lectures 7). Cambridge.

HENRY, F 1970 *Irish Art in the Romanesque Period. 1029–1170 AD*. London.

JEROME, ST 1936 The life of St Paul, the first hermit. In Waddell, H (trans) *The Desert Fathers,* 41–53. London.

KERMODE, P M C 1907 *Manx Crosses*. London (new edn with an Introduction by D M Wilson, Balgavies, Angus, 1994).

LACY, B *et al* 1983 *Archaeological survey of County Donegal.* Lifford.

LAING, L 1995 The date and significance of the Ardchattan stone. *Pictish Arts Society Journal* 8, 2–7.

LAWSON, G 1981 An Anglo-Saxon harp and lyre of the ninth century. In Widdess, D R and Wolpert, R F (eds) *Music and Tradition: Essays on Asian and Other Musics, Presented to Lawrence Picken*, 229–44. Cambridge.

MATHEWS, T F 1993 *The Clash of Gods: a Reinterpretation of Early Christian Art.* Princeton.

Ó CARRAGÁIN, É 1988 The meeting of St Paul and St Anthony: visual and literary uses of a eucharistic motif. In Mac Niocaill, G and Wallace, PF (eds) *Keimelia: Studies in Medieval Archaeology and History in Memory of Tom Delaney*, 1–58. Galway.

RENSCH, R 1989 *Harps and Harpists.* London.

ROE, H M 1949 The 'David cycle' in early Irish art. *J Roy Soc Antiq Irl*, 79, 39–59.

RCAHMS = Royal Commission on the Ancient and Historical Monuments of Scotland

– 1975 *Argyll: An Inventory of the Monuments,* vol 2, *Lorn.* Edinburgh

– 1982 *Argyll: An Inventory of the Monuments,* vol 4, *Iona.* Edinburgh.

– 1994 *South East Perth: an Archaeological Landscape.* Edinburgh.

SANGER, K and KINNAIRD, A 1992 *Tree of Strings – Crann nan Teud: a History of the Harp in Scotland.* Temple, Midlothian.

SMALL, A, THOMAS, C and WILSON, D M 1973 *St Ninian's Isle and it Treasure* (Aberdeen Univ Stud Ser 152), 2 vols. Oxford.

STUART, J 1856–67 *Sculptured Stones of Scotland*, 2 vols. Aberdeen (vol I); Edinburgh (vol II).

TRENCH-JELLICOE, R M C

– 1991 A recent Viking-age sculptural find from Tynemouth Priory. *Archaeol Aeliana*, 5 ser, 19, 71–8.

– forthcoming A missing figure on the slab fragment no 2 from Monifieth, Angus.

YOUNGS, S (ed) 1989 *'The Work of Angels': Masterpieces of Celtic Metalwork, 6th–9th Centuries AD.* London.

Maelrubai, Applecross and the Late Pictish Contribution West of Druimalban

Douglas Mac Lean

In his *Life of St Columba*, Adomnán defines the border between Scottish Dál Riata and Pictland as *dorsum Brittaniae* (the 'spine of Britain'), the Latin equivalent of Old-Irish *Druim nAlban*[1] (anglicized as 'Druimalban'), the watershed that separates the West Highlands and Islands from the rest of Scotland. The boundary seems to have been established during the same period when Maelrubai was the first abbot of Applecross, while the last Class I Pictish symbol-stones were being carved in the Outer Hebrides, Skye and Raasay. The two contemporaries, Adomnán and Maelrubai, personify the two most important early medieval sculptural traditions that were to develop west of Druimalban. Although both abbots came from Ireland and belonged to different branches of the Northern Uí Néill[2], they operated professionally in distinct cultural milieus, Adomnán in the Gaelic context of Iona, Maelrubai as a foreign missionary among the Picts of Wester Ross. Surviving evidence suggests that it was the southern atmosphere of Iona that prevailed in the eighth century: there are no Class II sculptures, relief cross-slabs bearing Pictish symbols, found in the West Highlands and Islands. But there were two great sculptural centres in Dál Riata when the Vikings arrived, Iona and Applecross, and intimations of both traditions would later combine, huddling together on the same monuments in the aftermath of the Nordic onslaught.

Maelrubai and the foundation of Applecross

According to the *Annals of Ulster* and the *Annals of Tigernach*, Maelrubai sailed for Britain in 671 and in 673 founded Applecross in what must have been a Pictish neighbourhood at the time. He died there in his eightieth year in 722.[3] Maelrubai is described as 'abbot of Bangor' in the *Annals of the Four Masters*, one of whom, Mícheál

Ó Cléirígh, recorded the same detail in various martyrologies, although Maelrubai's name is not included in the list of Bangor abbots in the *Antiphonary of Bangor* of *c*691 (Milan, Bib. Ambrosiana, C. 5 inf, fol 36v).[4] But Applecross seems to have had some sort of connection with Bangor from its inception, perhaps because Maelrubai's mother descended from a sister of Comgall, founder of Bangor.[5] Comgall 's and Maelrubai's mother's people were the Dál nAraide of Antrim[6], who enjoyed friendly relations with Scottish Dál Riata in the later sixth century, when Comgall called on Columba at the latter's Hebridean foundation on *Hinba*[7]. Tiree held a particular attraction for the Dál nAraide. According to his Latin *Life*, Comgall himself founded a monastery in Tiree between 561 and 566, but returned to Ireland after an attack by Pictish raiders.[8] Áed Dubh mac Suibne, king of Dál nAraide, killed Diarmait mac Cerbaill of the Southern Uí Néill in 565, but was ordained priest at the Tiree monastery of *Artchain* by its founder, Findchán, before Áed resumed the kingship, only to be killed 'in a ship' in 588, in fulfillment of a prophecy of Columba's.[9] The Dál nAraide formed a military alliance with Scottish Dál Riata *c*600, although relations subsequently broke down, but Fiachra Cossalach of Dál nAraide served as a guarantor of the Law of Adomnán, promulgated at the Synod of Birr in 697.[10] There may have been earlier connections, however, between the Dál nAraide and the Hebrides, a name corrupted from the probably pre-Celtic *Eboudai* of Ptolemy's second-century map, which is related in turn to Old-Irish *Ibdig*.[11] A laconic entry in the *Annals of Ulster* for 672, *Deleti sunt Ibdig*, records the devastation of the inhabitants, not the islands themselves.[12] Genealogical tradition relates the *Ibdig* to the Irish *Cruithni*, who apparently descended from immigrants from Britain and included the Dál nAraide, who therefore could claim *Ibdig* ancestors[13], but by the historical period the Dál nAraide of Antrim were culturally indistinguishable from their Irish neighbours and are not to be confused with the Picts in Scotland.[14] In a conversation with Comgall of Bangor, Columba identified Comgall's people as *Cruithni*, but in Adomnán's account the two saints have no difficulty communicating in the same language.[15] Nonetheless, in establishing his monastery at Applecross, which remains best accessible by sea, Maelrubai may unwittingly have restored a connection of his maternal ancestors, thus imparting a curiously Pictish flavour to the enterprise.

Maelrubai was a closer witness than Adomnán of the collapse of the Pictish western province, although his Gaelic foundation at Applecross would later provide inspiration for a revival of Pictish sculptural taste in the region. The devastation of the Hebrideans in 672 occurred between Maelrubai's departure from Ireland and the foundation of Applecross, in a period of local instability. The annals also record the deposition of the Pictish king Drest son of Domnall in 672, an event which coincided with a Pictish revolt of *c*671-72 against Northumbrian overlordship, described in Stephen's *Life of Saint Wilfrid*.[16] Drest assumed the kingship *c*663, perhaps owing fealty to Oswiu of Northumbria, whose death *c*670–71 may have prompted the Pictish rebellion crushed by Oswiu's successor Ecgfrith. Interpretations of the evidence differ: either the Picts deposed Drest following Oswiu's death and then rebelled, or Drest led the revolt and failed, only to be expelled from the kingship.[17] In either case, Bruide son of Bili succeeded Drest, in circumstances which may explain the devastation of the Hebrideans in 672 and the opportunities afforded Maelrubai at Applecross. Bruide later 'destroyed' the Orkneys in 682[18], perhaps to consolidate control of the Pictish hinterland, while planning to overthrow Northumbrian overlordship, an objective he achieved in 685 at the battle of Dunnichen (*Nechtanesmere*).[19] The earlier destruction of the Hebrideans occurred in a similar context, although it is unclear whether the contemporary Pictish rebellion was led by Bruide or Drest. But Bruide would have had particular reason to bring the inhabitants to heel following the deposition of Drest, whose family was associated with Skye and Raasay, islands visible from Applecross.

Maelrubai's abbacy oversaw the protracted eclipse of the dominant Pictish kindred in the area. Isabel Henderson has called attention to a series of entries unique to the Annals of Ulster between *c*675 and *c*730, which displays a particular interest in Dalriadic and northern Pictish affairs, especially those centring on Skye. The evidence suggests an annotated set of Easter Tables kept at Applecross.[20] The earliest contemporary entries in the Irish annals reflect the existence of a lost *Iona Chronicle*[21], while the tradition of friendship between Iona and Bangor renders plausible any annalistic activity at Applecross.[22] Indeed, Applecross may have picked up where Iona left off, since both the *Annals of Ulster* and the *Annals of Tigernach* report 'the voyage of the sons of Gartnait to Ireland with the people of Skye' in 668 and their return from Ireland in 670, events probably recorded in the original *Iona Chronicle* before any Easter Tables could have been annotated at Applecross.[23] The 'sons of Gartnait' were unquestionably Pictish and constituted the most important of the three kindreds associated with Skye whom Henderson has identified in the subsequent entries in the *Annals of Ulster*, which seem to have originated at Applecross.[24]

The pivotal figure in the annals is Cano son of Gartnait. The description in the Old-Irish *Scéla Cano meic Gartnáin* of his departure for Ireland with 'the people of Skye' is that of a royal retinue sailing in currachs, complete with fifty well-armed warriors, fifty well-dressed ladies and fifty liveried gillies, each with the silver leads of two greyhounds in his right hand, a musical instrument in his left and the board of a *fidchell* game on his back, along with its gold and silver playing-men.[25] *Scéla Cano* is historical fiction and conflates Cano with another Cano son of Gartnait (a Pictish king who died *c*601), who was the son of Aedán mac Gabráin, the Dalriadic king who died *c*608, but the Skye Cano's antecedents were certainly royal.[26] His father, Gartnait son of Domnall, was a king of the Picts who died in 663, while his grandfather seems to have been Domnall Brecc, the king of Dál Riata killed by the Britons of Strathclyde at the battle of Strathcarron in 642.[27] Following the return of the 'sons of Gartnait' from Ireland in 670, the *Annals of Ulster* reports the capture of Cano's son Conamail in 673 and his slaughter in 705. Cano's uncle, the deposed king Drest, died in 678. Cano himself 'entered into religion' *c*683, according to the seventeenth-century *Annals of Clonmacnoise*, while various sources note that he was killed in 688 and his daughter Coblaith died in 690.[28]

According to *Scéla Cano*, Cano's father Gartnait was from *Inis moccu Chéin*, while Cano himself was from Skye.[29] Noting that the name of Raasay is Norse in origin, Dr Colm Ó Baoill has identified Inis moccu Chéin as its earlier Old-Irish name, used before any Viking settlement in the area.[30] The last contemporary usage of *moccu* surnames is in an early-eighth century poem[31], so the name must have originated by that period. Additional place-name evidence links Cano son of Gartnait to Raasay. Modern maps identify the highest point on the island as Dun Caan.[32] A late-seventeenth century account states that '*Duncan* (*sic*) takes its name from Cannus, whom they relate to be Denmark's son'.[33] The folk memory then current did not extend beyond the advent of the Vikings and both the older name of the island and the pedigree of the commemorated Cano had been lost in the interim, but Dr Sorley MacLean, a native of Raasay, informed Ó Baoill that the correct Gaelic place-name is *Dùn Cana*, or 'Cano's Fort'.[34] Taken together, the place-name evidence, the annals and *Scéla Cano* associate the kindred of Cano son of Gartnait with Raasay and Skye. Between his return from Ireland in 670 and his death in 688, Cano might have resided occasionally at the fort that still bears his name in Raasay, within sight of both Skye and Applecross, during the abbacy of Maelrubai. The location of Applecross follows the Irish tradition of placing ecclesiastical establishments adjacent to political power centres, as St Patrick did by founding Armagh near the Ulster capital of Emain Macha. In each case, the monastery outlived the secular power.

The tribulations of Cano's family in the later seventh century and their connections with Skye and Raasay offer a plausible context for the devastation of the Hebrideans in 672, when the Pictish king Drest son of Domnall was deposed. Drest was both Gartnait's brother and Cano's uncle.[35] According to Bede, after the mid-650s Oswiu of Northumbria had 'subjected the greater part of the Pictish race' and made tributary the Scots of Dál Riata; neither would escape the subordinate relationship until 685.[36] Thus Drest is usually viewed as Oswiu's vassal, whether or not he led the Pictish revolt against Oswiu's successor Ecgfrith c672.[37] Dr Henderson, however, has suggested that Cano's father and uncle, the successive Pictish kings Gartnait and Drest, may have ruled a 'free Pictland' in the north, based in Skye, which was still Pictish but beyond the southern Pictland dominated by Northumbria, a proposal challenged by D.P. Kirby, although he admits that the Northumbrians might not have advanced 'beyond the Tay' until 685.[38] The devastation of the Hebrideans in 672 may represent Drest's successor Bruide asserting control before attempting rebellion, as he later did in Orkney three years before Dunnichen.[39] Whether the Pictish revolt preceded or followed Drest's expulsion and the Hebridean expedition, Bruide had a pressing incentive to demonstrate his authority over Hebrideans loyal to Cano's kindred, who would then have been in no position to oppose Maelrubai's foundation at Applecross.

The momentous consequences of the battle of Dunnichen in 685 had more local implications along the Inner Sound between Applecross and Raasay. Bede informs us that as a result of the battle, the Picts 'recovered their own land which the English had formerly held', while the Scots and some of the Britons regained their freedom from Northumbria.[40] Adomnán's identification of Druimalban as the border between Pictland and Dál Riata describes the situation at the end of the century, one changed since the 'sons of Gartnait' returned to Pictish Skye from Ireland in 670. Gaelic infiltration of their territory, indicated by the foundation of Applecross, became an ongoing process. The killings of Cano in 688 and his son in 705 fit the context offered by the Andersons' conclusion that the boundary was redrawn following Dunnichen, when Bruide may have forsaken his fractious western province; he is described at his death in 693 as 'king of Fortriu', in southern Pictland.[41]

Incised Pictish sculptures in Skye and Raasay bear mute witness to the transition. The three symbol stones in Skye, including Clach Ard in Tote, Tobar na Maor near Dun Osdale and Fiskavaig Bay, Bracadale display the Crescent and V-rod symbol, as does the dressed slab near Raasay House in Raasay.[42] All four are examples of the typologically late 'Dome and Wing' group in Robert Stevenson's classic typology.[43] The Raasay stone places its Crescent and V-rod and a 'tuning-fork' symbol beneath an incised Chi-Rho monogram, which so closely resembles another, on a rock outcrop near the Old Pier in front of Raasay House, that both are likely to have been carved by the same sculptor.[44] Each is fitted with a shaft and comprises four arcs compass-drawn in a square, creating the expanded arms of the cross, with almond-shaped interspaces between them. Simple incised spirals define the loops of the Rho in both monograms. But there are subtle differences between the two. Triangles are carved in the interiors of the cross-arms on the symbol stone, which also has a small circle at the centre of the cross, while the shaft of the monogram on the outcrop has a central line the other lacks. The shafts, however, are similar in outline: squared at the end, narrowing at the neck, with pointed projections on either side, suggestive of the knops on processional crosses.[45] A suggested late-sixth century date for the Raasay Chi-Rhos depends upon the dedication of the nearby church to St Moluag of Lismore, who died in 592, but Mrs Curle's late-seventh century date is preferable, in view of the local activities of Maelrubai and the link between Applecross and Bangor; Moluag was also of the Dál nAraide and studied at Bangor during Comgall's abbacy.[46] Maelrubai of Applecross or Cano son of Gartnait may well have seen the Raasay Chi-Rhos. The combination of Christian monogram and Pictish symbols on the Raasay slab invokes an accommodation between Irish abbot and Pictish prince. Its Crescent and V-rod symbol is an early or 'prominent' member of Stevenson's typologically late 'Dome and Wing' group, while at least two of the examples in Skye are 'devolved' and thus perhaps chronologically later[47], extending even into the early-eighth century, as final memorials of Pictish defiance against new Dalriadic rulers. The abandonment of the Pictish western province by Bruide son of Bili and the subsequent mayhem affecting Skye foreshadow later phases of West Highland history: the existing power was overthrown, creating a vacuum that a few symbol stones were not enough to fill. Cano's old neighbourhood had little apparent political importance when the Vikings arrived at the end of the eighth century. Applecross, however, may have been a different story.

Applecross after Maelrubai

Cano's kindred disappears from the annals after 705, but Applecross lasted another century. Fáilbe mac Guaire, the successor of Maelrubai, was lost at sea with 22 sailors in 737.[48] The annals mention Applecross once more, when Mac Oigi of Applecross, abbot of Bangor, died *feliciter* and *in pace* in 802, the same year Iona was burned by Vikings, not for the last time.[49] The early-sixteenth-century *Breviary*

of Aberdeen anachronistically reports that Maelrubai, who died in 722, was himself martyred by Vikings at Urquhart in Ross and buried at Applecross, a garbled association of the monastery with a Viking raid.[50] Mac Oigi's death may have been peaceful at Bangor, but Applecross departs from the annals after 802, lost in the Scandinavian maelstrom.

Conflicting oral traditions surround an unfinished cross-slab at Applecross, still known as 'Mac Oigi's Stone'. A story recorded over a century ago identifies it as the tombstone of one Ruairidh mór mac Coigean, a proprietor of Applecross said to have been killed by 'Danes', whom Reeves and Skene identified with Mac Oigi.[51] According to another tradition, surviving to the present day, Mac Oigi's body was placed on the slab in Belfast Lough when he died at Bangor and it floated him home to Applecross, where it was set up over his grave.[52] In either case, the tall, narrow slab displays the incised outline of a ringed cross, with circular pellets in the armpits.[53] The sides of the broad shaft curve outwards at the bottom until they meet the vertical edges of the slab, turning most of its lower half into a Calvary. The stone cut away above the upper ring quadrants, on both sides of the short upper cross-arm, implies that work was abandoned while converting a cross-slab into a freestanding cross, an unusual procedure in its original context more probably indicative of modern tinkering. The carefully drawn outline of the cross covers less than half of the slab's visible surface above the Calvary, leaving a broad zone below, suggestive of decorative intentions left uncompleted. It thus meets the basic criteria Dr Henderson has identified for a late phase of Pictish sculpture, heralded at Rosemarkie in Easter Ross roughly *c*800, when cross-slabs grew taller and narrower and their crosses were often set on bases, while the dimensions of the crosses grew smaller in relation to their slabs.[54] But there are no Pictish symbols on Mac Oigi's Stone, although they still feature on a number of diagnostic exemplars of Henderson's ninth-century type. The absence of Class II Pictish cross-slabs west of Druimalban need not imply that there were no Picts left to carve them, but rather that there were no Pictish patrons in a position to commission them.

Maelrubai's successors at Applecross, however, exercised sculptural patronage and the sculptors they employed were probably Picts. Only three surviving fragments, carved in relief, are left of their finished work[55],

a **b**

1 *Cross-slab fragment, Applecross:* **a** *front* **b** *edge*

but they provide evidence of an Applecross workshop equal in quality to, and contemporary with, the early medieval Iona School. The mutilation of the Applecross fragments owes little to any Viking destruction of the monastery and reflects more recent iconoclasm. According to local tradition, *a' Chomraich*, the 'girth' or 'sanctuary' of Maelrubai had a six-mile radius around the monastic church, marked by 'stone crosses' (or cross-slabs), at least one of which is known to have been smashed by a 'bigoted mason' *c*1870.[56]

Carving survives on one principal face and one edge of the largest of the three fragments (**1**).[57] The edge shows a small human figure with bent knees above a double row of Stafford knots with repeated cruciform breaks, over a running spiral (**1b**). The slab apparently bore a cross with

pierced quadrants. But there is no cross-ring, other than a narrow bead outlining the cable moulding beneath the remaining hollow quadrant. A similar bead divides the decoration on the main face into two zones, the lower supporting the shaft of the unringed cross superimposed over its pierced quadrants, much as Rosemarkie places its V-rods behind its Crescent symbols.[58] Pierced quadrants are rare on Pictish cross slabs; of the three Perthshire examples, the Applecross fragment is closer to the Gask 'Bore Stone' than either Carpow or Gellyburn.[59]

The Applecross slab's lower decorative zone had a rectangular border with a double row of interlaced roundels, based on a six-cord plait with S-shaped bends, of a late sculptural type found in Ireland, South Wales and the West of Scotland, 'but almost entirely absent in other parts of Great Britain'.[60] The interlace border frames a key pattern also found on the St Andrews Sarcophagus (mixed with interlace), at Nigg, Rosemarkie, Tarbat 8 and in the ninth century on Shandwick, Meigle 4, Farr (Sutherland), the St Andrews 14 cross-shaft, and on the very late Reay slab in Caithness.[61] The framing of the Applecross key pattern recalls Dr Henderson's observations on analogous devices used on the St Andrews Sarcophagus, Nigg, Hilton of Cadboll and Rosemarkie 1, perhaps placing the Applecross fragment slightly before the period inaugurated at Rosemarkie, where the symbol side also features an unbordered key pattern, something unknown at Applecross, while 'the use of all-over key pattern to fill lower panels is characteristic of later Pictish sculpture'.[62] The broken edges of two vertically adjacent key patterns represent the Applecross slab's cross-shaft and recall Rosemarkie 2.[63] The upper pattern appears on Rosemarkie 1, Farr and Inchbrayock 1 in Angus.[64] The panel to the right is complete and of particular interest, comprising six pairs of triple-spiral medallions, with an extra one under the outermost curve of the quadrant's cable moulding. The spirals terminate in lobes and the heads of humans, ducks and birds of prey, paralleling the St Vigeans 7 cross-slab in Angus, which Dr Henderson describes as 'a clear instance of a Pictish sculptor's behaving exactly like a Book of Kells artist but not in fact copying a design used in the Book'.[65] One Applecross spiral medallion employs snakes with bulging eyes, of a type seen in the Book of Kells but not at St Vigeans.[66] The Applecross

2 *Cross-arm fragment, Applecross*

3 *Corner fragment, Applecross*

medallions have triquetras in the interspaces, sub-ordinating interlace to spiral patterns, as does a panel on the Nigg slab.[67] But Nigg has bossed spirals, while those at Applecross are flat. Bossed spirals dominating interlace also characterize aspects of the Iona crosses and the related Saint-Germain bronze objects.[68] The flatter ornament of Applecross and St Vigeans is equally 'reminiscent of metalwork techniques' and akin to that of the Irish Ahenny group.[69] The largest Applecross fragment thus provides a link between major Pictish sculptural sites in Easter Ross and southern Pictland, as well as Iona, the Book of Kells and Ireland.

The other two Applecross fragments belonged to different monuments. One of them seems to be a cross-arm with small rounded armpits, chamfered arms and a circular central setting (**2**). The interlace pattern on its single carved face is also found on the St Andrews Sarcophagus, in northern Pictland at Nigg and Golspie and in the tenth century, with an Anglian runic inscription, at Thornhill, Yorkshire (West Riding).[70] The remaining Applecross piece is a corner fragment bearing double spirals linked by C-scrolls, merging along one edge of the right angle, but not on the other, with an enframing rare interlace pattern (**3**).[71] Of the spiral panels known in Easter Ross, Hilton of Cadboll has broad borders on opposite sides, but Shandwick does not, while C-scrolls combine with surrounding interlace elsewhere in the north at Skinnet in Caithness, which, Dr Henderson notes, 'shares interlace

patterns with Rosemarkie'.[72] The recurring evocation of Rosemarkie by Mac Oigi's Stone and two of the fragments at Applecross lends credence to the *Aberdeen Breviary's* association of Rosemarkie with St Moluag, who founded Lismore in Lorn after leaving Bangor during the lifetime of its founder Comgall, himself a member of the Dál nAraide, to whom Moluag and Maelrubai's mother also belonged.[73]

After Applecross

The Applecross and Iona workshops ceased functioning at about the same time and for the same reason. But Applecross continued to exert sculptural influence west of Druimalban. Surviving Applecross sculpture is aniconic, except for the little bent-kneed figure with splayed feet atop the edge of the largest fragment. The posture of the figure on the front of the Canna 2 cross-shaft is similar (**4a**), although the arms are in different positions.[74] The left side of Canna 2 (**4d**) pairs the same interlace over double-spiral patterns found on the edge of the Applecross fragment[75], while the interlace on its right side (**4c**) is of a widely distributed ninth-tenth century type.[76] The back of Canna 2 (**4b**) reflects both Iona and Applecross. Its bottom panel's fish-tailed eared serpents combine features seen separately on Glamis 2, the St Andrews Sarcophagus, Rosemarkie 1, Shandwick, St Oran's Cross at Iona and complete in the Book of Kells.[77] Examples of its upper panel's spiraliform key pattern range in date from the early Aberlemno 2 to the late slab at Reay; a related version was used on the large

ERRATUM *page 179*

The photographs **4c** and **4d** have been mistakenly transposed, with the result that the left side of the cross is now shown in **c** and the right side in **d**

a

b

c

d

4 *Canna 2 cross-shaft:* **a** *front* **b** *back* **c** *right side* **d** *left side*

5 *Canna 1 cross, back*

Applecross fragment's cross-shaft.[78] But its central panel's interlace pattern is otherwise found only in County Durham, in the late-ninth to early-eleventh century, placing Canna 2 firmly in the Viking period.[79]

The figural ornament on two Hebridean crosses, Canna 1 and another on Eilean Mór in the Sound of Jura, has no known counterpart at Applecross, but their other decoration echoes the connections of the Applecross-influenced Canna 2.[80] The upper shaft panel's key pattern on the back of Canna 1 (**5**) also appears at Ulbster in Caithness, Nigg, Aberlemno 3 and in tenth-century Argyll at Ardchattan and on the Kilmartin cross.[81] The quadrupeds in the adjacent Canna shaft panel, with interlocking, although addorsed bodies and interlaced ears and tongues, follow in the tradition of those on the shaft of the Iona School's Keills Cross and the top cross-arm on the Nigg slab.[82] Cruder but comparable affronted creatures, with interpenetrating necks, figure on the west face of the broken Eilean Mór ringed cross, within double-ribbon

interlace borders of a late sculptural pattern known on St Andrews 15, in the west at Jordanhill and Govan and found earlier on a Pictish brooch from Perthshire.[83] Eilean Mór's east face includes an expanded version of a key pattern seen on Rosemarkie 1 and a flat, circular interlaced boss also known on the crosses at Dupplin in Perthshire and Kilmartin.[84] Eilean Mór displays two features that Stevenson identified as typical of Pictish sculpture in the later ninth and tenth century, 'two-ply interlace' and prominent key patterns, details characteristic of the Dupplin and St Andrews 14 crosses[85], although Dupplin is now known to be earlier than previously thought, while Canna 1 and Eilean Mór may both belong to the tenth century.

Dupplin provides the earliest applicable historical context for the fusion of Pictish ornamental taste with the Gaelic preference for the cross over the cross-slab, as demonstrated at Canna and Eilean Mór. The recently recovered Dupplin inscription names Constantine son of Fergus, who obtained the Pictish kingship in 789, the Dalriadic kingship in 811, ruled from Forteviot near Dupplin, 'built Dunkeld' and died in 820.[86] But in the west, the second decade of the ninth century was too unsettled for the invention of new Hebridean cross types, given the continuing Viking depredations that led to the martyrdom of Blathmacc at Iona in 825 and the still nascent coalescence of the hybrid Gall-Ghàidheil, whose full emergence belongs to the mid-century, with their conversion later still.[87] Intermarriage between Viking and Gael certainly occurred by the period of Constantine's joint kingship; Gofraidh mac Fergusa, who had a Norse personal name and a Gaelic patronymic, was adult enough c835 to leave northern Ireland for service with Kenneth mac Alpin in Scotland, where he died as 'lord of the Hebrides' c851.[88] But the annals only recognize the marauding Hebridean Gall-Ghàidheil c856.[89] Following the destruction of the Iona and Applecross workshops, the first half of the ninth century was a barren period for sculpture west of Druimalban; the sculptor of St Matthew's Cross at Iona had to be imported subsequently from Ireland.[90] The intimations of Dupplin lay fallow for decades in the west, before reaching fruition at Canna and Eilean Mór.

Late cross-slabs with Pictish associations are also found west of Druimalban at Ardchattan on Loch Etive in Lorn and

6 *Cross-slab, front, The Lodge, Eigg*

the interlace border below the cross-shaft on the largest Applecross fragment, and as late as the unframed example under the cross on the Reay slab, which has another key pattern, seen on Canna 2, related to one on the Applecross slab's cross-shaft.[97] Although its cross-head has a more complex form, Eigg is especially comparable to Reay; both have short, ringed crosses set above key patterns and belong to the last phase of Pictish sculpture on both sides of Druimalban.

In its heyday, Applecross was an artistic conduit between east and west, probably overland to Easter Ross via Glen Torridon, Glen Docherty and Strath Bran. Almost a century after its demise, its sculptural affinities with the Pictish heartland were briefly resuscitated, answering a handful of yearnings in the old Pictish western province and those of displaced Picts from the north, or others moving west, following the final unification of Picts and Scots under Kenneth mac Alpin.[98] The foreigners' sea became the corridors of the sculptors' galleries, linking Applecross, Canna, Eigg, Eilean Mór, Ardchattan and Iona, where the Book of Kells spent much of the ninth century.[99] 'In Insular art, variety invariably goes hand in hand with quality', as Dr Henderson observes.[100] Into the tenth century, sculptors west of Druimalban sought both at Applecross.

on the more Pictish island of Eigg. Ardchattan shares a key pattern with Canna 1.[91] Stevenson's identification of its bifurcated and pelleted, triple-ribbon interlace as Scandinavian features assists in its dating, although Rosemarkie 1 made earlier use of bifurcated double-strand interlace[92], while the Applecross corner fragment's merging of spirals and interlace along one edge (**3**) prefigures Ardchattan's related ornament.[93] The broken cross-slab from Kildonnan, Eigg (**6**) was sculpted on the reverse of an older Pictish monument.[94] The rectangular terminals, central square and protruding top arm of its encircled cross recall Meigle 2, although the double-ribbon interlace of the Eigg cross-head and ring are better comparable to Invergowrie 1 and 2, or the unringed crosses on Kirriemuir 1 and St Andrews 15, which shares another pattern with Eilean Mór.[95] Eigg's interlace is uncontrolled, lapsing into a simple twist inside the ring.[96] The key pattern filling the area beneath the cross appeared earlier, within

Acknowledgement

Isabel Henderson served as the external examiner of my PhD thesis (cited below), parts of which provide the basis for this essay, although I have now expanded my earlier conclusions and identified some Applecross patterns that previously proved elusive. In the process of writing I was reminded precisely why I welcomed Dr Henderson as one of my examiners and offer my new appreciation of Applecross in token of that admiration.

Notes and References

1 A.O. and M.O. Anderson, *Adomnán's Life of Columba*, rev ed, Oxford, 1991, xvi, xxxiii, lix, 62–3, 138, 139n, 166–7, 178–9, 200–1; T.F. O'Rahilly, *Early Irish History and Mythology*, Dublin, 1976, 219, 385.

2 Adomnán was of the Cenél Conaill; see F.J. Byrne, *Irish Kings and High-Kings*, London, 1973, 258; Máire Herbert, *Iona, Kells and Derry: The History and Hagiography of the Monastic Familia of Columba*, Oxford, 1988, 47–8,

310. Maelrubai was of the Cenél nEógain; see Whitley Stokes, *The Martyrology of Oengus the Culdee*, London, 1905, 118–19; idem., *The Martyrology of Gorman*, London, 1895, 80; John O'Donovan, *The Martyrology of Donegal*, ed J.H. Todd and William Reeves, Dublin, 1864, 106; Alan Orr Anderson, *Early Sources of Scottish History A.D.500 to 1286*, 2 vols, Edinburgh and London, 1922, I, 219–20. For both Adomnán and Maelrubai, see Pádraig Ó Riain, *Corpus Genealogiarum Sanctorum Hiberniae*, Dublin, 1985, 6 (no 17), 54 (no 340).

3 Seán Mac Airt and Gearóid Mac Niocaill, *The Annals of Ulster (To A.D. 1131)*, Dublin, 1983, 140, 142, 176 (hereafter: AU); Whitley Stokes, 'The Annals of Tigernach Third Fragment. A.D. 489–766', *Revue Celtique*, 17, 1896, 202, 228 (hereafter: AT); A. Anderson, *Early Sources*, I, 181, 183, 219; John Bannerman, *Studies in the History of Dalriada*, Edinburgh and London, 1974, 114; Alfred P. Smyth, *Warlords and Holy Men; Scotland AD 80–1000*, London, 1984, 109–111. For Pictish place-names in the area, including that of Applecross itself, Tornapress on Loch Kishorn and Arinacrinachd (*Airigh nan Cruithneach*, 'the Picts' shieling'), see W.J. Watson, *The History of the Celtic Place-Names of Scotland*, Edinburgh and London, 1926, 14, 78, 359, 420, 458; Ian A. Fraser, 'Pictish Place-Names – Some Toponymic Evidence', *The Picts: A New Look at Old Problems*, ed Alan Small, Dundee, 1987, 70–1.

4 John O'Donovan, ed, *Annals of the Kingdom of Ireland by the Four Masters*, 7 vols, Dublin, 1856, I, 282, 320 (hereafter: AFM); idem., *Martyrology of Donegal*, 106. In 1633, Ó Cléirigh copied the single surviving manuscript of the twelfth-century Martyrology of Gorman (Brussels, Bib. roy., 5100–4, fols. 124–197v), identifying Maelrubai in a gloss as abbot of Bangor; see Stokes, *Martyrology of Gorman*, vii, xvi, l, 80. For Ó Cléirigh's manuscripts of the Martyrologies of Donegal and Gorman, see James F. Kenney, *The Sources for the Early History of Ireland: Ecclesiastical*, New York, 1929, 482–3, 485. The earliest manuscript to associate Maelrubai with Bangor is the twelfth-century Book of Leinster (Dublin, Trinity College Library 1339 [H. 2. 18]), in its version of the ninth-century *Martyrology of Tallaght*, a text also copied by Ó Cléirigh from another exemplar; see R.I. Best and H.J. Lawlor, *The Martyrology of Tallaght*, London, 1931, xii–xix, 35, 182. For the list of Bangor abbots in the *Antiphonary of Bangor*, see Whitley Stokes and John Strachan, *Thesaurus Palaeohibernicus*, 2 vols, Cambridge, 1901–3, II, 282; Kathleen Hughes, *Early Christian Ireland: Introduction to the Sources*, Ithaca, 1972, 122–3; Kenney, *Sources*, 266, 710.

5 The genealogy of Maelrubai's mother, Suaibsech or Subthain, in Ó Riain, *Corpus Genealogiarum*, 175 (no 722.50), 178 (no 722.86) makes her Comgall's sister in an obvious compression of generations, since Maelrubai was born *c*642, while Comgall died in 602, in his ninety-first year; see AT, 163.

6 For Comgall's genealogy, see Ó Riain, *Corpus Genealogiarum*, 16 (no 97), 63 (no 419), 69 (no 506), 103 (no 205), 185 (no 729.2). The *Vita Comgalli Abbatis de Bennchor* makes clear his Dál nAraide origins; see Charles Plummer, *Vitae Sanctorum Hiberniae*, 2 vols, Oxford, 1910, II, 3.

7 Anderson and Anderson, *Adomnán's Life of Columba*, lxxii, n228, 206–7. *Hinba* remains unidentified, with suggestions ranging from Eileach an Naoimh in the Garvellachs to a site in Jura or others north of the Isle of Mull; see William Reeves, *Life of Saint Columba, Founder of Hy*, ed W.F. Skene, Edinburgh, 1874, 318–324; Watson, *Celtic Place-Names*, 81–4; Marjorie O. Anderson, 'Columba and Other Irish Saints in Scotland', *Historical Studies*, 5, 1965, 30–1; Royal Commission on the Ancient and Historical Monuments of Scotland (RCAHMS), *Argyll: An Inventory of the Monuments*, 5, *Islay, Jura, Colonsay and Oronsay*, Edinburgh, 1984, 27, 182, 340, nn 92–3.

8 Plummer, *Vitae Sanctorum Hiberniae*, II, 11; A. Anderson, *Early Sources*, I, 52–4.

9 Anderson and Anderson, *Adomnán's Life of Columba*, 64–7; Bannerman, *Studies in the History of Dalriada*, 3–4; AU, 84, 94.

10 Bannerman, *Studies in the History of Dalriada*, 2–8, 88, 98, 101, 105–6, discusses relations between Dál Riata and Dál nAraide in the later sixth and seventh centuries. The gaurantor list of the Law of Adomnán anachronistically describes Fiachra Cossalach as *rí Cruithne* (the Dál nAraide), a position he did not attain until 709; see Máirín Ní Dhonnchadha, 'The Gaurantor List of *Cáin Adomnáin*, 697', *Peritia*, 1, 1982, 201.

11 Watson, *Celtic Place-Names*, 37–8.

12 'The Hebrides were devastated', according to AU, 140–1; but O'Rahilly, *Early Irish History and Mythology*, 377, n2, 538, shows that *Ibdaig/Ibdig* identifies people rather than places. Eoin MacNeill, 'Early Irish Population Groups: Their Nomenclature, Classifications and Chronology', *Proceedings of the Royal Irish Academy*, 29C, 1911, 100–02, was the first to associate the *Túatha Iboth*, the *Ibdaig* of *Lebor Gabála*, with 'the old traditional inhabitants of the Hebrides'.

13 Watson, *Celtic Place-Names*, 38; *Lebor Gabála* suggests that some pre-Dalriadic Hebrideans also came from Ireland; see O'Rahilly, *Early Irish History and Mythology*, 377, 487, 538, n6.

14 O'Rahilly, *Early Irish History and Mythology*, 344–6; K.H. Jackson, 'The Language of the Picts', *The Problem of the*

Picts, ed F.T. Wainwright, Edinburgh and London, 1955, 159; Byrne, *Irish Kings and High-Kings*, 8–11, 39, 108–9.

15 Anderson and Anderson, *Adomnán's Life of Columba*, 88–9.

16 Bertram Colgrave, *The Life of Bishop Wilfrid by Eddius Stephanus*, Cambridge, 1927, 40–3. The Pictish kings' lists call him Drest or Drust and give his father's name as Donuel; see Marjorie O. Anderson, *Kings and Kingship in Early Scotland*, rev ed, London, 1980, 248, 262, 266, 272, 280, 297. The Irish annals call him Drost son of Domnall; see AU, 140, 144 ; AT, 202, 205.

17 A.O. Anderson, *Early Sources*, I, 181, n 5; A. O. Anderson and M.O. Anderson, *Adomnan's Life of Columba* (1st ed), London, 1961, 52–3; Isabel Henderson, *The Picts*, London, 1967, 54–5; idem., 'North Pictland', *The Dark Ages in the Highlands*, ed Edward Meldrum, Inverness, 1971, 41; D.P. Kirby, '… per universas Pictorum provincias', *Famulus Christi: Essays in Commemoration of the Thirteenth Centenary of the Birth of the Venerable Bede*, ed Gerald Bonner, London, 1976, 290–1; Smyth, *Warlords and Holy Men*, 62–3; M. Anderson, *Kings and Kingship*, 172.

18 Ibid., 174–5; Isabel Henderson, 'Inverness, a Pictish Capital', *The Hub of the Highlands: The Book of Inverness and District*, Inverness, 1975, 96; AU, 146; AT, 207.

19 A. Anderson, *Early Sources*, I, 192–3; F.T. Wainwright, 'Nechtanesmere', *Antiquity*, 22, 1948, 82–97.

20 Henderson, *The Picts*, 167–8; idem., 'North Pictland', 41–2; ibid., 'Appendix A: Applecross and the Pictish and Dalriadic Entries Unique to the Annals of Ulster, circa 675 – circa 730 A.D.', 43–9; the suggestion is favourably received in M. Anderson, *Kings and Kingship*, 8–9.

21 The fundamental study is Bannerman, *Studies in the History of Dalriada*, 9–26, first published as 'Notes on the Scottish Entries in the Early Irish Annals', *Scottish Gaelic Studies*, 11.2, 1968, 149–70, which relies in part on Henderson, *The Picts*, 165–8; additional discussion in Alfred P. Smyth, 'The Earliest Irish Annals: Their First Contemporary Entries and the Earliest Centres of Recording', *Proceedings of the Royal Irish Academy*, 72C, 1972, 33–41; best summary in Hughes, *Early Christian Ireland*, 116–9.

22 Bannerman, *Studies in the History of Dalriada*, 14; Smyth, 'The Earliest Irish Annals', 41. Henderson, 'Applecross and the Pictish and Dalriadic Entries', 48, argues that the Applecross material may have been combined with the *Iona Chronicle* at Bangor; M. Anderson, *Kings and Kingship*, 11–12, attributes all the relevant entries to Iona.

23 AU, 138, 140; AT, 200–1; A, Anderson, Early Sources, I, 181, n 6; M. Anderson, *Kings and Kingship*, 11–12.

24 Henderson, 'Applecross and the Pictish and Dalriadic Entries', 46–8. There are no exclusively Pictish names

among the families of Conaing son of Dúnchad killed in Skye in 701 or the Oengus son of Maelanfaith killed in Skye in 710; both kindreds indicate Dalriadic encroachment on Pictish Skye. For fuller discussion, see Douglas Grant Mac Lean, II, *Early Medieval Sculpture in the West Highlands and Islands of Scotland*, unpub. PhD thesis, 2 vols, University of Edinburgh, 1985, I, 43, 129, nn 117–24.

25 D.A. Binchy, *Scéla Cano meic Gartnáin*, Dublin, 1975, 1–2. Gartnán (nom.) is a hypocoristic form of Gartnait; see Bannerman, *Studies in the History of Dalriada*, 54, 92, n 8. For gaming boards in the Pictish context of the Northern Isles, see Anna Ritchie, 'The Picto-Scottish interface in material culture', *The Picts: A New Look at Old Problems*, ed Small, 60–2.

26 *Scéla Cano* makes Cano's father Gartnait the son of Aedán's 'brother', the ahistorical Áed mac Gabráin, whose invention for literary purposes may depend upon manuscript variants of the *Senchus Fer nAlban*, which call Aedán *Aed find*; for discrepancies between the annals and conflicting interpretations of the evidence, see A. Anderson, *Early Sources*, I, 76, 122–3, 169, 178–9; Rudolf Thurneysen, 'Eine Irische Parallele zur Tristan-Sage', *Zeitschrift für Romanische Philologie*, 43, 1924, 386–8; O'Rahilly, *Early Irish History and Mythology*, 359, n 4, 361, n1; Binchy, *Scéla Cano*, xviii–xix; Henderson, 'North Pictland', 41, n 1; Bannerman, *Studies in the History of Dalriada*, 33 (the *Aed find* variants), 80 (the date of Aedán mac Gabráin's death), 92–4, 114; M. Anderson, *Kings and Kingship*, 154–5; fuller discussion in Mac Lean, *Early Medieval Sculpture*, I, 44–8, 129–31, nn 125–60.

27 For Gartnait son of Domnall, see Bannerman, *Studies in the History of Dalriada*, 93, 114; Henderson, 'North Pictland', 41. Anderson and Anderson, *Adomnan's Life of Columba* (1st ed), 52, and M. Anderson, *Kings and Kingship*, 154–5, 172, identify Domnall as Domnall Brecc; idem., 'Picts – the Name and the People', *The Picts: A New Look at Old Problems*, ed Small, 10, suggests that he may have been a Briton. For the relevant annal entries, see A. Anderson, *Early Sources*, I, 166–7, 178. Smyth, *Warlords and Holy Men*, 63–7, 70, 79, 120–1, is cautious about equating Gartnait son of Domnall Brecc with Gartnait of Skye, but expands on the identification of Gartnait as the son of Domnall Brecc by arguing that the Picts, after a period of Strathclyde overlordship at the beginning of the seventh century, may then have been subject to Dál Riata until the battle of Strathcarron, when they reverted to Strathclyde overlordship, before coming under Northumbrian domination in the reigns of Oswiu and Ecgfrith; W.D.H. Sellar, 'Warlords, Holy Men and Matrilineal Succession', *Innes Review*, 36, 1985, 40, characterizes Smyth's arguments for a seventh-century Strathclyde overlordship of Pictland as 'purely

speculative'. Kirby, '. . . per universas Pictorum provincias', 311–13, casts doubt on the identification of Domnall father of Gartnait as Domnall Brecc.

28 AU, 140, 144, 150, 152, 164; A. Anderson, *Early Sources*, I, 182, 184, 198, 211; Denis Murphy, *The Annals of Clonmacnoise*, Dublin, 1896, 110, may be a seventeenth-century English translation of a lost Irish source, but Herman Moisl, 'The Bernician Royal Dynasty and the Irish in the Seventh Century', *Peritia*, 2, 1983, 123–4, has demonstrated its reliability in precisely this period. The genealogy of the Conamail killed in 705, who was the son of Cano son of Gartnait son of Domnall, echoes that of Conamail son of Cano son of Gartnait son of Aedán mac Gabráin given in the *Genelaig Albanensium*, which accompanies all manuscript versions of the *Senchus Fer nAlban*. The similarity probably contributed to *Scéla Cano*'s conflation of the the two Canos; see Binchy, *Scéla Cano*, xix; Bannerman, *Studies in the History of Dalriada*, 27, 66–7, 92, 109; M. Anderson, *Kings and Kingship*, 154.

29 Binchy, *Scéla Cano*, 1, 7, 21n, thought it unlikely that *Inis moccu Chéin* 'is just another name for Skye'; Watson, *Celtic Place-Names*, 99, suggested that it might have been 'off the coast of Skye', an inland loch or a crannóg.

30 Colm Ó Baoill, 'Inis Moccu Chéin', *Scottish Gaelic Studies*, 12.2, 1976, 267–70.

31 MacNeill, 'Early Irish Population Groups', 74.

32 Ordnance Survey Sheet 24: Raasay and Loch Torridon, 1:50 000 2nd ser, 1979.

33 This 'Description of Skye' was given to Sir Robert Sibbald by a 'Mr Macmartin', who received it from the chaplain of Clanranald; see Arthur Mitchell, *Geographical Collections Relating to Scotland Made by Walter Macfarlane*, Edinburgh, 1907, II, 222. 'Macmartin' may have been Martin Martin, according to whose *Description of the Western Islands of Scotland*, 2nd ed, London, 1716, 164, '*Dun-Cann*' takes its name from 'one *Canne*, Cousin to the King of *Denmark*'.

34 Ó Baoill, 'Inis Moccu Chéin', 268–9. I am grateful to Dr MacLean and Prof Donald Meek for advice on this point.

35 According to the Pictish kings' lists; see M. Anderson, *Kings and Kingship*, 248, 262, 266, 272, 280, 297

36 Bertram Colgrave and R. A. B. Mynors, *Bede's Ecclesiastical History of the English People*, Oxford, 1969, 150–1, 294–5 (*gentem Pictorum maxima ex parte regno Anglorum subiecit*), 428–9.

37 A. Anderson, *Early Sources*, I, 181, n5; Anderson and Anderson, *Adomnan's Life of Columba* (1st ed.), 52–3. Smyth, *Warlords and Holy Men*, 62–3, follows Kirby, '. . . per universas Pictorum provincas', 290–1, in thinking that Oswiu may have imposed a two- or three-year interregnum on the Picts after the death of Gartnait,

before his brother Drest became Oswiu's 'puppet', which would explain the year-length of his reign in the kings' lists, but other discrepancies in the same sources cannot be explained in reference to direct Northumbrian rule; see M. Anderson, *Kings and Kingship*, 117, 172–3, where it is argued that Drest was Oswiu's vassal but revolted against him.

38 Henderson, *The Picts*, 52–5; idem., 'North Pictland', 41; Kirby, '. . . per universas Pictorum provincias', 290–1

39 Mac Lean, *Early Medieval Sculpture*, I, 41, 121

40 Colgrave and Mynors, *Bede's Ecclesiastical History*, 428–9: *Nam et Picti terram possessionis suae tenuerunt Angli.*

41 Anderson and Anderson, *Adomnan's Life of Columba* (1st ed.), 59–60; discussed in Henderson, 'North Pictland', 41, n 8. For Bruide son of Bili as 'king of Fortriu', see A. Anderson, *Early Sources*, I, 200; Henderson, *The Picts*, 59; M. Anderson, *Kings and Kingship*, 173–4; Smyth, *Warlords and Holy Men*, 69–70.

42 Graham Ritchie and Iain Fraser, *Pictish Symbol Stones: A Handlist 1994*, Edinburgh: RCAHMS, 17, with additional references.

43 R.B.K. Stevenson, 'Pictish Art', in *The Problem of the Picts*, ed Wainwright, 102–6, fig 15 (C2, C6, C12, C14), map 4. The Double Disc and Z-rod symbols on Clach Ard and Fiskavaig are also typologically late; see Mac Lean, *Early Medieval Sculpture*, I, 82–91; additional discussion in Gordon Murray, 'The declining Pictish symbol – a reappraisal', *Proc Soc Antiq Scot*, 116, 1986, 223–53.

44 J.S. Richardson, 'Note of an Undescribed Sculptured Stone with Symbols in the Island of Raasay', *Proc Soc Antiq Scot*, 41, 1906–7, 436–7, figs 10–11; RCAHMS, *Ninth Report with Inventory of Monuments and Constructions in the Outer Hebrides, Skye and the Small Isles*, Edinburgh, 1928, 184–5, fig 265; J.J. Galbraith, 'Donations to the Museum' and 'The Chi-Rho Crosses on Raasay: Their Importance and Chronological Relationships', *Proc Soc Antiq Scot*, 67, 1932–33, 63–4 (figs 1–2), 318–20.

45 Mac Lean, *Early Medieval Sculpture*, I, 175, 177, 181–3.

46 Galbraith, 'The Chi-Rho Crosses on Raasay', 319–20; A. Anderson, *Early Sources*, I, 95; Cecil L. Curle, 'The Chronology of the Early Christian Monuments of Scotland', *Proc Soc Antiq Scot*, 74, 1939–40, 74, pl. XVIIIc. For Moluag's genealogy see Ó Riain, *Corpus Genealogiarum*, 20 (no 121); Watson, *Celtic Place-Names*, 292, n 3; for his association with Bangor, see H.J. Lawlor, *St Bernard of Clairvaux's Life of St Malachy of Armagh*, London and New York, 1920, 28.

47 Stevenson, 'Pictish Art', map 4.

48 A. Anderson, *Early Sources*, I, 236; M. Anderson, *Kings and Kingship*, 8–9, points out that 'this may be a complete record of the abbots of Applecross down to the point

(c 740) where Scotian annals cease to be plentiful'.

49 AU, 256, 258; AFM, I, 404, 406.

50 Williams Reeves, 'Saint Maelrubha: His History and His Churches', *Proc Soc Antiq Scot*, 3, 1857–60, 265–9; A. Anderson, *Early Sources*, I, 220.

51 Reeves, 'Saint Maelrubha', 274–5, 279–280; William Forbes Skene, *Celtic Scotland*, 3 vols, Edinburgh, 1876–80, II, 412.

52 According to Mr Murdo Gillanders, Personnel Officer of Edinburgh University, who heard it from his father, the former Registrar of Glasgow University, the late Lt-Col Farquhar Gillanders of the 7th Gurkha Rifles, a native of Applecross.

53 Joanna Close-Brooks, *Exploring Scotland's Heritage: The Highlands*, Edinburgh, 1986, 123; RCAHMS photo RC/1261.

54 Isabel Henderson, 'Scupture North of the Forth after the Takeover by the Scots', *Anglo-Saxon and Viking Age Sculpture*, ed James Lang, Oxford (*British Archaeological Reports*, British Series 49), 1978, 49–52; idem, *The Art and Function of Rosemarkie's Pictish Monuments*, Inverness, 1990 (unpaginated), dates Rosemarkie to 'the very beginning' of the ninth century, 'or more probably, to the end' of the eighth.

55 Close-Brooks, *The Highlands*, 123.

56 Watson, *Celtic Place-Names*, 124–5, 125 n; G.A. Frank Knight, *Archaeological Light on the Early Christianizing of Scotland*, London, 2 vols, 1933, II, 210, 223, n 28; see also Charles Thomas, *The Early Christian Archaeology of North Britain*, Oxford, 1971, 41, fig 15. The same means of marking the monastic precinct was employed on Raasay, where the Chi-Rho-bearing symbol stone may have served such a purpose, one still recognized in the eighteenth century by the Rev Donald MacQueen, who so informed Johnson and Boswell; see *Samuel Johnson: A Journey to the Western Islands of Scotland and James Boswell: The Journal of a Tour of the Hebrides with Samuel Johnson, LL.D*, ed Alan Wendt, Boston, 1965, 48, 223; Galbraith, 'The Chi-Rho Crosses on Raasay', 319.

57 Close-Brooks, *The Highlands*, 123; Mac Lean, *Early Medieval Sculpture*, I, 410–11.

58 Henderson, 'Sculpture North of the Forth', 51; idem., *Rosemarkie's Pictish Monuments*.

59 J. Romilly Allen and Joseph Anderson, *The Early Christian Monuments of Scotland*, 3 parts, Edinburgh, 1903 (hereafter ECMS) (repr 2 vols with an Introduction by Isabel Henderson, Balgavies, Angus, 1993), III, 290–1 (Gask, now at Moncrieffe House, identified as 'a transitional type of monument between the upright cross-slab and the free-standing cross'), 311–13 (Carpow, removed to Mugdrum in Fife), figs 307, 307A, 327A–B; C.S.T. Calder,

'Note on a Pictish Cross-Slab from Gellyburn, Perthshire', *Proc Soc Antiq Scot*, 85, 1950–51, 175–7, pl XVIII. Gask has semicircular quadrants, as does Applecross. Carpow has the round pierced quadrants of a quadrilobate ring, although the cross-ring itself is circular. Gellyburn has a shafted cross with a pierced quadrilobate ring on one side and an encircled cross of arcs with round, pierced interspaces on the other.

60 ECMS, II, 213–14 (nos 544–7). The Applecross pattern seems to be a reversed variant of Romilly Allen's no 545, with a looped knot (no 304, pp 165–6), between each four roundels.

61 Ibid., II, 353 (no 974); III, 36, 68, 73, 82, 86, 93, 299, 352, 359, figs 32, 79, 83, 94, 313A, 365, 373A; better photographs of Rosemarkie 1 in Ritchie and Fraser, *Pictish Symbol Stones*, 16; and Shandwick in Henderson, 'Sculpture North of the Forth', pl 3.4; idem., *Rosemarkie's Pictish Monuments*, discusses northern examples of this pattern, adding Nigg and Burghead 14 to Romilly Allen's list.

62 Ibid.; idem., 'Sculpture North of the Forth', 51.

63 ECMS, III, 86, fig 83.

64 Ibid., II, 351 (no 969); III, 53, 63, figs 53, 53A, 61, 235A.

65 Mac Lean, *Early Medieval Sculpture*, 411; Close-Brooks, *The Highlands*, 123; Henderson, *Rosemarkie's Pictish Monuments*, n 89 and idem., 'The Shape and Decoration of the Cross on Pictish Cross-Slabs Carved in Relief', *The Age of Migrating Ideas: Early Medieval Art in Northern Britain and Ireland*, ed R. Michael Spearman and John Higgitt, Edinburgh, 1993, 216, finds comparable the lost Birnie 2 (near Elgin), another northern example; see John Stuart, *Sculptured Stones of Scotland*, 2 vols, Aberdeen and Edinburgh, 1856–67, I, pl XLII. For the St Vigeans spirals, see Henderson, 'Pictish Art and the Book of Kells', *Ireland in Early Mediaeval Europe: Studies in Memory of Kathleen Hughes*, ed Dorothy Whitelock *et al*, Cambridge, 1982, 90, pl XIIIb; ECMS, III, fig 278.

66 For the Kells type, see Isabel Henderson, 'The Book of Kells and the Snake-Boss Motif on Pictish Cross-Slabs and the Iona Crosses', *Ireland and Insular Art A.D. 500–1200*, ed Michael Ryan, Dublin, 1987, 56–65.

67 ECMS, III, 80, fig 72.

68 D. Mac Lean, 'Snake-Bosses and Redemption at Iona and in Pictland', *Age of Migrating Ideas*, ed Spearman and Higgitt, 245–53, figs 30.3–4.

69 Nancy Edwards, 'An Early Group of Crosses from the Kingdom of Ossory', *J Roy Soc Antiq Irl*, 113, 1983, 11.

70 ECMS, II, 235 (no 607); III, 48, 82, figs 48, 72A, 81; for St Andrews' broken right end panel, see Henderson, The Pics, pl 63. For Thornhill, see W.G. Collingwood, 'Anglian and Anglo-Danish Sculpture in the West Riding', *Yorks Archaeol J*, 22, 1915, 243–5, 244c.

71 ECMS, II, 291 (no 748A).

72 All three examples use triple spirals; ibid., III, 33, 62–3, 73, figs 29, 59, 66A, 70; Henderson, 'Sculpture North of the Forth', 51, 53, pl 3.4. Idem., 'Art-historical comment' in Elizabeth Okasha, 'The Non-Ogam Inscriptions of Pictland', *Cambridge Medieval Celtic Studies*, 9, Summer 1985, 63, finds these Applecross spirals comparable to Hilton of Cadboll, Shandwick and the fragmentary spiral-work on the inscribed Tarbat 10 in Easter Ross, which seems to have had both double and triple spirals; see ECMS, III, 94, fig 96; John Higgitt, 'The Pictish Latin inscription at Tarbat in Ross-shire', *Proc Soc Antiq Scot*, 112, 1982, 302–3, pl 26b.

73 Moluag is said to have been buried at Rosemarkie; see A. Anderson, *Early Sources*, I, 19n; Watson, *Celtic Place-Names*, 292; Henderson, *Rosemarkie's Pictish Monuments*, discusses Moluag's connection with Rosemarkie; cf n 46 above.

74 ECMS, III, 109, fig 112, illustrates two adjoining fragments; a third was recovered by Mrs Margaret Shaw Campbell of Canna, whom showed me them in Canna House. For the iconography of the Canna figure and its relations to others on Pictish sculptures at Balblair, Golspie, the Brough of Birsay, and on a Pictish pin from Golspie, see Mac Lean, *Early Medieval Sculpture*, I, 415–16. Henderson, *Rosemarkie's Pictish Monuments*, assigns Birsay, Applecross and Rosemarkie to 'a distinctive northern school of shallow relief carving'.

75 ECMS, II, 232 (no 598); III, 110, fig 113. Romilly Allen thought the spiral pattern unique, but did not know of the Applecross fragment.

76 Ibid., II, 220 (no 568); Henderson, 'Sculpture North of the Forth', 53, concludes that this pattern 'occurs on later slabs only'.

77 Mac Lean, *Early Medieval Sculpture*, I, 417; Henderson, 'Sculpture North of the Forth', 52; idem., *Rosemarkie's Pictish Monuments*, notes that 'fish-tailed creatures are characteristic of Kells and common in mature Pictish sculpture'. For examples in the Book of Kells, see idem., 'The Book of Kells and the Snake-Boss Motif', 60–4. A papal bull of 1203, confirming Iona's ownership of land in Canna, may merely recongnize much earlier connections between the two islands; see Ian Fisher, 'The monastery of Iona in the eighth century', *The Book of Kells: Proceedings of a conference at Trinity College Dublin 6–9 September 1992*, ed Felicity O'Mahony, Aldershot, 1994, 47, n 47.

78 ECMS, II, 351 (no 971: 'of the same class as no 969'); III, 36, 210, figs 32, 227A; see n 64 above for no 969 at Applecross. The fragment of a cross-head from Edzell in Angus should be added to Romilly Allen's list for no 971;

see R.B.K. Stevenson, 'The Inchyra Stone and Some Other Unpublished Early Christian Monuments', *Proc Soc Antiq Scot*, 92, 1958–59, 42–3, pl VI.

79 Canna 2 uniquely creates a square with four repeats of the same pattern; ECMS, II, 294 (no 758); III, 110, fig 112A; For the late Anglian and Anglo-Scandinavian examples, see Rosemary Cramp, *Corpus of Anglo-Saxon Stone Sculpture*, I, *County Durham and Northumberland*, Oxford, 1984, pt 1, 42–3 (Aycliffe 1B), 54 (Chester-le-Street 1A), 66–7 (Durham 1A), 73 (Durham 11C, with 'space-filling pellets'); pt 2, pls 7.26, 20.102, 37.189, 49.235.

80 Mac Lean, *Early Medieval Sculpture*, I, 412–15, 417–20.

81 ECMS, II, 348 (no 958); III, 35, 81, 108, 215, 378, 395, figs 31, 79, 228B, 393, 411A. For Ardchattan, see also RCAHMS, *Argyll: An Inventory of the Monuments, 2, Lorn*, Edinburgh, 1975, 22, 110–11, fig 99; for Kilmartin, see idem., 7, *Mid Argyll and Cowal: Medieval and Later Monuments*, Edinburgh, 1992, 129–31, no 68 (4). Kilmartin displays all the features characteristic of 'later ninth- and tenth-century [Pictish] taste' identified by Stevenson, 'Pictish Art', 126, but its structure is of a Gaelic type related to that of Canna 1, while its small circular armpits and short side-arms recall the Iona School's Keills Cross in Knapdale. Its dependency on a late Pictish ornamental repertoire testifies to the impoverishment of the declining Gaelic tradition west of Druimalban; see Dorothy Kelly, 'The Heart of the Matter: Models for Irish High Crosses', *J Roy Soc Antiq Irl*, 121, 1991, 114–16, 142, fig 44; Mac Lean, *Early Medieval Sculpture*, I, 433, 436; idem., 'Technique and Contact: Carpentry-Constructed Insular Stone Crosses', *From the Isles of the North: Early Medieval Art in Ireland and Britain*, ed Cormac Bourke, Belfast, 1995, 172.

82 Stuart, *Sculptured Stones of Scotland*, II, pl LI (Canna 1); ECMS, III, 76–7, 108, 391, figs 72–3, 408. For Keills, see also D. Mac Lean, 'The Keills Cross in Knapdale, the Iona School and the Book of Kells', *Early Medieval Sculpture in Britain and Ireland*, ed John Higgitt, Oxford (*British Archaeological Reports, British Series* 152), 1986, 182–3, pl 8.2; RCAHMS, *Argyll*, 7, *Mid Argyll and Cowal*, 87, no 45(1). Relationships between the Nigg animals, Rosemarkie 1, Shandwick and the Pictish St Ninian's Isle Treasure are discussed in Isabel Henderson, 'Variations on an Old Theme: Panelled Zoomorphic Ornament on Pictish Sculpture at Nigg, Easter Ross, and at St Andrews, Fife, and in the Book of Kells', *The Insular Tradition*, ed Catherine Karkov, Michael Ryan and Robert Farrell, Albany (forthcoming).

83 ECMS, I, fig 27 (Perthshire brooch); II, 213 (no 544); III, 381, fig 396B, identifies the Eilean Mór figures as 'a swastika key pattern', a mistake corrected in RCAHMS, *Argyll*, 7,

Mid Argyll and Cowal, 70–2, no 33 (4). For the brooch found near Clunie Castle, Perthshire, see also *'The Work of Angels' Masterpieces of Celtic Metalwork, 6th–9th Centuries AD*, ed Susan Youngs, London: British Museum, 1989, no 109.

84 ECMS, II, 302 (no 789), 348–9 (nos 960–1); III, 68, 320, 381, 395, figs 60A, 63, 334A, 396A, 411.

85 Ibid., III, figs 334B, C, D, 373, ; Stevenson, 'Pictish Art', 126; Leslie Alcock and Elizabeth A. Alcock, 'Reconnaissance excavations on Early Historic fortifications and other royal sites in Scotland, 1974–84; 5: A, Excavations & other fieldwork at Forteviot, Perthshire, 1981 etc', *Proc Soc Antiq Scot*, 122, 1992, 240–1, ills 14–5 (Dupplin). Henderson, 'Sculpture North of the Forth, 55, notes that the sculptor of St Andrews 14 'was familiar with a number … of patterns found on Nigg, Shandwick, Rosemarkie and Farr', at least one of which was used at Applecross; cf n 61 above.

86 Katherine Forsyth, 'The Inscriptions on the Dupplin Cross', *From the Isles of the North*, ed Bourke, 237–44. For Constantine son of Fergus, see A. Anderson, *Early Sources*, I, 253–5, 262; Henderson, *The Picts*, 88–9, 94–6, 134; M. Anderson, *Kings and Kingship*, 174, 191–4, 249, 263, 266, 273, 281, 287, 292; idem., 'Dalriada and the creation of the kingdom of the Scots', *Ireland in Early Mediaeval Europe*, ed Whitelock *et al*, 108–11, 114–15; Smyth, *Warlords and Holy Men*, 177–80, 186.

87 For Blathmacc, see A. Anderson, *Early Sources*, I, 263–5; for the Gall-Ghàidheil and Viking settlement and conversion west of Druimalban, see Barbara E. Crawford, *Scandinavian Scotland*, Leicester, 1987, 47–51, 96–8, 101–3, 118–19, 126–7, 140, 146–8, 162–3, 167–8, 179–84, with additional references.

88 AFM, I, 452, 486; discussed in W.D.H. Sellar, 'The origins and ancestry of Somerled', *Scottish Historical Review*, 45, 1966, 123–42; K.A. Steer and J.W.M. Bannerman, *Late Medieval Monumental Sculpture in the West Highlands*, Edinburgh, 1977, 201; John Bannerman, 'Comarba Coluim Chille and the Relics of Columba', *Innes Review*, 44, 1993, 33–4. The eleventh-twelfth century 'Prophecy of Berchán' suggests that a brother of Kenneth mac Alpin was also the 'wanton son of a foreign [Viking] wife'; see A. Anderson, *Early Sources*, I, 292; Smyth, *Warlords and Holy Men*, 190–1.

89 A. Anderson, *Early Sources*, I, 285–7, 290. For differing interpretations of the sources, see Alfred P. Smyth, *Scandinavian Kings in the British Isles 850–880*, Oxford, 1977, 104, 115–26, 152; idem., *Warlords and Holy Men*, 154–66, 190; Donnchadh Ó Corráin, 'High-kings, Vikings and other kings', *Irish Historical Studies*, 21, 1979, 296–303.

90 RCAHMS, *Argyll: An Inventory of the Monuments, 4, Iona*, Edinburgh, 1982, 19, 208–9, 211; Mac Lean, *Early Medieval Sculpture*, I, 436–8.

91 See n 81 above.

92 R.B.K. Stevenson, 'The Chronology and Relationships of Some Irish and Scottish Crosses', *J Roy Soc Antiq Irl*, 86, 1956, 93–4, fig 1.4; idem., 'The Inchyra Stone', 55; for Rosemarkie, see ECMS, III, 68, figs 64–5, discussed in Henderson, *Rosemarkie's Pictish Monuments*; see also Mac Lean, *Early Medieval Sculpture*, I, 421–3.

93 ECMS, III, 378, fig 393.

94 Its hunting scene, 'erased' by an incised cross indicating its re-orientation, is still visible; see RCAHMS, *Outer Hebrides, Skye and the Small Isles*, 220, no 688d; Walter Runciman, 'Donations to the Museum', *Proc Soc Antiq Scot*, 67, 1932–33, 65, fig 3; Mac Lean, *Early Medieval Sculpture*, I, 420–1.

95 The ring of Invergowrie 1 has a key pattern, as does the related Aldbar in Angus; see ECMS, II, 213 (no 544); III, 227, 246–7, 256, 297, 360, figs 239A, 259A, 266A, 311A, 374A. Henderson, 'Sculpture North of the Forth', 56–7, places Invergowrie and Kirriemuir in a group of 'markedly smaller late Pictish slabs'. For the connection between St Andrews 15 and Eilean Mór, see n 83 above. The letters 'Ihu' and 'XPI', incised in the upper border on either side of the top cross-arm on the Eigg slab, fall beyond the seventh to early-ninth century limits of Okasha, 'Non-Ogam Inscriptions of Pictland'.

96 Compare the interlace in the unringed cross on Inchbrayock 2; ECMS, III, fig 264A.

97 See nn 61 and 78 above.

98 Mac Lean, *Early Medieval Sculpture*, I, 423–4, 459–60, 479–80; idem., 'Technique and Contact'. It was presumably the descendants of Pictish refugees fleeing the Northern Isles, Caithness and Sutherland *c*800 whose sculptural taste had recourse to Applecross.

99 Paul Meyvaert, 'The Book of Kells and Iona', *Art Bulletin*, 71, 1989, 6–19; George Henderson, *From Durrow to Kells: Insular Gospel-books 650–800*, London, 1987, 185–95; for the wider context, see also Herbert, *Iona, Kells and Derry*, 70–3; Bannerman, 'Comarba Coluim Chille'.

100 Henderson, *Rosemarkie's Pictish Monuments*.

Isabel B. Henderson
A Bibliography of Her Published Works

Compiled by Carola Hicks

The origin centre of the Pictish symbol stones. *Proceedings of the Society of Antiquaries of Scotland,* 91 (1957-58), 44–60.

Two Pictish symbol stones, (i) Flemington farm, Aberlemo, Angus.... *Proceedings of the Society of Antiquaries of Scotland*, 95 (1961-62), 219–21.

The Picts. London, Thames and Hudson (Ancient Peoples and Places Series), 1967.

with Lloyd, D M *Celtica* (exhibition catalogue). Edinburgh, National Library of Scotland, 1967.

A printed text of a portion of Macpherson's Ossian. *The Bibliothek*, V (1968), 111–13.

Introduction and entries in *William Blake* (exhibition catalogue). Edinburgh, National Library of Scotland, 1969.

Entries 170–176. In Piggott, S (ed) *Early Celtic Art* (exhibition catalogue). Edinburgh, Edinburgh University Press, 1970.

The Chadwick Bibliography (a list of the published writings of H M and N K Chadwick). Cambridge, Will and Sebastian Carter, 1970.

with Holland, S *Scandinavia* (exhibition catalogue). Edinburgh, National Library of Scotland, 1970.

The problem of the Picts. In Menzies, G (ed) *Who are the Scots?*, 51–65. London, British Broadcasting Corporation, 1971.

North Pictland. In Meldrum, E (ed) *The Dark Ages in the Highlands*, 37–52. Inverness, Inverness Field Club, 1971.

The meaning of the Pictish symbol stones. Ibid, 53–68.

The Picts of Aberdeenshire and their monuments. *The Archaeological Journal*, 129 (1972), 166–74.

Bass of Inverurie and Pictish symbol stones. Ibid, 193.

Pictish sculptured stones. Ibid, 198–99.

A Pictish cross-slab. Ibid, 203.

Scandinavian books in the National Library of Scotland. *Northern Studies*, I (1973), 17–20; 3 (1974), 28–32.

The published writings of David Talbot Rice. In Henderson, G and Robertson, G (eds) *Studies in Memory of David Talbot Rice*, 317–25. Edinburgh, Edinburgh University Press, 1974.

Inverness, A Pictish capital. In Maclean of Dochgarroch, L (ed) *The Hub of the Highlands*, 91–108. Inverness/Edinburgh, Inverness Field Club/Paul Harris, The Albyn Press, 1975.

Pictish territorial divisions. In McNeill, P and Nicholson, R (eds) *An Historical Atlas of Scotland c.400–c.1600*, 7–8 (text accompanying distribution map 7). St Andrews, Conference of Scottish Medievalists, 1975.

The monuments of the Picts. Ibid, 9–11 (maps 8–10).

Pictish archaeological sites. Ibid, 11–13 (map 11).

Sculpture north of the Forth after the take-over by the Scots. In Lang, J (ed) *Anglo-Saxon and Viking Age Sculpture* (*British Archaeological Reports, British Series* 49) 47–74. Oxford, 1978.

The silver chain from Whitecleugh, Shieldholm, Crawfordjohn, Lanarkshire. *Transactions of the Dumfriesshire and Galloway Natural History and Archaeological Society*, 3rd ser, 54 (1978–79), 20–8.

Early medieval Scottish sculpture. In Daiches, D (ed) *A Companion to Scottish Culture*, 350–52. London, Edward Arnold, 1981.

Pictish art and the Book of Kells. In Whitelock, D, Dumville, D and McKitterick, R (eds) *Ireland in Early Medieval Europe: Studies in Memory of Kathleen Hughes*, 79–105. Cambridge, Cambridge University Press, 1982.

Pictish vine-scroll ornament. In O'Connor, A and Clarke, D V (eds) *From the Stone Age to the 'Forty Five – Studies Presented to R.B.K. Stevenson*, 243–68. Edinburgh, John Donald, 1983.

Entries for early medieval Scottish history and art. In Thompson, D (ed) *A Companion to Gaelic Scotland*. Oxford, Basil Blackwell, 1984.

with Ritchie, J N G *Pictish Symbol Stones: A Handlist*. Edinburgh, Royal Commission for the Ancient and

Historical Monuments of Scotland, 1985 (new edition 1994).

Art-historical commentary. In Okasha, E The non-ogam inscriptions of Pictland. *Cambridge Medieval Celtic Studies*, 9 (1985), 43–69.

The 'David cycle' in Pictish art. In Higgitt, J (ed) *Early Medieval Sculpture in Britain and Ireland (British Archaeological Reports, British Series* 152), 87–123. Oxford, 1986.

The Book of Kells and the snake-boss motif on Pictish cross-slabs and the Iona crosses. In Ryan, M (ed) *Ireland and Insular Art: A.D.500–1200,* 56–65. Dublin, Royal Irish Academy, 1987.

Early Christian monuments of Scotland displaying crosses but no other ornament. With a gazetteer of sites with cross-carved stones. In Small, A (ed) *The Picts – A New Look at Old Problems,* 45–58. Dundee, Graham Hunter Foundation, 1987.

The arts of Late Celtic Britain, AD 600–900. In Ford, B (ed) *The Cambridge Guide to the Arts in Britain,* vol 1, 206–19. Cambridge, Cambridge University Press, 1988.

Françoise Henry and Helen Roe: fifty-five years' work on Irish art and archaeology. *Cambridge Medieval Celtic Studies,* 17 (1989), 69–74.

The Art and Function of Rosemarkie's Pictish Monuments (Groam House Lecture Series I). Rosemarkie, Groam House Museum Trust, 1990 (revised edition 1991).

Pictish sculpture at Glamis, Aberlemno and St Vigean's museum. In Pounds, N J G (ed) *The St Andrew's Area: Proceedings of the 137th Summer Meeting of the Royal Archaeological Institute,* 17–18. Supplement to *The Archaeological Journal* 148 (1991).

with Okasha, E The Early Christian inscribed and carved stones at Tullylease, Co. Cork. *Cambridge Medieval Celtic Studies,* XXIV (1993), 1–36.

The making of *The Early Christian Monuments of Scotland.* In Allen J R and Anderson, J *The Early Christian Monuments of Scotland,* 2 vols (the Introduction to the facsimile reprint of the original edition (Edinburgh, Society of Antiquaries of Scotland, 1903)) 1, xx–xlviii. Balgavies, Angus, The Pinkfoot Press, 1993.

The shape and decoration of the cross on Pictish cross-slabs carved in relief. In Spearman, R M and Higgitt, J (eds) *The Age of Migrating Ideas,* 209–18. Edinburgh/Stroud, National Museums of Scotland/Alan Sutton Publishing, 1993.

Zoomorphic ornament on the cross-head of the cross-slab at Nigg, Easter Ross, and two panels of the St Andrews sarcophagus. *American Early Medieval Studies,* III (1992-93).

The Insular and Continental context of the St Andrews sarcophagus. In Crawford, B E (ed) *Scotland in Dark Age Europe* (St John's House Papers 5), 71–102. St Andrews, 1994.

The Picts: written records and pictorial images. In Burt, J R F Bowman, E O and Robertson, N M (eds) *Stones, Symbols and Stories: aspects of Pictish studies (Proceedings of the Conferences of the Pictish Arts Society, 1992),* 44–66. Edinburgh, Pictish Arts Society, 1994.

Pictish art and its place within the history of Insular art. In Nicoll, E H (ed) *A Pictish Panorama: the Story of the Picts and a Pictish Bibliography,* 15–20. Balgavies, Angus, The Pinkfoot Press, 1995.

Pictish monuments (four distribution maps with accompanying text (one with NM Robertson)). In McNeill, P G B and MacQueen, H L (eds) *Atlas of Scottish History to 1700.* Edinburgh, 1996.

Anglo-Saxon stone sculpture. In Hicks, C (ed) *Cambridgeshire Churches,* 216–232. Stamford, Paul Watkins, 1997.

Pictish Monsters: Symbol, Text and Image (H M Chadwick Memorial Lectures 7). Cambridge, Department of Anglo-Saxon, Norse and Celtic, University of Cambridge, 1997.

In Press

Variations on an old theme: panelled zoomorphic ornament .... In Karkov, C E and Ryan, M (eds) *The Insular Tradition.* New York, SUNY Press.

with Okasha, E, The Early Christian inscribed and carved stones of Tullylease, Co. Cork: addendum. *Cambridge Medieval Celtic Studies.*

The Dupplin cross: a preliminary consideration of its art-historical context. In Hawkes, J and Mills, S (eds) *Proceedings of the Conference on the Golden Age of Northumbria.* Stroud, Alan Sutton Publishing.

Pitti. Entry in *Enciclopedia dell'Arte Medievale.* Rome, Istituto della Enciclopedia.

J. Romilly Allen. Entry in *New Dictionary of National Biography.*

Monasteries and sculpture in the Insular pre-Viking Age: the Pictish evidence. In Thompson, BJ (ed) *Proceedings of the Eleventh Harlaxton Symposium 1994.* Stamford, Paul Watkins.

Forthcoming

with Harden, G A jet pendant from Erchless, Strathglass, now in the Inverness museum. *Proceedings of the Society of Antiquaries of Scotland.*

Book Reviews

Argyll: An Inventory of the Monuments, vol IV, *Iona* (RCAHMS, 1982). In *Medieval Archaeology*, 27 (1983), 235–8.

Roe, H *Monasterboice and its Monuments* (Co. Louth Archaeology Society, 1981). In *Cambridge Medieval Celtic Studies,* 6 (1983), 98–9.

Wilson, D M *Anglo-Saxon Art from the Seventh Century to the Norman Conquest* (London, 1984). Backhouse, J, Turner, D and Webster, L (eds) *The Golden Age of Anglo-Saxon Art 966–1066* (London, 1984). In *Medieval Archaeology,* 29 (1985), 235–7.

Smyth, AP *Warlords and Holy Men: Scotland AD 80 to 1000.* In *English Historical Review,* CII (1987).

Neuman de Vegvar, C *The Northumbrian Renaissance* (London, 1988). In *The Burlington Magazine*, December 1988, 934.

Driscoll, S T and Nieke, M R (eds) *Power and Politics in Early Medieval Britain and Ireland* (Edinburgh, 1988). In *Medieval Archaeology*, 34 (1990), 283–4.

Bonner, G *et al* (eds) *St Cuthbert. His Cult and His Community to AD 1200* (Woodbridge, 1989). In *Archaeologia Aeliana*, 18 (1990), 238–42.

Bailey, R N and Cramp, R J *A Corpus of Anglo-Saxon Stone Sculpture* II (Oxford, 1988). In *English Historical Review*, 106 (1991), 968–9.

Horn, W *et al* *The Forgotten Hermitage of Skellig Michael* (University of California Press, 1991). In *Cambridge Medieval Celtic Studies*, 23 (1992), 114–16.

Harbison, P *The High Crosses of Ireland*, 3 vols (Dublin/ Bonn, 1992). In *Antiquaries Journal*, 72 (1994), 212–14.

Review in press

Tweddle, D, Biddle, M and Kjølbye-Biddle, B *Corpus of Anglo-Saxon Stone Sculpture* IV *South-east England* (Oxford, 1995). In *The Journal of Ecclesiastical History.*